W9-ARG-073

TARNISHED
ANGEL

TARNISHED
ANGEL

Surviving in the Dark Curve
of Drugs, Violence, Sex, and Fame

A Memoir

by

Jennifer Lee

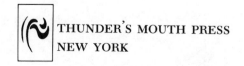
THUNDER'S MOUTH PRESS
NEW YORK

Published by
Thunder's Mouth Press
54 Greene Street, Suite 4S
New York, NY 10013

Library of Congress Cataloging-in-Publication Data

Lee, Jennifer, 1949–
    Tarnished angel : surviving in the dark curve of drugs,
violence, sex, and fame : a memoir / by Jennifer Lee.
        p.   cm.
        Includes index.
        ISBN 1-56025-025-9
        1. Lee, Jennifer, 1949–   . 2. Motion picture actors and
    actresses—United States—Biography.   3. Models,
Fashion—United States—Biography.
4. Singers—United States—Biography.
I. Title.
PN2287.L294A3   1991
791.43′028′092—dc20
[B]   91-25080
                                                             CIP

Text design by Harold Nolan

Printed in the United States of America

Distributed by
Publishers Group West
4065 Hollis Street
Emeryville, CA 94608
(800) 365-3453

For my brother
Byron Brewster Lee

ACKNOWLEDGMENTS:

I would like to thank my father for his Irish genes and assistance through the lean times; my dear sister and best friend, Cindy, for all her love and never ending belief; my mother, Patricia Brewster Lee, for her gardens and other magic; my dearest enfants, Livia Lee and Emmet Fox Kelly Lee, whose companionship, profound love, and great sense of humor made it possible; my publisher, Neil Ortenberg for his faith and patience especially during the "nightmare of the green box"; Associate publisher, Anne Stillwaggon; Joan Fucillo, for editorial assistance; John Stark for his friendship, support, and guidance; Geraldine Smith, for being there; Barry Beckerman, for loving me; Gary Fisketjon, for his advice and friendship; and my darling Tiberius, who spoke like a true poet and had the attitude of Socrates.

The rest of the hard working crew at TMP: Marian Cole; Amy Guggenheim; Eric Brandt; Laura-Ann Robb; Jennifer Ginsberg; Eric Meyer; and all the speedy angels at Breakaway Messenger Service.

I would also like to thank: Sandy Bodner; Liz Smith; John Prine; Mickey Newbury; Garth Batista; Gerard Malanga; Martin Sheen; Marysa Maslansky; Adina Michaeli; Patti Towle; Dr. Kathy Cox; Ann, Nancy, and Karen; and John and Hasan at Discount Books.

Thank you Magic Fawn, all the cowboys, and tarnished angels!

Your halo is the neon
Your heart is a jukebox song
Your heaven is a honky tonk
You love to live so wrong

I know you're not a'changin'
As a saint you'd gain no fame
My angel's kind of tarnished
But I love her just the same.

"Tarnished Angel"
Roger Miller

THEN

Just like you always told me,
the men would want to hold me,
and they do

And, it's "Hello, Cowboy, buy me one,
I might go home with you"

They all call me baby,
It's driving me crazy,
but it's slow
When you fly like an Angel,
but the devil's got your soul.

"High Like an Angel"
L. J. Dalton
R. Pierce

1953

My first memory is of my mother, Pat, standing in front of the small white sink in the downstairs bathroom. She is looking in the mirror, pressing a towel against her face; her nose is bleeding, the smell of liquor fills the room. It's dawn.

"Your bastard father hit me," she says. I say to myself, *I will never be like you. I will never be like them*. . . . At the time I believed it.

1965

We've been waiting all day for Pat to come home. Harry is in a quandary since we got the phone call that Pat's brother, Gregory, was found dead in a Las Vegas motel room. It is the drugs and alcohol that killed him. Gregory Byron Brewster—Pat idolizes him. He could do no wrong. (Gregory. His brilliant legal career ended when he was caught forging the signature of a judge—who happened to be his father.)

"Look, Pat, I have something to tell you," Harry says as Pat stands in the dining room, her coat not yet off. The lights in the room seem brighter than usual.

"Gregory's dead." Harry tells her it was a heart attack.

She freezes.

"Harry, what are you talking about? Is this some kind of joke?"

"No, Pat. It's not a joke. It's real."

As the news starts to sink in Pat sucks in the air around her, and slowly exhales. She begins to breathe harder and faster then, as though she'll die if she stops. She starts to thrash and scream like wild animal. She picks up the chairs around the dining room table and pitches them in all directions, smashing everything in their path: the bay window, her treasured antique toys, ironstone china on the jelly cupboard shelves, the brass hurricane lamp, flower pots, candlesticks. Harry tries to restrain her, but the pain gathers momentum. She's yelling, "My Gregory. My Gregory. None of you knows. He's the only one who loves me. He's the only one who understands me."

God . . . Gregory. His shiny green Jaguar pulling into the driveway, seeing him from my bedroom window, looking up at me, waving. He was tall and handsome. He crawled into bed beside me and wrapped his big arms around me. In his vise-like grip, I was frightened, unable to move; I thought, *This is the way a man holds a woman when he loves her.* . . . I knew something was wrong. How old was I?

Pat's been downing martinis and popping Miltowns. She's been dressing like Isadora Duncan, modern dancing in scarves and leotards, and reciting Dylan Thomas for four days now. "Do *not* go gentle into *that* good night," she emotes, over and over and over . . . Enough of that damn good night stuff! I hate Dylan Thomas! I hate my mother! The walls are tumbling down; we can't hold them up any longer. These "outbursts" have usually lasted no more than twelve hours, well, sometimes two days. But this one is the worst. Thank God Harry's living in the Henry Hudson Hotel. He would have killed her by now. He's at the end of his rope, and was about to snap when I packed his suitcase.

We've gotten Harry out before just in time to prevent disaster. One time, Pat destroyed my room. I can no longer recall what set her off, I remember standing on the stairs holding onto Harry, keeping him from going up after her. While the crashing and banging thundered above our heads, I held his arms tight whispering in his ear, "It's *okay*. It's only my room."

Now things are really out of control. Pat has the scissors and is cutting up her necklace. Pearls bounce, roll, and ricochet across the hardwood floors. We'll never find them all, never string them back together. I go to call Nancy, Pat's sister, to tell her I'm coming over with Cindy and Byron. It's definitely time to grab the younger kids and make a getaway. But I pick up the phone and see that its cord is cut, too. Furious, I go to find Pat, taking the receiver with me, swinging it 'round and 'round by its cord. Pat's sitting on the

4

couch now, clinging to Byron. I hit her on the legs with the receiver. I feel its impact, too, along with my own deep shame. I try to grab my brother away from her.

"You're not taking my Lord Byron!" she screams.

"I am taking him! Cindy, get your things! We're leaving this madhouse!"

She holds Byron even tighter. At this instant I realize that Byron has become her Gregory. Now Byron is her love. She has always called him Lord Byron, a name that slightly sickened me. And now he is her "precious Lord," the apple of her eye, the light of her life. Her needs are played out in his young soul. I must save him. I grab one arm; she grips the other. I know she will never let go, so I must, before an arm comes out of its socket. Byron is petrified and unable to make a sound. He's so little, fragile. I can't rescue him, at least not now. I have to leave him behind in her clutches.

Cindy and I pile into the station wagon and I drive us to Aunt Nancy's. I get there, and call Harry, who rushes to the house with our family doctor. There's a struggle. Harry wrestles Byron away from Pat. She bolts, throwing herself down the stairs. The doctor shoots Pat up with a sedative, straps her into a straitjacket, and brings her to the Mosher psych ward at the Albany Medical Center.

1967

Fall: NYC

I'm now at Finch, a college of matching shoes and handbags, located in the Seventies between Madison and Park. "The entire city is the campus," the brochures tout. Finch's biggest claim to fame is senior day student Tricia Nixon, and its biggest claim to shame is Grace Slick, Drop-Out. Dean Harris is a perfectly coiffed, impeccably groomed, pewter-haired spinster who wears pink wool dresses, speaks with a shrill, overly cultured voice, and has a neck stretched long and thin from looking down at everyone. Finch is her knight in shining armor, the love of her life, and she runs it with an iron hand in a white glove. It fills up her entire life; I think it's all she has. Her disdain for me is inevitable. I'm not polished or rich enough. The typical Finchite is more like Khristy, the first girl I've met here—tall and thin, legs up to her shoulders, and hair halfway down her back—the epitome of the elegant WASP. An athletic one,

5

too! Climbs the stairs two steps at a time, a large suitcase tucked under each arm. Khristy's a vision of sophistication in designer gray and pearls—even her gray alligator clutch purse has a pearl clasp. "Hi, I'm Khristy Howard," she says warmly, in a rich, gray Philadelphia lockjaw. Her arm thrusts out to shake my hand, her elbow not even slightly bent. But underneath the sheen, I can detect something irreverent. Until meeting Khristy, I had felt confident in my first-day-at-Finch-outfit—red suit, white blouse—which I'd thought rather Chanel-esque. But now I feel its clumpy, naive shape and I think to myself, *You're country.*

Is Khristy really my age? A lot of these girls look like some of my mother's friends—grown up and *very* well put together. In fact, Khristy looks just like her mother who's dressed exactly the same, though in a deeper shade of gray. All this chicness is painfully intimidating.

1968

Spring

Dean Harris has caught me sneaking out after midnight, so I have to go before the House Committee. That's how they handle bad girls here. I stand before twelve upper classmen, a blinding symmetry of color-coordinated headbands, Pucci dresses, Gucci and Pappaggalo shoes. The verdict, of course, is guilty. So now I'm "campussed"—not allowed to go anywhere after 8 P.M. for two weeks. (God, if they knew I've been paying the security guard $20 a week to let me in and out when I want.) I have to get out of this ski resort! Am I the only non-virgin here?

I call my father Harry to tell him I'm leaving. I cannot bear the thought of anyone telling me what to do, especially anyone named Muffy, Puff, Bunny, or Salina. Not a good solid name within a block of this place. No one here cares about anything except how they look. Isn't anyone concerned about what's going on out there? Vietnam? Martin Luther King? Medgar Evers? Robert Kennedy? I wonder how many other girls loaded helmets onto a plane with their mothers to send to Selma? The day Robert Kennedy was shot, Pat, who'd been campaigning for him, called to tell me. I delivered the news and no one seemed to care, at least not as much as I. This school is a study in obsolescence. Probably the only thing that would cause a student riot is somebody showing up in a duplicate Givenchy.

Harry, always the lawyer, reasons with me, telling me to hang on for a few months and finish out the year so at least I'll get some credits. Credits for what? My major is Art History, but so far all I've got to show for this year are some stretch marks on the inside of my thighs from eating too many marshmallow sundaes. Harry also points out that this is one of the few schools that will take me with my grades. Apparently a contribution from him helped. Fuck 'em! . . . I agree to hang on, but make it clear that I'm never coming back to this country club.

It's late and I'm awake, as usual. Lying on the top bunk in my tiny dorm room, I look out across the street. I can see into Woody Allen and Louise Lasser's townhouse. They're fighting, as usual. The fight moves from room to room. I watch them until their lights go out. I think of Pat and Harry.

Summer

All I know is when I leave a place I'm gone. Good-bye, Finch! Hello, Cropseyville! Despite how hard things can get at home—we have always lived in the eye of a hurricane, never knowing—there are good times here as well, which make all the bad times that much worse.

Cropseyville is a hamlet at the foot of the Berkshires, between Williamstown, Massachusetts and Troy, New York. It was named after Crazy Judge Cropsey, who brought his "painted women" here on weekends in his horse-drawn surrey "with-the-fringe-on-top." Our house was built in the thirties. It is big—a white, green-shuttered, two-story farmhouse that's gotten bigger as we've added on to it. As land comes up for sale Harry buys it, so that our house, on its private road, has remained isolated. We are surrounded by woods, pastures, and brooks, and have a swimming hole, a red barn, and our very own teepee. And there are Pat's gardens . . . such beautiful gardens that bloom from early spring to the first snow. She's created a world, a kaleidoscope of color: pink peonies, purple lilacs, yellow snapdragons, bronze tiger lilies, blue delphinium, white daffodils, lilies of the valley . . . but the most amazing flowers are her favorites—the red bleeding-hearts that hang delicately from the white threads that attach them to the rest of the plant. They are so beautiful, little red puffs that look as if someone has breathed sighs of air into them. From the upstairs bathroom window, I can see Pat sunbathing in her white bra and shorts amidst this abundant display. She loves the earth, loves getting her hands dirty, really seeing what mysteries lie under the rocks. "Look! Spring is really here," Pat announces, opening up her fist to show me a handful of writhing baby snakes. She even had a pet one, Penelope.

Our closest neighbors, up the road on a dairy farm, are Norm and Gladys Burdick. Sometimes we'd run to their house, when Pat and Harry fought, to the smells of home-baked bread and cookies and pies. After Norm's barn burned down the dairy farm went bust. So Harry bought it, renting it to Norm and Gladys for only $40 a month. (Only years later did we learn the truth, that Byron had set the barn on fire, playing with matches in the hayloft. Scared to death, he ran away from the fire. He always kept the secret hidden in his heart, believing that he was the reason for the demise of Norm's farm.) Truth was, things were already bad and getting worse when the barn burned down.

Pat creates wonderful dinner parties, which I always look forward to—Cornish game hens, beef bourguignon, Lobster Newburg —setting the table with red-and-white china, brass candlesticks, shining silverware, a chaotic bouquet of just-picked flowers, and bottles of burgundy at each end. And that big cracked wooden salad bowl, black-brown from years of use, sat waiting. The house fills with warm smells, dancing candlelight, and the voice of Nina Simone moaning low on the stereo, "Trouble in mind I'm blue—but I won't be blue always . . ."

Pat dresses dramatically for her parties. She looks so glamorous in her red Chinese vest and purple pants, or maybe she's wearing black Berber pants with a turquoise toreador jacket and silver lamé slippers. The children weren't allowed to sit with the guests, but we helped serve, clear, and pour. I love the dinner conversations. The guests are usually artists and writers and professors, people well-known or accomplished in their fields: Dorothy and Granville Hicks, Georgia and Bill McKinley, Ann (Hank) and Tom Littlefield. Jim and Liz Westbrook, Libby and Carl Korté, and Ann and Bernard Malamud (on whom Pat had a mad crush). They talk and ar-

8

gue—about World War II, civil rights, abortion, Adlai Stevenson, free will, and Erich Fromm. And sometimes Pat doesn't drink too much—so after the guests leave we don't hear the sounds of breaking china and crying.

Harry often defends people who can't afford to pay him. Buck Washington, a muscular construction worker who's always getting into trouble, is a proud man who does some work around the house in exchange for his legal fees. He's helped my father build a stone wall and dam up the stream to make the swimming hole. I love to see him walking down the road carrying the mast to my father's sailboat. He can balance it on his shoulder, holding it lightly with one hand, bare chested and showing off. Buck is a very warm man whose smile and greeting I always look forward to. More than anything, I love to hear him laugh. One time, we were driving past his house in the city and Pat stopped to say hi. When he came up to my side of the car he leaned inside the window, dropped something in my lap, and simply said, "Give this to your father." I looked down and saw a gun in my skirt. Buck was the first black man I knew. I've always been proud of my parents' stand on the issue of racism. The dinner party discussions sometimes result in heated arguments about this topic. I can remember hearing the question, "But would you want your daughter to marry a black man?" And I remember my father's answer: "I don't care who she marries as long as he loves her and can provide for her in the manner to which she's become accustomed." I know he meant it!

Right now, the house is empty. Pat's on the Cape with Byron and Cindy, and my older sister, Georgia, is still at college. After a few days at home it's time to go, to get on with my life. I have a white 1964 Jaguar with red upholstery to use for the summer. Harry has gotten this car as payment for some legal fees. I hit the road, careen around Dead Man's Curve, and drive non-stop to Long Island in a raging thunderstorm. My destination—Southhampton, where I'll be spending the summer. I had gone there for the first time with Khristy Howard over Memorial Day weekend. To my surprise we're friends. Under all that gray perfection, there really is a sister in disguise, another rebel. She, too, hates Finch and is looking for an off-ramp. She's got a live-in poodle-sitting job in Quogue for some elderly lady who has an extravagant house on the beach. It all seems so easy. Just pack the car and head off. I feel so fearless, and so sure. Of course I'll find a place to live. Of course I'll find a job. Of course I'll find a boyfriend. Of course I'll be happy.

June

I find a charming upstairs room in Water Mill, in a Victorian house run by somebody's grandmother. It's right around the corner from Mitty's General Store, the local night spot where everybody hangs out. Now all I need is a job. So I walk into Jax, the chicest women's store in Southhampton. I feel really confident in myself and my ability to do anything, and easily convince Barbara, the manager, that despite my lack of experience, with my enthusiasm I can sell anything. She hires me on the spot. I sell tons of silk matte jersey dresses, tops, and cotton slacks during the day and spend my nights dancing at Mitty's, often not coming home till dawn.

Called Harry this afternoon from the Sip'n'Soda. He's livid. Georgia's run off to Haight-Ashbury and Jordan* has flown off to find her. Georgia's found out that I've been sleeping with Jordan, and Harry knows, too. Jordan, the two timing schmuck, must have suddenly developed a conscience and confessed. "For God's sake, think of your sister!" Harry screams. . . . "But Harry, it's over. It doesn't matter." Harry wouldn't let it go. "It does matter. You hurt Georgia. You know how fragile she is."

When Jordan finds Georgia, she's all freaked out on acid. She's always freaked out about something, especially on holidays. One Easter she tried to kill herself with pills and one Christmas I had to dig her out of a snowbank, half-frozen. She doesn't ignore the minor holidays, either, like slashing her wrists on Memorial Day. . . . always something.

When I met Jordan I was fifteen. He was my first lover. I was working as a junior counselor at Camp Ce-De-Ca, a Jewish day camp in Grafton, the next town up from Cropseyville. I was sitting on a blue ice chest, a red bandana around my neck, when I first laid eyes on Jordan, a graduate student at Syracuse. A real knock-out—tall, lean, and dark. He's fond of quoting Paul Newman in *Harper:* "Only the cream and scum rise to the top; the rest sinks to the bottom." Jordan's also a scoundrel and a true terrorist of love.

---

*Names followed by an asterisk have been changed along with other identifying characteristics.

10

But when I see him, I decide then and there I want him, even though Steve, the senior counselor I'm dating, is trying to set Jordan up with Georgia. Jordan wants me, too. "I'll take *you*," he says. "It's not possible there's any more at home better looking than you." Then I think, *Wait until you meet Georgia. She's drop-dead gorgeous, but what a nightmare! You'll end up liking me much better.*

Georgia and Jordan begin dating, but my flirtation with him continues. Soon I develop a full-fledged crush, leaving Steve in the dust. Toward the end of the summer I'm left home alone for a few days when Pat, Harry, Georgia, Cindy, and Byron go to Cape Cod—I'm to join them when my job is finished. But now, I'm alone, and Jordan knows it. One Friday night there's a terrible storm. The lights go out. The phone rings. "Are you all right, Jenny?" . . . "Yes, I'm fine." . . . "Do you want some company?" . . . "That would be fine, too." I knew what he had in mind. I'm a little frightened when Jordan calls but a lot more when I hang up. (Looking back, this moment was the most exciting part of the entire affair. Wanting Jordan was far more erotic than actually having him.)

He drives out and our cheating begins in the guestroom that's over the barn. His hands are in my pants, his mouth on my breasts, and he's a part of my heart. I no longer want to be a virgin. But it's not in the stars, not on this hot, rainy August night. It's more complicated than I thought it was going to be. I'm cheating on Georgia, and I'm betraying my family, too. Although my feelings for Jordan are strong, I'm filled with doubt, and I'm afraid. I have to rethink this plan.

After several hours of passionate making out I decide not to go through with it. Jordan doesn't press the point, and a few days later I leave for the Cape. When we all return, I try to avoid Jordan, who's having a full-fledged relationship with Georgia. But one night Steve, Jordan, Georgia, and I double-date. After dinner and a movie we go make out in Jordan's blue Mustang in the Camp Ce-De-Ca parking lot. Jordan's in the front seat kissing Georgia, staring back at me. No more equivocation. I can't stop obsessing about that night over the barn. I have to have him.

It happens that fall, in Syracuse, shortly after my sixteenth birthday. A friend of Harry's, Uncle Bill, calls the house to say he's going to a homecoming reunion at Syracuse.

"Would Jennifer like to come with us? I'm bringing our daughter, Suzy." Bingo! Divine intervention! I immediately call Jordan and tell him when I'll be arriving. After a four-hour drive we're on campus by early afternoon. Jordan and I meet at the student union, then take a long walk through the woods to the off-campus apartment he shares with two other graduate students. My heart is beating fast and I'm swallowing air. Jordan asks where I'm spending the weekend. "Suzy and I are staying at Uncle Bill's fraternity house." . . . "No you're not. If you ever want to see me again you stay here tonight. That's the way it is." Gulp! "All right. I guess I'm staying with you." Although this somewhat military approach strikes me as cold, my desire for him keeps me obedient. I do as I'm told. I go back to the fraternity house, get my bag, and leave Suzy a note. That evening Jordan takes me to some frat parties, where there are kegs of beer and live bands. I'm impressed and intimidated by this older college crowd, who, shit-faced and stoned, are singing and dancing wildly to "Woolly Bully," "Louie Louie," and "Mustang Sally." Even though I feel out of place, the music is familiar and at least I'm wearing my preppy uniform—matching pink wool skirt and sweater, knee socks, and Bass Weejuns. Every time I look at Jordan I panic. The hour is fast approaching.

When we go back to his place, there's another party in full swing. As I walk down the hall, I wonder if any of them knows I'm about to get my hip card punched and my cherry broken. Standing in the bathroom, staring in the mirror, I say good-bye to the little girl who's still wearing braces. I tell myself, *Be brave and fake what you don't know. Hide your fear. You're going to become a woman now.* I remember not to look in the mirror too long—Pat says it can drive you crazy.

I go back to the bedroom, and Jordan's sitting on one of the twin beds, watching me. "Are you going to wear your matching outfit to bed?" . . . "What?" . . . "Aren't you going to get undressed?" . . . "Yes, but can we please shut off the light?" He shakes his head and snickers as he turns off the lamp. He gets a great big kick out of my naiveté.

I take my clothes off by the light of the full moon shining through the window and slip into bed beneath the thin orange blanket. Smoothly, he takes his pants and underwear off and slides in beside me. He holds me for awhile, then begins kissing me. Suddenly, he's on top of me, forcing himself inside. It's too quick and too soon. I'm not ready. And it hurts. I want him to take longer, to caress me, to touch me tenderly the way he did before. I groan and gasp for air as he pushes deeper. Jordan's having a great time and I am the spectator. I'm rigid and can't turn off my mind. Is this the way it's supposed to be? I just want it to stop. He pushes further inside me. With his palms on the bed, he props himself up. And from the top of his mountain, miles away, I hear him say, "Jenny, I love you." Then he slaps me across the face. He continues to move inside of me. "I love you," he tells me again and slaps me even harder. I'm stunned and stung. "I'm going to come!" he shouts, which confuses me even more. Why this announcement? After it's all over, he pulls out of me, turns his back to me, and begins to cry. I lie there and feel the warm trickle of blood roll down the insides of my thighs. *If he loves me why did he hit me?* I ask myself over and over. *Is he angry that he loves me? Why is he crying?*

On Sunday Jordan drives me to the airport for my flight home on Mohawk Airlines. I am so sore I can barely walk or sit down. How can I face my father? How can I hide my guilt and sadness? I am continually on the verge of tears. "Look, Jen," Jordan tells me as we drive, "it's not as though you've changed. You're the same person." I'll never forget this moment, the bend in the road, or the cool way he says this. I don't feel like the same person. I feel like a de-virginized, dehumanized piece of shit. Waving to him from my airplane seat I begin to cry. I am in love and I will stay caught in its various shades for the next two years.

Although Jordan never hit me again, he controlled me with his sarcasm and manipulation. After two years of our sneaking around, I'm glad it is finally over. The thrill of the danger and duplicity has worn thin. So, too, my gullibility. It's time to move on.

I meet a guy at Mitty's that I really like. Bill's from South Carolina, drinks Tanqueray on the rocks, and always has a Marlboro dangling from his lips. He wears Gucci loafers without socks . . . . so cool. He plays backgammon all the time.

Shit! Jordan's tracked me down at Mitty's. I am talking to Bill when Jordan storms in and orders me outside to the parking lot for a talk. "I want to marry you," he says. I can't believe what he's saying! "Go back to Georgia. She needs you." . . . "But I love you. I really love you." . . . "Well I don't love you. Leave me alone." I have never seen Jordan look so lost. I feel embarrassed for him. "Jordan," I say quietly, "please just go away." He gets it, walks to his Mustang, turns around and gives me one last pleading look. I don't say good-bye. As he peels out of the lot, the dust flies and the gravel crunches. "The End."

Khristy calls. I've hardly seen her all summer. She's got terrible news. She's out of work. She was taking the poodle for a walk when it got run over by a Mercedes.

Fall

The summer ends on the heels of the Democratic convention, leaving Chicago a riot zone. I feel far away from these events. But thank God I've got a TV, so I can watch this disastrous chapter unfold; the highlight for me being the Buckley-Vidal debates. I don't feel as if I'm part of the brave souls who are helping to end the war. Not like my sister Georgia, who's become the family activist, always getting arrested. They're out in front—between me and the ditch. Right now, I'm more concerned with the direction of my own life.

The logical move is to go back to New York City and start a career. Over Labor Day weekend I meet a model, Matthew*, who invites me to stay at his apartment on Eighty-third and First. He thinks I should try my hand at modelling. Why not! I feel too gangly, but I go to his agency, Stuart 5. They send me out for test shots and go-sees. I even pose for a photography class at the Fashion Institute of Technology. But it's such a demeaning world I can't stand it. They look me up and down, say yes, say no. I climb up dirty, urine-stenched staircases to dark studios. Strangers tell me I'm enough or not enough.

Since I began sleeping with Matthew things haven't been working out. He's asked me to leave . . . . With pleasure! Matthew is the epitome of the narcissistic model—chiselled features and lean, taut body, blond, blue-eyed, and concerned only with his looks. I'm always tempted to slap that posed, self-consumed pout off his face. I need a place to stay, so I go see Jordan at Maxwell's Plum*, the bar on First Avenue that he's managing. I swore I wouldn't see him again, but I'm desperate and he's still carrying that torch. He gives me the keys to an empty apartment around the corner that belongs to some friend. It's a typical New York walk-up—small, depressing, furnished, and all mine—if only for a brief time. After two weeks, an eviction notice appears on the front door, followed by a phone call telling me I have twenty-four hours to clear out. Guess nothing's for free. So now I'm standing on York Avenue in a bitter wind with my down pillows, a portable TV, overstuffed suit-case, and my modelling portfolio, looking for a phone booth. I call Bill, who's easy to track down; he's at Churchill's, a bar on Third Avenue and a well-known backgammon hangout. He tells me to come over and get the keys to the apartment he's sharing . . . . Ah, Bill. He's slumped over a backgammon table with his winter drink, Drambouie, in hand. Out of the Southhampton sun, in his tweed jacket and argyle socks, he looks too complete. It clashes with his debauchery. His apartment is on Eightieth, in a fashionable brownstone between Madison and Fifth. The addresses are getting better.

I'm sitting on the couch watching my TV when the door opens and in walks Bill's roommate, Chris Dewey; a tall, lean, blond WASP, very attractive, but a little jumpy. "Who are *you?*" he asks. "I'm Jenny Lee, a friend of Bill's. I needed a place to stay." . . . "Good old Bill, I haven't seen him lately." Pointing down the hall, he says, "The bedroom's that way." . . . "I found it, thank you. Can I fix you a drink?" After a few days Bill leaves for South Carolina. Lucky for me.

It's not long before I move into Chris's bedroom. I'm never in love with him, but he's fun to be with and even more fun to sleep with. Since I need a job, Chris offers me one at a film company he had founded a year earlier with a pal Dennis Friedland—Cannon Films. It's in a small office in the East Fifties between Park and Madison, and it's like a family—a small group of young people determined to make the company a hit. (It's since become one of the most successful, independent film companies in the world.) I start out as a receptionist and start dressing up in mini-skirts and wearing makeup, realizing, finally, I'm pretty. Young Wall Streeters and in-vestors—Chuck Pheifer, Taki Theodorcropolous, Dimitri Villard, James Oppenheimer Clark—come into the office, flirt, and ask me out. I also meet and date filmmakers, such as Axl*, who's just won an award at a prestigious film festival for a documentary about his wife, who'd been a top model.

Now that I'm making money, it's time to be more independent. With two co-workers, I move out of Chris's into a two-bedroom apartment in the East Seventies . . . . Three real bachelorettes. One was having an affair with a wealthy married man and is trying to convince me that it's the only way to go. I try going out with Ted* a few times, but I don't like it. It makes me feel cheap and I'm not willing to pay the price. Besides, I'm not looking for a boyfriend; I've discovered Max's Kansas City on Park Avenue South, where I've been spending many nights dancing till dawn to live music—including Bruce Springsteen.

1969

Spring

After a few months at Cannon I'm put in charge of investor relations where I keep everyone apprised of the current status of the projects in which they've invested. I love working at Cannon. But then it goes public and everything changes. We're all given company stock. One day, Norman Friedland, Dennis's father, comes in and claims the certificates need correcting and asks for them back. None of us realize that it's a trick; the certificates are never returned. Norman has balked at Chris's and Dennis's generosity. So, for me, Cannon's all over. Although everyone's hurt and angry no one is willing to do anything about it. Except me; I have to let them know what I think. I walk into Dennis's office while he's in a meeting with his father and Chris, hand over my Rolodex and say, "Good-bye, I don't like this new set of rules." I walk out of the building right into a thunderstorm. An omen? I know that this is a turning point. I go to a record store and buy a Nina Simone album, kick off my shoes, and run all the way home in the rain. Laughing all the way!

Pat's mother Mimi has died after a long and painful bout with cancer. She'd hated me ever since Harry made me do my imitation of her picking things up off the floor. He roared, she scowled. We all go to the big house in Elizabethtown for the funeral, and Pat's sisters forbid me to go to the cemetery in my black mini. I stay home and read pieces of adhesive tape. On every stick of furniture throughout her huge house, Mimi had stuck a piece of tape on which she'd written the name of the person who'd get it when she died. I search for my name . . . finally locating it on a small table in a hallway. Well, she couldn't have hated me all that much. Aunt Jane arrives with a U-Haul for her share. Pat is depressed to see the locusts descending.

Summer

Find work as a production assistant on *The White Whore and the Bit Players*, based on Tom Eyen's surreal Off-Broadway play, one of those artsy-fartsy, "who cares and why bother anyway" kind of films. It never gets released. I'm still going to Max's, and I'm seeing Axl a few times a week. I wonder if he and I will go anywhere? He has sure turned me on to sex—taught me to relax and experiment, even try my first three-way with another woman. He's probably the most well-endowed man I've ever met, and I don't mean financially. He knows it, too, and has even given me a matted blown-up photo of himself holding his erect manhood. When *White Whore* wraps I take some odd modelling jobs, work nights checking coats at a Third Avenue bar, take acting classes at Herbert Berghof Studios, and do some post-production work on *End of the Road* that stars James Earl Jones and Stacy Keach. I hear Georgia's at Woodstock. Good place for her, rolling around in the mud with all those hippies. I'm glad I turned my car around when I heard on the radio what a mob scene it is. Anyway, I'm not a flower child; grass makes me paranoid and I don't have to take LSD to know that it scares the shit out of me. Was it Picasso who said, "I don't need to take acid—I see the trees melting anyway?" Joining groups of anything scares me even more. All the hippies I've ever met seemed unable to focus or concentrate, and being oblivious is a frightening thought to me.

Fall

Meet director Arthur Hiller at a private screening, and he offers me a job as Ali McGraw's stand-in on *Love Story*. Arthur's warmth, and the childlike way he searches your face when he talks to you, makes him very attractive. He is genuinely interested in others and has a nurturing presence. I accept; I need a job and this will get me my Screen Actors Guild card. But I find standing around all day being lit excruciatingly boring and demeaning. I almost freeze to death sitting in the snow on the bleachers at Wolman Rink as they shoot the ice-skating scene. Everyone thinks Ali's so sweet but not a very good actress. She flares her nostrils to show emotion, reminding me of Pat.

17

1970

Winter

After the film wraps, Ryan O'Neal asks me out. We go to a party with publicist, Bobby Zarem, which model Carol Mallory gives for her lover, Claude Picasso, in her Upper East Side, cubist high rise. Ryan goes crazy over a gorgeous topless photo of Carol by Hero. Who wouldn't?

Spring

Cindy calls me, she's crying. Things are a real mess at home. Pat's picked up a hitchhiker on Route 2 and brought him home to stay. Joe-Jim-John is tall, skinny, sandy-haired, and at least ten years younger than Pat. He's got stooped shoulders, sneaky eyes, pale skin, and hands that look as if they've never done a day's work. Cindy also says he's very nervous and soft-spoken.

You never know who Pat might bring home. Sometimes, she gets it right. One summer, when Harry was the attorney for the Capitol District Chapter of SNCC—the Student Non-violent Co-ordinating Committee—she had the Freedom Singers camped out downstairs. I loved it. I'd go to bed at night listening to Rutha, Chuck, Cordell, and Bernice singing *a cappella* in four-part harmony, "Ain't Gonna Let Nobody Turn Me Round," "Pick a Bale of Cotton" and "We Shall Overcome." I was already in love with music, but this music, with its special harmony, remains tattooed on my soul. One winter she had the Beers Family move in while they were trying to get a record deal.

But this Joe-Jim-John is a different story. Cindy and Byron have rifled his backpack, finding passports with different names on them, bankbooks from Texas and Massachusetts, and an A&P name tag from Louisiana. Pat and Joe-Jim-John are sleeping together in the bunk-bed room; Cindy and Byron see Pat sneak in by him every night. What's Pat doing? Doesn't she give a damn about Cindy and Byron's safety, let alone the emotional impact this must be having on them? How can Harry allow this? Jesus, does he love her or is he just trying to keep the peace? Isn't anyone thinking of the kids?

At Peter's Strongwater's studio I meet Berry Berenson, who's working as a staff photographer for *Vogue* magazine. We hit it off immediately. She's tall, with slouching shoulders, svelte—an aristocratic Peter Pan. Her square jaw, sweet blue eyes, and shaggy, shoulder length, sandy hair give her an androgynous sensuality. A handsome woman, she's also one of the hippest women I've met, with her chic, kooky outfits. Berry invites me over to her duplex in the East Eighties, which she shares with her small spaniel, Squiggy, and Suzy Engelhardt. The apartment, with its custom-built, Afghan-pillowed couches draped with Indian tapestries, French movie posters with amber necklaces and scarves hanging from the frame, and mismatched, brightly colored dishes and mugs, reflect her elegant, gypsy sense of style and taste. She definitely inherited her flamboyance from her grandmother, Elsa Schiaparelli. When she shows me Suzy's room she mentions that her roommate is leaving in June, and would I like to move in? I would love to. I know Berry appreciates who I am, but I can also tell that she wants to take me under her wing a bit. Sometimes she looks at me as if I'm "that wild, little waif from Cropseyville."

I'm told that Joe-Jim-John left last night. Harry finally took a stand and ordered him out, and Pat left with him. The sleaze started walking out the door with Harry's luggage and Cindy started shouting, "Dad, he's got your suitcase! Hit him, Dad!" Then Harry cold-cocked Joe-Jim-John in the jaw. Pat started yelling, "You shanty Irish bastard, you can't keep a woman with your fists." Then Harry tells her, "I didn't hit him because he took my wife, I hit him because he took my suitcase."

This has been cataclysmic. It is the straw that has broken my father's heart. Pat is finally, truly, gone. Sometimes my father's strength has looked like weakness. They loved each other so much once. One letter I have from Harry to Pat reads, "I know that I would never, never be happy again if I had to go on through life without you. Indeed, I would not want to go on at all." Perhaps he once thought that his love would save her. When that failed, he began to indulge her. He let her bring people home to appease her, and also to enjoy these magical misfits himself—from his distant role as benign provider. But it became a dangerous habit, some sort of fractured sublimation for Pat's need to create something other than a family, a beautiful garden, or a great dinner. Even her role of wifely social Democrat—pouring tea and organizing benefits when Harry was legal consultant to Governor Harriman—wasn't fulfilling enough. Finally, Pat began creating her own departure, breaking away through her outbursts of madness. And Dad has had to become more stable in the face of her increasingly idiosyncratic and inconsistent behavior, no longer reacting to her outbursts with violence. In the process he has, to some degree, become a martyr to her convulsive interior self. Sometimes he has had to be both father and mother to her as well as to the children. I wonder to what extent this has inhibited his own identity, growth, and the direction his life has taken. Are we all the results of the people with whom we share our hearts and lives? Despite the suffering, everyone in our family loved the colors and textures Pat created in our lives.

June

Life at Berry's is one big whirl. Because of her job at *Vogue* and, more important, her social status—her sister Marisa is on her way to becoming a top model—everyone wants to know Berry. And Berry couldn't be more generous . . . introducing me to her friends and world—a weekend in Southhampton at Giorgio Sant' Angelo's house, parties at Halston's, tea with her dowager-legend grandmother at the St. Regis. I meet Kitty Hawks, Lou Lou de la Falaise, Lucy Saroyan, Paul Jasmin, and Marisa. We share clothes, diet doctors, haircuts, and mutual dislike of each other's boyfriends. She doesn't like Axl, and I don't like Thomas, the German aristocrat-social-climber. Berry brags to her friends about how strong and mature I am for my age; she always moves with an entourage, while I'm more of a loner—going to Max's by myself, studying acting. She claims to admire my courage, which helps me see my strengths. "It's incredible how your father leans on you," she says. "This must be painful, yet you seem to deal with it. You're so strong and so giving." Sometimes even I think Harry's putting too much on my shoulders. He's sent me four, grainy, eight-by-ten photos that some detective took of Pat and Joe-Jim-John outside a package store in Williamstown. Harry's filed for divorce. Took him long enough. Twenty-three years.

Pat and Harry met during World War II, when he was a captain in the Marines. During combat in Okinawa, Harry met a fellow Marine who asked him to look up his wife, Jane, in Elizabethtown,

N.Y. when Harry went home on his next leave. Pat was working there as a hostess at the Deer's Head Inn. She was having breakfast when Harry walked in wearing his officer's uniform decorated with campaign ribbons. He asked her if she knew Jane Brewster Evans. She answered, "I'm Pat Brewster, Jane's my sister. Please, join me." He was so handsome with his rocky Irish jaw, kind hazel eyes, and wavy black hair that Pat drank the maple syrup and poured her coffee over the pancakes. She was in love.

Harry tells me that he's always known the truth about Pat. "I was walking in Central Park with Pat after I returned. We were engaged to be married and I was happy. The war was over and I was in love. I was filled with the horror and sorrow of what I had seen and very much needed to talk about what I was feeling. I wanted to be able to tell someone else for the first time all that I had been through . . . . I began to open up my heart. At last someone I loved and who loved me would be able to understand the sadness that I felt. I began to cry as I talked about the men and boys I had watched die, of all the grief. At that moment, Pat began shouting, 'Look! Look!' as she pointed to a faraway pond. 'Look at the swans! Aren't they beautiful?' To tell you the truth, Jenny, all I could see was the mistake I was about to make."

But that didn't deter Harry, neither did the news from Pat's father. At the age of twenty-one Pat, severely depressed by a boyfriend's rejection, was committed to Stony Lodge Sanitarium in Ossining, New York. There she was diagnosed as schizophrenic and given twenty-one electric-shock treatments. This resulted in withdrawal, followed by further severe depression, loss of contact, complete confusion, amnesia, and severe back pains. Despite her mental history, I think Harry believed that love would fix whatever was broken. Besides, Pat was pregnant, she didn't want go through a second abortion, and Harry wanted this baby too. (As Harry was fond of telling us, "You were all wanted.") She was an extraordinary beauty, with chestnut brown hair and an exuberant personality.

Pat's ancestors go back to the Mayflower (William Brewster), something she never lets Harry forget. After a few drinks, she'd snarl and call him "Shanty Irish." Pat's father, Osceola Byron Brewster, was a New York Supreme Court Justice, named in honor of the great Seminole chief who had a child with one of the Brewster women.

Martha Evelyn Brewster, Pat's great-aunt, married Oliver Brown, one of the abolitionist John Brown's sons. He and all his brothers were killed along with their father in 1859, after their raid on the arsenal at Harper's Ferry, Virginia. With Judge Brewster's help, the bodies eventually found their way back to North Elba, New York, outside Lake Placid, Brown's home at the time he was killed.

When we were children, Pat took us to the graves. We stood over them, held hands, swayed from side to side, singing, "John Brown's body lies amould'ring in the grave . . ." Sometimes at home she'd get out a small wooden box that had belonged to John Brown. Inside, attached to the wood, was his compass, and Pat would let us hold the heirloom while she read to us from family letters dated 1860. "Oh! how my heart has ached for those suffering ones at The Ferry. What must have been their feelings to have a band of murderers and thieves come upon them without a moment's warning! In some parts of the world sympathy is for Brown's family, but not here." Pat explained how greatness can look insane!

Now, as I stare at the photos of Pat and Joe-Jim-John getting into her station wagon, about to head off down a highway to who knows where, I'm sad and frustrated that I can't stop her desire to live a life fulfilled. She's always causing pain. I hate her. I don't have a compass to point her in a safe direction. I'm worried about the kids. Cindy says Byron's taking it especially hard. He feels abandoned and keeps asking, "What did I do wrong?" I'm worried about Dad, too.

Cindy calls to say that Joe-Jim-John has left Pat. He walked out of their motel room, went to get cigarettes, and never came back. Then Pat went looking for Joe-Jim-John. Cindy went looking for Pat. And Pat's been found. . . . living in Albany in an apartment down the street from Georgia. Of course Georgia's been no help. She can't handle any of this.

Pat's been calling Cindy, telling her about her new life, living with drug dealers and selling mescaline. When Cindy knocks on the door of Pat's sleazy apartment, a man answers, stark naked. Inside, everyone's naked, including Pat. "Don't be upset, Cindy. This is perfectly natural." . . . "No it's not! No it's not!" Clay, the tattooed leader of the group, tells her, "You're just an uptight kid." Everyone is tripping.

Cindy figures Pat has already spent more than $8,000 on gifts for her "roommates." Cindy tries to steal the Minolta camera and the Harley-Davidson motorcycle from them, figuring Pat will need the money when she comes to her senses. But when Cindy goes for the camera, Clay catches her, slams her against the wall, and says, "How dare you, you little motherfucker!" Undaunted, Cindy gets Georgia's musician-biker boyfriend to come and help her retrieve the Harley. Again they're caught, but not before Cindy cuts the wires on the bike, making it inoperable. A scuffle follows. Cindy gets away. Furious, Clay tosses the bike into Pat's Karmen Ghia and drives off to have it fixed. On the way back he totals the car, hops on the bike, and rides off into the sunset. A few days later the rest of the guests at "chez Pat's" check out, leaving her alone again. Desperate, she shows up in Harry's office trying to sell him her antiques. She needs money to continue her search for Joe-Jim-John, who she now believes is George Harrison. Harry puts her into Mosher.

But not for long. Pat gets arrested trying to sneak past security at the Plattsburgh Air Force base. Somehow, she's managed to get on the roof of the Albany Medical Center, convince a construction worker to hoist her down in the bucket of his crane, and hitchhike to Plattsburgh. When the security guards at the base ask her what she is doing, she tells them, "I'm trying to stowaway on a plane to London. George Harrison is waiting for me. He told me so in his songs." Pat gets locked up in the Ogdensburg State Hospital with "loss of memory and severe withdrawal," then transferred back to Albany Medical. Later she becomes an out-patient, and is put on Lithium.

Summer

Dad calls me at Berry's to tell me Pat's kidnapped Cindy! Pat shows up at the house, tells Cindy if she loves her she'll come with her, giving her time to leave a quickly scrawled note on the kitchen table. Thank God Byron is in school. Cindy grabs her Siamese cat, Yasmin, and they hitchhike to Provincetown in a rainstorm. This whole trip is especially dangerous because Cindy has diabetes. After arriving in Provincetown, Pat and Cindy spend the night in a tent with some black hippies. Cindy refuses to smoke pot with everyone, next, they take a room at Mrs. White's* boarding house (where we had spent some holidays). Then Pat splits and moves in with the Hare Krishnas. Cindy tries sleeping there on a mat on the floor one night, but wakes up past midnight with a diabetic

23

reaction. When she tries to leave to get some food they tell her, "No one's allowed to leave Krishnas's house." . . . "I'm fucking leaving," she says, pushing them out of her way. When Cindy refuses to dress up in robes and beg for money, Pat throws a fit. Cindy leaves and goes back to Mrs. White's. The Krishnas are happy. They don't like her threatening attitude or the hissing cat perched on her shoulder. Besides, she's what stands between them and Pat's money—several thousand dollars—which they eventually get. One morning, Cindy shows up and Pat's not there. She's on a bus with the Krishnas—something about a rally in Boston. Cindy waits a few days for her to return but she never does. Broke, she can't pay her board. Sweet Mrs. White throws her out and Cindy finds a cheap room on the bad side of town and gets a job at a fishstand on the pier . . . . Pretty gutsy for a fourteen-year-old. She even covers for Pat, telling Harry that everything's all right and not to worry. Then Cindy gets sick. She has an abscessed tooth and is about to go into a diabetic coma. Her fellow boarders make her call home. Harry rushes to get her and puts her in a hospital in Troy. Cindy tells him, "I always believed she was coming back for me."

I'm on a beach digging with my bare hands, looking for a knapsack full of valuables that Pat has buried in the sand. But where? This is ridiculous. I can't remember Cindy's exact directions. Which rock? Which bush? Forget it. I'm in Provincetown to clean up Pat's mess after first picking up her station wagon at the Greyhound Bus Depot in Boston. (This car was abandoned often during Pat's many travels.) I settle with Mrs. White and collect Pat's belongings. I go visit Cindy in the hospital. Her face is smeared with iodine from the oral surgery. Freaked, I scream, "What have they done to you?" which freaks her out, too. We end up laughing. I'm so relieved she's okay. "Would you and Byron like to come to East Hampton with me and Axl this summer?" I ask. Then I spend some time at home with Harry, comforting him over the divorce. He's lonely and drinking more martinis than usual. (I have seen him weep over a martini glass before, watching his tears fall straight into the clear liquid.)

One night I'm standing in the kitchen when Pat suddenly appears in the back door. "Hi, Jenny," she says, nonchalantly as if I had just seen her yesterday. "What are you doing in Cropseyville?" I notice something on her forearm, and ask, "What is that?" . . . "It's my new friend," she says, yanking up her dirty denim shirt sleeve, revealing a nine-inch-long tattoo of an American Bald Eagle with the word FREE underneath it. I ask her how she's been, all the while checking her out—blue jeans tucked into hiking boots, her hair in a long braid, looking like she definitely needs a bath. "Fine, I've been travelling, you know. Hitchhiking around the country. Meeting all kinds of people. Sleeping where I can." I don't know what more to say to her. A few moments later she asks me to drive her to the Beerses, who now have a house about fifteen miles up the road. As she gets out of the car I ask what she's doing here. "I'm staying with Evelyn and Bob."

The next morning we get a call from the Beers, who seem rather shaken. They tell us that Pat has broken in and is sleeping on their living room couch. I go get her while Harry calls the shrink. When the shrink arrives, I tell this charlatan off. "You're an incompetent asshole. Pat's crazier than ever.". . . "Calm down," he says. "How dare you take my father's money for all these years and tell me to calm down. Fuck you! I've got a lunatic for a mother! *You* calm down!" Pat sits there, mute. Evelyn's got a look of self-righteous pity. Maybe she's forgotten how much Pat helped her and her family when they were down and out. It's time to get *serious*. No more Albany Medical Clinic. That afternoon, Harry and I drive Pat to the Poughkeepsie State Hospital. They're waiting for us, and immediately give Pat a dose of Thorazine. Then a matronly aide takes Pat's hand and leads her down a green corridor. She goes willingly, like a child; I watch her fragile back as she walks away. Suddenly, I realize I have been wearing a shield, and my heart breaks. Pat doesn't look back. I wonder, will she be safe here? Will she get better? Lucky me, I'm chosen to describe all the gory details to some anonymous psychiatrist as my father sits silently behind me. Harry allows me to take charge of this situation, perhaps because it is too painful, or perhaps because he has managed to evoke eternal sympathy from me throughout the years. It's been my job to be the caretaker of his pain. In the process, the shield returns. I have come to loathe my mother for causing this pain. I see my father as the victim of a wild and tortured soul. I wonder if Pat could ever really love me.

Fall

I decide to try living with Axl in his small carriage house in the Village. We've had a fairly nice summer together in Easthampton so maybe it'll work, even though he's still married to someone who's "getting it together" in some faraway hippie-style rehab. Cindy and Byron spent a few weeks with us. It was good to be with them even if Byron's temper, as well as my own, were exhausting. They're back home in Cropseyville where Harry's much loved, well intentioned, but drill-sergeant sister, Aunt Agnes, is in charge. I send Harry a copy of Nancy Milford's *Zelda*, telling him how much Zelda reminds me of Pat.

Talk to Berry about moving out. "Good timing," she says. "I've been looking for a loft. This'll make me do it." She hopes, but doubts, that moving in with Axl is the right decision. Well, I'm not mad about her new boyfriend, either. Tristan Stark* is a flamboyant performance artist who lives in the East Village. I just don't get *what* he and Berry are doing together.

Dad's now seeing someone Pat introduced him to, named Yvonne. She's divorced, Swiss, the mother of two children, and very into yoga and Krishna Murti. At night I work with Axl on some film he's making about Buckminster Fuller. During the day I model for Yves St. Laurent and Issey Miyake and continue to take acting classes. Sex with Axl is still creative, even though he's asking for too many threesomes. It doesn't feel like an experiment anymore. He doesn't like me to go to parties, or to Max's, without him. He especially hates it when I tell him about the types of people I'm meeting: like Gerard Malanga, a poet-photographer who I like and who writes me poems, poems, poems; Sven Lukin, who wears his apathy like a shield; sad Robin Clark; Paul Morrissey, who seems more neuter than gay; and Sylvia Miles, who talks for hours on the topic which interests her most—herself. His wife calls all the time, talking to Axl as if *he* were the crazy one, and ordering him to do-this-or-do-that regarding their two-year-old son, who's living with us. I feel very much the interloper. She seems to be everywhere. When I go to the drugstore she's staring at me from boxes of cherry red hair coloring. She has the face of an angel, but those eyes, with their haunting *sampaku* . . .

26

1971

January

Axl has begun smoking mean little cigars, making him look like a pimp. He behaves like one too, especially since he's given me a couple of social diseases. I call a halt to the threesomes, put my heart on hold, decide to have a talk with Harry, who drives down to see me. We meet at the Palm Restaurant, where Pat had gone into labor with me twenty-one years ago. Feeling blue and kicking the sawdust on the floor, I listen to Harry's lecture on love. As we eat our steaks Harry tells me that it all boils down to one sentence: "Love is about socks and shoes." . . . "Socks and shoes?" . . . "It's about responsibility and taking care of the ones you love." . . . "What about you and Pat? Have you taken care of each other very well?" . . . "That's a whole other matter, but I have provided for all of you."

I think about socks and shoes on my way back to Axl's, the House of Bare Feet. A few days later I find out I'm pregnant, adding insult to injury. But I know I can deal with it. Over dinner, I tell Axl that I want an abortion and my own apartment. The veal goes flying and I do too, right out the door. Halfway out, he grabs my arm, spins me around, and slaps me across the face.

I move into a fourth floor walk-up in a renovated brownstone on East Eighteenth Street near Gramercy Park. A week later, in the dead of winter, I go to Beth Israel Hospital, and am among the first group of women who have legal abortions in New York State. It's a decision I feel very clear about. Of course I pay the entire bill. While at home recovering, Axl drops by with a can of Campbell's soup. Thanks Axl.

February

Max's Kansas City has become the backdrop to my life. I usually go around midnight and stay until four, or whenever it closes. It feels like a private club and I'm happy to be a member. *Everyone* comes to Max's—from Andy Warhol to Gloria Vanderbilt to Nicholas Ray. Then there are the rock stars and their groupies, the Euro-flash, the jet-setters, painters and poets, and international good-time girls. Anything is possible here. From Frosty Myers's loft on

Park Avenue, a red laser beam shoots south, then veers left into Max's picture window, continuing overhead until it hits the wall of Max's back room. I bounce from booth to booth downstairs and then head upstairs where I dance for hours on end. I hang out in the back room sometimes, but never feel too comfortable there; it's mostly filled with Andy's stars and groupies who look as if they're following the pied piper while at the same time they're trying desperately to be some sort of self-contained, walking sideshow. There's Eric Emerson and his high-tech bisexuality; Andrea Whips and her X-rated champagne bottle routine; the gorgeous and sweet siliconed transvestite Candy Darling. (All dead. Including Mickey Ruskin, who conceived this nightly three-ring circus.)

Spring

Fix up the apartment: a few cheap Orientals, some tapestries, and some plants displayed against the living room's brick wall. That'll do. I'm never home. Days are spent modelling. . . . Get an album cover for some German choral group. Demonstrate Berber makeup at Bendel's. Work a few days at the Moroccan consulate before they find out I can't speak French. Well, I tried. Since Berry's moved to her loft we've become even closer. She's upset about Tristan. She doesn't understand why he keeps going to Europe without her. She cries a lot. I go to a party at Frankie Welch's with them, where they goad me into doing my Gloria Vanderbilt imitation. Paul Jasmin tells me the reason why some of his guests freaked out is because they were on acid and thought I *was* Gloria. . . . Join Max's softball team playing left field.

Closing time at Max's last night, I'm outside unlocking my ten-speed bike, listening to René Ricard spin a poem—pretty Jenny—pretty penny—when I notice Roger Vadim and Jane Fonda watching my every move. They've been showing up at Max's almost every night lately. I say, "Hi." Jane, statuesque, is wearing a snug-fitting, suede-fringed mini dress and boots, lookin' *good*. Vadim, wearing slightly tinted glasses, is standing behind her, hands in his pockets, smiling lasciviously. "What are you doing tonight?" Jane asks. "Well," I say, relieved that my lock has finally opened, "I'll be going home and reading some diaries. Good-night."

This strikes me as a much better alternative than becoming an-other little trophy of Vadim's and Jane's, like Geraldine Smith or

Eric Emerson or Patti D'Arbanville or Andrea Whips—with whom they've been spending *beaucoup* nights! I've been compulsively reading all of Anaïs Nin's diaries after Gerard had given me a gift of Volume Four, which he'd had inscribed by her to me. (Years later, I saw Anaïs Nin wandering down a hospital corridor in Los Angeles, looking frail, like a translucent angel.)

I run into Nancy Allen (who later married Brian DePalma and starred in his movie *Dressed to Kill*) at a magazine shoot for some hair product. Afterward, we walk back to her place in the East Seventies, where she shows me around the apartment she's sharing with another model, who just happens to be dating Axl. "Poor Laura, she's a mess over him. Lucky you got away." Nancy also mentions she's good friends with Warren Beatty. "Do you want to meet him?" . . . "Sure." Although I'm aware of him because of *Bonnie and Clyde*, I don't feel in awe of him. But, why not meet a movie star! So Nancy and I go over to the Carlyle, where Warren is staying. I'm not sure that I'm dressed right for the occasion in my Betsey Johnson corduroy top and faded dungarees, but it doesn't seem to matter. Meeting Warren is no big deal. In fact, he seems instantly familiar, sort of like seeing an old friend that you haven't seen in a while.

Warren greets us wearing a terrycloth robe and mumbling something about "just getting out of the shower." As we sit in the living room of the suite, he really tries to make us feel at ease, offering us drinks, chatting about how Nancy and I know each other and how much he'd heard about me from Nancy. He's very warm and sweet and adorable! Although he's about thirty-three years old, he's like a young boy, with a strong, tight body and lots of energy. When the phone rings, he runs off to get it in the bathroom, then comes back in and picks up the conversation. Finally, he suggests getting a bite to eat and rushes off to get dressed.

After our bite we're all standing under a streetlight, waiting for a cab. It's obvious that Warren is leading us back to the hotel. Nancy extricates herself, saying, "I've got to go home right now." Warren makes her promise to call later, and for a second, I wonder if I've been set up. Shit. Do I want to be alone with this knockout? I hem and haw. "Maybe I should go home, too." . . . "Nonsense, you're coming with me." I know what he'd had in mind for the three of us, and now there's just us chickens. "Aww, come on. I'm not going to bite you." Well, *carpe diem*. We go back to the hotel. "Nancy's

29

messed up your plans, huh?" I say. "Yeah, but I always have a back-up. I don't think I'll use it tonight. We'll save that for later."

For the next few weeks I see a lot of Warren. Sometimes, we go out for dinner and to the movies. He likes an unusual assortment; one night it's a double bill, *Freaks* and *The Night of the Living Dead*. Another night it's Renoir's *The Rules of the Game*. And we make love. (Often, we're interrupted by phone calls from his then-girlfriend Julie Christie, which he takes in the bathroom, a towel draped around his hips.) Sometimes we're alone and sometimes there's another woman.

I do like Warren a lot; he's a good lover, strong, passionate, and sensual. But, for all his reputation, he's not a particularly great lover. [He's not *that* well endowed no matter what Madonna said in her *Advocate* interview]. In fact, it's almost as if his reputation gets in the way. His need to be "great" in bed transcends any true consideration of his partner's needs, so it all boils down to *his* experience, *his* conquest. When he tries to relate intimately it's too hard—it's like crossing a line into serious narcissism. He likes to give directions, not only about positions, but about how you should feel and react. The pressure to have the biggest most earth-shattering orgasms can get a little relentless. I've definetly had to fake a few.

During the threesomes I never feel truly present; I feel like a camera, watching and recording the multilayered dynamics of these triangles. The extra person becomes just an object in the process, one that guards against the dangers of intimacy, but during these sessions Warren and I can connect in a way that we can't when we're alone. This third woman, whoever she may be—a top model, a wealthy married lady—becomes *our* object, *our* device. So a strange thing happens beyond the sexuality, Warren and I become freer to communicate. We enjoy another kind of intimacy, one that's borne out of complicity: shared glances, private jokes, awkward moments. If I drift, even if only for a moment, he gets concerned, asks if I'm okay, and pulls me back into this mad reality. Although he's the ringleader in our sex games, he's imbued me with an ego-gratifying authority and a sexual savvy, often allowing me to take charge. After our lady leaves, we discuss the experience, compare observations and personal moments. And the silence is filled with tenderness and relief, if only for a brief time.

One night Berry, Tristan, and I drop some mescaline and go to

Tristan's loft. He changes into full black leather regalia and takes us to Gianna's, a trucker-lesbian bar on Nineteenth Street. What *is* the message here? After twenty-nine seconds Berry starts crying. We rush out of there, and Tristan and Berry drop me off at my apartment. I'm feeling terrified! Thank God I only took half a tab. It's the first, and last, time I'll ever do that stuff!

Summer

Warren's good friend, Roman Polanski, is in town. Warren wants me to meet him, so we go up to his suite at the Essex House. The brutal murder of his wife Sharon Tate occurred two years ago, but it's immediately clear that Roman is still on the mend from that horrific experience. There's a strange kind of party atmosphere; not particularly joyous, it just seems designed for forgetting. There are several nameless young women who seem to be just lounging around.

Roman is an unusually short man, but he more than makes up for it with his intensity and energy. He's very much the man-child. I like him. It's also clear that he's amazingly egocentric, talking about *his* this and *his* that. He yearns to be the center of attention at all times, jumping up and down to emphasize a point, or even acting it out, hands constantly in motion, pushing his hair back off his forehead or wiping his lips of the spittle that flies out of his mouth in his exuberance. He gets as excited by the way he describes the rudeness of the hotel telephone operator as he does when describing a scene in a movie. One of the main themes of these monologues/performances is the inferiority and stupidity of many people. I realize the women in his entourage are his audience. Roman talks about *Macbeth*, which he's just finished shooting. It occurs to me that "the Scottish tragedy" is an odd choice for a man who's experienced such a devastating loss; perhaps it's an exorcism of some sort. (The only thing I've ever heard Roman say about the murders is, simply, "If I had been there it wouldn't have happened." And I believe him. There's a fierceness about him. A Polish Jew who survived the Holocaust, he's been a fighter since childhood.)

Later that evening, I'm with Warren in one of the dimly lit bedrooms. There are two queen-sized beds; Warren and I are on one of them, and we're about to make love. Suddenly, Roman walks in

31

with a porcelain-skinned, black-haired woman who is introduced to me as Soraya. Warren gives her a kiss. Clearly, they're more than friends. Roman and Soraya sit on the other bed. I extend my hand and say, "Nice to meet you." Warren whispers, "Soraya is a fascinating woman." I can tell that this gal is no slouch. Even in this light I can see her exquisite beauty. Who is she, and what are we all doing together in this room? It's obvious that something is supposed to happen here. Sometimes, three's company, but any more's a crowd. I'm uncomfortable, and decide to leave.

Roman, Warren, and I become a threesome of sorts—hanging out, going to Elaine's for dinner, going to screenings. I think that they appreciate knowing a woman who isn't a burden, who can be one of the guys. I consider myself lucky to be spending time with these two powerful, intellectual, productive, and complex individuals.

Fall

Warren and I go to an afternoon soirée at Sam Spiegel's stunning Park Avenue duplex. Sam and Roman are talking about their upcoming trip to London and Roman says to Sam, "Why don't you bring Jenny along?" . . . "Jennifer, would you like to come to London with me?" . . . "I can't. I'm modelling for Diane von Furstenberg." . . . "Who?" . . . "It's a new company. I'm her first showroom model." . . . "I'll pay your salary." I look at this overweight, seventyish, cigar-smoking man who produced such classics as *The African Queen* and *Lawrence of Arabia* and wonder, *What does he want?* I tell him I'll think about it.

The next day, I ask Warren what he thinks about this offer. I've come to trust Warren, to respect his opinions, and to take his advice. Although I know I'm one of his many lovers, I also know I'm the main one of many—the last stop before the ball-and-chain main squeeze, which is what Julie is. I am content with my status, as Warren is, since we are truly, good friends. He answers me, "No big deal, I think you might have fun" . . . "But what about my acting?" . . . "You can't just *say* you're an actress, you have to work hard at it." . . . "I've studied, and I'm working with Paul Grey." . . . "You haven't studied until you've gone to Stella Adler. Go to London, come back, and I'll pay your first term's tuition. I promise you, you're going to learn a lot."

It occurs to me that Roman and Warren have "pimped" before for old Sam, but I do want the adventure. Besides, I've never been to England. An experience is being offered, so why not? I'll go, and figure out the rest as I go along. But no way am I going to sleep with this man, even if he is paying my way. Diane's definitely not thrilled at my leaving. She's just starting her company; it's in two small rooms in the West Fifties. Anyway, I look like shit in the clothes she's making—common little wrap-around dresses in simple fabrics and boring designs. (I still don't understand how it's become the huge company it has. These dresses have sold like hotcakes to the housewives of America. I think it's the name—Diane is really clever at marketing. After all, she had a title—Princess—which she used, from her marriage to Egon von Furstenberg, whom she eventually divorced.) Diane and Egon are a young, attractive "in couple," who throw great parties, and they're very much a fixture at the "in"clubs. I met them through Berry one night at Hippopotamus, and am completely taken with Diane's European accent and continental charm. She calls everybody "darling" and kisses the air. So ethereal, so delicate. But underneath it all, Diane is one tough businesswoman.

Come home to find another poem by Gerard Malanga in my mailbox. This one's titled "R O U T E   2 :"

> *i follow you as far as it takes me*
> *where you have vanished*
> *27:ix:71 nyc*

There are two kinds of people in the world: toxic and nourishing. Gerard is both, but it's fun to be immortalized with hip haiku in his books dedicated to the beautiful and/or social women.

Cindy comes down from Cropseyville to visit and to work with Gerard, who's become obsessed with the idea of photographing her with Joe Dallesandro, the hunky star of Andy Warhol's *Flesh* and *Trash*. Gerard thinks they look like twins. We all spend the afternoon in Berry's loft, watching Gerard imitate Diane Arbus. [A photograph from this session turns up a few years later in *Screw* magazine.] I agree to let Gerard stay in my apartment while I'm away.

33

November

Finally, I'm on the flight to London! I'm excited. I'm also worried. What kind of situation have I gotten myself into? I've purposely arranged to follow Sam a week later to avoid going *a deux* and all that that implies. I'm glad Roman's in London now. I think about my life—do I really want to be an actress? I like my adventures. I believe I should be able to move as freely as any man can as long as I use birth control and I don't judge myself. A writer friend quotes Dag Hammarskjöld: "Never, for the sake of harmony, deny your own experience." The minute I heard this, I knew I would be true to it.

Hope all is well back home in Cropseyville—but that seems debatable. Yvonne has moved in with Harry. It seems awfully quick, but Dad needs someone there for the children; he needs someone there for himself, too. From everything he tells me, she sounds very caring, but Cindy's last letter was angry—she seems unhappy with his decision. She thinks Yvonne's taking over. She also says that Yvonne hates animals and has gotten rid of Wynkin, our sweet Brittany Spaniel. Cindy's convinced she's sent him packing off to the land of Nod. To further complicate matters, Yvonne's two children have moved in as well. Pat's taking her medication, but she's living with a man named Ace* who collects empty coffee cans, makes spider webs out of string, and talks to the kitchen sink. Ace met Pat when he picked her up hitchhiking (a variation on an old theme!). Every old sock finds an old shoe! Cindy says he's five hundred miles of bad road. Sounds to me more like five hundred miles of potholes. Think I'll have a Bloody Mary—maybe several.

I arrive in London to find that my room is in Flat 115 of Grosvenor House, on the same floor as Sam. I'm eating peanuts, drinking white wine, and looking at a dozen roses that David Puttnam (years later, the head of Columbia Pictures) has sent. David was waiting in the lobby when I arrived. He's got a crush on me; I don't feel the same way. I can't sleep—jet lag, nuts, vino.

The next couple of days I spend exploring London and shopping with money that Sam's given me. There's been no further mention of "paying my salary." Have dinner with Roman and some of his friends at Mr. Chow's: Sandy Whitelaw, Andy Braunsberg, and many beautiful, nameless women. I tell Roman that I'm uncomfortable at the Grosvenor House; he says that I can come stay at his place if I want to. At dinner one night with Sam, I suggest this. Although Sam's been a complete gentleman, never even suggesting a pass, the situation makes me feel uneasy. I thank him for his kindness and generosity. He says he understands; I feel a tad guilty. But Sam is mostly interested in appearances, so after a week in the hotel I feel as if I've fulfilled that obligation. I tell myself it was a fair exchange.

Roman's home is charming, a two-story carriage house in Eaton Place Mews. It's got a few strange pieces of furniture, though, such as the coffee table in the living room. It's a sculpture of a woman, crouched on all fours, with a plate glass top across her back. She's has large breasts, long blond hair, knee-high black leather boots, and leather gloves. Occasionally Roman changes her wig. Although I sleep with Roman, I've got my stuff in the guest room, which has a rather spooky vibe to it. The closet has some of Sharon's clothes in it; a shirt, a skirt, a pair of slacks, a pair of clogs, a pair of high heels. Sharon was a tall woman and the clothes, especially the shoes, seem particularly large, and almost animated. They have a kind of presence that feels too real. Everything is neatly hung on the left side of the closet. I keep my things on the right. I believe in ghosts.

Roman is fastidious and disciplined—he has a daily housekeeper so the house is spotless. He's up early every morning, eating the same breakfast—espresso, toast, and two wedges of Laughing Cow cheese. I like staying here and I like making love with Roman—as they say, it's not the size of the ship but the motion of the ocean. Despite his gargantuan ego, I've found him to be a real *mensch*. There's a festivity about everything he does. He seems to sweep people up into his world and they follow his irresistible force. He has no patience for self-pity or laziness; he is all will. Though somewhat jaded, there is an innocence about him; he laughs like a child at the simplest things. As mad as I can get at Roman, I can never stay mad, always maintaining a genuine affection for him. Never afraid to speak his mind, whether it's a surly waiter or a racist remark. And he's taught me to celebrate my own qualities of strength.

Staying at Roman's is never dull; people are always coming and going: Gerard Brach, Roman's screenwriter, Simon Hessara, and Gene Gutowski, one of Roman's producers. I share Roman's bed with him and with Eva, a Swedish model who's been staying at

Roman's, and who is more or less his girlfriend. Eva's incredibly beautiful—blond, blue-eyed, classical features, a real Greek goddess. She's really nice, too. Not terribly bright and, of course, very quiet, but a real buddy. During our threesomes, we use a lot of poppers. I have never really enjoyed that particular high. It has a stinging, nasty chemical odor, and it causes a tremendous rush that's very disorienting—sweat, spinning head, difficulty seeing or hearing—and lasts only a minute or so, so you end up on this intense roller-coaster ride. One night, Roman sets up the video camera and gets into bed with me and the gorgeous Swede. He's videotaping us and shoving poppers under our noses. Eva and I are lying on our backs. She's fondling me and he's on top of Eva, getting more and more excited, and yelling out, his Polish accent getting thicker and thicker. Then I start giggling at the puzzled look on Eva's face. Roman leaps up, "What's wrong?" I begin laughing even harder and, by now, Eva's giggling too. Roman gets furious. "Why are you laughing at me?" Now I can barely talk. "Roman, I'm not laughing at you." . . . "Get out of this bedroom now," he orders. Feeling like a banished bad child, I go into the guest room, sit on the bed, and look at Sharon's clothes. I'm not laughing anymore. A few minutes later, Roman calls, "Come here. Jenny, I want to show you something. I rewound the tape. You're right. You're not laughing at me." . . . "I'm really relieved, Roman," I say as I return to the room of dead clothes. As it turns out, this is my room for the remainder of my stay. Roman and I have clearly moved into friendship, and he tells me to stay as long as I like.

After a couple of weeks Eva leaves London, and I become the "bedroom hostess." Often, Myna, A Nigerian stewardess, or Fiona, an English actress, join Roman and me, but they never stay the night. It's funny how threesomes have become *the* way to make love. It's as if each of us is one of a series of interchangeable parts; we all come and go in different combinations.

I spend some time with Roman at Shepperton Studios, while he does dubbing and other post-production work on *Macbeth*. When I see a finished print at a screening, I cannot believe how violent a film he has made; it's a bloodletting. One afternoon, while alone in the house, Jon Finch—Macbeth himself!—knocks at the door and I take him to bed. "Double, double, toil and trouble/Fire burn and cauldron bubble . . ." I like being here, but what am I *doing*? Endless restaurants, parties, sex, and late evenings at

Tramps—the current disco. I haven't been at Roman's that long, only a week or so, but already I'm getting blue. I start exploring the house and wander into the garage, there's space for a car, but other than that, the rest of it's taken up with boxes and trunks stacked fully to the ceiling along one wall and about three-quarters of the way along the other. I find that they are all filled with newspapers, magazines, periodicals, and clippings about the murders, in every conceivable language. I leave . . . fast!

Shopping in the neighborhood, I find an album by Georges Moustaki in a record store and buy it for the song "Non Je Ne Suis Jamais Seul Avec Ma Solitude." Back at Roman's, I play it and play it and play it. He loves it, too, and translates the lyrics for me.

But Roman's Napoleon complex occasionally results in tyrannical outbursts that can be completely intimidating, and sometimes cruel. One night there are guests over for dinner and we order Indian take-out, which Roman tells me to put in the oven. When it's time to eat I serve the food—coagulated curry. Roman screams in front of everyone. "What did you do?" . . . "I put it in the oven, just as you said." . . . "Jennifer," he yells, "you have to turn the oven on!" So I'm not domestic; still I don't deserve the humiliation. Another time, he decides to challenge my desire to act in the middle of a crowded disco. "You want to act? Okay. I ask you to give me the expression of pity." Sitting in that dark room with its flashing strobes, blaring music, and dancing bodies doesn't inspire the vulnerability required for this emotion. He continues. "Show me sorrow!" I just sit there, intimidated and still. "Just as I thought!" he proclaims.

Usually, however, I give as good as I get, and Roman gets a kick out of it. During one heated argument with Sandy Whitelaw, Roman stops us by interjecting, "Sandy, don't bother arguing. She's a hermaphrodite." Sandy and I both look at him blankly. "She has a cock in her head." In a house where the women seldom speak, let alone engage in arguments about issues, I take this as a compliment.

We go to a dinner party at Gene and Judy Gutowski's. Among the guests is Soraya Khashoggi. "Hi, remember me?" she asks. "Yes. How've you been?" I ask, thinking, *how could I forget!* "Fine, darling," Soraya replies. We sit down to dinner. Afterward, Roman, Soraya, and I walk back to his house, which is just a few minutes away. We go up to Roman's bedroom where Soraya gives Roman a blow job. I help her out. Then we go back to the Gutowskis' for dessert. During coffee, Soraya asks me, "How long will you be here?"

"I haven't decided."

"Good, then you'll come on a trip with us."

"Where are you going?"

"To L.A., maybe Las Vegas. Who knows where else."

"Who's going on this trip?"

"Gene, Judy, me, my husband, and you. It'll be fun."

"Sounds like a great invitation. Let me think about it." The following week Soraya takes me to lunch a few times and we get to know each other. Judy and Gene urge me to come along and promise to be my chaperones. Roman tells me not to worry, that I'll be in safe hands with Gene there. "Besides," he adds, "Soraya's husband is a fascinating man. You'll definitely have an adventure."

I'm at Heathrow with Gene and Judy, we're waiting for Soraya and her husband, Adnan. We're in a DC-9 that A.K. intends to buy from Kirk Kerkorian, who's head of MGM. Adnan deals in arms and oil and is rumored to be one of the world's wealthiest men. Enter Soraya, wearing a full-length, leopard skin coat. Yikes! Twenty cats must have sacrificed their lives for that little wrap. She's followed by A.K., who's trailed by eight Arabs in full-length white sheets. Adnan immediately goes for a nap in the bedroom in the back of the plane. Roman was right! This will be an adventure! We're hardly off the ground when Jackie Williams, Soraya's assistant, a tall, bony, English aristocrat, serves us hot curried hors d'oeuvres from Tandori. At least *she* knows to turn the oven on. After dinner and several bottles of Cristal I find myself dancing with one of the sheets. I look up and see a fat, jolly man smiling at me. A.K. has just emerged from his nap. "You must be Jennifer." . . . "And you must be Adnan." . . . "Call me A.K." He watusis with me briefly before disappearing. I feel as if I'm in a dream or underwater; I'm not sure this is real. Then I overhear Soraya harshly reprimand her assistant. From the look on Jackie's face I can see that there's cruelty here. Suddenly, I look at Soraya in a new light. Her body, which has borne A.K. five children, is fleshy and untoned, short-legged and large breasts, a body built for breeding. I wonder if her looks are so legendary after all. What was it that got her out of Leicester, England, and her working-class background? Was it merely the porcelain skin and the chiselled features, the gorgeous

38

but vacuous face like those I've seen in a million cosmetic ads, or is there character and intelligence here? The story goes that A.K. and Soraya met in London at a gambling casino, and she brought him luck.

After landing in L.A., a fleet of stretch limos deliver us to the Beverly Hills Hotel. Since this is my first trip to L.A., I immediately have to hug a palm tree. That afternoon, Soraya, Judy, and I have lunch at the Bistro and shop on Rodeo Drive. Later, Warren calls and drops by my room. So does Soraya. Warren and I have just made love. A threesome is suggested, but for some reason Soraya seems nervous, so we abandon the idea. The next morning Soraya calls and says, "Pack a few things, darling. We're joining A.K. in Vegas tonight. He's there on business." Things do move swiftly in the world of oil and arms!

Our first night in Las Vegas, we have dinner with the heads of Lockheed, Northrop, and Raytheon. I feel as if I've got an obligation to fulfill—look beautiful and be charming for all these suits. I know something serious is going on here, and I feel slightly intimidated by the ambiguity of it all. There are a few other beautiful women at our table; supplied by whom and from where, I wonder? And the money—it's amazing! I'm continually bowled over by Soraya's wardrobe, while I'm stuck looking through the racks of green and yellow satins in the lobby dress shop. I'm trying not to worry about money, though I haven't worked for some time. Facials, steams, saunas, kinky underwear, all go on A.K.'s tab or Soraya's charge card.

The next night at dinner at the Desert Inn, I meet the stunning Prince Mohammed Bin Fahad of Saudi Arabia (who is now Governor of the Eastern Province—where all the oil fields are). He's tall, dresses impeccably, sports a mustache, is very formal with me, and smiles as if he knows everything, but isn't telling! Then there's Prince Faisal Al Sahud, his cousin, who's adorable, but in a different way. He's also well-dressed, but has a much more casual demeanor, a bigger, more open smile, and a hearty laugh. He also stutters amidst his broken English, but he doesn't seem to give a damn. These Arab fellows are just beginning to go outside their closed world with all their serious wealth, and it's clear that Adnan is a guide in sophistication, social tactics, and the pleasures of the decadent West. A.K. acts as though he's host of the casino . . . of the world. We go off to the gaming rooms, where I take a seat at the baccarat table next to Mohammed, who becomes even more formal and distant. But he does stake me a couple of thousand dollars. This is a sophisticated game for high rollers, so I don't think I'll be here long, but, an hour later, I'm ahead. Mohammed, however, isn't doing well. But just at the point when he runs out of money some mysterious man always shows up with a clipboard that Mohammed signs, and he's back in the game. On my way to the ladies' room, A.K. stops me to ask, "How much did Mohammed sign for? How many times?" It's dawn and I've won several thousand dollars. It's easy for me to stop—now I can pay some bills. I excuse myself and go to the dice-rolling table and watch Adnan play. This is a fool's game; with baccarat, I feel, there's some measure of skill involved. I watch Adnan drop nearly $600,000, and he doesn't blink an eye. Amazing—as though it all means nothing! I imagine that it would be quite easy for it *all* to mean nothing. After his final toss, A.K. turns to me, giggling, and says, "I'm starving and broke. Will you take me to breakfast?" After a few more days of Vegas-ing, we finally get our marching orders—it's back to L.A. I'm happy to be leaving Sin City, though. The neon lights, the pancaked showgirls, the incessant ringing of slot machines, the pastel wedding chapels, the hostile geometric carpets, the Dean Martin show, the banal waste of money, the half-eaten eggs benedict left outside anonymous hotel doors (next to half-empty glasses of watered-down bourbon filled with cigarette butts). This clockless glitz and insatiable hedonism is driving me around the bend. This is where gaudy goes when it dies. I'm getting paranoid. LET ME OUT!

At the Daisy in Beverly Hills, Adnan turns to me and says, "I've had your rooms bugged, you know." . . . "You're kidding, A.K.!" . . . "No, I'm not. You certainly speak to Mr. Polanski and Mr. Beatty a lot." Gulp. I remember Judy and Gene telling me that Adnan has detectives on Soraya all the time and rooms full of files about her activities. Whoops! I must be included. No wonder Soraya got nervous when she and Warren were in my hotel room. "Don't worry," he tells me, patting my hand and cackling. "Now, dear, where would you like to go for the weekend?" . . . "Acapulco!" It pops right out of my mouth and, a bit embarrassed, I look at all the other guests at the dinner table. "Great," says A.K., "pack some things. Tomorrow we're all leaving."

We land in Acapulco on a bright afternoon in early December.

Immediately, there's a controversy over Soraya's jewel case. She throws a tantrum at the customs gate, surrounded by her beaucoup bags. Following her instructions, I've brought a carry-on, while she must have twelve suitcases. Customs insists on keeping her jewels, though God knows what she needs them for. We have two pink villas at Las Brisas, each with it's own camellia filled swimming pool, pink Jeep, and view of the polluted Acapulco Bay. Adnan, Soraya and I are in one of the two villas, while Judy and Gene are in the other. Bob Sheheen, A.K.'s assistant, and Jackie stay in the hotel part. The next few days are spent in the pursuit of happiness and tropical drinks. We charter boats, picnic on a private island, watch the pearl divers at La Perla, and have catered dinners at our villas complete with flamenco dancers and mariachi bands. One night, after drinking tons of tequila and diving into the pool fully clothed, my suspicions come knocking at my bedroom door. "Jennifer." . . . "Yes. . . ?" . . . "Soraya and I would like you to join us tonight." "Oh, A.K., that's a great idea but I'm throwing up!" It works. Don't have to pay the piper, yet. On the way out of Acapulco, Soraya throws another fit when she finds that her jewel case is not under lock and key, but is sitting in the customs office next to a refrigerator full of *cervesa*.

December

Back at home in New York, a letter from Harry greets me:

Dear Jenny—
Everyone is excitedly looking forward to your return to the fold. I heard you took the pros at Las Vegas. I want to hear how you did it. . . . Byron went through a bad period at school and at home but Yvonne was magnificent. . . . and sought to change his hostile attitude by love, understanding, and persuasion. She bent to her purpose with absolute selflessness. Day after day she went to school, argued and cajoled with teachers, encouraged Byron, and even convinced teachers to upgrade his marks on the slightest evidence of effort. Her plan was to instill confidence. . . . The result has been little short of miraculous. . . . The boy felt defeated, stupid, incompetent. This feeling of

41

defeat turned to despair. Despair turned to hostility, hostility deepened and was hardening with an anti-social attitude that bordered on criminal mentality. All that is changed. Cindy's hold on him has been broken and that is good for both. Byron is his own man and no longer Cindy's serf. Cindy can find her way now. The future has promise. If I could only be sure that you are not losing your way my anxieties would be at an all-time low. This is not to suggest that I am disappointed in you. I am not. You have something special—something the others do not have—Yvonne calls it "openness." The openness is only the window through which the fire inside can be seen brightly burn-ing. We shall talk of that more when you come home. . . . Hurry home for Christmas.

Love, Dad.

I find this letter disturbing.

1972

February

I'm taking classes with Stella Adler. Even though she attacks me sometimes, I know it's because she believes in me. She's *so* dramatic—wears big false eyelashes and sits in a red, throne-like chair. She's excessive, intelligent, vivid, extreme, filled with enormous energy and love. During class she tells stories about Stanislavski, whom she adores, or Strasberg, whom she criticizes, "All that method could give you is a nervous breakdown. Just read *An Actor Prepares*. You'll understand everything." After one particular class I feel so inspired I send Stella flowers. During a private assessment of my work she tells me, "You're very talented, but you have a problem. You're very beautiful. You don't know yet that you didn't earn it."

Go to a party in some high rise with Jack Nicholson. I met Jack through Bert Schneider while bicycling down Park Avenue one sunny day. At the party, I meet Art Garfunkel and we hit if off immediately. It's as if he's some long-lost brother, funny and sweet, observant and interested in people. He appreciates his position in life, but doesn't let it distort his view. A pretty regular guy. Soon after, Art goes to Yugoslavia where he sends a card from Dubrovnik asking me to meet him in Austria for a week of skiing. "This place is filled with groovy boys and girls. You might want to touch a few." I decline. A week seems too long to be away from Stella.

Spring

Stella's not real pleased that I'm missing class. Prince Mohammed, who I met in Vegas, goes to school in Santa Barbara, and he's invited me out for a long weekend. I remember how attractive he was, with his tailored English suit, silk tie, and bedroom eyes. One of his employees, who's wearing designer jeans and a partial white sheet, meets me at the airport. Immediately, he presents me with a blue velvet box. Inside: a gold watch. He acts as though I should be thrilled with this; instead, it makes me feel prepaid for something—an instant turn-off. I'm taken to a split-level house somewhere in the hills above Santa Barbara that's swarming with young men—some in designer jeans, some wearing sheets. Mohammed enters, dressed in a sheet. His imperious walk makes me want to slap him and say, "Go upstairs and put on a suit! You're in America!" The house is really tackily furnished—it reminds me of a penthouse suite in a Las Vegas hotel. Lord, I can see that this is going to be a long weekend.

The conversation here is very odd. There's no depth to it; it's never more than snippets, and everything, no matter what the remark, is laughed at. I think that these oil princes only come to the West to play and shop. They seem to believe that since they are richer than anyone else they are more worthy of the pleasures the West has to offer. Their incredible wealth, coupled with the fact that they are royalty, makes for an arrogance that allows them to see others, especially women, as chattel. The palpable chauvinism is frightening, and it occurs to me I could be abducted and sold into slavery.

After closing time at the local disco, the inevitable has to be faced. It's as if all that money has insulated him from emotion and passion as well as from everything else that has to do with real life.

We spend the next few days in a Bloody Mary haze: brunching, bowling (those wild Western activities) partying, and driving around Santa Barbara in various Mercedes with members of the entourage.

One evening they give a party in my honor, that's what I'm told, and I meet some of the local talent. All the men are Middle Eastern. All the women are American, wearing high-heeled sandals, shiny dresses, necklaces that spell out their names, and the inevitable gold watches. These fellows are having a ball in America! And these women are glad they've arrived! At the airport I go into the bathroom, take off my watch, and deliberately leave it on the stainless steel counter.

Art is back from Europe, so we drive down to Atlantic City to visit Jack Nicholson, who's making *The King of Marvin Gardens*. Meet Jack's girlfriend, Michelle Phillips. She's so into ballet that she's got her rather large, pink satin ballet slippers on display; they're draped over the cheesy lamp that hangs above the formica table in their hotel room. It seems as if she's making a territorial statement, one that's probably intended to remind Jack of her claim when she's away. Michelle is anything but warm to me. Perhaps she's insecure—must be tough to be the girlfriend of a movie star. I also meet Bruce Dern, who looks half-frozen after jogging. I feel invisible and this place is like a ghost town. Big hotels and ghettos. We hightail it out.

A.K.'s in town with "Contessa Laura," his travelling companion. We go to dinner at Café Nicole with a group of people. Adnan tells me that I'm a very beautiful and intelligent woman. "This is a good combination for a spy." I just look at him: "What?" . . . "You would make a good spy, Jennifer." Giggling, I say, "Thank you very much." . . . "I'm serious. With a little training you'd be terrific. Would you like to work for me?" I realize he *is* serious. "I could make you a very rich woman." . . . "Let me think it over, Adnan." It was fun to entertain the thought for about three seconds. "No, thank you," I say. (When A.K. and Soraya eventually split up, one of her claims during the divorce settlement was that she had assisted her husband in amassing his fortune by doing "whatever was necessary" to obtain helpful information. Some years later, Jackie Williams told me that after Adnan had remarried he remarked "I turned my wife into a whore and my whore into my wife.") I know that I would have to sleep with this businessman, that diplomat, that prince, in order to be an effective spy of the sort that A.K. wants, it would have certainly been *beaucoup* bucks, and I'd have probably been a drug addict and dead by the time I was twenty-five.

Get a letter from Artie, who's in London. He's clearly upset that our weekend in Montauk didn't go well. There had been all the makings for romance, too—foggy and cold and on the beach. We'd rented one of those old two-bedroom cottages with a fireplace at Guerney's Inn. On Saturday afternoon he and his friends, a gay couple, also musicians, took mescaline, but not me. I'd learned my lesson. But I felt left out. Then Artie and I couldn't make love very well. I got angry and said some things, and questioned his sexuality. Actually, I said, "I think you probably prefer men." I hurt him, and I'm sorry about it because I like him. In his letter he refers to our sexual awkwardness and wonders if we can have a relationship anyway. God, this seems so complicated. I don't like sleeping with him very much. I think he's in touch with his feminine side, which gives him a sensitivity that most men don't have, and I appreciate that vulnerability. He's always searching, always trying to figure things out—the world, others, and especially himself. He says things like, "I noticed I was feeling jealous about this and I didn't like that—I tried to tell myself, 'Artie, calm down, you know better . . .' " I think all this self-examination is brave. He does it with me, too. "Jen, what do you think you really meant?" or "Jen, do you think you did that because you wanted to or because you felt you had to?" Or he'll look at a couple holding hands: "Do you think she's holding his hand because she wants to or because he's holding hers?" The kind of stuff I'm always doing silently in my own head and heart. It's fun to have a buddy to talk it over with!

Meet some interesting men this month. . . . I see David Blue perform at Max's and am smitten by his gloomy songs. Bob Feiden tells me that Leonard Cohen had given David his last name; originally, it was Cohen. David's part of that group of New York City folksingers, such as Tim Hardin and Eric Andersen, but David hasn't really made it. Still, he keeps struggling. (David died of a heart-attack in 1982 while jogging in Central Park.) When I get home at four A.M. I call David, who's finishing his set at Max's, introduce myself and invite him over for coffee. He chain smokes and pops blues (10 milligram Valiums) all night.

At Berry's loft I meet Peter, a gorgeous-blond-rancher-hemophiliac from Taos. He's married to Rory, a friend of Berry's. We have a nice weekend anyway. . . . At the Bitter End, Bob introduces me to John Hartford. Wake up with him in my bed. Too many Tequila

45

Sunrises. Incredible fiddle player, but John's such a strange person. He moves like a mime and isn't very sensual. In fact, it's as if he's become that high-pitched, speedy fiddle music he plays. His entire being is music—he's a fish out of water without a fiddle under his chin and a bow in his hand. One night, during the break, we're next door having a drink when in walks a wiry, energetic guy who sits down and introduces himself. "Hi, I'm Bobby Neuwirth. You remind me of Edie Sedgwick. Who are you?" . . . "Hi, I'm Jennifer Lee. Edie's dead. I'm going to live." His statement makes me uncomfortable, but I have an immediate crush on this lanky, glasses-wearing, fast-talking, fast-moving, legend-muse-songwriter. Bobby's got a whiskey flask in his cowboy boot, and he knows every word to every George Jones song. The following morning I say good-bye, hoping I'll see this rambling rogue soon. I've heard that he's quite a ladies man, and now I can understand why. He's elusive, hip, clearly an outlaw; always on his way to something, somewhere, or someone. He seems to know everybody. All doors are open to him, and he never has to tread water. Perceptive, intelligent, with a great sense of humor, Bobby makes you feel as if you're the only person in the world. But it's only for a moment, because the trouble is, that for Bobby, there are many other "only" persons in the world. The big love of his life is Phyllis Major, the beautiful model, and that relationship is on and off. (She eventually married Jackson Browne, with whom she had a son. After he left her, she killed herself.)

A.K. calls. He's staying at the Waldorf and wants me to come and have dinner with him and some friends. I hate to ask, but I take this opportunity; "Adnan, do you think you could give me a small loan? I'm still studying with Stella and I haven't worked in a while." . . . "No problem, we'll talk about it later." I meet him at the hotel, where as usual, he's staying in Nixon's suite. He introduces me to Odile and Marique, two drop-dead gorgeous, impeccably dressed French women, who have come with him from Paris. Immediately, I think of the notorious Madame Claude. I wonder when I'll get the opportunity to talk to him. Over caviar and champagne, I kiddingly stand on a chair and peer into the crystal chandelier saying, "I'm looking for a bug." Adnan gets a kick out of my "paranoia." At dinner at Lutèce there are clearly sexual vibes in the air. In the candlelight, I can see that these women, in their black sheaths and diamond drop earrings, have passports to the major bedrooms of the world. Back at the hotel we stand in the lobby and start to say good night when Adnan places an envelope in my hand. I can feel the money inside. "You're coming upstairs for a drink, aren't you?" I guess I am now. "Sure." I have to think fast. He wants me to sleep with him in exchange, and I decide before I get to the room that I will. He has been incredibly generous with me. After several glasses of champagne A.K. leads me by the hand into one of the bedrooms, where Odile and Marique are involved in full-swing cunnilingus. Reluctantly, I join in, and A.K. watches from the sidelines. As though choreographed, long French legs hit me in the head as black garter belts snap, stockings are peeled off, soft breasts collide, and creamy skin rubs against my inner thighs. Only French is spoken here; these girls are pros. I suddenly feel awkward and out of place, tense and a little ashamed. In all my other threesomes I've never been the object, I've been the one in control, the camera, the one experiencing. I do not like the emotional impotence of being the object, and I begin to feel a deep interior silence. A.K., sensing my discomfort, takes my hand and gently leads me into his king-sized bedroom, to his king-sized bed—for the kill. I feel like a child as this short, rotund man climbs on top of me. Thank God, I can barely feel him. He is finished with me in moments, and there is no further interest in me, in my comfort or lack of it. It seems that for Adnan, sex is just another unpleasant bodily function to be done away with as swiftly as possible. Somehow this makes sense. Nothing can distract him from his pursuit of power and money. When I check my envelope it contains $5,000. Officially, I guess, I have turned a trick. God, what does this *mean?* I have to think seriously about this. Does this make me a whore? Naah. Here's how I see it: I got paid for paying the piper.

I'm in L.A., the land of blond tits and whispered syntax, looking for work and staying at the Sunset Marquis—the "S & M"—an upscale rock 'n' roll motel. The low-rent one is The Tropicana, just down the hill. The S & M's clientele mainly consists of actors and musicians: some on the way up, some on the way down, and many who have already hit bottom. There I meet Christopher Jones—the beautiful debauched boy who was in *Wild in the Streets*—his one hit movie—and now walks the streets barefoot and stoned. Then there's the Barrymore grandson, who runs through the lobby drunk and, minutes later, performs off the balcony where he retches and vomits his insides out—all over the green Astroturf that surrounds the pool.

Meet with Mike Medavoy, head of IFA (which became ICM. Eventually, Mike becomes head of Tri-Star pictures). He's very cute. His enthusiasm and his shock of red hair remind me of Huckleberry Finn. I meet him through a New York IFA agent, whom I met through Roman. Mike and I begin an affair that is played out at the S & M and in borrowed apartments throughout Hollywood and Westwood. I enjoy being with Mike; he's supportive and fun.

I visit Ryan O'Neal in Malibu. We've kept in touch since meeting in New York during *Love Story*. Meet his daughter, Tatum, who's smoking a joint when I walk in. *A tad young for that,* I think. She's a real tomboy and a real smart-aleck. I spend the night with Ryan. He's a nice enough guy, but he's got a huge ego and he's really self-conscious. I can't be buddies with him like I am with Warren. Making love with Ryan can be a little disconcerting. He doesn't have a mirrored bedroom or anything like that, but he's really into his technique and he poses a lot. It's as if there's a camera on him. He knows all the angles, so he always knows how he looks during every move of our love-making. At times I feel like saying, "Hey, I'm down here."

Stella's out for her annual summer classes. I take a few. Run into Bobby Neuwirth, the rambling rogue, at the S & M. I do like the boy, but I really don't see much hope. Fly up to see Art in Tiburon—a small, tony village across the Golden Gate Bridge from San Francisco. He says it's like Europe, and that I have to see it. As we explore Marin County we sing Everly Brothers songs in the car, and Art draws the notes in the air with his finger. Sometimes we harmonize in public bathrooms—gas stations and airports—for the acoustics.

> *Please mister conductor don't put me off of this train*
> *The best friend I have in this world, sir*
> *is waiting for me in pain.*

We look at guitars in a music store. Later, we're sitting under a tree in a park and Art excuses himself, saying, "I've gotta get something from the car." A half an hour later he returns with a guitar case, hands me a nail clipper, and says, "Come on, Jen.

48

Cut those nails off and learn something." I open the case, the Yamaha guitar I'd admired in the store. So we're never going to be Dick and Liz, and I don't sleep with him anymore, but we enjoy being with each other and that's what matters. Art draws some lines and notes, and starts teaching me a few chords—G-C-D! It's frustrating, but I start to get it, and practice late into the night in the motel room.

Back in L.A. I cross paths with Bobby, who's on his way to Cincinnati to visit his mother. We go to Barney's Beanery, drink some Mexican beer, and make some cheap, fast love. Bobby likes to do it with his cowboy boots on. If he's not turning you on to the latest greatest song or album or songwriter or singer he's singing one of his own songs to you. Bobby grabs my guitar and spontaneously creates a terrific tune. I pick up mine and write my first song: "Holding in Ohio." It's your basic three-chord country melody, which I've loved since childhood. (When I was small, Gene Autry was the love of my life. Our babysitters always listened to country and one of them could even yodel.) I sing to Bobby:

> How bold you were when coming on strong
> How shy and frightened you grew
> I kept myself going with some sad country songs
> And the dream that you fell in love, too.

I get my first speaking role, in a TV movie-of-the-week called *Footsteps*, starring Richard Crenna. I play a glamorous *femme fatale*.

Fall

Start fall classes with Stella and move to a new apartment on East Seventeenth Street, right around the corner from Max's. How convenient. I spoke to Cindy, who's been living at Norm Burdick's all summer to get away from Yvonne—Norm has died and Gladys has moved. Cindy doesn't want to move back to the house.

Tristan, Berry, Bobby, and I are all at Lucy Saroyan's apartment on Second Avenue in the Fifties. As we're leaving Lucy asks, "Is everybody going?" Bobby turns to her and says, "I'm staying." I can't believe it. It's a shower of razor blades to my heart. Lucy's one of my friends! I've often relied on her support. I don't understand why she's doing this. Maybe it's because of her recent suffering over Marlon Brando. She was so distraught she even tried to flush her long, thick hair down the toilet. She's always being rejected by men. It started with her father, William Saroyan. He'd exited the family more than once, having been twice married to, and twice divorced from, Lucy's mother, Carol. Carol's happy now; she's married to Walter Matthau. But Lucy is still in pain. Her father has not been a loving father, and this was her deep wound, a source of great anguish to her. Even so, I consider Bobby to be a part-time boyfriend with full-time possibilities. Still, I try not to show my pain; I'm hip, after all. I decide this is a lesson to show me that Bobby doesn't consider me to be a romance, but rather someone on whom he's shining his light. Bobby collects special people—the talented, the famous, the larger than life. His avocation is to celebrate and nurture talent. This is a gift, but it's used at the expense of his own talents: song writing, performing, and painting. I wonder if he's hiding behind others. What is he afraid of? He's become a legend as a muse to the likes of Bob Dylan, Janis Joplin, and Kris Kristofferson, and is rumored to be an uncredited co-writer on some of their songs. His friends include Waylon Jennings, Willie Nelson, Johnny Cash, Ramblin' Jack Elliott, Dennis Hopper, Billy Joe Shaver, the late Edie Sedgwick, and on and on and on. Bobby likes to bring artists together, creating an atmosphere in which anything can happen: a new song or a three-day party. I think many of us need and want his approval. So, I decide to appreciate Bobby's appreciation of me. By staying with Lucy, he's clearly making a statement—no involvement—for my own good. Intimacy is something he considers dangerous, a waste of time and not for people who are going places. As Kris wrote about "Bobby —and Dennis Hopper, Funky Donnie Fritts, Paul Seibel, Jerry Jeff Walker, Johnny Cash, Ramblin' Jack Elliott"—in *"The Pilgrim— Chapter 33."*

> *He's a poet (he's a picker)*
> *He's a prophet (he's a pusher)*
> *He's a pilgrim and a preacher and a problem when*
> *he's stoned*
> *He's a walking contradiction*
> *Partly truth and partly fiction*

Taking every wrong direction on his lonely way back home.

Berry shows up at my apartment one afternoon after having interviewed Tony Perkins for *Interview* magazine. She's in love, radiant and gushing. She sits on the floor and turns on the tape. "Listen, isn't he wonderful? I told him I had a crush on him since I was fourteen. Oh, God, he's so gorgeous. We sat on the terrace of his Chelsea brownstone. I think he likes me, too. He asked me out." Suddenly I know her future, "Berry, you're going to get married and have a baby right away. No, wait. First you move in with him, then you get pregnant, then you get married." (This is exactly what happened.) But there's been a glitch in the process. Tristan, who is still "officially" Berry's boyfriend is the only one who doesn't know she's dating Tony. She doesn't want to face this problem until she has to. And, one night—she has to.

Tristan stops by my apartment around nine, dressed in black leather and stoned on Mandrax and Seconal. He's out of control, and he's angry. "Yeah, Berry's seeing Tony. She finally told me. I suppose you knew all about it. Everybody else did." I try to calm him down as he raves on. "Everyone's so full of shit. Do you know what they say about you?" I don't want to hear it. "They? Tristan, I think you better go." . . . "Berry and Lucy, they call you a groupie and a whore and Lucy says sleeping with Bobby, your cowboy boyfriend, was a forgettable experience. She even described his ragged family jewels." . . . "Tristan, you need help and it's time to go." He can barely stand up. "Yeah, I'm going. I'm going. I'm going to kill myself, too." He staggers across the threshold, stumbling down the stairs. Right away, I call Berry. "Tristan's in trouble. He's taken all these pills. Something bad's going to happen." Immediately, Berry reacts like a little girl. She can't handle too much. "I don't know what to do!" she cries. At three A.M. my phone rings. It's Lucy. "Jen, Berry and I, we're at St. Vincent's Hospital. We need you." . . . "Is it Tristan?" . . . "Yeah, he took an overdose. Luckily, he told a woman friend who found him. Berry's a mess and I don't know what to do. You're more experienced, with your mother and all. Can you come down, please?" Apparently, Tristan has tried to emulate Tony Perkins's suicide in *Play It As It Lays*—the scene where he asks Tuesday Weld's permission to kill himself.

When I arrive, Lucy and Berry are in tears. I go in to see Tristan. He's strapped to an old wooden wheelchair, wearing a white hospital gown, and drooling. His front teeth are knocked out. "Hi, Tristan. You're going to be all right." He barely acknowledges me; "Jennifer." He slurs, nods, looks up, and then looks past me. Berry wants him transferred uptown to New York Hospital. Since both Berry and Lucy say they are too upset to ride in the ambulance, I climb in beside Tristan while they follow in a cab. Why should I be in here? It's not my job. What Tristan had told me earlier that evening keeps playing in my head: "They think you're a whore and a groupie." We're up all night.

In the morning, Berry calls Tony who makes an appointment for her to see his shrink, Mildred. I go with Berry, who's a basketcase. When we come out of the building a few hours later, Tony's leaning up against the hood of a car, waiting. We all go for a walk in Washington Square Park. I trail behind them, feeling rather depressed myself. Tony's a hard guy to figure out. I don't have the veil of love over my eyes, so I'm able to see him more clearly. He knows this and I think this makes him uneasy. He's recently ended a relationship with a man, a dancer that he'd lived with for nine years. Now he's decided he's straight! I can't help thinking it's all just a little too convenient. He is angular, bony, and rather quiet. He asks questions but doesn't offer much. He plays it safe. I feel uncomfortable in his presence; I always feel as if he's judging me. In fact, the one expression he wears almost constantly is one of irony. He is tremendously self-conscious and aware of his every movement and gesture—little spontaneity. I want to like Tony, but it's difficult. Perhaps he gets a kick out of me, but I don't think he likes me. Berry loves him madly. I'm think he loves her but I can't tell for sure. It's as if he possesses her.

Warren's in town, so's Art. Both are staying at the Carlyle. After a date with Art I complain of a headache, leave his room, press the elevator Up button, and knock on Warren's door. "Just happened to be in the neighborhood . . . "

Halston wants Berry and me to perform in the Coty Awards ceremony at Alice Tully Hall, where he's receiving his second award. Yikes! But I'm game. I'm also flattered that he's asked me, since I know him casually through Berry. She isn't game; I have to talk her into it. I tell Halston that we're on as long as we get to sing a country-western song. I'll write it. One night in Berry's loft, Tony and Art cheer us on as we rehearse. They know each other from *Catch 22*. The big night comes—October 19. In her reviews Eugenia Sheppard proclaims this to be "the most swinging evening the Coty Awards ever had," adding that "the fun and games came with the Halston section."

The dressing room is a jumble of silk matte jersey and nervous friends and models. I'm excited, but poor Berry's a nervous wreck. I keep pouring her shots of Southern Comfort to help her calm down. It's the usual, predictable, choreographed fashion show until we all tumble out on to the stage. Pat Cleveland emcees while Donna Jordan tap-dances, Apollonia sings, Naomi Sims vamps as only she can, China Machado plays the bongo drums and corpulent Pat Ast, in a black sequined tent, leaps out of a giant birthday cake, singing "Happy Birthday to me. . . ." Modelling Halston's evening dresses are his conservative contingent of customers—Lilly Auchincloss, Betsey Theodracopolus, Jane Holzer, Kitty Hawks, Nan Kempner, and Eve Orton. Pat Cleveland keeps moving the mike during our song, which really pisses off Berry.

> *As we sit here tonight in our Halston dresses*
> *We know how very good it feels to look our best*
> *You may see him in* W.W.D. *or* Vogue *magazine*
> *Now you have to wear a Halston to try and make the scene . . .*

Afterwards we all go to Halston's for a party and we toast him over champagne and disco-disco.

Sitting in a booth at Max's with Bobby, I meet Michael J. Pollard, who's drunker than the Lord. Drink Sunrises till dawn, wake up with Michael, and realize he's uglier than homemade sin. That's not a judgment call because Michael capitalizes on his off-beat looks, which get him weirdo roles in *Bonnie and Clyde* and *Little Fauss and Big Halsey*. And there is a beauty beyond ugly, where ugly in all of its grotesqueness becomes beauty. Michael's got a boyish, impish quality that cries out for love. When drunk, he vacillates between raging beast and poet-child. In his stupors he, too, calls me Edie. I've never identified with Edie Sedgwick, the child-waif who self-destructed. I realize that boys like Michael are really mourning themselves and that her overdose punctuated the end of a chapter in their lives. The only antidote for Michael's morose insanity is making love. This need has resulted in an intense sexuality, making him one of the best lovers I've ever had, and also one of the most out of control people I've ever met. He's impossible to have a relationship with. A couple of times I've had to call his parents in New Jersey to come get him, like the time when he threatened to jump out of my window, I was living on the second floor. (He's back on his feet, working again and going strong.)

Have dinner at Elaine's with Roman and Jerzy Kosinski, who looks like a bird and who strikes me as being cold and rather rigid. He has a darkness that's similar to Roman's. Jerzy's wife, Kiki, is with us, as is Charles Riachi, an A.K. associate. Charles is upset with me. "You blew it. You should have worked for Adnan. You'd be a very wealthy woman now." . . . "Yeah, Charles, wealthy and dead."

Halston throws a fantastic Halloween party. He's given everyone instructions to come in costume, but I can't face that and wear hot pants and high suede boots instead. Halston's place looks great. There's lots of small tables to sit at, tons of lit candles, and wonderful food. Everyone's dancing to the blaring music. Tony and Berry are there. Tristan Stark arrives wearing a hat and suit made of buttons—the button man. Countess da Vinci*, the jewelry designer, arrives on her purple Harley wearing black leather pants and black leather bra with a purple leather cape. She looks like the seducing spiderwoman.

Later that evening, I go with the Countess and her effete Baron boyfriend back to their house for a nightcap. I tell her one more time how much I like her onyx and gold slave bracelet. She's standing at a big corner window, looking at the snow falling on Park Avenue. Then she turns to me and says, "Dahling, if you spend the night with me it's yours in the morning." With her alone, or with her and the Baron. It makes me nervous. Anyway, where would I wear it?

1973

January

In search of work, I take the New Year's Eve red-eye to L.A., where I get a small part in a TV movie, *Skyheist*. It's my second job, and I play a woman named Edie who gets killed. Weird. At the S & M I see Michael P. hanging out on the couch in the lobby, reading Blake, drinking, and imitating Bogie . . . artistic angst? I think of Pat. Meet Warren at the Beverly Wilshire, who introduces me to Gary Hart from Colorado. Warren says he's a political hopeful, but he seems more like a poor man's version of Warren. He flirts, and not well. He's too eager and too goofy, and what an ego. He acts as if he's arrived at a party given in his honor, smiling at every woman, every waitress, *anybody* whose eye he might possibly catch. He stretches his arms almost completely across the white tablecloth, it's kind of a grasping gesture—and I notice the sleeves of his navy-blue blazer are too short. Gary's constantly perusing the restaurant-bar, focusing every now and then on us, his actual companions. All the while he's unconsciously dipping his hand into the peanut bowl, shaking off the salt off by tapping the table, as though he's playing an imaginary piano. He laughs and laughs at everything Warren says. Good ol' Warren. He looks like the big brother here who knows his way around the block and is going to show this country boy! Gary calls me a few times later on, but I'm busy.

February

Mort Viner, the agent, takes me to a dinner at his client, Dean Martin's gigundo house in Bel Air. I like Dean, but not his transparent girlfriend. Serious gold-digging vibes. At the Troubador, I run into Ramblin' Jack Elliott and Evel Knieval—now *there's* a good combo. Hoyt Axton, whom I know from the Troubador and Tana's, asks me to join him on stage. I decide to sing a Kitty Wells song "Honky Tonk Angel." It's her women's lib answer song to Hank Thompson's, "The Wild Side of Life." And in my best imitation of Kitty, I sing:

> *It wasn't God who made Honky Tonk Angels*
> *As you said in the words of your song*
> *Too many times married men think they're still single*
> *That has caused many a good girl to go wrong.*

Lee Clayton, a singer-songwriter friend from New York, and I run into Waylon at the Palamino and then later that night at the Troubador (Lee wrote "Ladies Love Outlaws," which was a big hit for

Waylon Jennings). I'd met Waylon in New York when he played Max's—Lee had introduced us—and developed a crush on him and still have it! Gary Hart calls, again; I'm busy. Waylon calls; I'm free! Visit him at the Universal Sheraton and emerge two days later. . . . crazy 'bout that man. Have a few nervous moments though, because Waylon's wife, Jessi Colter, is staying in another suite in the hotel. Things are a bit rocky between them. She knows Waylon's fooling around, but she doesn't know with whom or when or where. Whew!

Send Stella a letter after hearing that her husband, Mitchell Wilson, died. She is my artistic conscience and keeping in touch with her gives me some sense of connection to art and my center. Meet Woody Allen at MGM about a part in *Love and Death*. I'm uptight; he just stares and stares. Maybe telling him how I used to watch him and Louise fight from my dorm window at Finch might have lightened things up a little. Maybe not.

March

At the Playboy Mansion meet Hugh Hefner, who was wandering around in gold silk pajamas, and Buck Henry, who's in the cave-enclosed Jacuzzi with foggy glasses and a girl under each arm. Beautiful, slow-motion women are floating everywhere. "I can't take this," I tell Paddy Chayefsky in the dining room where I'm taking temporary refuge from the fray. "Neither can I." Thank God, a life-line. He asks me to take him to the Château, where there's a round-the-clock, two-week party in progress, to meet The Band, Emmett Grogan of San Francisco counter-culture fame, the legendary songwriter Bobby Charles, (who wrote "Walking To New Orleans" for Fats Domino), and anybody else who drops by. Bobby Neuwirth pops in and out, playing sometime host. Everybody's on drugs and playing music. Paddy loves it. Richard Emanuel, Bobby Charles, and I end up locking ourselves in a room for a couple of days—drinking Courvoisier, taking Desbutol, and making love. Nobody feels left out. We become incredibly close, enjoying an intimacy that goes beyond sexual.

Dinner at the Beverly Hills Hotel with Prince Faisel, the "stuttering prince" I'd met in Vegas. Although conversation with him is very light and superficial, he somehow seems more real than his cousin,

Prince Mohammed, and I think we can be friends. I don't stay with Faisel. He *does* give me a plane ticket back home to New York, however. Bless his heart.

Dinner with Tony and Berry, who are living together in Chelsea. They seem really happy. Date with Roman, it's always nice to see him. Couple of lunches with Paddy, who says he wants to help "advance my career," but what will he really do? So far, he's just hit on me. Going out on a lot of interviews and modelling for Issey Miyake. Meet Willie Nelson through Bobby, and we all go to the house of a friend of Bobby's for a serious picking session. I love to hang out with guitar players, listen to the songs, and learn what I can. Bob Feiden introduces me to Merle Haggard, one of my idols. He's one of the *real* McCoys. . . .

At a party at Caroline and Chip Monk's triplex nicknamed "Heartbreak Hotel," Kris Kristofferson and Rita Coolidge show up. She's wearing black leather jeans and has a black leather patch over a wounded eye. Great look: a lady outlaw. I visit Willie at the Warwick, and emerge two days later. Willie's a really sweet guy and we've had a good time, but he can be kind of boring. He's so interested in getting along with everybody he seems strangely passive—the stereotype of the laconic, slow-moving country man. His interest in the world is noncommittal. When he shakes hands he only squeezes your fingers. His love-making lacks true passion, as well. He smokes a ton of grass, which may be the cause of his passivity . . . as well as the lines on his face.

More trouble in Cropseyville, so I head home for a quick visit. Pat has announced to Cindy that she's not Harry's daughter and that Jack Williams, a family friend and musician, is. Yvonne butts in with her own form of logic, and tells Cindy that this makes absolute sense because she's musical, has diabetes like Jack Williams and anyway, all the Lee children are crazy, with the exception of Cindy. Devastated, Cindy talks to Pat's shrink, who says it's a lie. Dad says it's the furthest thing from the truth and gives Cindy a portrait of his mother to prove how much she and Cindy look alike. Then Yvonne accuses Cindy of sleeping with Byron and tells her that Harry believes it, too. Poor Cindy, she's so upset she's moved out again and is staying in a tent in the woods with her boyfriend. I tell her I love her, to stop worrying, and to stay put in her tent.

I do have a terrible memory of a fight. I hear two men screaming and yelling in the middle of the night. It was Dad and some other man. The sounds were coming from the guest room. Then I was standing in the guest room, too, in the middle of the fight. I saw my mother was there. She was yelling and screaming and trying to separate this man and my father. But their bodies kept slamming and crashing up against each other. They were puffing and gasping for air. My mother got hold of my father, and bit him. There was a lot of blood. And then it was quiet. The next morning was beautiful, perfect spring day. The sun was shining, the dew was still on the lawn and the air smelled like fresh-cut grass. My father and the man from the night before (who I now think is Jack Williams), sat on the white chaise lounges, looking very sad. My mother served them coffee and dirty looks. I picked some tiger lilies and made two bunches. When I gave my father his bunch, I saw where my mother had bitten him. There was a piece of his ear missing. I picked extra tiger lilies for him. I never found out what they were fighting about.

The place to go after Max's closes is my place, just around the corner. My second floor brownstone apartment is the gathering spot for the still wide-awake, those who need more tequila to get them through what's left of the night. It's a cozy place to hang out, with a fireplace in the living room and a hand painted mural, the gift of a stoned artist, on one wall. Shoulder-height molding runs all the way around the kitchen, creating a narrow ledge where I put all the empty Cuervo Gold bottles. One by one, all in a row, they form a Cristo-like motif. Over endless shots of tequila we discuss politics, especially Watergate; we all love watching the hearings and we know all of the senators' and the sinners' names. But mostly, we sing, play guitar, and write songs. And the hip and the happening float in and out—Brice Marden, Gregory Corso, Bobby Neuwirth, Rip Torn, Larry Poons, John Hammond, Jr., and François DeMenil. Some nights things get a bit reckless but someone always keeps a cool head. One late night when the music's right, as is the combination of men and drugs, I suddenly decide, during a haunting live rendition of "Send Me Someone to Love" to take off all my clothes. But as I start to undress Bobby decides it's time for everyone to go get breakfast. *Whew*, saved by the Bobby!

Another evening, I walk into my kitchen and spot Gregory Corso quickly hide something in his hand. I ask him what he's got. He sheepishly opens his palm to reveal a blank check from my checkbook and a photo of my sister, Cindy. He's stealing from me! "Wait," I say, "there's something I want to read to you." I return with a copy of his poem "Friends," one of my favorites, and I read it to him. When I finish the last line I tell him, "Now you may leave." The following day, he calls to apologize.

Summer

It's summer in New York. I hear Willie Nelson's having a "First Annual Fourth of July Picnic" at Dripping Springs. François DeMenil wants to make a movie of the event and badly needs a liaison to the producers and the talent involved. Since I know Willie, Francois gives me the job!

I fly to Austin and meet with Eddie Wilson of Armadillo World Headquarters, who's co-producing Willie's picnic. We all go out to Willie's house on Lake Austin, where we're greeted by his sweet, and very pregnant wife, Connie. Naturally, Willie is a little surprised to see me, but he relaxes when we start talking business. Immediately I feel at home in Texas, although I realize that I will have to deal with their innate mistrust of Yankees, especially of François DeMenil, who's not only a Northerner, but a rich kid to boot. Eventually, I manage to earn the trust of everyone involved. While I'm waiting to give François the okay to come down, I begin the pre-production work; I secure film releases from artists' labels, coordinate talent, get film and location permits, and get insurance. This is not an easy task. Some labels won't give permission even though the artist will. Then there's the problem of differentiating the film's responsibility from the festival's as far as who gets a stage built, who hires a crew, who secures parking permits, who gets tickets printed, and who arranges for security and first aid stations. All this plus the problem of being a woman having to circumvent all the male egos. I work hard, but I have to tread lightly. Willie isn't a savvy businessman; he's been ripped off before, making him instinctively mistrustful and resistant to the whole idea of a François. And when François finally does arrive, he manages to insult Eddie, Willie, and their business people as well. They think François is an effete New Yorker, a snob-schmuck. It's a disastrous first meeting, a fight breaks out, leaving François and his people running with their tails between their legs. The film is cancelled, and naturally I'm depressed over that, as well as out of a job. At the Armadillo office the following day, Willie asks me to stay on as one of the associate producers of the festival. I'm thrilled. I already feel part of the event and very much at home here. Although I realize it's no utopia, I do like this atmosphere much better than that of the more pretentious social scenes of New York or London. This place is much more embracing, more authentic, and somehow more alive. Even the Texas way of speaking is more lyrical. The metaphors sound like pure American poetry to my ears. Things like, "You knock my hat in the creek," or "my dick in my watch-pocket," or "she hung on, like a tick on hound dog's tail." Everything just seems to have more texture and more color here.

A few days later Willie asks me to go on a promotion tour with him to publicize the festival. After Willie plays at an afternoon fair in Seguin, we go to San Antonio to see Charlie Rich perform and to make sure he'll keep his promise to appear at Willie's bash on July 4th. We also stop in Willie's hometown, Abbot, population three, and give away festival tickets to the man who runs the cotton gin where Willie once worked. I love riding down the Texas highway listening to the local country stations fade in and out. I feel like I'm following the ghosts of Patsy Cline, Hank Williams, and Jimmie Rodgers, especially when we stop for some shade and Shiner beers in dimly lit roadside honky-tonks on hot afternoons and hear "Crazy" wailing from the blue-and-yellow jukeboxes.

Sometimes a little hard reality interrupts our travelling tryst. One night in a motel room with Willie, we hear a woman's bloodcurdling screams pierce the wall. "We've got to call the police, Willie." . . . "Jennifer," he tells me, "there's something you should know about country people. We don't interfere in one another's domestic squabbles." Willie's a tender, caring man but too laid back. Maybe he's afraid that he'll be caught with me. The fighting continues, on and off the whole night long. The following morning, I tell Willie I'll meet him in the coffee shop, then I slip over to the front desk to report what I'd heard, hoping the screaming woman is still alive.

Still we have a few great nights. The best one is at J.T. Flore's Country Store outside of San Antonio. Willie performs here, standing on a bandstand under the Texas stars. Accompanied by his sister, Bobbie, on the piano, he sings, "Yesterday's Wine" and "Stay All Night" while hundreds of couples, young and old, waltz and sashay the Cotton-Eyed Joe. I am moved by the elegance, ease, and agelessness of all these cowboys and cowgirls as they glide expressionless across "the world's largest patio." They take their dancing seriously here. And I feel such an affinity with it all.

We all keep working hard on final preparations for the festival. One afternoon we're at the site, about thirty miles outside of Austin on Bert Hurlburt's 74,000 acre ranch. A bunch of guys who are building a stage toss me and the beer cooler into the back of a pickup truck. We all pop some Pearls and hightail it into the dusty, bumpy heat till we get to a nearby creek. Off come the shit-kickers and the denims and we all dive in for a soothing skinny dip. Now this is my idea of fun! "Texas: Where men are men and women are women." The bad news is I end up with a serious case of chigger bites and have to paint my abdomen with clear nail polish to smother the little darlins. But I feel more comfortable here in my dusty, chigger-bitten skin than I do in a silk matte jersey anywhere!

Countdown: We make a fast trip to leave tickets in legendary Luckenbach where they're already celebrating the 4th with men in Confederate uniforms firing cannons and simulating battle. They take their celebrations seriously here. On July 3, around three A.M., I'm driving back to my room at the Ramada Inn when out of the night two blinding headlights pop up over a hill as a car comes speeding straight at me. I know that this is going to be a head-on collision; I *decide to live and be all right*. The second after impact I jump out of the mangled metal. I keep telling myself, *Just keep moving, you'll be fine*. (I've applied this philosophy to everything!) I'm lucky to be alive. The crash, as it turns out, is the easy part.

Belligerent, and badly shaken, the two drunks in the other car want to know what a Yankee woman is doing out alone in the Texas night. As one slowly approaches me, with a bottle in his hand, I start babbling about Willie and the festival. Luckily, the state troopers arrive, although they are much more suspicious of me than they are of the two inebriated Neanderthals. Then I remember the bottle of Jack Daniels that I keep in the glove compartment for emergencies. I promise them all passes to the festival which diffuses serious Texas tension. The troopers give me a ride back to the Ramada. I shower and change, feeling proud that when challenged, I was able to back my way out of a dangerous and difficult situation. I'd never even considered that I might have been hurt. Hey, it's all part of the Texas experience, part of the larger experience. Forget about sleep, I grab a ride back out to the site. Ride 'em cowgirl!

* * *

Word's out that the festival is going to be a major event. The performers, and some 6,000 fans, begin arriving the day before. The energy and excitement about this new wave of country music has been brewing in L.A., Nashville, and New York. Cowboy music is *in* and Dripping Springs is making it official. On July 4, 1973, the phenomenon of "C & W" begins. The music has crossed over, no longer played only in back road honky-tonks for beer drinking good ol' boys. In their performances Waylon, Willie, and Charlie Rich knock out the sophisticated city folks. Everyone, it seems, is starting to wear cowboy boots, cowboy shirts, fringe, and cowboy hats! C & W is hotter than a firecracker!

Yikes! Seventy-five thousand people are here. They're mostly young, spread out across the dusty fields. Some in tents, some with sleeping bags, some in bathing suits. Amidst this sea of cowboy hats are the hardcore, older country fans who've come out to see their favorites. The seven miles of access road are jammed with Winnebagos and trailers, surpassing Willie's wildest expectations. The music begins at seven A.M. on July 4, with Willie and Leon Russell singing some Hank Williams tunes followed by a duet of "A Song for You." From there it's non-stop wailing from the likes of Sammi Smith, Rita Coolidge, Kris, Lee Clayton, Tom T. Hall—who ends his set by happily tossing his Ovation guitar into the audience after breaking a string—Billy Joe Shaver, Charlie Rich, Waylon, Bobby Neuwirth, Kennèth Threadgill, and John Prine, who I've had my eye on. There's even an onstage wedding around sunset, complete with illustrated invitations. Willie's drummer, Paul English, marries Diane Huddleston. The day's a real scorcher, and I haven't slept; but I don't feel tired. I take a break, wandering into a group of parked trailers where I have a beer with a cowboy who's hauling his horse and his two bowed legs to the next rodeo. "Where men are men."

The day's events don't end till way past midnight, culminating in a set by Willie and the sweet harmony of some of the other performers who wander out to join him. When it's over and I walk out onto the empty stage and watch as the last drunken stragglers try to find their way home, tripping over abandoned coolers, and getting tangled in the forgotten sleeping bags that blanket the land. Empty Pearl and Shiner beer cans glint under the bright moon, making it look like a field full of diamonds. John Prine sits on the edge of the stage, swinging his legs, a cigarette dangling from his lips. I've been watching him coming and going and performing all day. He smiles like a child, unsure and open. He looks like a child, too, with sleepy eyes, his black messy hair, and scruffy beard. Every time I've passed him, I've had to resist the impulse to give him a hug. I go over and sit down beside him. I've long been a fan—"Sam Stone," "Paradise," "Hello In There," "Angel from Montgomery"—and after hearing him play today I'm convinced he's one of the best new songwriters around. His voice sounds like an angel's with sleep in it. This boy has touched my soul. "Look at those stars," he says, swinging his legs and gazing up. "They're so beautiful they embarrass me." I feel my heart click into place. "I watched you all day. You worked hard. You must be tired. Would you like a ride back to town?" he asks. I don't tell him that I've been watching him, too. I never make it back to the Ramada.

The following evening Willie comes to my room. High on the festival's whopping success, we make love. Then he gives me my salary and a generous $1,500 bonus. "Thanks, we couldn't have done it without you." Willie has even more to celebrate as Connie has just given birth to a girl, Amy Lee. After Willie leaves, Waylon shows up at my door with a brown paper bag filled with $1,000 in cash. "Thanks, we couldn't have done it without you." I take Waylon into my arms. Because I've slept with both of them in the space of a couple of hours, I feel as if I'm inside my own country song, "Hot Cheatin' and Cold Sin with Two Best Friends at the Ramada Inn."

Waylon's here for the weekend, doing a concert in Central Park. We have a great time walking around New York in the July heat. I suggest to him that he record "Amanda," a minor country hit. (Waylon makes it a big hit.) I really enjoy Waylon's company. As we pass a bookstore on Third Avenue he sees copies of Norman Mailer's *Marilyn* in the window. Waylon marches right in, plunks a copy down on the counter, and buys it for me, saying, "You remind me of the best part of her." This is really typical of Waylon; he's very direct and has a generous spirit. There are a lot of fake cowboys around now but Waylon's the genuine article. Big, hardy, and lusty, impossible to slow down. Drinks, smokes, does a lot of black beauties—claims to have once stayed up for twenty seven days straight. When we make love he looks directly at me; if I get up to go to the bathroom he's waiting open arms, ready to enfold me as soon as I get back. He's sensual, tender and fun, and he's always concerned about how I'm feeling. A bit clumsy at times, but it's endearing. When the combination of drugs and alcohol are too much and he can't get it up, he works up a good sweat trying. All in all, Waylon's probably one of the best lovers I've ever had. It's wonderful having him here for an entire weekend, just the two of us. He's always had a rocky relationship with Jessi, but he loves her a lot, and I think they'll make it.

August

Dinner at Tony and Berry's. There's a lot to celebrate. They got married this month, she's pregnant, it's my birthday, and I'm moving to L.A. Suddenly, my life in New York feels as if it has come to an end. The hanging out at Max's, the socializing always with the same old people. This scene's over. I want to act.

Andrew Wiley, a poet who always sports a black beret, (he has since become one of the most successful and aggressive literary agents in New York, getting mega-bucks for his clients) gives me key money and takes over my lease. Lee Clayton steals my bed and Helen Marden, Brice's wife, chases me down an aisle at Max's, bopping me over the head with a book.

Fall

Sleeping on Jonathan Axelrod's couch at the French Hill Apartments on Olive Drive in West Hollywood. My friend Alan Sharpe says he's working on a script called *The Long Distance Piano Player*, and using me as the prototype for his heroine, Jennifer Swift. Lunch with Clint Eastwood and Lee Clayton at Universal Studios. I meet some friends of his and become their female cohort and mascot: Barry Beckerman, who calls me America's guest; John Milius, who's funky, large, and larger than life, and who's always spouting the best lines, like, "A great surfer once told me, 'Just try and surf like me. If you're really good enough, you can't do it because it's gonna come out your own' "; Walter Hill; and Sidney Chaplin, Charlie's son. We all hang out at Dan Tana's, the Italian restaurant-bar right next to the Troubador, on Santa Monica Boulevard. Tana's, with it's red leather banquettes and a maître d' named Guido, is always warm and friendly and crowded. I make friends with Tana's regulars—Harry Dean Stanton, Ed Begley, Jr., Jimmy Woods, Warren Oates, Seymour Cassel, Ned Doheny, Bud Cort, Helena Cantanta. I borrow Jonathan's Porsche and immediately find my way around. I like L.A.; driving in the hills, the bougainvillea, the sense of space. I do feel at home here. All these beautiful women driving shiny new cars. Who buys them? People are generally nicer in L.A., but there is a weirdness underneath, something going on that you cannot see. Except for the vagabonds, people don't really walk here, and you can often go an entire day without relating to anyone. And, naturally, the Sharon Tate horror is still on everyone's mind. At least in New York if you get mugged, you usually know what they want—your money, your jewelry. Here, they could want your eyeballs for some satanic ritual. Run into Neuwirth at Tana's who tells me that David Blue's written a song about me, "The Ballad of Jennifer Lee." "It's really good. You should hear it."

Have a date with W.S.* for dinner at Tana's. I've been feeling a bit frustrated lately about my acting career and talk to him about it, saying things like, "Well, I'll show them someday." W.S. advises patience and explains that my attitude is *not* a good motivation for acting. "You'll get parts. Above all don't be bitter." Afterward we go to Saul Chaplin's house for a party with Gene Kelly, Sky Aubrey, Adolph Green, and Betty Comden. Betty and Adolph play and sing and I'm mildly impressed, although I find them all to be a bit stuffy! W.S. turns out to be a better lover than I'd thought. I was afraid that he'd be a bit cold. After all, he is rather intimidating, very much like his on-screen characters, a real, rugged, macho mystery man. He's very quiet and well-mannered, making me feel I should be on my best behavior when I'm with him. It's hard to know what he's thinking; he doesn't really react to anything. He is a very predatory creature, and that famous cool goes out the window when we make love. It's a real shock to see him get so wild. He loves to give head, and is almost ravenous about it, which, for me, can be a bit off-putting. I prefer the entire gestalt of lovemaking.

I'm reading three books, the biographies of Janis Joplin, Frances Farmer, and Marilyn Monroe. See Warren and Willow*. See Warren and Sally. Catch John Prine's show at the Troubador. Afterward I go backstage to say "Hello in there." He's with his wife, who looks angry and frazzled. I don't let M.J.P. into the apartment so he breaks Jonathan's window. Michael is so out of control. Go to a screening of *Day for Night* with Dimitri Villard, who gets angry when I don't sleep with him. Warren calls, "Willow gave us the clap." I rush to the doctor for penicillin shots. I'm starting to feel anxious causing my confidence to waver. Then the insecurity grabs hold of my entire being and doesn't let go until I'm on my knees with morbid depression. When that gets unbearable I find some way to pry myself loose, get moving, and start all over again. But I wonder if it will always be like this? I'm sure working will help. I feel as if I've got to be on my toes all the time. This social disease doesn't help. It makes me feel careless and angry. Warren's a bit too flip and doesn't even offer to pay the bill! Lose out on a soap part that paid well. I call home and cry like a baby. Georgia's preggers and getting married to some loser-musician.

Co-write a song with Larry Murray:

> *Somewhere there's someone who loves me*
> *Somewhere there's someone who cares.*
> *If I die before he finds me*
> *I'll rest just knowing he's there.*

Jonathan's coming home in a week, so I'll have to move. Acting classes are going well, but Lou Pitt, my agent at ICM, suggests I go to a "smaller" agency. Thanks, Lou! I do; Jimmy Hyde at Jack Fields. Jimmy's father, Johnny Hyde, is mentioned all through *Marilyn*; he was her agent-mentor-lover. Jimmy is incredibly nurturing and supportive. Move into the S & M, eating my meals at Ben Frank's coffee shop and Dukes at the Tropicana.

Hooray, my first job since I've moved here! Second lead in an AIP film called *Rape Squad*. I play Nancy, a lady of the canyon who joins up with a group of vigilante women who've been violated and are seeking revenge. Have a lot of meaningful dialogue to learn: "You treat women like slabs of meat! Well, your time is coming, mister. . . . " So, it's not going to get me an Oscar nomination but it feels good to work. Jack Nicholson began working in this genre so it seems fine to me. I've never been raped, but I actually like the concept of this movie—A group of women refuse to accept the fact that these men are going unpunished, and they fight back by going after the men themselves. Very liberated and determined women who simply refuse to remain victims. Good idea!

Reward myself with a trip home for Christmas.

Christmas Dinner by Norman Rockwell, in DayGlo: Seated around the harvest table are Yvonne and her children, Caroline and K.K.; Byron, Cindy, Georgia and Eddie and their bundle of joy; and Pat and Ace. At the head of the table is Harry, who wants everything to be perfect and thinks it can be. I'm unable to look at Ace, the creature Pat lives with, without going into a silent rage. He could be Manson's father, with his scraggly beard, unkempt head of hair, and Cro-Magnon posture. I expect him to be on his knuckles when he greets me. He behaves aggressively toward Harry—Pat's on a real safari with this one. I can't relate to her at all; I don't know where she lives in her head. I just know that I can't reach her, and don't want to. I feel contempt and pity towards her, but no compassion. Yvonne acts like Nurse Ratched overseeing the inmates, flaunting her mediocre culinary skills and kissing Harry on the cheek at every opportunity. Her kids, the corpulent, humorless Caroline and the skeletal K.K., are dismissive and rude, treating Cindy and Byron as if they are guests who have overstayed their welcome. Caroline's thick limbs make her movements slow-she seems weighed down with bitterness. K.K. is almost the opposite—skinny and fast, like a ferret; her darting eyes, unable to give a steady gaze. I don't trust her. And then there's Georgia's husband, who looks like caveman Ace's sibling. This entire scene is so fraught with weird territorial and competitive dynamics that it's easy to feel hostile, and it's hard to figure out why I came home. I watch Harry bend over backward to make things pleasant. Bending especially way over for the children who are not his own. I want to scream.

1974

Winter

After a grueling month of shooting, *Rape Squad* wraps and I need a new place to live. Although the S & M is colorful, it's taken all of my salary. It's also not a good place to live if you're not working—too many unemployed actors hanging out around the pool, drowning their sorrows in booze and sun.

Barbara Steele and I meet one afternoon in the Bank of America on Sunset and Doheny. Lucy has always said we would "just adore each other." Barbara's with Tom Baker, a Warhol star and a method actor I know from New York. He looks like the missing link. Tom's main claim to fame is that he was friends with Jim Morrison. (Tom eventually died of a heroin overdose.) He introduces us, and Barbara and I like each other immediately. She's edgy, hyper, part of my tribe. "Where are you staying?"she asks. "I'm at the S & M, but not for long." With exaggerated English syntax, she says, "You just get out of that taaaaacky hotel and come to Malibu. Come see the ennnnnndless horizon." I do, and move into a small wood-panelled room off the living room in Barbara's tract house, on an affordable stretch of Carbon Beach. Staying there is like being at summer camp; Saturday afternoon tea parties and barbecues on the sundeck. There's something instantly familiar about Barbara—I feel as if I've known her forever. Barbara's thirty-six years old, has an extraordinarily high forehead, and a slight overbite. She's striking; tall and lean, long legs, large breasts, with blue black hair that she often forgets to wash for days, which makes her seem pathetically out of place in the L.A. sun. You can see where great beauty had been and lingered still, though it's fading fast with the help of too much Mexican food, too many bottles of Beaujolais, and not enough reality. Royal Academy of Dramatic Arts–trained, Barbara botched her first film job as Elvis Presley's co-star, when she insisted that a pair of skin tight, canary yellow, thousand-dollar custom-made pants be covered with dirt in the name of realism. The studio balked and replaced her with Barbara Eden.

So Barbara left for Rome and became a star of Italian movies. She appeared in films such as: *Revenge of the Blood Beast, Terror Creatures From the Grave* and *Nightmare Castle*. She rarely got the opportunity to do classier parts, with the exception of *The Pit and the Pendulum* and Fellini's *8 1/2* where she played "the lady with the whip." A horror movie queen, she lived a life of excess, losing track of time the way she lost her call-sheets, drinking cognac while shooting, and falling asleep in her coffins. One director had it written into her contract that she not be allowed to apply her own lipstick as it always ended up on her jaw. Several sad affairs and bad films later, she met James Poe, who had won an Oscar for co-writing *Around the World in Eighty Days*. The affair with Louis Malle had soured. Anthony Quinn was long gone, and

Barbara was tired of dungeons. So she married Jim, who promised to have her teeth capped, write a film for her, and take her back to America with some renewed dignity. They moved into a big house on a Malibu hill and the slow mudslide began. Although she did get her teeth capped, the film he wrote for her, *They Shoot Horses, Don't They?*—that's where she met Tom, who was her fellow-actor for the screen test—was made without her, and Jim began drinking and stopped writing. He eventually joined AA, but nobody told him the coke had to go, too. They fought continuously for eight years until one night Mr. Cocaine invaded Barbara's bedroom where she was sleeping with their son. He shouted, "UFOs are landing!"and emptied a bottle of Cuervo Gold over mother and child. Barbara packed her bags, took their son, and rented the house on Carbon Beach. That's when I moved in.

I've never known anyone as theatrically lyrical as Barbara. She speaks like the horror movie queen she was, stretching and pulling her words like straps of leather on a torture-chamber rack, pushing the air away with her palms, beating her chest, blinking her eyes, and waving her arms. She has a repertoire of gestures and move-ments to accompany every thought she yearns to express. I think she's magnificent and exceedingly profound. One afternoon, while driving down the Pacific Coast Highway, we see a dog sticking his head out of a car window, catching the wind. Barbara screams, "Just think, he's smelling sounds we will neveh, eveh, heeear!" Damn! Where did she learn to say things like that? She tells me that "all parts fit together. Everything is in the air—including Cleopatra's bed." One morning, with Margarita hangovers, we drive through the gray smog to the L.A. Convention Center to take est training and really "get it," once and for all. But when we arrive all we do is try to figure out what we are doing amongst these blond, page-boyed, razor-cut, smiling, gold-chained robots who are registering people and getting them ready to sit in rows of orange Naugahyde chairs for hours at a time. . . . And no breaks—not even for the bathroom. Clutching our required pillows and our embarrassment, we shake from the paranoia of our hangovers. We run to the bath-room. "Barbara, I think they inject transistors up your ass to turn us into one of them. Would Picasso take est?" . . . "Oh my God, Jennifer—neveh. You're brilliant!" She explodes, clutching her long pale neck in shock. She really can make me feel brilliant. We make our escape and hightail it to the closest Mexican restaurant and drink several Margaritas. Barbara wants to know how she will ever "get it." I suggest she start by cleaning her pocketbook. At the bottom of her bag are open lipstick tubes, dirty Valiums, combs with missing teeth, used Kleenex, pearl earrings, and loose change covered with old tobacco from crushed cigarettes. Just like my mother's.

I play a lot of Lefty Frizzell and tell Barbara about my cowboys. She's not very talkative about her Italian days. But I know she's seen the dark side; there are clues. Once when I asked her if she believes Dracula existed, she says "Yes." I ask how she knows. "There are some things you just know," she says, staring into the mirror. I feel a cold north wind and for a split second I can't see her reflection. Barbara tells the story of being in a massive castle in the hills of Tuscany with a gray haired Italian count who pasted peacock feathers all over her body and slapped them off, one by one, with a black antique whip. She pulls the neck of her black turtleneck sweater up over her ears as she tells me this. Weird! And those grotesque, pre-Columbian figurines in her bedroom—I can't get them out of my mind. Perhaps they are conduits to Satan.

Like Pat, Barbara can't stand to be alone. She's another animal crashing up against herself. So the house is always filled, and it's an odd assortment—Malibuites, ex-Warhol superstars, horror-movie fans, weak men, sad wives. These people are all that stand between Barbara and madness. In the middle of an afternoon tea she might ask who is going to keep her company during her nap. And she can be a deceiver, once seeing two therapists at the same time, keeping it a secret from both. She's asked me to forge an abstract painting that Jim wants back. Though my first, and my last, forgery, I do a credible job, but Jim wasn't fooled. The fun is turning into a kind of chaos that's beginning to make me sad. Besides, the longer I stay the more I realize that Barbara's addicted to pain. I don't want to be around it. As she lies on the sundeck I can see her night-before bruises from Tom. Although I feel sort of protected in this environment, I'm growing tired of her insincere friends and drunk neighbors. I feel lonely and cut off out at the beach and want to be around people who have a sense of hope. Three months after moving in, I say good-bye to Barbara. It's a Sunday afternoon and she's standing under the blazing sun watching the ennnnndless horizon. A tattered red Mexican robe covers her tired heart, her black-and-blue tattoos, and her Margarita hangover. I feel sorry for Barbara, grand Barbara, Barbara the horror-movie queen. I shout good-bye and leave her standing at the edge of the sea, the sun glinting off all her beautiful capped teeth.

Spring

I feel as if I'm an official starlet. While at Barbara's I had a disturbing interview with a well known director who hit on me. I report him to the newly established SAG Morals Committee. Definitely learning fast here in Hollywood! New photos with Keyan, a terrific photographer, with whom I do endless shoots. Bobby Neuwirth introduces me to Peter Boyle. So far it's a fabulous phone flirtation! Much fun at "Hidden Valley," a house in the hills Johnna Kirkland shares with her boyfriend Danny. People drop by—rompin' Ronnie Hawkins, Bonnie Bramlett, Peter Boyle, Don Everly, T. Bone Burnett, Stephen Souls. We play and listen to a lot of good country music. There seems to be a lot happening now; people are striving in their careers and sharing their work. There is a core tribe, and then there's an outer circle that's forever changing. See Jack Nicholson—we go to Elliott Gould's house. Elliott's live-in, Jennifer Bogart, is there. Drunk, we go back to Jack's house where he plays all of Willie's albums. Drinks, drugs, and dicks don't mix—not with Jack anyway! The phone keeps ringing, it's Jennifer Bogart—"telephone interruptus." Willie sings on . . . Fix up Dana Rushe with Levon Helm. When I join them later at Imperial Gardens, it's clear they've hit if off really well.

It's been a month since I've seen John Prine. When I say good-bye, I never know when I'll see him again. He tells me, "I'll see you in Europe." What the hell does that mean? It's rough sometimes. John's married, so non-involvement is written into our affair, but I do wish I could get a straight answer from him now and then. John tends to be oblique and passive. But he's so sweet. There's a naivete about him that keeps his music pure, but it can work against him. I've seen others take advantage of that innocence. John's got a wonderfully skewed sense of humor that meshes with mine. When we make love, he's tender and affectionate. He looks directly at me and talks to me; he's very attentive. I do miss him.

I've moved into a furnished studio for $90 a month in a building on Sycamore Avenue in the middle of Hollywood that's filled with sad older people with worn-out dreams. Sign contracts for *The Wild*

Party, a James Ivory film starring Raquel Welch. I'll play Madeline True, thespian-lesbian. Go to a tacky party at Roman's house in the hills, filled with wannabes. Go with Peter Boyle to a great party at Darryl Diamond's house. Guests include Gene Wilder, Cloris Leachman, Marty and Loretta Feldman, Mel Brooks and Anne Bancroft. Cloris tap dances and Anne pays me a great compliment. She says that she'd seen me at the wrap party for *Young Frankenstein* the night before and that "You really stood out, you're very striking. I feel as if I've discovered you." Levon tells me that Richard Emanuel is not doing well—his girlfriend is carrying his needles around. He can't kick heroin. (Eventually, he hanged himself.) It's Mother's Day—wish I had a mother to call. Life is speeding ahead. Relationships forming, shaping, changing. Peter arrives carrying a dozen roses and a membership to the Sanctuary. I say, "Just friends." My hair is growing and so am I.

Go to Waylon Jennings's opening night at the Troubador with Kris, Ronnie Hawkins, and Bobby. After the show we go backstage to see Waylon, who's with his wife, Jessi Colter. Jessi's a great singer-songwriter, and I really admire her talent. When I give Waylon a big hug and kiss, she waves her hand and says, "I see ya, darlin', I'm sitting right here next to him." Whoa! I like her style. You don't mess with a country wife's territory! There's been a vague attraction between Kris and me since we met in New York and this evening there's an unspoken agreement—we'll spend some time together later. But while we're backstage Joan Baez walks in and leaves with Kris, almost as if he belongs to her! No big deal. I made a date with Donnie Fritts, the keyboard player. We go back to Hidden Valley for Chi-Chis and Margaritas, and I sing with Bonnie Bramlett and Ronnie Hawkins. Bonnie has the most soulful voice I've ever heard from a white woman—from any woman! It can break your heart in two. Bonnie's friend, Patsy, threatens me with a knife. "I'll cut you," she says. I guess she's jealous. I introduce myself and she replies, "You'll know when we meet!" I get a kick out of her serious Southern white-trash caricature—I've never met anyone like her. Bonnie's crazed, breaking glasses and dropping cigarettes. Ronnie thinks I should go to Toronto with him and sing. "No thanks, gotta kick off my acting career." In walks Kris, minus Joan. After a few more Chi-Chis, we skinny dip in the pool, mimicking dolphins. "Where's Rita?" I ask. "Home, about to give birth any minute." I swallow half the pool. Although we end up at the Holiday Inn, guilt, Chi-Chis, and an idea whose time has come and gone, results in talking and hugs. "Two studs unable to make love," I tell him. "Yeah, but not worth shooting," he says. We talk about many things—father-hood, daughterhood, broken hearts. Each of us just needs to be held. He tells me, "I remember what you said the first time I met you and what you had on." (He never told me.)

See Waylon before I leave town. He's troubled so the sex isn't that great, but what is great is that I really like him. He has such a kind and generous spirit. He feels like a friend.

Staying at the Howard Johnson's in Riverside, California, while filming of *The Wild Party*. Principal shooting is at The Mission Inn, which serves as the mansion of Jolly Grimm, a character based on Fatty Arbuckle, played by James Coco. The nineteenth century inn is beautiful, Spanish-style hostelry with gardens, gargoyles, flying buttresses, and bells that go gong in the night. James Ivory is very sweet and his partner, producer Ishmael Merchant, makes curried food everyday for lunch. Meeting nice people on the set: Perry King; David Dukes; Michael Childers, who's the set photographer and the companion of John Schlesinger; Bruce Weintraub, set designer; Rick McCallum, assistant director; Hallie Smith, make-up artist; and Pat Birch, choreographer. Raquel Welch steps all over my lines. God, I don't have that many! I've been warned that she might do that. Step on them? She's been mashing them to a bloody pulp! And I've been fighting for what's left of them. Anything sets her off. She's been screaming at Jim Ivory and walking off the set, telling him to go get another actress. Poor Jim. He just stands there in stunned silence, getting beaten down by her constant tantrums. Ron Talsky, Raquel's boyfriend and designer, is the only one who supports her cruel tirades. I actually feel sorry for Raquel. After hearing her sing and seeing her dance, I know this must come from insecurity. But I don't know why she wants to sabotage this film by undermining the director and all the talent around her. With the exception of Raquel, it's a warm and fun set. I get a kick out of playing a Theda Bara–type. Have to do a love scene with Marya Small. "Clear the set!" She really threw herself into the part. Rick McCallum, the A.D., becomes my boyfriend. In the bar at HoJo's I sing C & W with the band every night.

Summer

My agent calls with good news Arthur Hiller wants me to play the part of Lauren Shavelson in the American Film Theater's Production of Robert Shaw's play, *The Man in the Glass Booth*, which stars Maximilian Schell. It's a small but good role. Become friends with Max, who has a daunting amount of dialogue to memorize, the film is practically all him. Max sips cognac all during shooting. Arthur wears a tux to direct the formal dinner room scene, which I find sweetly empathetic. That evening, I have dinner with Max at the Château. Why don't I read the signs? Max is a method actor, and once he gets in character he stays in character. In the film he plays Arthur Goldman, a Jew who becomes an enthusiastic—and violent—Nazi collaborator. My character, Lauren, is a Jewess. I make love with Max—*big mistake*. He treats me like an object, like a rag doll, flopping me this way and that. When I attempt to assert myself, to say I don't like the way he's handling me, he shoves me back down and ignores what I'm saying. Max doesn't seem to care if he's causing pain, and in fact, seems to feel it's a big part of sex. There's a terrible expression of angst on his face. Maybe the only way for him to achieve pleasure is through pain, too. I hightail it out of there and never want to see his ass again!

Take a trip to Ottawa with Warren Oates for *The White Dawn* premiere. Meet Canadian Prime Minister Pierre Trudeau, Eskimos (!), and discover that Warren and I are only friends, not lovers. From there, we go to New York, where we see Peckinpah's new film, *Bring Me the Head of Alfredo Garcia*. It makes me sick. I go on to Cropseyville. Yvonne and her kids are in Europe and I spend time with Dad, Cindy, and Byron. I drive Dad and Byron to Montreal. They're flying to Milan to meet Yvonne. Byron is growing into a sensitive and strong young man, but I feel his intense solitude. On the way back I stay in Plattsburgh, and the next day drive on to North Elba to visit John Brown's grave. The caretaker gives me a photograph of my great aunt, Martha Evelyn Brewster, with her husband Oliver Brown, and I realize that Byron looks like her! I am consumed by the blues, and wish that I had someone to talk things over with. Why am I always by myself at the wrong time? Perhaps I'm meant to be. My own solitude can be intense. I try to "be here now," to live life and to enjoy it. But my freedom to do that always seems to get trapped by an overwhelming loneliness, a deep desire to be held and loved, to share all that I see as well as my present burdens and memories that cause me to suffer. Sometimes I feel invisible. If a heart breaks and no one is around to hear it, does it make a sound?

Get a letter from Dad who's now in Switzerland with Yvonne after dropping off Byron at a summer camp. He says that "we both know that the occasion was a turning point in his life and our relationship. It was like a bird taking an overdue first flight from the nest. Neither of us knew how strong his wings would be, and now there is cause to believe he was not ready for flight." Eventually Byron does acclimate well to camp. But Harry adds that he is aware Byron is still taking the divorce very hard, and that "he has no sense of his personal worth." But nevertheless Harry is hopeful, believing that "the past is the past and now everywhere there is light within and without."

Poor Dad. He's struggling to be a good father, but beyond that, he also understands that Pat's problems have left deep scars on Byron. Harry wants so much for everything to be all right, and he keeps telling himself, and me, that with Yvonne's help, everything will be fine. But it's clear that something is nagging at him, and that he's not sure that everything will be all right.

Fall

Feel as if I'm living across the street from Cinque, Patty Hearst, and the whole SLA army. After watching the shoot-out on TV I decide: It's time to move! A friend of Warren Oates's, Warren Miller, turns me on to a quaint little place in West Hollywood called Windsor Gardens. The set up here is a courtyard, with three white cottages on each side and two two-story apartment buildings in the back. Fuchsia-colored bougainvillea pours over the trellises and doors; I love it! I decide to rent a cottage and convince my friends to move into the other empty ones, creating my own Garden of Allah. I paint the walls and floor of my cottage white and get a cat named Marilyn. The courtyard is managed by Mrs. Williams, an elderly, overweight woman, who sits on her porch in a green plastic lawn chair, keeps her eyes on all the action, never missing a trick. We all wait on her hand and foot to keep her happy and from complaining about our noise. My friend Bruce Weintraub moves in; then songwriter Paul Jabara; Sally Kirkland; Joey Townsend, who arrives with her sometimes-visiting lover, Maria Schneider; and Warren Miller. Hiram Keller, dubbed the most beautiful boy in the world, shows up on Paul's steps one day. Paul and Hiram had performed together on Broadway in *Hair*. "Back from Brazil, darling," Hiram announces, ending a five-year hiatus that, from the looks of things, has been spent lying in the sun and powdering his nose. He stays and stays with Paul, who calls him Blanche (as in DuBois), Paul never tires of reminding Hiram that he's "just another pretty face." Hiram has not yet come close to his starring role in Fellini's *Satyricon*, but he sure is versatile! One day I walk over to say "hi," and find him in bed with Joni Mitchell! Aside from Hiram, Paul always has interesting people coming around. Even his manicurist, Sandra Bernhard, is a trip. Here in Windsor Gardens we struggle together in our careers, fight and love, share lonely evenings, have communal dinner parties, afternoon lunches in the garden, rehearse together, and exchange advice. I feel safe with all of these gay/bi people—they don't want anything from me but my friendship. I'm in heaven. It's my first real home in L.A.

Taking ballet lessons—good for the body and the soul—from Stefan Wenta. He's Polish, and he's also good friends with Roman—know him from the "old country." Michelle Phillips is there too, getting in shape. *Playgirl* shoot with Bruce Weintraub—in a Rolls! There's a little bit of nudity, but it's tasteful! Dream that I'm being chased through a forest by a mulatto monkey who's trying to bite me and then I run into Mel Brooks. I won't even guess at the symbolism here! Need to escape from this town so I take a quick trip to Fayette, Mississippi, where I visit new friend-cowboy/farmer-Lionel and go to a concert he's produced. No one comes except the mayor, Charles Evers. I dance with him and try to engage him in conversation about his brother, Medgar Evers, the NAACP field director who was gunned down in front of his home in Jackson, Mississippi, on June 12, 1963. Charles does *not* want to talk about Medgar. I wonder if Charles, who'd marched alongside his brother and worked hard to register voters, has turned into some version of a fat cat, or maybe he just wants to have a good time and not be inhibited by one more discussion about his dead brother-hero.

I return back to my life and my cat, on whom I depend for much of my emotional sustenance. Work three days on a TV movie-of-the-week, *Contaminated*. Horrible. We have to wear gas masks and pretend we're dying of some mysterious toxic poisoning. Dating Guy Dill, a sculptor from Venice, California. He builds me a queen-sized bed, and gives me a Plexiglas box that contains the sawdust residue, a picture of a heart, and a verse from one of his favorite songs—"Blue Umbrella" by John Prine. I visit a friend at the Château and go for a swim. While sitting by the pool, I see Leonard Cohen, who's studying a rhyming dictionary. Somehow, this disappoints. John Prine's in town, recording. He tells me, "Last February when you drove me to the airport you should have kidnapped me." Eric Andersen plays us a tape of his new stuff. John's polite; I'm uptight. We see Martha Reeves at the Troubador and give Joni Mitchell a ride home to Bel Air in my 1964 black Cadillac convertible that pal Alan Sharpe gave me. I've met her several times before—once with Hiram! I think she's funky and good, but she's a bit cool and keeps her distance. John tells me I look like Miss Indiana with my "buttermilk skin." We try to cook hot dogs over a gas jet in the fireplace and make love. He also tells me a great story: "At one time Hank Williams was married to a woman named Audrey. She broke his heart, and then she fleeced him. Anyway, when she died, the preacher walked up to her casket, looked in, and said, 'Hey, good lookin', what ya got cookin'?'" . . . Party at the S & M, where I sing all night with Eric Andersen and Phil Ochs. This is fun, although Phil gets very drunk and very gloomy. Eventually, Eric, as always, bores me to death.

1975

Winter

I'm taking acting classes with Milton Katselas and going on lots of interviews. I run into Warren, who says he's in love with Michelle Phillips. "Michelle knows me the way you knew me. She's seen me all ways." He asks who I'm seeing, and says, "You look better than I've ever seen you." It was good seeing Warren, but when he calls later, wanting to gossip *and* have a threesome with Michelle, I say, "No!" *I'm* not the object. While waiting for John at Tana's, I run into the magnificent Barbara, who's with Warhol-star, Viva, and Tom Baker. Then I join Bonnie Raitt, her boyfriend, and Harry Dean for a few drinks. When John shows up, we brownbag some wine and go back to the Château.

Have a meeting with Herb Ross, who's going to direct *The Sunshine Boys* for Columbia Pictures. Herb thinks I may be too tall to play Harvey Keitel's wife. "Take your shoes off." I do; I'll even saw an inch or two off my legs! . . . Do a role on "Harry O" opposite David Janssen, who's very sweet, very supportive, and appears to be very drunk. John calls at 4:30 A.M. Throw a black cape over my pink nightie, and hop in the Caddy. John tells me, "Your hair is always windblown, like you're standing on the edge of a cliff. You remind me of Natalie Wood in *Rebel Without a Cause.*" Ah, John, you silver-tongued devil! Harvey Keitel's fired from *The Sunshine Boys*. He's asked Herb one too many times what his *motivation* should be. "Your salary!" snaps Herb. Harvey's replaced by Richard Benjamin and I get hired to play his wife.

Wearing a white suit and a purple beret, I go pick up John and his band at the S & M and we head out to a party at Bonnie Raitt's house in the Valley. All the Eagles are there and everybody sings. Sometimes this works, but this evening everyone seems especially self-conscious—maybe everyone's too stoned. Bonnie can be hard to figure out—sometimes she's real friendly to me and other times the refrigerator door is open. Maybe she's got a crush on John.

Lucy Saroyan's been living in a sad apartment, right across from Ralph's Supermarket off Sunset; she is being driven crazy by her neighbor, who for three days straight, has been battling with her husband. When the police arrive they discover the woman's schizophrenic and has been fighting with herself! Only Lucy would have this experience.

The *L.A. Times* gives me a good review for *Rape Squad*. Linda Gross writes: "Miss Lee stands out as an actress with sensitivity and potential that she is unable to fulfill in this film." A lot of prison inmates must feel this way, too, because I've been getting fan mail from them and they're asking for photos, too. Somehow this haunts me . . . in the movie we were stalking and now I feel as if I'm being stalked!

Alan Sharpe killed his dog—shot him in the head. Shit! At the Bel Air Hotel at a party honoring Clive Davis I see Bonnie who tells me that John and Ann Carol are doing fine. "Who? . . ." His old lady, Jen." . . . "Ooh, isn't that nice. So good to see you again, Bonnie." Who does she think she is? The romance police? Cocaine everywhere! Afterward, I go to Don Henley and Glenn Frey's house and hear two new Eagle songs, "Hollywood Waltz" and "After the Thrill Is Gone." I also listen to jive jargon that drives me crazy—and home! Don is the more mature of the two, but both are very competitive with one another. After a little coke men seem to get really extra macho! Back at the hotel, John tells me his favorite song by him is *Far From Me*, "about a girl named Kitty who dumped me for no reason a long time ago."

I'm sitting in a car in the driveway of Carol and Walter Matthau's house waiting for Lucy, when Walter sticks his head out of the front door and motions me inside. He apologizes for Lucy's rudeness and says he's glad we're getting a chance to meet since we'll both be working on *The Sunshine Boys*. Walter seems kind and generous. He tells me that I look like Oona Chaplin—and a little like his mother! I get a tour of the house, which is so colorful, like being in a rainbow. Flowers and floral motifs are everywhere.

Paul Jasmin fixes me up with Jimmy Connors. I don't know if I like him. Jimmy's sweet but very immature and vulgar. He does things like belch and fart in public, and the group he hangs out with thinks this is the height of humor. They also think a woman with "big tits" is the height of eroticism. It's like being with a group of high school boys, ones with large bank accounts and fast, fancy cars. Jimmy's only a couple of years younger than I am, but I feel way too old for this one. Maybe Jimmy's immaturity stems from the fact that he's had to give over his entire life to tennis, and this has left no time for *anything* else. And he doesn't seem to have any desire to learn about anything else—even women, even sex. I haven't slept with Jimmy, and I don't know if I'm going to. John returns and I introduce him to Warren Oates and they love each other.

Life on the set of *The Sunshine Boys* has its ups and downs. I have a really bad time during one scene, and Herb yells at me in front of everybody. I'm humiliated—confused. And I still don't understand what he wants! Now we're all off to the East Coast to finish shooting at the Actors' Home in New Jersey. Dick Benjamin has a massive crush on me. Yikes! He and his wife, Paula Prentiss, are close friends with Tony and Berry, with whom I'm staying in New York. This gets a little awkward, on more than one occasion. But it doesn't go further than a sweet harmless flirtation. I really like Paula. Art drops by a couple of times for dinner. We're just friends now; he's in love and very happy. I go with Berry to see Tony in

Equus. God, that's a seriously disturbing play and all that dialogue, and I don't even know what it's about.

Spring

Tony's a man with a lot of self-control; he's very disciplined about his diet and exercise. But to me he looks really wound tight and lately he's been acting a bit strange. One afternoon, I'm taking a shower and Tony walks into the bathroom and begins to shave. He's just got his briefs on and I'm standing behind a foggy, but see-through, shower curtain. We're alone in the house. I try to act cool, as if this is nothing, but I know Tony feels my discomfort. I'm getting paranoid, remembering the Bates Motel and I can also feel the sexual vibes in the air. Tony and Berry seem to see me as a kind of modern-day Moll Flanders, so I wonder if Tony wants some sort of approval or reaction from me. He's obviously preening and very nearly naked. Maybe because he's gay and has only limited experience with women, he feels he has to prove something. Or it could be just plain exhibitionism. Maybe he just likes to show off his taut and sinewy body. Whatever it is, I don't like it. And he keeps on shaving—for what seems an eternity.

I take Tony and Berry to see John Prine at Avery Fisher Hall and backstage afterward to meet him. Make a quick trip to Cropseyville to say goodbye to Harry, who's on his way to Ireland. Yvonne is too much, talking about "the East," "nature," and the "motion of non-motion." Go to Caesar's Palace in Las Vegas to see the first big money match in the game of tennis, between Jimmy Connors and John Newcombe. I tell Jimmy, "If you win I'll give you a present. Something of mine you've always wanted." I arrive halfway through the match to see him win. In his room after the game he's having a massage and talking to Angie Dickinson. "Angie, could you excuse us? It's time for Jimmy's present." Game-set-match. A very short time later I join Angie at the bar downstairs for a much-needed vodka and tonic. "Angie, don't ask."

Back to L.A. With the top down on the Caddy, I drive Kris Kristofferson, Barbara Steele, and Bobby to Santa Monica Civic Center where John is performing. In his dressing room, he's got the sterling silver roses I'd sent him. "They were so beautiful, Jen, I didn't know whether to admire them or eat them." I go to a dinner with Art at Richard Perry's art-deco house. He's just produced

Art's new album. Gwen Welles and Dyan Cannon fly into the room from the Jacuzzi. Wrapped in towels, giddy, and breathless; they ignore me. At dinner, they make a conspicuous effort to make me invisible. Dyan and Gwen are stars. I am not, and therefore, "worthless." They tell Art—out of earshot—"She's ambitious." And they're not? Since when is ambition a dirty word? Especially in Hollywood! Here, one must either be a star or have some sort of show-biz power, but what does that really mean? What's that really worth? God, the collective taste and mindset of so many people in this business is intensely mediocre.

Summer

Lucy takes me to a party at Jim Brown's split-level house in the hills. We arrive at twilight on a Saturday night in July. Some guests are swimming, some are eating, some are just sitting around on the wall-to-wall shag carpet. Loud disco music is everywhere. Women of all colors abound; they all want him. Jim's not just a movie star, but a legend and the king of his lair. Dressed in shorts, he ambles through his sparsely furnished house with its crooked electrical sockets. I've heard Jim once tried to throw a girlfriend through a plate-glass window. I go looking for the window. Lucy gives me Quaaludes, and when Jim takes me by the hand to show me the guest house below the pool, I'm high. It's musty and dark inside; there's only a little light refracted from the main house. I sit on large, squishy, square pillows. All of a sudden Jim's on top of me. While he's inside of me, I see someone, peering over his shoulder, straining to watch. I'm crying; I'm being smothered; I try to push him off. "Tell them to leave" are the only words I can say. I feel that I am a sacrificial lamb. I did not want this. . . .

Visit Cropseyville, and go with Harry to the Williamstown Theatre to see *Six Characters in Search of an Author*. Byron and I visit Darrow, the boarding school he'll be going to in the fall. He seems so sad and so lost. I go to Leadville, Colorado, to do a small part in *The Duchess and the Dirtwater Fox*. I hear that Byron's in the hospital; his leg is broken in several places from a soccer accident and he's got a cast up to the waist. Harry's angry about the accident, and this has got me worried. I get a small part in *Marathon Man*. John Schlesinger tells me a funny story. When Dustin Hoffman was trying to work himself into a cold hysterical sweat for his role jogging madly and not sleeping, Lawrence Olivier suggested, "Dear boy, you'll wear yourself out. Just act!" . . . Getta "Baretta," and pose with Won Ton Ton, "the dog who saved Hollywood," for an *Esquire* piece on up-and-coming actresses.

Fall

Through Harry Dean I meet Gordon Lightfoot. I run into Gordon a few more times at Tana's before he asks me out. Again, we go to Tana's. Drunk on champagne, we stumble back to my cottage after dinner at—where else—Tana's where all the musicians hang out. Gordon's big and clunky; a sweet guy, but not completely on the ball. He's kind of boring, kind of like his music—safe, no rough edges. We make drunken, fumbly love. In the middle of the night, I get up and go into the bathroom, somehow managing to lock myself inside. I try and try but can't get out. HELP! I rattle the knob and pound on the door, yelling and screaming. The bathroom is down the hall from the bedroom, so it takes Gordon about twenty minutes to get up and rescue me. He opens the door, and there's this moment of stunned silence. Neither of us has a stitch of clothing on. We're both in shock. We've just made love, but somehow this moment is much more intimate, too intimate. He calls a few times after this but once was enough.

Stefan Wenta tells me I remind him of Tysus; some fictional character who had any man she ever wanted, whenever she wanted. But she was also like a monk and led a life of spiritual purity. I am not naive by any stretch of the imagination but I *am* innocent. All of my affairs have been experiences, not conquests. Above all, my main desire is to learn and to grow. Experience is the greatest teacher; it simply demands that you be honest with it. That's the only way experience can be effectively assimilated. And, through this process, I have learned to pursue the truth about myself, my past, the world in which I live and the people in it.

Christmas in Cropseyville. Byron appears healed. Go with Tony and Berry to Woody Allen's New Year's Eve party at the Harkness House. Seeing Woody has become a milepost of sorts—I see him and I measure the distance I've come since Finch.

1976

Winter

A blue year. I'm getting very little work, so far, just *The Private Files of J. Edgar Hoover*—in which I run screaming out of a burning building. I'm also doing some modelling and going on a lot of interviews. Well, that's to be expected. Reporting a director, who wanted "to secure a relationship with me," to the SAG morals committee hasn't helped. I guess it makes me look like a trouble-maker. Lord, some of these people seem to think they're finding the cure for cancer, they've such huge egos. And it's such a simple, often embarrassing, and demeaning, profession. My focus on acting is beginning to dissipate more than just a little bit. My endless small parts never fill me with a sense of accomplishment. Would a nice large one? I wonder if it would and I wonder if I can, or even care to, maintain the patience and motivation needed to make it in this vain and superficial business! I am always slightly humiliated to say I'm an actress. Once I believed that if I were a "star" I would be loved. Now I realize that this attitude may court disaster. God, I am so lonely. I would love to have a relationship. I adore John, who's in and out of town more than ever, but that's clearly a dead-end street. All the other men I see I feel very little for, and my greed for experience is beginning to make me feel like a subway stop. I firmly believe that, as a woman, I can do the same as a man—at work, play, or in bed. But boy, the price is mighty high. And the judgment, it's fierce—from both men *and* women.

Summer

After watching Jimmy Cagney in *Yankee Doodle Dandy*, I suggest to Paul Jabara that he do a disco version of the song for the Bicentennial. He loves the idea and, with Bob Esteys, produces a good rendition of it. We work up a routine and I learn to tap in a week. Patti D'Arbanville, two professional dancers—Chris and Geri Boccino—and I dress in little red, white, and blue outfits from Frederick's of Hollywood and perform "Yankee Doodle Dandy" on the "Dinah and Her New Best Friends" at the MGM Grand in Las Vegas and on "American Bandstand." We also perform in L.A.,

New York, and San Diego. A couple of times we use a flatbed truck as a stage, appearing on behalf of local radio stations. Paul dresses in a World War II wool army uniform, complete with rifle, and does his best Jimmy Cagney, sweating profusely. Did I ever get credit for my idea, let alone royalties? No. But fifteen years later I see I'm included under a Special Thanks Section of Paul's Greatest Hits CD. Me and 100 others.

Although drugs have always been around, there seems to be more of them and even easier access—cocaine and Quaaludes mostly. Everyone who comes to Windsor Gardens seems to be carrying. Even a shrink shows up on my doorstep after my first visit to him—vial in hand. I ask, "Is this unethical or is this just Hollywood?" People I know are starting to die—Phil Ochs has hanged himself. I realize I don't want to die. I go home to Cropsey-ville for Cindy's wedding. Yvonne is wearing Pat's jewelry—which enrages everybody! Not a good move. Pat's there sporting a long braid, dressed like a hippie, looking sad and confused. I drive Byron back to Winchenton, his new boarding school. I'm sure he feels abandoned by Cindy's getting married. Twenty-four hours later, I get the news that Byron has tried to kill himself. He tells Cindy that he feels like the problem child Dad and Yvonne want to get rid of; he truly believes he must be the cause of their fights. Yvonne has analyzed him, saying that all of his troubles are caused by his "too close relationship" with Cindy. It sounds to me as if Byron has become the conduit for Yvonne's anger over Dad's refusal to marry her.

Once again Lucy is fiercely unhappy over a man—Richard Pryor. He does sound like a magic man. She went on location for *Greased Lightning*, she had a small role and he ended up having an affair with Pam Grier!

Lord, everyone's unhappy. And to top it off, the IRS is after me for the erroneous tax refund that I already spent. Yikes! Ten thousand dollars! I'm completely frantic and feel terribly guilty. Everyone says, "Screw the IRS," but it is theft.

What's it all about, Alfie? Endless parties at John Schlesinger's house where Michael Childers is, as always, the impeccable host. At these gatherings are an abundance of stars who, no matter how big they've become, never seem to really believe that they've made it. They still act insecure, preening and fawning, jockeying for posi-tion, wanting to be on the "A" list at the best parties. My name's been in the columns almost daily—big deal! I feel like a fag hag or a beautiful armpiece. I cannot find the center of this town or the center of myself. I even try group therapy with an overweight, overly friendly shrink, Vivian, and five sulking lost souls whose problems and whining bore me to tears. I hate it. Have a brief affair with Don Johnson. We've written a song together, "Bartender, Please Don't Sell Me Anymore." Don is a sweet soul who loves to party hardy. Drugs and drinks till he passes out, but he's a lot of fun until he gets there. And he can hold on for a while—lots of energy! More than anything, Don wants to be a star, but I think he's really a country boy at heart. He's got a funky little treehouse house on Lookout Mountain in Laurel Canyon. Don takes me out to the sticks where Dickie Betts lives, and we play guitar, get ripped, and sing till daylight. I play guitar too—which is rather a hoot since Dickie is soooo good! But then the great ones learned that way too, and they never put you down for learning!

Fall

Looking through books and smelling incense at a metaphysical bookstore on Melrose. Lots of gym and bike riding at Venice Beach—obsessed with my body, the shape it's in, how much it weighs. Lots of Fassbinder movies. Obviously I'm searching, but I don't know what for. I spend Labor Day weekend with John and Michael on Natalie and R.J.'s boat, sailing to Catalina. Bruce and another pretty boy join us. Gay-gay-gay. I flirt with the cute, blond Harbor Master and feel as if everyone's looking on and giggling at the lonely woman I am. Many of my friends are gay; they can be very supportive—I feel comfortable and safe with them. But sometimes I feel a lot of conflict about these friendships because they can be dismissive and hostile toward women, which makes me crazy. I have plenty of stupid evenings. Like the night I go to see Lynyrd Skynyrd, whom I loathe. End up snorting coke with Linda Blair—the actress from hell! Even have a walk down three-some memory lane with Warren, et al!

Back home to Cropseyville. God, why do I keep going? I do crave love and affection, but is this the place?

I hear that David Blue's in the studio making an album. I also hear that he's recording the song he wrote about me. I decide to drop by. I walk into Clover Studios late one afternoon. Suddenly I hear my name being sung by a chorus of black back-up singers. David sees me: "Perfect timing!"

Jennifer Lee won't you listen to me
Time moves on quickly
You're living in a prison believing you're free.
Oh, baby, that's no way to be
Oh, baby, that's no way to be.

Although I have heard some of these lyrics before it feels as if it's the first time. I like this as a song, but it makes *me* sound like a victim. A real male interpretation.

I go to Sea Ranch with Alan Sharpe, some of his children, and Toby Raffleson. He says something cryptic: "You're like a great soccer player trying to be good." Alan is a good Scotsman—which is why he relates everything to soccer—a good writer and an especially a good friend. But sometimes I wonder if a truly platonic relationship between hetero men and women is possible; there always seems to be sexual tension in the air.

I run into Warren, thank God! My Caddy's gotten towed, so he drives me to pick it up. I sell it then and there for $100. It's time for some changes—a new car and some real love. My poor cat Marilyn has leukemia. It *is* always something. Like that heartbreaker John sings, "If heartaches were commercials we'd all be on TV."

At least I go to a good New Year's Eve Party, at Peter Bogdanovich's house in Bel Air. He's very grand, with his windswept collar. Warren plays the piano and Cybill sings, Dick and Paula are there, and guess who—Jim Brown. I totally ignore him. Lucy gets dreadfully drunk and melancholy and can't get up off the floor. I meet Ken Tynan, the film and theater critic and author of *Oh, Calcutta*, who's mesmerized by the seams in my black stockings, which inspires him to tell stories about Louise Brooks, who he profiled in *The New Yorker*. Ken says when he visited Louise in Rochester, she told him that when she masturbates she is able to ejaculate several feet. Then she had him go look in the stereo, to see where "it" lands. I guess that didn't get in the magazine! What a story! And Ken is so terribly English and so dignified that it makes the story seem even stranger! It's a nice party—not too many people. Gore Vidal dropped by as did one of the Smothers Brothers—who appeared to be three sheets to the wind.

1977

Winter

Feeling blue and thinking about John, I fuck around on Paul's piano and come up with a good line: "My man ain't man enough for me." From there I come up with three chords, I keep going and Paul helps me out on the chorus.

Decide to throw a little party for the Alpha Band. I'm making guacamole and the next thing I know, my little cottage is filled with people: Boz Scaggs, Heather McRay, Joni Mitchell, Alan Jones, Susy Allan Blakely, Ron Cooper. It looks like a good party, but I decide to leave. It's too crowded!

Do some opium—my first and last time—with a brilliant, wiry, little fellow, Van Dyke Parks. He's a songwriter-producer-actor, endlessly nourishing, and takes me around to meet some of his friends: Terry Melcher, the good-looking son of Doris Day; Lowell George, creator of Little Feat; Dennis Hopper; Kinky Friedman; and Piers Ackerman. Van Dyke tells me that I can do anything and not to let that frighten me. He talks and walks like an old man, but is seriously hip. We do lots of coke and 'ludes, and have a great time but this affair comes to a crashing halt when his girlfriend Sally comes by one morning and drags him out of bed. Marlon Brando comes by Windsor Gardens to pick up an old girlfriend, a Jamaican actress who's staying with Paul and Hiram. She's a petulant child who's always screaming, "I'm the victim!" and "blood clot" this and "blood clot" that. Marlon's really sweet; he does this odd embarrassed little dance, kicking up one leg like a chorus-line dancer. Since he's a tad overweight, this makes a touching image. He's all vulnerablility, with "I'll do anything for love" written all over his face. See him a few days later at a Filmex screening for Bud Cort's film, *Why Shoot the Teacher?* where he tells me I look ravishing!

Spring

Waylon comes by with a vial of coke, pulls out my guitar and begins to play and sing for hours. Afterward he talks about Jessie, who he's visibly tormented over; publishing troubles in the music business; and rocky friendships. He tells me about wanting to be a preacher when he was young and spins tales about his great granddad, a Cherokee. Says he wants to make a film about Hank Williams. He's sincere when says he's proud of me for the independent way I've lived my life. We end up in bed for hours; he's extremely passionate, but I'm way too full of coke and it takes time. I do love his large body, his rugged hands, the tender way they touch my breasts. Waylon's in terrible physical condition; he's overweight and sweats easily. And he tells me he has to go into the hospital for "general exhaustion." I'm sure it's the drugs. He fights his demons on a daily basis. All that macho-ness and sensitivity fighting to be number one—it has to be particularly hard for a man, especially for someone like Waylon! But he fights on, with a spirit and integrity I greatly respect. His openness has touched me more deeply than ever; this is true intimacy, far more important than sex. Waylon's special and good and I feel close with him in a way that I don't with anybody else; he's like family. I'm glad Jessie loves him so much. I give him a copy of *My Wicked Wicked Ways* by Erroll Flynn. The very next day, I run smack into Jessi Colter. I wonder if she knows, and you know, I feel a little ashamed.

I visit John at the Château and he plays me a new song, "Chain of Sorrow." It inspires me to think about Pat, Harry, Cropseyville, and the bad old days: the fights, the drinking, the Dylan Thomas. I knew then that I was already old. (A friend tells me you can figure out at what age you were born by how old you are when you reach a "spiritual plateau." But he didn't tell me how you know when you *hit* a "spiritual plateau"!) But I also think of birch trees, tiger lilies, a snake called Penelope, butterflies, a graveyard across the highway. I write a song about my parents called "Pat and Harry."

Summer

It starts out as a short trip. I ride to Phoenix for the weekend with Al Bunetta, John's manager, to see Steve Goodman, Jerry Jeff Walker, and Joe Ely perform. Then it's on to an all-night party, followed by an afternoon of driving mini-Trans Am formula cars around a track. Forty-eight hours later, I'm on a private plane with Jerry Jeff and Joe Ely, heading for Vegas. Joey claims to be a "vagabond meeting the queen of Spain." After gambling, little sleep, and lots of pills, coke, and gin, we fly on to Reno. Briefly, we give in to our exhaustion, but then we decide to go on to Tahoe. Driving on the winding mountain roads we all sing, "That's the Way the World Goes Round," by John and "Your Sweet and Shiny Eyes," by Nan O'Byrne. We keep moving, energized by a mix of coke, beer, gin, and speed. While hanging out with Larry Mayan's group, I'm completely puzzled—why am I on this junket? Sure, I can hold my own with the boys, but all of this is becoming a disorienting blur. My mind feels as if it's got a neon sign flashing *HELP! Get me out of here*!

Nan O'Byrne asks me to join her on the road; we'll go to Texas and play in some clubs. Warren Zevon says this will be a good way for Nan to figure out if she wants to be a performer as well as a songwriter. Nan's another ex-girlfriend of Bobby's I'd met when she was on what she calls her "re-entry." I've never understood from what. Nan's older, petite, and attractive, with sandy-colored hair, tiny hands, and a slight, hip Texas drawl. She's got an overly determined walk; each step makes a statement. Before leaving for Texas, we go on a trip to Twentynine Palms, outside Joshua Tree. There we sing, play guitar, and finish up a couple of songs. One is inspired by my Phoenix-Vegas-Tahoe-Reno-Joe Ely sojourn, called: "The Woman's Getting Tired of Running with the Men." On July 20 we leave for Texas in my second-hand Volvo.

At 4:15 A.M., we stop at a gas station in Peachtree, Arizona, where we meet creepy, SLA-probables who have a pet tarantula in a peanut butter jar. The gas station attendant tries to give us a small yellow dog, but we're in a hurry so we name him Rudy and take him with us only in spirit. We drive straight through the remainder of Arizona—accommodations in Flagstaff and Winslow really sucked. And straight on through to Gallup, New Mexico and see its red desert and our even redder eyes. At this point, it doesn't make sense to stop, so we forge ahead, making it to the Dollar Motel in Albuquerque, falling asleep nearly twenty-two hours after leaving L.A. I put us on a potato skin diet because it's full of lithium—we need all the help we can get. We hit the road again, passing Cadillac Ranch (Cadillac front ends shoved into the earth with the rest pointing to the sky), and arriving in Amarillo in time for an audition that I'd arranged in L.A. Some Neil Simon dinner-theatre play I really don't want to do. I read for the part, they ask me to come back for a second audition.

When we get back to Motel 6 we find our door open and nothing gone. It's an omen. I feel as if we're in the Twilight Zone and it's time to get out. Besides, I'd rather play music with Nan than be in some dinner theatre production. We drive on to Fort Worth and check into the Green Oaks. Nan's sister, Bitsy, comes to see us and tells us about Johnny Bell, a great psychic whom we must visit. Johnny's an old, crippled, bed-ridden black woman who lives on the bad side of town. She's holding a long, polished shillelagh, which has a blue floral handkerchief secured by a rubber band at the end. Every time I ask a question she wipes her brow with the hanky and says, "Put it all in a box for Jesus." There are no revelations here—but not disappointing. A few more days of r & r in Fort Worth; we get a great cowboy hat for Nan; visit the new Bluebird Café with old friends Barney, Lionel, and Janie; and go to Nan's hometown, Tyler. We visit her family, then go searching for her father's grave so we can sing "Satisfied Mind" to him. After wandering around in the dead of night looking for his plot, we give up and serenade the entire cemetery.

Once more, I need to *move*. I can't get out of there fast enough, so we head on to Austin. On our way, we stay at the Blue Bell Motel*, a rundown clapboard-covered motel in Rockdale. No cars—motorcycles and semis, parked *everywhere*. This is sinister! I'm convinced that we're surrounded by wild men and nickname this place "the Murder Motel Court." I prepare for the onslaught by dragging out a chest of drawers and pushing it against the door. "This is healthy paranoia," I tell Nan. Fully clothed—in case of the need for a quick escape—we wrap ourselves up like a taco in a paper-thin blanket and giggle ourselves to sleep. In the car the next day, we write a song: "Put It in a Box for Jesus."

> *If you've got a cross and a burden to bear*
> *Just put it all in a box and send it to Jesus.*
> *Send it to Jesus*
> *If you think nobody cares and you're waiting*

For someone to knock
Put it all in a box and send it to Jesus.

In Austin, meet some friends of Nan's, George and Carlin, who book us into some clubs around town. We all drop by the Split Rail to see Butch Hancock perform. The first club we play in is called The Hole in the Wall. There are no mikes and we have to tune up in the kitchen. Nan, who's more nervous than I am, calls Tom Waits and gets some advice. "Don't worry. It'll be all right. Just keep your zipper up," he tells her. And we do all right, singing four songs, "Margarita Cantrel," "Right, Left and Wrong," co-written by Nan and me; "The Day Will Come," by Nan; and Paul Sibel's "Anyday Woman." When we leave the stage the crowd gives us a standing ovation. We get the same warm response at Gordo's Pizza Parlor, the Lake Austin Lodge, and on the back porch of a honky-tonk in Jollyville, called Our Place. At the Good-bye July party at the Split Rail I pick up Gil Thomas, who's the bass player from a small band that's joined us for our last performance there. Gil and I go back to the hotel, drink tequila, make love, and write a new song, "So Little Time." At this point, Nan and I have had actually developed a little following—some fans are asking us, "Where are you gals playing next?" We're invited to open for Gary Nunn and the Lost Gonzo Band at the Soap Creek Saloon but Nan doesn't think we're good enough. I think we're doing fine. I wonder if her fear is based on the tenets of her religion, Scientology. I've been having a ball. Despite a few moments of paranoia, I've approached our trip with excitement and enthusiasm. I'm looking for experience and keep in mind *my* tenet; _Never, for the sake of harmony, deny your own experience._ And I love everything about it. Before a show we tune up our guitars, do a little harmonizing, get all dressed up, have a couple of vodka-tonics and hit the boards! It's all right not to be Linda Ronstadt. We can still communicate some heart and some soul and sing on key. I love all these honky-tonks and the hole-in-the-wall dives. I love the Texas nights, the beer drinking audiences who respond to us with genuine heart and soul, and I love the pure spontaneity of the whole experience. Anything could happen—even true love! There's a freedom here that I deeply appreciate because I'm not dependent on casting people, producers, my eight-by-tens, or even a good night's sleep. I can go beyond how

91

I look when I'm singing the songs I love. My voice may not shake the timbers of the world but I can give it all I've got. Most importantly, though I feel such interior joy when performing here, relaxed and safe. Even flaws are sweet—the mistakes are honest and true. Then there's a whole other world after the set is over—catching another good songwriter at another club, having some beers with some admirers, riding home at dawn in the sweet country air. I don't know what I'm going to do with this discovery or where it may lead but I feel as if I've finally uncovered some secret part of myself.

Outside Fort Worth the Volvo's clutch gives way and Nan and I are barely speaking. Over enchiladas at Delbert McClinton's where Nan is behaving like "serious songwriter," she announces she's flying back to L.A. I get my car fixed and head on back alone. Another adventure! I check into the KoKo Motel in Lubbock and hit the Cotton Club where it all began for Buddy Holly and the Crickets, Waylon being one of 'em—thank God he didn't get on that plane. The next morning I pick up the phone book and call Mrs. Holly and she tells me how to find her son's grave. It's etched with a guitar and his name. I say a prayer and sing "Waltz Across Texas."

I drop some Escatrol, put on the straw cowboy hat Joe Ely had given me and drive all day. Stop at a garage sale in Clovis, Texas, and buy a small porcelain jewel box. It's green with white cloverleafs. It's my Jesus Box. I drive on, through Muleshoe, Albuquerque, Gallup, New Mexico—I have to leave my peaches at the state line. Travel on through Holbrook, Winslow, and Flagstaff, Arizona. Too noisy at the Western Hills Motel, so I change my room even though I'm riding into Vegas on a shoestring! I reach Kingman, the outskirts of Vegas. Can't decide whether or not to stop in Vegas and see Jerry Jeff—flip a coin with the gas station attendant and I lose. Call Lucy who's now in love with Nick Nolte. Ha! I'd written those love letters she'd sent—they obviously worked! Another Escatrol and I drive straight through the purple and pink sunset to L.A. Life is good and getting better. I feel such a profound sense of anticipation! (I should have guessed that there was a big bend in the road of destiny right up ahead.) Exhilarated, broke, and dusty, I pull into the driveway at Lucy's place on Almont Drive. I'm walking in, she's on the phone:

"Hey, Jenny just walked in. You need a job, Jen?"

"Sure do, why?"

"She looks adorable, Richard. She's wearing a cowboy hat and two inches of dust. So what do you think?"

"Jen, I'm doing some work for Richard. You can be my assistant."

"Richard . . ."

"Richard Pryor . . . we're just friends now. Right, Rich? I'm decorating his house. I'll bring her out a week from today!"

I'm not familiar with Richard's work or any of his movies but I'm aware of him, mostly through Lucy. For all her troubles, Lucy, like Bobby, collects the special and the brilliant, and I guess, she tries to help them. I'm aware that Richard's a controversial character who's had his share of troubles and he's been getting more press every day. Even though their affair has ended, Lucy believes that he's misunderstood and still describes him as an erotic-genius-icon who must be revered!

RICHARD

If you had not've fallen
I would not have found you
Angel flying too close to the
   ground.

"Angel Flying Too Close to the Ground"
Willie Nelson

1977

August

Lucy and I drive out to Northridge, in the San Fernando Valley, to see Richard's house. We pass 7-Elevens, McDonald's, and self-service gas stations. It's a peculiar kind of redneck suburbia—expensive homes amidst some that are obviously very low rent. This had nothing to do with the Los Angeles I know. All the way there, Lucy talks. Her main theme is how much Richard depends on her—ever since she got him that good role in *Blue Collar*. Of course, she's tight with Paul Schrader, the director. In exchange, Lucy got herself a nice little part as Harvey Keitel's wife, and she got a finder's fee—$5,000—smart cookie. Now Richard's got her on the payroll, as a "creative consultant." Lucy's going to help him crossover and get noticed by *all* of Hollywood. She is certain that she can do this with all her connections: her stepfather, her mother, and then all her other friends, like Marlon, Paul, and Mike Nichols. Lucy collects "special" people, does them favors, then holds on to their markers. There is something Machiavellian about Lucy. I'm the interesting vagabond wandering waif and she'll be controlling my income. With Richard, she's the patron-like white woman. I can see trouble ahead—I think Lucy is still in love with Richard. I am impressed by the way she rings the buzzer and yells into the intercom, "Mercy, it's me." *Very* familiar. The rusty gate wobbles open and we drive up a long circular driveway towards a low-rider version of a rather large, Spanish, ranch-style house. It's has terracotta tiles on the roof and is painted that popular California beige-

pink-salmon color. Lucy keeps talking, "Richard recently pur-
chased this house way out here because he got a really good deal
and good acreage. It's the old Wrigley estate. As you can see, it
needs a lot of work." It's in complete disrepair. Richard has been
here about a year and the only thing he's renovated is the office.
The front lawn is filled with orange trees that need pruning and
grass that needs mowing. All the grounds are overgrown and
shaggy in a way that strikes me as ghostly and sad. As a matter
of fact, I think, *ghost house*. The gardens at the back of the house
are full of roses dying in the cracked dirt. Overripe pomegranates
hang heavy and low (like bloody teardrops). There's a tennis court
with a torn sagging net and rotting bleachers along one side.
There's a guest house, a gym, two garages and a dog run—all of
which need work. I see an unhappy looking Great Dane staring at
me, as if asking for help or some sign of affection. Lucy becomes
more and more animated, showing me around. "See all the work
that needs to be done . . . it's endless!" The swimming pool is full
of water, leaves, dead mice, and a wilted yellow air mattress that
drifts from one end to the other. The pool house doors are falling
off and the indoor-outdoor carpet smells of mildew and urine! It's
obvious that no one cares about this place, except maybe Lucy.
On one edge of the property, a run-down cottage can be seen
through hedges and trees. Screaming children play in its small dirt
backyard. On the other side, is a sedate white house; its windows
are boarded up. There is a depressing kind of isolated splendor
to this place. And when I walk into the house I am immediately
overwhelmed, kind of Salvador Dali meets Norma Desmond. Palpable doom and gloom smack me in the face—almost knocking me
off my feet like a hot desert wind. God, even the streaks on the wall
look like tears.

Lucy introduces me to a small, rather attractive dark-haired
woman in her late thirties. "Jen, this is Mercy, the best housekeeper
in all the world." Lucy goes on, saying that Mercy's been with
Richard for years and that he couldn't live without her. Mercy beams
at every word. I immediately see that Mercy runs the show. She's
Richard's "executive housekeeper" and he's given her carte
blanche, making her feel indispensable. She is certainly the lady
of the house. Sometimes, Lucy says, he even takes her on location
with him. A Salvadoran, she's hyper, flirtatious, and a giggler.
Mercy speaks in thickly accented broken English. Nevertheless,

she is a very shrewd lady. She reacts with too much enthusiasm to everything Lucy says. It looks as if each of them thinks the other one has the power. Mercy makes me uncomfortable; she seems to feel threatened by everyone who walks through that door. And, she's too familiar for a housekeeper. While serving us coffee and cookies, she sends us a message, *This is* my *turf, folks.*

We sit in the kitchen, which is just as depressing as the outside of the house. Renée, Richard's eldest daughter, saunters in wearing tight, tight jeans, leans on the counter and throws her ass out to Malibu. She looks at Lucy with contempt.

From here, we tour the empty dining room, then into the living room, which has a large globe-like aquarium filled with oddly shaped, brightly colored fish swimming in slow motion. "Some of these," Lucy whispers, "are poisonous." As I stop to look at the deadly fish, I can see through the French doors into the atrium where Richard is being photographed for a *Newsweek* cover. He spots us, flashing an embarrassed smile. Richard seems painfully shy when he walks in, waiting for Lucy to introduce us. She presents me as if she owns me and is sharing me out of the goodness of her heart. Nervous and talking nonstop, Lucy's practically selling me to Richard, telling him how beautiful and wonderful I am and how I just don't know it. Richard offers me his hand. "Hi, Jennifer, I'm glad you're going to be working here. You are, aren't you?" Then it's my turn to be shy. "Yes, thank you, so am I . . . happy to be working here . . . happy to meet you." I know him instantly. Immediate kinship—complete affinity! I see his shyness isn't the whole story; his eyes dominate me and tell me that he *knows* about me, much more than what Lucy has told him. And like his house, he looks broken and unloved. As Lucy chatters, I realize she is still completely besotted with him, and that he no longer cares for her. I keep my eyes on her but I can feel what Richard is feeling, hear what he's thinking. His quiet demeanor is mysterious and powerful—everything his reputation is not! There's no sign of the vitriolic madman here. Then Prophett, a painter friend of Richard's, walks into the room. He wants to take a picture and tells Richard to sit next to me. I sit down, Richard leans into frame. It's an SX-70, so we see the photo within minutes. Richard looks dazed. Handsome. I look as if I've swallowed a canary. I'm also in shock; I've just been struck by Cupid's arrow. The over-bloomed roses in front of us look like a wedding bouquet. Lucy is chirping away about how great Richard and I look together, an odd thing for her to do. Maybe she's finally letting go. I look at the photograph and I am immediately struck by the contrast of his deep black skin next to my whiteness. I think it's incredibly sensual. And I can't help wondering what making love with him would be like. I can *see* the connection I've been feeling today. Amidst all this gloom there is something I want to be part of, his magic, power, danger, mystery. I feel a reverence for Richard.

I begin working this week. I'm Lucy's assistant, an arrangement she adores. She's decided to redo the house in a basic French country theme. Lucy's mother, Carol Saroyan Matthau, is advising her, as is another friend, Joan Axelrod, who's the mother of old friend Jonathan. Joan has a great store from which Lucy gets ashtrays, chairs and beaucoup *objets d'art*. Mostly, Lucy does the shopping by herself while I stay at the house—greeting workers, accepting deliveries, making phone calls, supervising the dirty work. I stand in the dusty air, watching workmen pull up faded green linoleum, sandblast the walls in the atrium and strip cupboards. There's a Cinderella aspect to all of this that I can appreciate.

I look forward to coming to work every morning—that's when I usually see Richard. More often than not, a low-rent leftover from the night before surfaces before he does. These girls come in varying shades of black and white wearing tight leather, satin, or denim on their spent thighs and last night's faded dream on their face. When they pass the table where I'm doing my paperwork, they feel compelled to tell me their names. I feel like their confessor. It's as if my acknowledgment will cleanse or validate them and make their one-night stands real and lasting. The names are similar—lots of Cherry Anns and Sharondas. Sometimes I feel a twinge of jealousy, but I also have a feeling of superiority. The likelihood of any one of them passing my table again is slim. (Later, I found out that this little routine was designed to make me jealous.)

Eventually, Richard comes by looking well-scrubbed, bashful, and smelling of some wonderful cologne. Some mornings we have coffee together and chat about the work on the house. Then he goes off to his office. I love these mornings with him; they're private, solemn and intoxicating. I know I'm falling love.

Lucy sleeps late, so I work for a few hours and then she shows up carting her latest acquisition for the house. As long as I remain

her serf-waif I am her friend. It's hard playing to Lucy's High Priestess. And she's growing more desperate; she can't believe her
affair with Richard is really over. She quizzes me, "Did you see
anybody here this morning? Is Richard seeing somebody? Was
somebody here last night, Jennifer?" . . . "I don't know Lucy. It's
none of my business." I have to fudge because God knows I can
be replaced! Lucy could fire me but if I tell the truth and she says
anything about it to Richard, he'll think I'm a snitch. But Lucy
presses on, "Well, it's my business Jenny Lee, so if you ever see
anybody here you must tell me. You owe it to me. After all, look at
all I've done for you." Lucy and her markers. I'm getting tired of
hearing how much I owe her! She even tells me I "owe" her for my
friendship with her mother. "I've *given* you my mother as a surrogate since you really don't have one." Whenever Lucy does something for her friends, she uses every opportunity to remind them of
her generosity, and she's been doing this ever since I've known
her. We all used to feel sorry for her because of her neediness and
laughed it off but the simple truth is we're all bullied by Lucy. I
wonder if it would be easier not to receive. I decide I'll never tell
her anything about Richard's women.

August

It's been a long day of deliveries, workmen, and drop cloths, and
it's my birthday! It's one of those magical Southern California nights.
The air is clean and sweet with the scent of jasmine. The light at
dusk makes everything look pink and green. Lucy usually hates
my birthday because it's also her father's, but she decides that we
should celebrate. She makes a big fuss about giving me a "special,
special" gift; it's a colorful hand-painted plate, trimmed in gold-
leaf, of people dancing in a wedding procession. She explains,
"You are the bride and here is Richard. He's the groom and here
are all the people who love you, dancing behind in the wedding
party. That's me, I'm first."

Yikes! This seems really crazy since Lucy's still in love with Richard. In fact, Lucy's been hinting in a variety of ways that Richard
and I would make a great couple. It's got to be one of her tests of
my loyalty and devotion to her. Richard gives me an envelope with
"HAPPY BIRTHDAY" written on the outside. It contains two grams
of cocaine; generous, but odd. We all get higher and higher as the

evening wears on and end up in Richard's bedroom, snorting more coke, drinking more vodka, and playing sad songs on his guitar. Lucy and I sit on the huge brass bed while Richard sits on the floor, leaning against the wall. His eyes are closed and in stream of consciousness he begins to play a song about a woman he loved and lost, creating a spontaneous soul-poem. "A man loved a woman, she broke his heart, she made him cry, he couldn't forget her," he moans, like an animal skinned alive. Tears roll down his cheeks as his long brown fingers play un-fucking-believable guitar riffs. His hands move like Django Reinhardt's, up and down the neck, barring chords all over the place, picking the strings as if he's been doing it all his life. And his voice—it's from heaven. If Billie Holiday had had a brother who sang, he'd have sounded like Richard. Smooth and lilting with incredibly intricate phrasing. But these words were from hell. Demons and angels are out together tonight.

I think about the part Richard played in *Lady Sings the Blues*—Piano Man—a broken-down junkie. Here he is again, Blues Man. I'm moved by his sorrow, his love for this girl, Deboragh; his heart's been ripped out. But I also know that this need for love, this pain, was my pain. I can recognize his torment, identify with it, and understand it instinctively. We come from two different worlds, but there is much common ground. We are two people in pain who need to be fixed by love. I want to hold him so badly. Silently, I vow that I will get him over this heartbreak. He'll love me. Richard hands me the guitar. I don't want to sing about a man, so I sing "Pat and Harry."

> Well, they swore their love and devotion so strange
> As the rubble and the scars did grow
> And now the girl was feeling deranged
> Figuring she might reap what they sow.
>
> Don't you worry my child
> If they maim and destroy—they're still together for thee
> See the light, hang on tight, and try to enjoy
> 'Cause it's simply meant to be.

Richard likes it, begins to sing the chorus and says he wants to make a demo of it. There are more tears, including my own.

I am relieved when he decides to call it a night; we are becoming dangerously maudlin. I'm liable to play, party, and weep until dawn. Then Richard announces, "No one is driving home loaded, so you can stay in the guestroom." Sage advice from another stoned soul—thoughtful, too. But Lucy has other plans.

"I'm fine and I'm driving home, Richard. Thanks anyway. Come on, Jennifer." Lucy looks really shaky but she's trying to play it cool. Definitely a tad late, though.

"She's not going anywhere, Lucy. She's got sense. Now, come on. You are too stoned, and you are staying here. You'll kill yourself if you try to drive." Lucy fumbles through her oversized handbag until she finds her car keys, which Richard grabs from her and shoves into his pants pocket.

"Richard! Give me my keys! We haven't made love in over two months and I *know* you're sleeping with somebody else. Now let me go!" I think, *Somebody else? Well, that's one way of putting it.* When Lucy lunges at him, trying to get at her keys, he laughs at her. I feel sorry for her, the expression on Richard's face—utter contempt. Lucy must see that look, too. Suddenly, she begins to cry and rage at him. Richard shoots me a sheepish grin, trying to look innocent. I realize he's enjoying this drama. I leave them wrestling and yelling in the hallway as I go sleep in the guest room. Clearly, they have some issues to work out.

The next time I see Lucy, the sun is coming up. Crouched on the floor by my bed, pale and quivering, she is going through her purse, telling me she has to leave. The edges of her mouth are white and her lips stick together when she speaks. Her nose is red and cracked; dried blood clings to the rims of one of her nostrils. I can recognize the symptoms; Lucy is coked out of her skull. They've stayed up all night, snorting the demon drug.

"Luce, what happened?"

"Oh, Richard just tried to kill me, that's all. I've got to get out of here *now*! Are you coming with me?"

I'm blurry-eyed, but I can see that there's a *whole* story in here somewhere. I'm not going anywhere.

"Lucy, I've got to work here in a couple of hours anyway."

A familiar, ice-cold fury suddenly comes into her eyes. I'm disobeying her. This is not in her game plan. I should be following her like a lost puppy. I hear her speeding down the driveway, ramming her clutch, grinding her gears in her rage as I go back to sleep.

An hour or so later, Richard comes in wearing a tattered, blue terry-cloth bathrobe; he looks like the lost puppy that Lucy thought I should be. He is a wreck as he sits on the edge of the other twin bed. After several silent minutes, he says, "I fired Lucy. The price was too high. I pay the cost to be the boss."

Despite a serious hangover, I sit up. I don't want to miss this.

"She teased me. A woman shouldn't tease a man. Do you tease men, Jennifer?" I don't answer this question.

"She wouldn't let me fuck her. That's what she said she wanted. You heard her. So I told her to give me a blow job instead. I guess she thought she was too good for that. I had a gun. I just meant to scare her. It did. I put the gun away and then she started getting real nasty. So I just thought I got to end this game or I might really end up killing the bitch. You know what I mean? So I fired her ass." Despite all the macho bluster of words, I manage to sympathize with him. I want to show him that I can fix anything that's broken. (I didn't take Lucy's fear seriously; I was completely in denial. And I'd never really been around guns. To tell the truth, maybe I was a little excited by it.)

Richard grins as he tells me how he scared Lucy. Then he looks for my reaction. I give him my best shrug and a pout, as if to say, "Sounds reasonable to me." I don't want him to think that I'm shocked by this, or that I'm scared, or that I'm going to run away. I'm familiar with physical violence but there are some new elements here. This story is uglier than I'd imagined. Nevertheless, running out is the last thing on my mind.

"Well, at least you didn't kill her," I say, mustering a little giggle!

"Shit. I wouldn't go to prison for that silly bitch."

Jesus! I was only kidding! I wonder who he *would* go to prison for—a serious one? My head is pounding. The valley heat is beginning to crawl up into the day. Richard continues his confession.

"I was afraid to come in here. I thought she took you with her."

"Yeah, well, she did ask me to go." . . . "I'm sure she did. She wants to put my balls in the sand and leave me with my house all torn up and no one to fix it. Well, I guess you messed up her little plan. You didn't leave. I'm surprised myself. I thought she had you under her wing. Will you stay Jennifer? Will you stay and fix my house without her? I know you can do it. I see how you dress, the work you've done so far. You've got good taste. I'll give you a raise. I need you. Please say you'll stay."

He's so vulnerable and lost. I would do anything for him. And I actually think I should have been in charge all along. So, while I'm a little nervous about taking on the whole job, I also feel liberated, like a slave set free. Just pay attention, be responsible and everything will be fine.

"If you want me to."

I am ignoring the signs: BRIDGE OUT! DANGER AHEAD! I am going to fix his house, his heart, everything! Wild horses can't drag me away.

I dress for work and what a wonderful day! No Lucy. Freedom! Even the house seems more welcoming. Then I hit a snag. I needed some information from Lucy and that's when I find out how mad she really is. She hangs up on me three times. On the fourth call she says, "You should've left with me. You are betraying me. You are supposed to be working for me. I am your friend. You are a sneaky cunt, Jennifer."

"Lucy, I need the work and what's the big deal?"

"The big deal is that you are there because of me."

"Well, what am I supposed to do about that, Lucy?"

"Obviously, Jennifer, not a fucking thing. Don't ever call me again. Consider me your enemy. And forget about my mother loving you anymore. She only did so because of me."

"Well, Luce, what about the paperwork?"

"I'll give everything to Richard's secretary. Meanwhile, lose my number."

Click.

Poor Lucy, she's always on the lookout for betrayal. And, she has finally found it in me. But I want Richard, I want this job and I want to end her control of me. I am worried however; her wrath is frightening. I know there will be a high price to pay.

I call Lucy's mother. "Carol, this is Jennifer."

"Please don't call me anymore. You must understand, Lucy is my daughter."

Click.

Lucy is gone, and now so is Carol. Carol has been loving and supportive of me. And I know she trusts me and has relied on me as a friend. But Lucy has negotiated the contract for that friendship; she created it, and now she's taken it away. I feel terrible. Mother love, that's my weak spot, my black hole. (Lucy's weak spot is father love—or lack of it. So I was saddened but not surprised, when a few years later I heard this story about Lucy and her father. When William Saroyan was dying, Lucy went to see him, hoping for a bedside reconciliation. She arrived eager, carrying a basket of goodies. Lucy was not there five minutes before her father told her, "Leave my room. I can't stand the smell of your perfume. Allow a dying man the privilege to die in peace." There is a happy postscript to this story. Lucy later told me she went back and asked her father, "Papa, do you love me?" He nodded yes.)

The end of my friendship with Lucy helps cement a bond that's been forming between me and Richard. He has been really sympathetic with me and the pain I'm in. Lucy has been scandalizing my name and Richard's, telling everyone who'll listen that I stole Richard Pryor from her, and that she was now in pathetic misery all because of me. To trash me has become her *raison d'être*. To carry out the mission she's enlisting all her friends and, even some of *mine*.

At lunch at Le Dome I get a message from Lucy. I'm there with Joan Buck and Marisa Berenson to celebrate a metaphysical bonding we'd experienced the previous night. We had a kind of seance at Michael Childers's house, where I'm living, telling stories about ghosts and fulfilled premonitions. So excited by our experience I buy little, hand-painted angels at the religious shop at Farmer's Market to put at each place, symbolizing our sharing. We're seated but haven't ordered yet when Marisa looks at me coolly and says, "Oh, Jen, I've got a message for you from Lucy." I brace myself. "She told me to tell you, now let me see—how did she put that? Ah, yes. 'You will turn out to be just like your mother and you know what that means.' Let me see, yes. I think that's it." Marisa may act like an airhead, but she's got the delivery of a scalpel-wielding surgeon.

"Got it, Marisa. You can tell Lucy you did a fine job." I look back at the menu and feel the blade in my stomach. I look at the angels and feel like a fool. I expect Marisa to order the blood sausage.

Richard and I are finding out about each other during our long afternoon talks about our hopes and dreams in his office. We share our desire to create without interference, our demons of self-destruction, our fears of bone-crunching loneliness and our endless search for eternal love. He tells me his ideas for projects he's working on, making me feel needed and relevant. Richard tells me about his childhood growing up in Peoria, Illinois, in a whorehouse

that belonged to his grandmother, Marie. He was born Richard
Franklin Lenox Thomas Pryor. His parents, Gertrude Thomas and
Buck Pryor, adhered to a family tradition and named their son after
Buck's brother Richard—a.k.a. Uncle Dicky. But his middle names
are also in honor of "uncles," which is what he called the pimps.
So Richard sort of belonged to everyone. He became a collective
teddy-bear child—played with, squeezed, hugged, and loved like
a boy-toy. And they all needed something or someone to love.
Amidst the violence, police raids, con games, and hustles, among
the pimps, whores, and johns. Somewhere there's a family in all
this, he tells me. You had to learn to laugh to survive—laugh and
fight. He's definitely come up the hard way. Hearing all this, I feel
I'm really getting to know him, that I'm falling in love with the real
man.

Sometimes though, I see another side. Richard sits behind his
desk and holds court with his friends, his entourage, his black-
macho club. He snorts coke, drinks vodka, and plays dominoes.
Everyone laughs at anything he says. I'm not welcome at these
gatherings, which is fine with me. I stop by to drop something off
one Saturday and find David Banks—a.k.a. Reverend Banks—and
Richard playing what looks like an endless game of dominoes. I'm
wearing skin-tight, pink cigarette jeans. David looks at me and
says, "Richard tells me you're real smart."

I look back at David. *Jive!* I want to say it, but don't. He sort of
flirts whenever he sees me. "Thanks," I reply.

"And we know you're a fox."

Richard tells him, "Ray Charles can see that, David."

David asks, "So, have you given it up yet?"

"Leave her alone, David." Richard sounds pissed.

I leave quickly but I'm only halfway down the stairs when I overhear the rest of David's comments. "Richard, she's got your nose
so wide open you could drive a Mack truck up it."

Scenes like this make me aware that there's a color issue that I
might have to face one day, if things go the way I hope and expect
them to.

I have a date with Richard. We go with David Franklin, Richard's
lawyer, and David's black starlet friend to a dinner for Andrew
Young. It's at the Beverly Wilshire Hotel, very sedate and political.
The nicest part of the evening is that Richard holds my hand under
the table. No question—I'm in love. On the way home, David's

friend makes a racist remark that's got my name on it, saying something like, "Only a *black* person can understand that kind of bullshit, right Rich?" I bristle, but keep quiet. When Richard walks me to the door he apologizes for the slur and gives me a soft kiss on the cheek. He's concerned that my feelings were hurt. It keeps surprising me that somebody who's so irreverent can be so tender and sweet. It's hard to believe that all the press on him is true. I believe that he's a tortured, lonely, misunderstood soul.

An incident occurred a few nights ago that has all of Hollywood buzzing, everyone's in a rage at Richard. It happened at the Hollywood Bowl, where a lot of serious movers, shakers, and dealmakers were attending a human-rights benefit, being held in response to all the recent attacks against gays. When Richard came out on stage, he proceeded to insult the entire audience of showbiz, human-rights activists. His tirade began when he asked them, "Where were you when Watts was burning?" and it continued until he spun around, lifted his jacket and told them, "You Hollywood faggots can kiss my rich, happy, black ass."

This left a very stunned and very angry audience. The press and the rest of the media have been after him all week. Richard looks like a hunted man. One afternoon he asks me what my friends are saying. I tell him that John and Michael are in league with all my gay friends and the rest of Hollywood, in saying—"Richard Pryor was out of line." Richard doesn't respond—he just looks sad. He has certainly vilified himself and, in the process, has raised an old and ugly question: How can someone who fights for the rights of blacks be homophobic and then have the nerve to call anybody a racist?

We're sitting in Richard's office when he says, "I have something to tell you." I can feel something big coming. "I'm going to marry Deboragh—this week." The girl he sang about, the one who broke his heart. I'm shocked. Saddened. I want to scream, "No!" Instead, I hide the hurt. Richard tries to look happy but I think I see guilt and confusion on his face. And somehow I believe Richard is getting married to end the relationship, not to have it. There's something weird about this—it's so totally out of the blue. I've never seen the bride-to-be around the house and except for the song of heartbreak he sang on my birthday, he's never talked about her. I've only seen them together on one occasion, a year ago.

I was having dinner at Mr. Chow's in Beverly Hills when Richard walked in—another star coming into Chow's. He was with Deboragh. Richard looked dapper in a well-tailored white suit, while she had on a white dress, which didn't fit her tall, buxom frame particularly well. "That's the guy Lucy likes," I thought. "But why does he look so uncomfortable and miserable?" Richard in person struck me as being utterly handsome, an impression I'd never gotten from seeing him on TV or in magazines. I also thought that he looked rather composed and dignified for someone that everyone said was crazy. He and Deboragh made a striking couple, with their white suits and dark skin and I wondered if he felt more at ease with a black woman than with a white one. But on closer inspection, the image lost its dazzle. They spoke very little. Deboragh seemed rigid and Richard looked as if he were about to make his First Communion. There was no joy at that table and it didn't look as if there were any love there either. I remember feeling sorry for him.

This afternoon, more furniture arrives. It's an antique child's desk and I place it beside his bed. When Richard sees it he says it makes him feel like a happy kid. We admire it together and that's when it happens. We're locked in a gaze for what seems like an eternity. Then he mumbles, "I'm feeling something dangerous I shouldn't be feeling." A frozen moment. He slowly puts his arm around my waist, pulls me to him, and kisses me. Then, he kisses me again. Then somehow, we're in the bathroom. He leans me up against the black marble and kisses me again, more passionately. I am relieved when the gate bell rings, but not when we hear the voice on the intercom: "Hi, Mercy. It's me, Deboragh, the bride-to-be."

I make a beeline out of there, through the living room, the pantry and run smack dab into Deboragh in the kitchen. I feel a frightening toxicity spilling off her. She mutters, "I've got the worst hangover—never again," as she fills a glass from the water cooler. She does not look me in the eye.

September

They are married this morning, amidst the chaos of torn-up floors, uncovered cabinets, and piles of lumber. What an appropriate metaphor! I'm beginning to feel like the witness to Richard's life. He's married, but somehow I know this story isn't over.

I'm still working at the house. The new floors are being laid in the kitchen, back entranceway, pantry, and breakfast nook and I study the direction of the grain in the wood. Everyone in the house seems sullen about this marriage—especially Mercy and Renée, who is living in the guest house. I figure that Deboragh will want to finish the decorating of her new home, so every day I expect the secretary or the accountant to fire me. But instead, Richard keeps calling from Maui, where they're on their honeymoon.

One thing Richard's asked me to do is to get rid of any extraneous workers that Mercy has hired. She's got tons of people, who she calls "cousins," employed here, all from El Salvador. Some days the grounds look like a third world country and many of the chores seem nebulous. One might feed a fish, another trim a hedge. Some run day-long errands. As requested, I cut back on the staff, which has put me on Mercy's bad side. Richard's also asks me to keep an eye on Renée—which is another matter. She has a terrible attitude and resents everybody. But nevertheless, he supports her in a way that most twenty-one year olds only dream of; she drives a Mercedes SL convertible and shops, shops, shops.

The newlyweds arrive; back from Paradise. Renée shows her father the assortment of Maud Frizons. As she models them she becomes coy and coquettish. She pouts and squeals, "Look, Daddy, what Jennifer and I bought for me." I think of Marilyn Monroe singing "My Heart Belongs to Daddy."

Deboragh hasn't fired me yet. It's clear that her heart is not into taking care of things around the house. She says things like, "Well, I intend to run a tight ship here, Jennifer." Then she disappears for two days! I would've gotten rid of me long ago!

(Later Richard told me that Deboragh had intended to fire me, but he figured out a way to keep me around. He told her what an awful job I had, going downtown to dusty warehouses full of unpleasant characters. It worked.)

Richard and I continue to share longing looks and even longer talks. He praises my work on the house, then tells me a sweet story, about how frightened he was when he and Deboragh went horseback riding on their honeymoon. He didn't want to let her see his fear, so he rode anyway. He's so macho yet so vulnerable. God, something about him breaks my heart. I want him. And, there's a strange thing happening: his marriage is bringing us even closer together.

The situation in the "Land of the Pryors" is getting gloomier and gloomier. After a trip to New York where Richard's been working on *The Wiz*, he goes on to Peoria to visit his family and ends up being hospitalized for a few days with some kind of "heart trouble." Lucy once told me that Richard had a heart problem—something about a hole in it. It sounds cocaine-induced to me, but I remove all the plants from the bedroom, which is supposed to be better for cardiac patients.

November

I go to meet the family. They're all here for Thanksgiving, and Richard has asked me to come out one afternoon for some turkey. What a scene. I meet the formidable grandmother, Mama Marie, who has the most jutting and elongated jaw of anyone I've ever seen. There's Aunt Dee; Uncle Dicky's ex-wife, whose main claim to fame is that when she was young she looked like Lena Horne. Then there's Pops Bryant, Marie's second husband, who barely speaks and can hardly walk; Richard's children: Elizabeth, Rain, Richard, Jr., and Renée. The minute I walk in, I can feel the knife-like vibes ricochetting off the walls. There's no joy here. The flowers I'd sent this morning are sitting on a dusty window sill in the dining room, card unopened. Mama and Aunt Dee sit on the caned stools at the new butcher-block counter in the kitchen, overseeing the others sitting at the pine table. Everyone's ripping at their turkey, clawing at each other with their looks of contempt and hostile silences. Even Deboragh's manners are missing in action; she's hunched over her plate as though she hasn't eaten in a week. No one says a word, except for "Pass the salt" or "More stuffing." Weird! It's clear that Mama and Aunt Dee don't like the new bride, and Deboragh makes it clear that she doesn't like them, either. I kind of admire her for that. She's not intimidated in the least; she's rather defiant! The children also seem to dislike Deboragh and she seems to dislike them. Richard sits at the head of the table, comfortable amidst all this discomfort. He brilliantly orchestrated this symphony of bitterness, playing them all against each other and saying almost nothing.

After dinner, Deboragh, Richard, Jr., Renée, Elizabeth, Rain, Richard, and I play a game of softball on the tennis court. Why not play on the huge grassy lawn? A little tender familiar bonding, perhaps? . . . No way! This game is vicious—an emotional blood-letting. It's a cut-throat competition with murderous undertones; people are getting hurt, including me. I badly skin a knee careening into home base. Richard asks Deboragh to help me. This gives a further look into the dynamics of their marriage (a look I could have done without). In an exaggerated way, Deboragh leads me to the big, black-marble and wood mirrored bathroom off the master bed-room and with her best Clara Barton manner, begins tending my wound. Slowly, and with too much care, she cleans and dresses it. I'm a bit tense and confused, then Richard shows up. He darts in and out of the bedroom, hovering near the bathroom just close enough so that I get a glimpse of his reflection in the mirror, stop-ping in the doorway only once to get a good look. Then I realize this little scene of Deboragh's is for his benefit. Richard's told me she loves to make him jealous and maybe I'm more threatening than any man would be. Or, perhaps, they share a fantasy about me. As I watch myself being used in this weird game of psychologi-cal S & M, I see that each of them is watching the other in the mirror, looking for some trick or sign of weakness. Richard's darting even faster and Deboragh's becoming even slower and I'm getting more and more jittery. It's like being in a French film where the game is tease, create jealousy and paranoia, to wound and win. Get the power, no matter what the cost. These two have it down; old pros in the game of pain. In over my head, it's time to exit. I'm leaving. Then Richard asks me to stop by his office. My head's still caught in the mirrors and black marble and *he* wants to talk about a Tiffany lamp I'd gotten for the house—where to hang the damn thing! I'm trying to zero in on an answer to this odd question when Deboragh shows up. She's carrying a silver tray and she places it on his desk. It's a protein drink, a pale pink frothy milk shake in a tall soda fountain glass. Richard begins to stare at it. Deboragh turns and slowly starts to walk toward the door. Richard continues staring at the glass. Finally he asks, "Is it poisoned?"

With the cool, rangy sexiness of Lauren Bacall, Deboragh keeps walking, looks over her shoulder and says, "I don't know. Taste it."

Whew! These two don't know when to quit!

"Well, O.K., I'll be leaving now," I say. Richard mumbles good-bye as he continues to study the milkshake. Deboragh offers to walk me out. I feel as if the devil herself is escorting me out of hell.

As we reach the dining room, I mention the lamp and indicate the spot where I think it should go. Deboragh gives me one of her detached looks and says, "I've nothing more to do with this house."

We walk into the living room. She points to the plants. "Look. They're all dying slowly."

Stopping by a basket of wilted foliage, she sighs and says, "No plants ever thrive in this house. Have you noticed that? My mother thinks this place is haunted. What do you think? I just think it's an unhappy home."

Well, that's a little food for thought. There *is* no joy in this house, no happiness here. This afternoon has proven that. I can't say that it's haunted but I remember my first impression. I am a believer.

Deboragh walks me out to my battered Volvo. For some reason, I've got it parked on the street, outside the gates—maybe in anticipation of a quick getaway. As I open the car door she says, "Jennifer, I need to ask you something."

I hold my breath.

"Do you know a good divorce attorney?"

I can't say I'm surprised, even though they've been married only about six weeks. But I also know it'd be very awkward for me to become an advisor in an impending divorce.

"Deboragh, I really don't think I should get involved in this." I mean it, it's the right thing to say but I feel so darn crummy saying it. Silent, she gives me a look that says, *Thanks, bitch*, turns her back on me, and starts walking to the house. I drive away; the car's transmission is heaving and so is my heart. I'm feeling a tad guilty. She should only know.

And I really don't think she does know. I think she has chronically overestimated Richard's obsession with her.

A few days later, I meet another family member out at the house. Richard's Aunt Mexine is a large and very warm woman. When she greets me she says "For a country girl with such good legs, no one would ever know you didn't have any money." Bordello wisdom. I like her instantly—more than anyone else in Richard's family. Mexine doesn't seem to think she owns a piece of Richard like the others do. She appears to care deeply about him and doesn't ask for much. Richard seems more comfortable around her, maybe for the same reasons.

December

I'm at the house less and less as the work winds down. Christmas is coming and I've made plans to go home to Cropseyville. Richard's asked me to come see him before I leave. I'm sure that'll be the end of my job. I'm sad, but there really isn't a reason to keep going there. Except for the fact that I'm in love with him.

Everything is painted, the furniture is in place, the floors are gleaming, and colorful plants spill out of large terra-cotta pots in the atrium. The house looks wonderful but Deboragh was right; it feels awful. When I arrive, Richard's sitting at his desk. He's got a chessboard in front of him and an oversized bottle of vodka by his side; he's already put a pretty good dent in it. I suspect that there are other substances around as well. He looks miserable and I hope that it's because I'll be leaving. I hand him a gift, a small gold diary and say, "It's for your secret thoughts."

Immediately he brightens and writes something in it. I can hear the wind howling in the valley and through the large windows, I can see the trees bend and pull. It's late afternoon, and chilly. The vodka warms me. Richard hands me an envelope. "Merry Christmas" is written on it. His handwriting is naive—like a child's. I think, *White powder? For Christmas?* No—inside is a thick wad of money. I look at Richard.

"A bonus. For everything you've done."

"Thank you, Richard. That's very generous."

"I'll miss you, Jennifer."

Tears leap to my eyes and I think I see them in his as well. "Me too, Richard."

This is the end. I'm never going to see him again. I stand up to leave and he asks, "How 'bout a game of chess?"

I'm surprised but happy that he doesn't want me to go. "I don't know how to play."

"I'll teach you. You're smart. You'll get it fast. Come on, it's time you learned, sit down."

As I pull up the chair, he pours us each another drink, reaches into a drawer, and places a small white packet on the desk. He explains the general object of the game and what each piece represents. We begin to play. He's patient and answers the same questions about the chess pieces and their powers over and over again. Every few minutes he takes a long, silver letter opener and

114

delicately places it under his nose, sniffs some "white lady" from the packet, and then offers it to me. As he brings the dangerous-looking instrument closer to my face I am reminded of a priest serving communion. About an hour into the game it looks as if I'm winning. He's saying things like: "Damn. I didn't think you'd catch on this fast. Are you sure you haven't played before? You're definitely killing my ego, Jennifer."

I, too, am surprised at how well I play and reassure him that yes, this is the first time. It's just "beginner's luck." When I ask him again in which direction the queen is allowed to move, I notice he's losing his patience. There is anger in his face; the first real anger I've seen. His eyes are becoming darker. Something about it excites me. It is dangerous and I can feel it in my stomach. I lower my eyes and start flipping through the *Guide to Chess* that's on the desk. Richard grabs the phone.

"Come on up here, Deboragh. I need some support. This bitch is kicking my ass."

Silence.

"Oh, come on up. Bring me some luck."

He puts the phone down. Silent, he looks back at the board and considers his next move. I feel embarrassed for him. A few minutes later, the back door slams. Richard turns around, looks out the picture window, and watches as Deboragh drives away.

Another of their cruel games. I would never leave my husband alone this long with any woman—much less leave the house. He turns around to face me.

"It's because of you. And she knows it too."

So much for concentrating on the chess game. I'm feeling nervous. I think we're alone in the house. I haven't seen Mercy or Raul, the house man, at all today. There's an eerie silence. All I can hear are the wind and my own heart pounding. I've lost track of whose turn it is. After a few endless moments of staring at the chessboard, neither of us making a move, Richard gets up, walks around the desk, and stands by my side. He looks down at the game he's losing. I study the board for guidance. Suddenly, he shoves it across the desk. The brown and white pieces go flying and so does everything else. Even the big vodka bottle hits the floor with a thud; the top is on. I look up at him. "Was it because I was winning?"

He laughs and pulls me to him. "No, it's because I want you."

115

He kisses me deeply and we melt slowly to the carpet. Passion overtakes us swiftly as we sink into the floor. Then I think I hear the muffled sounds of a car in the driveway. There is no mistaking the slam of the back door.

"Richard . . ." He hears it, too. He's off me in a flash. We pull ourselves together and quickly begin picking up the debris: chess pieces, coke, cigarettes, ashtray, the gold diary, and my envelope of cash.

I think she's returned because Richard hasn't gone after her. But she doesn't come upstairs. Good instincts. But she's a little too slow and has far too much pride.

He asks me, "Can we go to your house?"

I no longer want to put off the inevitable. It finally feels exactly right. And I've wanted him for so long. I try to give Richard directions, but he interrupts me. "I'll get lost. I'll follow you instead."

I race down the freeway; he follows in his green Mercedes. I bounce and sway over Laurel Canyon knowing full well that I'm stoned. I'm being reckless for love. I'm so glad that Michael's out of town. Up the steep hill, pull into the driveway, I race into the house to put on music and light some candles—quickly- before he comes in. Ann Peebles wails on the stereo, "There's a troubled mind, confused within/ Stumbling in darkness, because of sin . . ."

There he is, standing in the doorway, looking strong, vulnerable, and predatory—a terrorist of love . . . . "Slippin'—trippin' with somebody else's love/Taking bitter with the sweet/Travelling the wrong way down a one-way street."

I walk over to Richard and he hands me my envelope. "You forgot this." . . . "There's a sad heart, all wrapped with pain/ Look at the sad face, filled with shame . . ."

He pulls me to him, kisses me tenderly, and whispers, "Where's your room?" . . . "Walking on troubled ground where I don't belong/ Taking bitter with the sweet/Walking the wrong way down a one-way street."

God, my room. It's behind the kitchen. I wanted us to be in a larger and prettier bedroom for our first time. I can't let him see my cramped quarters in this grand house. I point toward the gray and white guest room. It has French doors and overlooks a garden. . . . "You know it's wrong/ This way of living/ Sometimes you have to take less than what you're giving. . ."

"Can I get you anything, Richard?" Stupid question! Only one thing on this man's mind. He shakes his head, takes my hand, and we walk to the bedroom. . . . "How unsatisfied, taking bitter with the sweet/ Travelling the wrong way down a one-way street." The cassette stops and I leave him, teetering on the threshold. I have to turn it over. I need the security of music, though this song was ripping at my heart, making me feel raw and even more vulnerable. I come back and already he's under the covers. He offers his hand. "Come here."

I walk over to his side of the bed.

"Get in."

I take off my black turtleneck, my boots, my jeans. I feel so shy. Glad to be wearing a sexy black bra and panties. Had I anticipated this? Does my body look all right? I try to push away these inhibiting thoughts, telling myself he wouldn't care anyway. I slide into bed alongside him; the sheets are cold and so, at first, are our bodies. He grabs me and whispers in my ear, "I'd love to see you and Deboragh together."

"What?" I don't want to hear this. So he did have a fantasy about me. Men—they love to think about women together. I move my head away and look at him. Again I say, "What?"

"Jennifer, I want you. I wanted you for so long." This is what I want to hear. His voice is full of affection, desire, love. But it's still an awkward intimacy. He moves swiftly, quickly. He kisses me, grabs me again, and then he's on top of me. Too fast—much too fast.

"Richard, are you trying to catch a train? Slow down, relax."

He laughs and rolls over on his back. The tension breaks. We can catch our breath, finally see where we are and who we are with. We begin to touch each other, slowly and sweetly now. I stroke his hair. It doesn't move; it's stiff and unrelenting like his cock against my leg. He is self-conscious when I touch his hair and I love him for it. I hold onto his neck, then move my hands over his back and shoulder blades. Fragile, like an angel's wings. His skin is incredibly soft, like no other skin I've ever touched. I've never felt like this before, so tender and so completely full of desire. In the dark I can see the silhouette of my white hand on his black shoulder. So sensual. My head spins as the passion sweeps me up. I want him beyond wanting and then he's finally inside of me. There are tears in my eyes as he looks at me. He pulls me closer as he goes deeper and deeper, all the while kissing my eyes, my

117

neck, my breasts. This isn't sex, this is not what I'm used to, this is making love. Desire engulfs us with its sweet wretched force and I hold him, cling to him for dear life. I press my lips, my face, to his velvet skin and he whispers, "Jennifer, I love you. I need you. Be with me." He moans a primal sob then lifts me to him. We are lost together. Imploding—exploding. And suddenly we are limp. Lying in each other's arms. Sweet scents, tears, and sweat cover us. Like two beautiful fighters who call it a draw. Then we fall asleep.

I look at the clock—eleven A.M. I see my hand on his almost hairless chest. White on black. The contrast is jarring and soothing at the same time. He sleeps on as I slide out of bed. I need time alone. Though I know I've slept, I feel as if I've been swimming all night. Maybe it's a hangover but I feel too happy for that. I head for coffee.

In a red and white Chinese robe, I sit at the glass dining room table looking out at the L.A. haze trying to peel an orange, trying to focus on my life. This is the first time I have ever felt that I have made total love. But what about John? I was in love with him but I always had to hide my feelings, making complete surrender impossible. John is really married, not like Richard and Deboragh. Deboragh! Will he tell her? None of my business. I recall some moments from last night and slowly replay them in my mind. The memories excite me. Then I think of the added pressures that black men have when making love because they feel that they are expected to perform in some legendary way—mandingo sex. What was that expression? "Once black, you can't go back."

I decide it's a myth. When it comes to sex all men are equally human and vulnerable and fallible. I will tell Richard how happy he's made me. I am bowled over, not by the size of his cock though Lucy was right, it is impressive. It is the love that has made me swoon. It was special, and it can only get better.

My orange tastes bitter. I put on Chopin and take some vitamins. Extra B, for the hangover. Then I look up to see Richard standing at the top of the stairs. I spill my coffee. I'm jumpy—all these feelings! I grab my napkin and mop up the coffee. "Hi. How'd you sleep?"

He smiles a half smile, walks over to me, and kisses me tenderly on the cheek. "Okay."

It's as if we've been there before and will still be there, together

118

like this, in days to come. Instant bonding. This makes me even more nervous. "Can I get you some coffee?"

"No, thanks. But do you have any string beans or ice cream?"

Surprised, I say, "Did I get you pregnant?" We both laugh, walk out to the living room, and stand in front of the big window looking into the smog, looking into the future. We don't need to say anything.

"Was this house pink when your friend bought it?"

"Yeah. It was once owned by F. Scott Fitzgerald." He thinks about that. "*Tender is the Night*?"

"Right. I wonder if he ever visits?" Richard just looks at me. "I believe in ghosts," I explain.

"You know, Jennifer, I can really talk to you, about everything. I really like that."

I look at Richard. He kisses me softly and walks into the bedroom. I need more coffee, maybe even a Bloody Mary. A few minutes later, he's standing in front of me.

"Merry Christmas, Jennifer."

"Merry Christmas, Richard."

"Are you going to visit your family now?"

"In a couple of days."

"Do you like it there?"

"Not a whole lot. More before I get there."

"Then why do you go?"

"Same reason anybody goes home. It's a place to go, I'm trying to figure things out—a whole bunch of mixed-up reasons."

"Yeah. I know what you mean."

Without saying another word, Richard walks out through the big front door, leaving it open behind him. I like this final statement. I realize that I've forgotten to tell him how happy he's made me. He's gone for now and the only thing left to fill the vacuum is his black jockey underwear.

Two days later, I fly out of L.A. to make the long, lonely trip home to Cropseyville. I'm in love! I think about my family but mostly I think about Richard. I remember some things he's told me: About the screams in the middle of the night that would wake him up. Were his mother and father fighting again? Or did they come from one of the strange men with one of his many aunts? He would lie awake all night, terrified, waiting for his grandmother, Madam Marie—King and Queen rolled into one—to make the screams stop. His grand-mother was tough, *is* tough—I remember her from Thanksgiving. Richard's parents had eventually married, but things didn't work out. His mother, Gertrude, left. Gertrude returned for her son but Madam Marie took her to court. Marie had complete control over Richard. When the judge at the custody hearing put Richard on the witness stand and asked him whether he wanted to live with his mother or his grandmother, he was too scared not to choose his grandmother. Marie won custody, but Richard would never forget the look on his mother's face. A harlequin was born—split and scarred.

Christmas

In Cropseyville, there's lots of snow and a lot of my own memo-ries. I take a long walk with my father, Yvonne, and Byron, and I tell them that I'm in love. No one comments on the fact that Richard's married. And no one says a word about his color, except Byron, "Wow, Jenny, a black guy! Well, I guess you can handle it." Byron's impressed. Not only is Richard a black renegade and a celebrity, but he's also notoriously volatile. Byron understands that no one plays it safe in our family, but he also sounds concerned. And everyone has an opinion about Richard's controversial behav-ior. I finally tell them to look at themselves.

This scene doesn't change from year to year, although the cast sometimes differs. I eat fruitcake and drink too much eggnog with all the familiar ghosts. We decorate the tree while our rage and pain smolders. Yvonne gives everybody and everything the benefit of her analysis. But I endure it.

1978

January

Despite a bad flu, I fly back to L.A. on New Year's Day filled with hope and anticipation. Too sick to go anywhere, I take to the couch with a bottle of champagne. Around midnight, Byron calls to tell me there's been a shooting at Richard's house. I turn on the news. A few more friends call to tell me and to make sure that I'm safe.

From the news reports and the gossip I get the story. There was a lot of drinking and drugging going on; a fight broke out between Deboragh and Richard—could it have been over me?—and she decided to leave the party with some of her girlfriends. Deboragh's big mistake was in trying to leave in Richard's vintage, green Mercedes. Pissed off, he went and got his .357 Magnum, which I remember having seen in his bedroom. With his black-macho entourage looking on he told her, "You can leave bitch, but not in my car."

She didn't listen and kept driving. Richard emptied several rounds of bullets into the car. First he shot the engine, then he shot all four tires. The police arrived and arrested Richard. Deboragh, the women in the car with her, and the L.A. County Sheriff's Department itself are all pressing charges. It seems you're not allowed to shoot a vehicle, even if it is your own and is on your own property. David Franklin had to bail him out. This has been hot Hollywood gossip for several days now—bad-ass Richard Pryor.

I know what Richard has done. This is his way of ending the marriage. Destruction and violence—he likes to experience the death of something in a big way. No slow fades, he prefers the smashed-lens effect; it insures the end. The bizarre thing is I understand. For him, it is easier to do it this way. I can relate.

Richard's secretary, Mary, has firmly told me not to call the house; she says that Richard's in a deep depression and doesn't want to be disturbed. I hear that an ex-girlfriend is in charge—manning the decks and the phones. I've been thinking about Richard all week, wondering if I'll ever see him again. Then, Mary calls to ask about the delivery of the dining room chairs. Suddenly, Richard's on the other end of the phone.

"Hey, Jennifer, why haven't you called me?"

"Well, Mary said . . . "

"Fuck her! I'm leaving tomorrow. Why don't you come say good-bye to me?"

"I'll see you around six."

I'm so excited. I walk into his office and into his arms. It's as though no time has passed. We eat steaks, watch T.V., and make love for three days. I don't ask him anything about the incident but he tells me that Deboragh has filed for divorce. He keeps putting off his departure. Finally, he asks me to join him in Hana in a week. Hawaii . . . with Richard . . . I can't wait.

A long stretch limousine picks me up early and whisks me to LAX for my flight. I am prepared. I've bought sexy island attire and new lingerie, and I've even borrowed a skimpy madras bikini from Berry. Of course, she's promised not to tell Lucy, but I know Berry's playing both sides of the fence. But who cares? I've never been to Hawaii, and here I am, going there to be with the man I'm in love with. I'm wearing new clothes, flying first class, drinking champagne, and imagining torrid love scenes on white-sand beaches. We land in Honolulu, where I'm met by Mike, a good-looking pilot who will be taking me to Hana, where Richard is waiting. Mike reminds me of Sky King—the TV hero who used to fly around in a plane saving people. He's dressed for the part too, wearing crisp clothes trimmed with gold buttons, and navy-and-gold epaulets. The sun flashes off his white teeth as he places a lei around my neck, and softly kisses me on each cheek. Young and eager to please, he's definite series material. He grabs my carry-on bag and goes to the carousel for the rest of my luggage. I wait in the clear Hawaiian air as the warm soft wind brushes my face. A few minutes later, Mike's back with my canvas suitcase—I wish I'd gotten a new one, it looks shabby in this light—and he's accompanied by an older gentleman wearing a gray uniform. Sky King tells me, "Jennifer, this is your driver, Norman. He'll take us over to the hangar."

A driver! "Happy to meet you, Norman."

Norman *acts* like a chauffeur. He uses big, grand gestures and keeps saying, "I'm just here to please." I feel required to respond to this profound sense of purpose, which makes me uncomfortable. We all pile into a shiny, gun-metal gray, vintage Silver Cloud Bentley, which strikes me as ostentatious and out of place here in the land of clean sun. I ask, "Where are we going?"

With a killer "Hawaii Five-O" smile, Mike says, "Relax, you'll be there before you know it."

I'm feeling spaced out and my new pink slacks and shirt are wilting. In silence, we drive the few minutes to a private airport. Norman brings us right up to a small, sparkling white plane. So far, everything in Hawaii looks like a toothpaste commercial. Norman opens the door and Mike hops out and takes my hand. "Come on, Richard's waiting for you."

God, Richard planned everything—a private pilot, plane, and

chauffeur. This is too romantic. I feel like the princess in a fairy tale, Mike puts on earphones and a white-and-gold pilot's cap, then begins talking to the control tower in a low, professional voice. I think Mike thinks he *is* in his own adventure series. Fantasies explode and ricochet in my mind as we fly over the deep, blue Pacific; I can see porpoises and whales frolicking and leaping. This is an adventure I'll never forget. Mike talks constantly all the way, pointing out the islands, giving me brief history lessons. "That's the island of Molokai—the old leper colony."

I realize that Mike is flirting with me and I assume that Richard's celebrity is the reason. Obviously, it's very prestigious to be a pilot for Richard Pryor and his girlfriend—we're not that far from Hollywood! Mike is in charge here and he takes pleasure in that. It puts him on the same level. An hour later, at sunset, we're ready to land at the tiny airport of Hana. From the air, I can see Richard in the distance waiting for me, waving. He's a small dark dot, standing in the middle of all that green and blue. I can't wait to be in his arms! My stomach turns as Mike banks the plane and touches down on the thin runway that hangs over the edge of the sea. I think, I've been beamed to the center of a Michener novel. Hana! It even has a small, pale-green weathered shack for a terminal. We bump and rock; Mike is in macho-pilot heaven! I climb out of the plane and Richard sweeps me up into his arms. The breeze is even softer here. It covers my face and fills my heart. I am in paradise.

As Richard's putting my bags in the back of his red Jeep, Mike kisses me on the cheek. Richard sees this—he doesn't miss a trick. Quickly, he thanks Mike and we drive away. On the ride to the house, he tells me that Lisa*, his secretary's assistant, and Rashon, his bodyguard have come with him. He is nervous, telling me that Lisa's there to help him pick out some land. As happy as I am I smell a rat and know I'll find out soon enough. Then, out of the blue, Richard tells me a story. When he was a teenager, he'd become engaged to some girl who was pregnant; she claimed he was the father. He was so pissed off, he took another date to their engagement party. We laugh. "Did you marry her?"

"Oh, yeah. Had to. But I divorced her mighty fucking quickly. Seems Buck was fucking her too."

"This is Renée's mother?"

"Yeah."

Why does he tell me this story now? Suddenly, I spot trouble ahead and beyond. But I, too, grew up in a house full of trouble; I can handle it. Even if everything they say is true—I want it all, all his thousand miles of rough road. I think we have a journey to go on together, almost as if it were predestined. Where it will ultimately lead I don't know, but I'm almost certain that it will have a happy ending. I want to know where the exact center of his raging storm lies. There are things I need to learn from him, and anyway, I can help him. All he really needs is the love of a good woman. And he'll love me, the way I need to be loved.

I soon learn that my happiness with Richard will always contain some elements of fear. It will never be a safe place, yet I have to be there. Almost from the beginning, I've understood that we have a job to do together: save Richard—from the world and from himself. So, we are conspirators, there is purpose to our being together. And if we fail, I would spend forever missing him, the way one misses a childhood, even a bad one. So I promise myself that I will feel all things deeply—my terror, my happiness, and possibly my execution. Here on the edge, I will love Richard better than anyone could and love him better than I have ever loved anybody. He is my passion; he is already the love of my life. I know this.

Rashon welcomes me warmly. He's Flip Wilson's cousin and I've met him before. Playful and smiling, Rashon can be like a big kid, but you know if need be he can flex those muscles and take care of business. He also seems to be Richard's buddy, not just his bodyguard. I'm a little concerned about that. Then I meet Lisa—trouble in paradise! She can barely look me in the eye and makes me feel as welcome as a tarantula at a Fourth of July picnic. Lisa's "high-yellow," diminuitive, wears glasses, not too pretty, not too plain. Richard shows me to my room, explaining that Lisa's been staying in the master bedroom suite and has refused to move. "I wanted you to have the big bedroom."

Right. My room is large; a double-door entrance, a big bathroom, and twin beds. I just look at him. What is the answer to this puzzle?

I get a tour of the house. It's in a ranch-style design, built in the 1920s; once grand, it is now on the funky side. The huge living room has a picture window along its sprawling length and is filled with frayed furniture, water-marked coffee tables, and shelves of musty books—*My Chinese Days* by Gulielma F. Alsop, Hemingway's *For Whom the Bell Tolls, The Favorite Short Stories of W.*

Somerset Maugham. There are mildewed appliances in the seldom-used kitchen. A swinging door separates it from the dining room, with its large, bulky pieces. Everything is indicative of a bygone era. I spot cobwebs in forgotten corners. Owned by the Hana Ranch Hotel and rented out at a hefty daily rate, it sits, surrounded by sloping pastureland and isolated on the top of a hill, overlooking the distant Pacific. A few hundred feet from the main house is the two-bedroom guest house, where Richard and Rashon are staying. Gorgeous tropical foliage lines the walkways, surrounds the buildings, covers everything in sight. It's a romantic setting indeed, though I'm not too pleased with the sleeping arrangements. I wonder what's really going on here.

I find out this evening as we walk to the dining room in the hotel. Richard tells me, "Well, ya know why she won't move? I slept with her, that's why. It was only once but I guess she was jealous when she saw you." I say nothing.

"She's not moving to be spiteful."

My suspicions have been confirmed, I tell him, "Forget it."

"Well, I didn't think she'd act like that. She's got a lot of nerve."

So, Lisa was on a romantic trip to paradise, too! But why is he blaming her? Well, hey, Richard and I don't have a commitment. I tell myself it's okay. I also tell myself that he's being kind to a woman he has used, while in reality he's being controlled by her and by his guilt over his behavior. I overlook it all.

Despite Lisa's sulking and broken heart, the four of us share a good meal and some nervous joking. Afterward we decide to have coffee and brandy in the hotel library. I prepare Richard's and mine and walk down the stairs balancing the steaming cups and the small, cognac snifters that teeter on the edges of the saucers. As I walk, I trip on my long, lavender gauze skirt, tumble down the stairs, spill the cognac and coffee, and land ungracefully on the floor, still clutching the saucers and empty cups. I am mortified. There's a horrible dead silence as the other guests sit frozen pretending they don't see the purple heap I am on the carpet. No one moves, except for Richard, who comes over and helps me up. He's also feeling awkward, but it's in empathy for me.

The week is bliss. Hana is a beautiful and serene environment. Richard has made a truly wonderful choice. Despite his experience here with Deboragh, Richard says he wants to go riding. So we hire horses and head out through the pastures to the edge of the sea. We have picnics and then swim in hidden coves where I dive off the high cliffs. Near the Seven Pools we discover a little waterfall where we make love in our own magic fountain. Richard picks up a piece of bamboo and does a little impromptu dance under the mini-falls, shaking the stick and chanting: "Iaho-ho-u-eee-I-li." God lives in Hana.

Richard asks me to help him pick out some land. This was to have been Lisa's job, but she's finally resigned herself to the fact that Richard and I are very much together; so Lisa accompanies me on these trips and acts as if she's my new best friend. As Richard and I walk hand in hand over the acreage I've chosen, among the lemon, papaya, and avocado trees, he asks me to help him build a house on the land. I look at the magnificent view of the sea and imagine waking up with him there. I meet builders and architects and decide on a prefab, Japanese-style design. We make a few changes in the plans and end up with a smaller version of a Kyoto farm house.

There's cocaine in Hana, too, which has led to a couple of drug-crazed nights where we all participate in the gloomy gaiety of getting high and higher. One night, Richard, Rashon, and Lisa are especially into what I call "blackisms"—hip street patois—that cut to the marrow with their down-home profundity. They're calling each other "nigger this" and "nigger that." Feeling left out, like an ostracized kid at a playground, I try to join in on the "get down" flavor of the dialogue by calling Richard a nigger. You could hear a straw drop. He looks at me, but his eyes are a cold dark black. He doesn't say a word, but takes me firmly by the hand and leads me outside. I don't know where we're going, but I am scared. Waiting for the outburst. Richard points to the sky full of stars and asks me, "Which one is a nigger, Jennifer? Can you tell?"

"No," I say, my head hanging in shame.

He tenderly lifts my chin and looks into my eyes. "Do you understand?"

He looks sad. I nod as tears run down my face. He kisses them away and holds me close. I love him deeply for teaching me something I already know. I love him for allowing me this mistake. I love him for understanding that I have no malice, have not meant to cause pain.

Two weeks of heaven and it's time to go back to reality. I cry as we drive to the airport. I know love thrives more easily in a place like this.

Back in L.A., it doesn't take long for us to figure out that time apart is sad and pointless, especially for me. Richard's been under pressure—finishing filming *California Suite*, dealing with the litigation from the New Year's Eve incident, as well as the divorce. He sees Deboragh occasionally, tells me how sad she is and how rotten this makes him feel. He says she wants him back and she regrets having initiated the divorce. It looks as if she's being beaten at her own game. And despite his sympathetic words, I suspect he's enjoying the position she's now in. One evening, as we're getting ready to go to the NAACP Awards with Elizabeth and Rain, she calls. I answer the phone. "Jennifer, this is Deboragh. I want you to take good care of Richard."

I tell her, "I intend to do just that."

Click.

But Richard is suffering terribly over the divorce and talks about it almost constantly. Finally, I've had enough and tell him so. "If I didn't cause your pain, I can't fix it. I don't want to hear about her anymore."

Well, Richard just loves hearing this and tells me several times he loves the strength it expresses. I think what he really likes is that it has distracted him from his own self pity.

(I wish that I'd applied this philosophy to more things.)

February

Richard's got a "lady friend" who's visiting from Germany. She's staying in West Hollywood with a friend of his and he wants me to meet her. Another rat? I ask why, and he tells me he wants to bring her out to the house to have a threesome, but if I don't want to he'll find somebody else to do it with. Then he tells me that "it will bring us closer together." I agree to do it; after all, I'm hipper than anyone on the block. I want to please him, no matter what the cost. I've been in plenty of threesomes, no big deal, but I overlook one crucial piece of information: I have never done it with anyone I have been in love with. No one is that hip. It's a catastrophe waiting to happen.

With all the party-down accoutrements, the cocaine and the booze, this exotic, high-yellow fraulein is all over me like white on rice! Maybe since Richard "helps" her she really wants to give him his money's worth. Not long into this soirée, he suddenly begins screaming and stalks out of the bedroom. I follow him into the dining room where he's started picking up chairs and pitching them in all directions. Looks familiar! Then he grabs a chair, whacks the $10,000 Tiffany lamp and heads into the living room, where he attacks the windows, smashing almost all the small panes. The velocity of his rage increases as he searches for new furniture victims. Next, the six-foot long, mirrored coffee table is shattered. He keeps screaming. He looks like the Incredible Hulk. I follow him around trying to calm him with a few frail words. I end up watching. Exhausted, he collapses on the couch, sobbing and choking, "Why did you do this to me?"

Wait a minute. He's turning the tables here. This isn't my fault. I tell him, "This was your idea, Richard."

"Yeah, but you shouldn't have done it."

He is right. I certainly shouldn't have done it, but I didn't know that in the context of threesomes, love hurts. Suddenly, I feel set up.

I take full responsibility—which is too much. The m.o. is firmly established.

Richard and I spend the night in the guest room. In the morning I go into the bedroom to apologize to the fraulein for the disturbance. She sleeps in the weirdest position: ass high in the air, head under a pillow, arms down by her sides—palms up. Richard and I stand there laughing in *sotto voce*. She wakes up. I give her coffee, Richard gives her money and we have a limo take her back to West Hollywood. Whew! Now, there's the house to fix. I call the glass men who arrive in the afternoon, look at me strangely, and fix all the windows; they also haul the shattered coffee table back to the shop. The lamp is another matter. I'll have to think up a real good story for that, since the fellow I bought it from—and the one who can fix it—is a real Tiffany lamp freak.

Richard tells me it'll never happen again. He says he was in pain. He goes from the Incredible Hulk to the Incredible Sulk. I console him, telling him it was all my fault.

I'm now at Richard's house almost all the time. Every morning I bring him breakfast on a tray with a rose from the gardens which I'm resurrecting. I've found that the attention helps assuage his dangerous morning moodiness. We talk about changing the entire gestalt—music to my ears! Each of us has had a painful childhood, which we've been dragging behind us like little red wagons filled with the leftovers and the souvenirs—pain, loneliness, rage. We want to help heal each other with our love. And I have no doubt we can do this. I continue making improvements on the house—inside and out. Everything is starting to come alive as I chase all the ghosts away.

We go out to celebrate our love and end up in quite a scene. After dinner at Chow's we go to Jack Hanson's Daisy on Rodeo Drive for champagne and dancing. On the way home, Richard decides he wants to visit the friend that the fraulein is staying with; it turns out this friend is also a coke dealer. Well, I don't think this is such a good idea and decide to speak up. With my usual tact I probably say something like, "Why aren't you listening to me? I don't want to go where you want to go. Don't you get it?" We start to exchange a few words and Richard gets so ignited that he suddenly pulls over to the curb, coming to a screeching halt, gets out, and begins assaulting the car with rocks, stones, and small boulders. At some point, he pulls me out of the car, ripping my corduroy slacks in the process, then continues his attack on the poor red Mercedes. Naturally, the police show up—two squad cars, four cops. By that time the car is in bad shape; the windshield and the windows are smashed, the body is dented and scratched. We're on a particular section of a West Hollywood street that is residence to mostly pimps, cocaine dealers, and hookers. The LAPD, who are no fools, immediately want to know what happened here. I start to answer, "Well, you see, officers, it's like this. . . "

Then they separate us, I guess to compare our stories. I give them one in a rather loud, enthusiastic voice so that Richard is able to hear it. "You wouldn't believe it." (I'm sure they didn't.) "Some phantom low-rider car full of kids ambushed us, throwing rocks and small boulders out of their moving car . . . then just disappeared into thin air."

Who knows where this babble is coming from? I just feel proud to be telling lies on Richard's behalf.

Then they ask about my torn pants. "Oh, well, you see, I have actually gained some weight lately and in my haste to exit the car, my pants must have ripped." God—I actually think I'm being clever.

And I am certain that Richard will love me even more for this marvelous, extemporaneous fabrication. I don't even consider the fact that I am condoning his behavior by trying to extricate him from this sordid, crazed mess he's made. I have become his rescuer.

The police do buy this story anyway; we are in Hollywood, where stars are gods who are protected at all costs. The famous and powerful in this town have the privilege of bending the rules to the breaking point. As they leave, a couple of the officers ask Richard for his autograph, give him a supportive, knowing slap on the back and say "Hey, good luck, brother." And that is the end of that.

As fate would have it, we are right in front of the drug dealer's house.

We snort coke and drink with Joe* the dealer, and some Chinese girl. I like to push the outside of the envelope with the big boys, the black boys; it goes beyond slumming.

I am reaching for a liberation from the unauthentic, unfeeling world of everyday and moving towards experience and pleasure. I get my hip-card punched and prove how cool I am by hanging with the toughest. As I listen to their jive, I try to find my way around the street mind, the black man's mind, my lover's mind. I like risky situations where there is the potential of crossing the border into danger. But usually I have pretty good instincts and split before I fall off the edge. This night, I cross that border.

The coke, the vodka, and the rap-a-dapping continues until I begin to black out. I remember sitting on the floor kissing the Chinese girl with the distant, underwater sounds of encouragement from the male audience. Suddenly the whir of a camera. I regain consciousness. My eyes pop open. I am on my back. A black face is looking into mine. I can feel his hot breath on my cheek. Someone is fucking me. In my head, I know it's Richard. But as I focus, I see that the person behind the camera, still whirring with the sound of pictures being taken, is Richard. Then who is this person on top of me? Inside of me? My God. As his face becomes clearer, I see that it's Joe, the drug dealer. What is going on here? Why is Richard taking pictures? And something worse. Why do I see contempt in his face? Then I know. I have been raped while in a blackout and not only is Richard letting it happen, but he's photographing it. I begin to scream, "Noooo!" I want to vomit. Confused, scared, I shove him off me and move quickly. I have to get out of here. I run out, leaving Richard and my nightmare behind.

When I get outside, the early morning sun is cruel, shining

brightly, exposing me even more. I don't have my sunglasses. I start walking east, down Fountain Avenue towards Sweetzer. A thousand questions. Didn't Richard know I was in a blackout? Even if he didn't know, why would he let that happen? I have to climb steep Sweetzer Avenue towards home wearing my red and gold Charles Jourdan high heels with their killer ankle straps. My head's pounding and my heart's breaking. The questions keep coming: How long was I unconscious? How long in that position? *Another Hollywood casualty*, I think, imagining how I must look. I am walking, which is conspicuous in West Hollywood, and at this hour with wild hair and torn slacks—a true vagabond. I feel even worse. In my desperate haze to reach safety, I forge ahead to the Pink Castle—my own house and my refuge. How could Richard let another man touch me? In front of him? My anger, shame and self-recrimination would all have to wait, along with the answers.

When I finally reach F. Scott's old house, I am feeling like Zelda. I collapse on the stairs, exhausted, relieved to be out of sight. I don't even know if I have my keys with me. As I sit studying the cracks in the steps, Michael pulls into the driveway. Shit. Michael, the beauty expert, just what I need now. When I see the expression on his face, I know I look worse than I'd even imagined. In his most sarcastic tone, he asks, "What happened to you?"

"Don't ask, Michael."

"Jesus, Jennifer."

"Michael, please not now."

I follow him inside the pristine sanity of the house and dive into the safety of my forgotten bed. I want to sleep this nightmare away.

A few hours later, I'm awake, in a panic. I *have* to get Richard. He's in trouble. I shower, dress, and head back to hell, hoping I can find it. Amidst the row of generic, Spanish-style stucco apartment houses, I will remember where Joe, the rapist-drug dealer, lives. I follow my sleuthing nose, buzzing bells and reading names on mailboxes until I find myself standing beside a bed, looking down at Richard, who's curled up in the arms of the Chinese girl.

No jealousy. I'm on a mission. I don't even have to wake him. He feels my presence and looks up. Ecstatic to see me, he begins talking baby-talk. "Ooh, Jenny, I don't feel so well."

I literally drag him out of bed. "Richard, get dressed. We're going home."

We're out of there in two shakes. On the way back to the pink castle he keeps saying, "Yippee, my lady came and got me. God, you do love me. You came and got me!"

I pour him into bed. He keeps muttering how grateful and happy he is that I've rescued him. He holds on to me for dear life.

Yep, I've gone and gotten him all right. Any other woman would have never seen him again. I'm in for the long haul. We never mention that dreadful night or the pictures. But I often wonder why. Perhaps Richard wants me to share his sense of shame.

Several hours later, we wake up and Richard realizes that he's promised to go to Mercy's daughter's wedding reception. No problem, I'll fix that. I make some phone calls and within a couple of hours, Raul delivers clothes to us and a limousine arrives in time to get us there before it ends. I also ask Raul to please take care of the battered car. He doesn't even ask a question. Nice to have people pick up the mess.

We arrive at the basement of some West Hollywood church. Mercy and her daughter Merna are thrilled that Richard has made the effort. Hungover and fighting remorse, we pretend to have a good time. All of a sudden, Richard begins to cry. And cry and cry, making quite a scene. I find Raul and we get Richard out of there, into the waiting limo. He cries all the way home, saying that it reminded him of his own wedding, and the loss of Deboragh.

It's raining. I sit him down in front of the fire, get us each a brandy, and hold him close. My mothering finally begins to calm him down. He suggests we seal our bond further and tell our worst secrets. "Do you have one, Jenny?"

"Is the bear Catholic?"

I sure do have one, and it's given me almost a solid year of sleepless nights and has me sweating bullets of shame. It's the entire matter of the erroneous tax refund from the IRS. I feel too guilty, too mortified. Nor do I see how I can tell Richard my horrible secret and risk his not loving me.

"I can't tell you, Richard. I'm too ashamed."

"Come on," he coaxes me, "nothing's that bad."

"Oh, yes, it is."

"I'll still love you. But if it will make you feel any better, I'll go first."

How sweet he can be.

"Please don't be shocked or disappointed in me but I have to get rid of it; it's eating me alive. Anyway, I know better now." He swallows a big gulp of air.

"I'm sleeping with [   ]. That's my secret. I have to tell you because she's holding it over my head and I didn't want you to find out from her."

Lord. I can't say a word. This is even beyond "Donahue"! I am stunned and starting to get angry. I feel used. I stare at him. He continues, unable to read my mind or feelings.

I am sorry that he's told me, and sad. My father has always confided in me.

"Why did you tell me?" I speak calmly, but I am beginning to feel a boiling in my stomach. I feel betrayed, not only by Richard, but by the world I live in.

"I needed to. And what's yours?"

In my rage-daze, I don't have a clue as to what he means. "My what?"

"Secret. Your secret."

"Oh, right. My secret. I received an erroneous tax refund. And then I spent it." He looks at me blankly.

"My father made some payments to the IRS using my social security number by mistake, so it looked as if I had made an overpayment."

"So?"

"They want it back. They got me an hour before the statute of limitations ran out on it."

"And you don't have it?"

"Bingo. You see, my accountant told me to put it in the bank and not to spend it, which I didn't do."

"Jennifer, is this your secret? The fucking IRS. This is what you were so ashamed of?" He is obviously disappointed. "Are you fucking kidding me? I went to jail for income tax evasion. I did ten days in jail, three years probation, and had to pay a fine, and *you* feel guilty. Damn, Jennifer, I really do love you. How much do you owe?"

"Ten thousand dollars."

"I'll take care of it."

I can't believe what I'm hearing. Nobody's ever done anything like that for me before.

The next day we go to a movie in Westwood and begin to slide into our love space once again. Back home we decide to watch

TV and have dinner in bed but first I have to call Michael. He's asked me to play hostess at a dinner he's having. Michael lights into me in solemn, judgmental tones.

"Well, Jennifer, we should have a talk about your life. It's time you give it some thought."

I'm immediately on the defensive. "Michael, what are you talking about?"

"Jennifer, you *know* what I'm talking about."

Unfortunately, I do. He's upset because of the shape he'd found me in the day before, all crumpled up on the steps of the pink castle. What he doesn't realize is that I like to go to the edge and come back. People call me wild and crazy, but I've never doubted my ability to survive. There's something about running along the cliff that feels heroic and brave; makes me stronger. Wiser. This is something that nobody knows about me. This is *my* secret. I'm an experience junkie.

I promise to meet Michael the next day, for lunch and a "serious" talk. Back into the bedroom, feeling blue and dejected, Richard wants to know what's up. I tell him about my conversation with Michael, and the next thing I know Richard's in the closet, ripping clothes off hangers.

"What are you doing?"

"Get dressed," he shouts back. "We're going to that dinner party."

"Are you serious?" *Please*, don't be.

"I'm serious. Get dressed."

"Please, Richard, let's just stay in bed. It's been a long weekend." *That's* an understatement. "Why do you want to go anyway?"

"He can't talk to you that way. It's important they see that you're okay. That's why we're going." There's more to this.

"But I'm scared. I don't want to go." He looks angry at this confession.

"Scared of what? Not having those people tell you what to do anymore?" He has a point but I sure don't feel like making it—not tonight, anyway.

"Jennifer, I'm going to show you how to mean what you say."

Damn! Why'd I have to tell him anything? Lord, there's going to be another scene. We're heading for the hall of fame with this one.

"Come on," says Richard. "Help me get dressed."

The closet's strewn with piles of rejected clothing. And they all look like pimp clothes; studs, zippers, and metal rings cover everything. I need to go shopping for this man. I find some benign black slacks, a black shirt, and a frayed leather belt with a peeling silverplated buckle. Richard needs to look good and he knows it. This is a showdown with a group of chic, bitchy queens.

But these people are important to me. They're not just my peers, they're my support system—my surrogate family. They are funny, talented, hip, and have great taste. They make me feel very loved and sometimes make me feel very lonely. At times their emphasis on appearances and social amenities could be cold and cruel, which can create a distance.

Richard doesn't understand why I'm nervous. In fact, I'm filled with dread as I climb into the Jeep and we bounce all the way over Laurel Canyon to Sweetzer. My hands shake as I turn the key. Richard steps across the threshold and walks through the door in front of me. Stunned silence. God, why am I here? They're all sitting around the high-tech dinner table drinking coffee and cognac and passing a joint. The guests include Bruce Weintraub; a set designer; Peter Lester, a writer; a very powerful and very closeted gay agent; and a couple of those pretty male faces that are always on the scene. Michael stands at one end of the table, slicing an apple tart he's just baked. The epitome of composure, he continues serving his guests while he asks us to sit down. "Glad you could make it."

We remain standing as I half-heartedly make introductions. Everyone except Michael seems pretty uncomfortable and they look to him for leadership.

Suddenly Richard turns toward Michael and tells him how upset I'd been about our phone conversation. Michael, however, remains unruffled and ignores his comments. Instead he says graciously, "This is *such* a surprise. I'm *so* sorry you missed dinner. How about some dessert or a drink?"

Richard tries to maintain his cool and simply says, "No, thank you."

"Richard, you know Brenda don't you? Brenda Vaccaro? Well, I was talking to her just this morning—"

"Michael," Richard interrupts, "why do you disapprove of Jennifer being with me?" You could cut the air with Michael's dessert knife.

"I don't, Richard. But I do care about her and I am a little concerned. But I don't think now is the time or place to discuss it." As he speaks he continues serving his tart, licking his fingers between slices.

"By the way Richard, have you seen that gorgeous topless photograph of Jennifer that I took? It's hanging in my office."

Richard's getting pissed. "There's no need to worry and it *is* the time and place."

Michael pauses in his cutting and says, "Richard, did you or did you not want something to drink?"

"Listen, Michael, I came here to say something to you."

Bruce's sing-songy sarcasm interrupts him. "Oh, are you going to take Jennifer away from all this?"

Richard's just about had enough. He spins around on the heels of his pimp-style black leather boots and says, "Yes. You've used her as long as you're going to. She won't be hosting any more of your dinner parties. Now it's my turn to try and make her happy."

Then Peter Lester's thin, English voice pipes in. "Isn't that sweet."

Michael is unflappable. He gestures delicately with his dessert knife.

"You know Richard, Brenda thinks you are just so fabulous."

Suddenly Richard pulls me to him, looks me straight in the eyes, and kisses me—a long warm kiss for all the boys to see. Then he calmly looks back at everyone and tells them all, "I love her."

YIPPEE! What a moment!

I've watched this shootout in silence, listening to Richard and my friends discuss me. Richard has become my Lochinvar; he has claimed me and is whisking me away from the mean pink castle and the sad young men. No one has ever done such a thing for me before. This is true love. I love that he's brave enough to embarrass himself for me.

When he thinks that Richard isn't looking, Peter flexes his muscles, pretending to be "macho man." Richard turns around just in time to catch him. For a moment there's the possibility of a fight. Instead, I take him by the hand and lead him out of there. We climb back into the Jeep and head for home. No one noticed his belt.

I am falling more deeply in love with Richard; he's teaching me a special kind of courage. I came to him a bit weary, but he has recharged my battery. He gives me strength, hope, a sense of purpose, and pride. I feel exalted by his need for me. In just the short time I've known him I've learned that I have been living with truth, but partial commitment, too concerned with what others think of me, not risking enough. No man before Richard has made me think about these things. I've never been so involved or intimate with any man—or felt so fully alive.

As I begin to understand the layers of Richard, I can see why his emotional life is such a shambles. His psyche is such a thundering mass of good and evil colliding and fighting for power. And Richard welcomes all of these battles, all forms of angst are divine because they are his sources; they comprise his life and his art. He is dedicated to his demons and his angels; from them he derives his truths. And I'm in awe. He's a man who doesn't compromise. So what if it gets a little messy.

One of his favorite poems is "If—," by Rudyard Kipling. Richard had learned it by heart. Sometimes, when he's high, he'll break out with a few lines:

> *If you can bear to hear the truth you've spoken*
> *twisted by knaves to make a trap for fools,*
> *Or watch the things you gave your life to broken,*
> *and stoop and build 'em up with wornout tools. . . .*

My old friend Teo calls and offers me a part in an American Film Institute project that another student is doing. The film is *The Necklace*, based on the story by Guy de Maupassant. A liitle something for me amidst all the Richardness.

We begin to live in some sort of altered state of domestic bliss. Still, there's Richard's terror of intimacy to deal with; my terror too.

Richard returns my tattered copy of *The House of Mirth*, rebound in red leather and embossed gold, with an inscription inside that reads, *To Jennifer, Because I Love You, Richard*. But I'll have a better end than Lily Bart, although I've identified with her at times in my life. I've given him another book to read, *My Wicked, Wicked Ways* by Errol Flynn. One night we're sitting in the office discussing the book and I tell Richard he could play Errol Flynn. He thinks I'm crazy, but I continue, saying Flynn's character transcends color. I even call Tony Perkins to ask what he thinks and he agrees with me. Richard tells him that he's crazy too. "Errol Flynn was a white man, Jenny."

"You can play white," I tell him. It's all sort of fun until Richard gets mad and says I don't understand shit. He says that in America to have even a thought like that is dangerous. In case I haven't noticed, it's a racist country.

I'm enjoying a new sense of purpose and power and the feeling that I'm invaluable to Richard. I've taken over a myriad of domestic and business details. I help out his studio business, lawyers, accountants, and the office staff. I deal with angry ex-wives, needy children, drug dealers, relatives, sycophants, friends, and business associates. I buy Richard's clothes and I'm still fixing up the house. I also fulfill other roles, such as shrink, confidant, and lover. It's busy as hell but I like it. Finally, I ask him to put me on the payroll—a thousand dollars a month plus a clothing allowance. Relieving him of some of the day to day decision-making has also helped alleviate some of his paranoia about people cheating him.

Drug dealer-rapist Joe comes over to play tennis with Richard. They set up a videocamera on a tripod to record their breathless athletic contest and review it afterward. It's a bad joke; they think they will look like McEnroe and Connors, but they look like two geriatrics, running in slow motion for the ball. Funny but not funny, 'cause after all it *is* drug dealer-rapist Joe. I pretend that nothing's ever happened and am a gracious hostess.

Dick Gregory comes out for a visit. He talks about his new fast-diet and the importance of jogging twenty minutes a day. He drinks water and eats cashews; rather, he chews cashews and spits them out before swallowing. He wants Richard to invest in his company. Dick's *very* thin, but he has tremendous energy and great enthusiasm. During the civil rights movement, Pat took me to hear him speak at the Albany Civic Center. What has become of that once-large body and booming voice? Richard does not enjoy watching his cashew routine but he is nice to him. Dick was once one of Richard's heroes. He leaves some of that powder and vitamins. We use it, but not for long.

I decide to try my hand at entertaining. Bill Cosby and his wife, Camille, are our first guests. The menu is simple but elegant: fish, steamed green beans, a good white wine. It's a nice dinner but tense; Richard barely speaks and I am uptight in the reflection of the Cosbys' perfection. They are refined and restrained. There is some discussion by Bill and Richard about their work on *California Suite* and about the business in general. Bill had been an early role model of Richard's and I think this increased his nervousness, but in general he's not good in these kinds of social situations. He gets really tense; it's as if somewhere in the universe there's a rule book on how to have a nice dinner with friends and Richard doesn't have a copy. At the same time, it's clear Bill and Camille have studied that book. The ease with which they converse and the comfort they feel is disarming. Bill strikes me as being a pretty generous guy, but he seems to lack a certain spontaneity. I think that maybe they look down on Richard a bit, because he's "one of our untamed brothers." (I feel as though I am perceived as a slumming white woman. I'm being too jumpy. I want so much for them to see the same dignity and magic in Richard that I do. I also want them to see that he's well taken care of.)

Then there's the matter of the battered lamp which dangles above us bent, broken, and screaming. "I'm a $10,000 Tiffany lamp that Richard smashed and no one has even bothered to fix me." No one comments on it, which makes it worse because you just know it's on everyone's mind. I think it embarrassed the perfect Cosbys. I curse myself for not having had it repaired yet. I also end up wishing that Richard and I were "perfect." Don't think I'll try this again for a while.

March

Enormous Uncle Dicky arrives, weighing in at approximately three hundred and fifty pounds. Uncle Dicky has been a pimp and knows his way around a cell block. Now he's "legit"; he's in the construction business and keeps hitting up Richard for large sums of cash to subsidize this floundering enterprise. He consumes food, money, and grass—always has a big brown bag of it—as if there were an endless supply. The original bottomless pit. He confuses me. As vulgar and greedy as he can be, he has wisdom, humor, and a gentleness that is disarming. He is a survivor who takes no shit. Once when David Franklin was giving Richard a hard time about something, Uncle Dicky simply said, "Why in prison we'd take a guy like that, throw him up against the wall and fuck'm." Right.

He knows I appreciate him and often enlists my help to get more money. Sometimes he doesn't have to ask me. One evening we're in the guest room and Uncle Dicky is telling Richard some story about recent bad luck. He's crying as he tells it. He needs $50,000 for equipment for his business. Richard listens patiently. I'm sitting on the floor only half-listening, when I look over and see Uncle Dicky's swollen feet with their long, splintered, discolored toenails. I am mesmerized by these toenails that have seen it all. I reach out and touch them. Something about these toenails move me, move me enough to say, "Richard, give Uncle Dicky the money."

Richard does, but later says that he's counting on me to help him say no. There are so many requests for money, especially from the family; these are the hardest. I tell him about the toenails, he shakes his head and smiles.

A few days later Uncle Dicky comes back to the house all duded up in a new sharkskin suit and sunglasses monogrammed with his initials in rhinestones. Nobody asks about the new truck he was supposed to buy. During this visit Mercy hatches a plan to get her green card; she and Uncle Dicky will go to Tijuana and get married. . . . And they do. We all think this is a hoot—until Mercy can't get back into the country because she's left illegally. No one thought about that. With David Franklin's help, she crosses the border back into the U.S.

On Friday night Ray Lafaro and Stu Levine, producers who are friends of mine, come over to discuss *The Charlie Parker Story* with Richard. It's a productive meeting; everyone has the same vision and the desire to achieve it. The trouble with evening meetings is that they can often turn into social events, which is what happens. We all drink and do the usual—cocaine. I'm sitting on Richard's lap when he says something to me that Stu doesn't like; he suggests that Richard "cool it." *Wrong!* Richard hauls off and slaps me in the face. *Smack!* As I'm holding my hand on my burning cheek, I notice the wounded expression on Stu's face. *That's sweet*, I think; I also think there's something odd about it. Is he so disturbed by the slap, or is he concerned about me? No one moves. Then Stu asks, "Richard, why'dja do that?"

I stay stuck to Richard's lap. He just looks at Stu and says, "Because I can. I'm showing you she's mine. Got it? I'll talk to her any fucking way I want to."

No one knows what to say. I like it. I mean, I want to be owned because it means that I belong to someone, it means I can surrender.

As Ray and Stu leave, Stu throws away his wedding ring on the lawn, because, so he says, the whole scene's made him feel awful about love. We never find the ring.

Later that evening I sit on the desk in front of Richard, both of us pretty high on love, booze, and drugs, when Richard asks me, "Hey, Jen what would you do if I asked you for some pussy?"

Without thinking, without missing a beat, I slug him with a hard right, smashing him in the nose. Suddenly the blood begins pouring out and he's on his feet, screaming, arms and legs flailing, he's like a wild animal. He lunges towards me, knocking the lamp off his desk, then finishes the job, wiping the rest of his desk clean; the phone and the huge vodka bottle crash to the floor. I'm outta there! I make tracks as he follows in hot pursuit yelling, "Uncle Dicky, she hit me. I'm bleeding. The bitch hit me, Unk. Where is she? I'm going to kill the bitch, Unk."

I'm outside in a stucco corner of the house, hiding beneath some cobwebs, praying he won't find me. If he gets hold of me—no telling. I wait, I figure about an hour, till he calms down, then test the waters. As I cautiously walk down the hallway, I see there's blood everywhere: on door knobs, all over the soft pink carpet. I walk into the bedroom and find that the doctor's here, stitching up a big gash in Richard's elbow. But I hit him in the nose! Seems that in his insane search for me, he'd broken anything he could find, using his elbows and fists as weapons. Thank God for the doctor; he makes housecalls. He leaves Richard a box of glass ampules, liquid Demerol for the pain, and plenty of syringes. The following morning, we are back in love with the help of Uncle Dicky, who mediates the truce for the video camera. He's really funny, pretending to be a black, street version of Perry Mason. "When exactly did the bitch hit you? And when did you know there was blood? There was lotsa blood, your honor, coming out of that nigger's nose. And lotsa yelling—he wanted to kill the bitch. No, don't know where she trained; they say she's a natural."

Richard tells Uncle Dicky, "Unk, she's got a mean right." And Unk says, "Maybe we should train her. I warn ya son, with an Irish bitch who's got a right like hers, ya better behave yourself. Say, Jennifer, didja know the Irish are niggers turned inside out?"

No, I've never heard that. We all laugh and I feel as if I have earned my wings. Richard keeps asking, "Why, Jen? I only asked you for some pussy."

I tell him, "It was disrespectful. And you hit me in front of my friends." I don't like the humiliation, but there's something primordial about the sense of being possessed; it feels like love, and I like it. Richard's well into the stash of Demerol, and he's a very mellow fellow. He looks like a pro at poking his arms. I've never shot up anything; here's my big chance. Another turn on the road of love—sharing a needle.

He ties me off with yellow rubber tubing that the doctor has left him. There is something dangerous and vaguely erotic about this although I already know that the entire sinister gestalt of this could never really seduce me. Richard sticks me and in a moment I feel the warm rush of the drug. He gives me more and more. I am now reeling, beyond high. I begin to panic. I'm losing control, my grip, I'm slipping, passing out. Then Richard pays attention and shakes me to keep me from going under. "No more," I tell him. "I've had enough."

A few minutes later, still dizzy, I vaguely hear the gate bell ring and a voice on the intercom. An old friend of Richard's announces herself; he lets her in—God knows why. Like thunder, B.B. Drake Hooks rolls into our cloud of Demerol. All I can remember is her face about two inches from my soporific one as she begins to berate me. "Look at you! You think you're somethin' now, but Richard's gonna fire you—oh yes, child. He fires 'em all. Just you watch, he'll fire your ass one day. Count on it."

I'm not too happy about her arrival but I'm too stoned to care. Then I finally realize what she's talking about, and that I'm in no condition to listen to this. "Yep, after ya give 'em all ya got," she continues. I'm not stoned enough to keep from wondering how the hell does she know just how much I've "got" and if this tirade is because I'm a white woman or simply because I'm just another woman in Richard's life? She keeps after me with this invective, until I finally find the energy to ask Richard to walk B.B. Drake Hooks to the door. Then I figure out maybe God has delivered her. Of all things—perhaps she's a guardian angel in disguise, who's been sent here to disrupt the dark pleasure I was becoming lost in.

Richard puts the needles away and we fall asleep; we need to rest. In a matter of hours we're flying to Peoria to see Richard's family.

Later that afternoon we all pile into the private Lear jet at the nearby valley airport: Uncle Dicky, Rashon, Richard, and I. It's cold when we arrive in Peoria. There's snow on the ground and no leaves on the trees. It's dismal and gray like the endless Cropseyville days.

Mama Marie lives on the outskirts of town in a simple white two-story house that Richard has bought for her. Family, friends and the pungent smells of home cooking fill the house. Mama is sitting in a low chair in a corner of the family room, wearing a gray T-shirt and purple stretch slacks. She's clutching something in her right fist. I extend my hand and remind her that we had met on Thanksgiving.

"Can't shake your hand. Got salt in it." Then she opens her palm, showing me the moist, wrinkled salt.

I ask her, "What's it for?"

"Got some pain. An old remedy, fixes it right up."

Mama's in her late seventies and walks with a little difficulty, sometimes needing a cane. She's a bit stooped, and has large sagging breasts, which look like some extra baggage that she's struggling to haul around. We have a meal of some serious home-cooked soul food; I can't eat much because the food's been sitting out on the kitchen counters covered with dishtowels, flies everywhere. Then we all settle down to a poker game that has apparently been long planned and long looked forward to. I don't want to play, so I take a seat next to Richard feeling like a moll in Armani. One of the players is Jimmy, an ex-con who's been in and out of jail all his life. He's always asking Richard for hand-outs and tonight's no exception. He's not the only one.

The evening wears on; cards are dealt and dice roll. Women flirt, innuendoes fly and everyone gets high. I am holding my own in a world that isn't mine. But it's where I want to be-close to the bone, to the marrow of Richard's world. So I try to show myself and everyone there that I'm one of them; that I'm tough and hip; that I can take the racist remarks and veiled insults, understand their stories, take the pressure of their environment. They will not judge me by my white skin alone. I'm different and special—colorless. I know that this is a test—that's why he's brought me here.

I watch all night. Richard slips into his coke-snorting, gambling, macho man role like a second skin. I am being tested; I stay by his side. He's lucky with the cards and the dice. He looks like a man who can't lose. Completely at home—rolling the dice, calling out the numbers, snapping his fingers, giving subtle, confident nods—he keeps winning. I'm in awe. He's King and he's my man.

The sun comes up; most of the players are gone and the rest are just trying to stay awake. Then come more requests—for loans, for help, for money—along with some reminders: "Never forget your roots, son. Where ya came from, boy. Who made ya." Suddenly it's too much. Richard explodes and turns on his family with all his fury and his pain. "You never loved me! Ever since I was a little boy you wanted me to do everything your way! You wanted me to be a pimp! I couldn't do it."

He's sobbing, pacing back and forth. "Let me be who I am, goddamn it. You want me to be like all of you, stuck here in Peoria doing nothing with your lives."

Mama has a stricken look on her face. "Now son, just calm down."

But Richard won't be calmed down. He keeps raging. "My father would never take money from me the way Uncle Dicky does. What do you think he'd think of that, Mama? What do you think your son Buck would think?"

I understand his frustration and anger. Now it's just family. He keeps sobbing and lands the final blow: "And you took me away from my mother. I loved her. Didn't you know that, Mama? How could you not know that?"

He leaves through the sliding glass doors, going outside to cry in the cold gray morning. I follow, trying to soothe him, but he recoils at my touch. Uncle Dicky comes outside and I leave; Richard is weeping in a white lawn chair. I go to sleep listening to the fading sobs, wishing he were in my arms.

Early that afternoon I wake up and he isn't beside me. The house is silent. I go out to the family room, the scene of the crime, looking for Richard, looking for signs of life. The room is clean, too clean. You can't tell that a heart shattered here just a few hours ago. I feel frightened. The emptiness is oppressive; even the ceiling seems lower. Then I see Aunt Dee and ask, "Where's Richard?"

She looks away, mumbles something I don't understand. Then Mama's in front of me and I ask her, "Where's Richard?"

"Richard's upstairs sleeping. He don't want to be disturbed." She's real grouchy.

"Where is he, Mama?"

"I told ya. Upstairs, but you best leave him alone now. Hear? He got sumbody with 'im."

I must be hearing things. "Excuse me? What did you say?"

Snapping at me, "Ya heard me. I wouldn't go up there now if I was you. He's with a friend."

Well, she's not me. I go up to see for myself and find that the spare bedroom door's closed; I decide not to open it. I don't need more humiliation and the worst part is, I think they're all enjoying it. Why they don't like me? I'm white, an outsider, someone who could come between Richard and themselves. Well, I will refuse to let them win. I will not show my pain. I will hold onto what's left of my pride.

I go get my guitar, put on my Panama hat, and sit on the cold, steel spiral staircase, and serenade them.

> *I know that I should leave but then*
> *I just can't go, you win again . . .*

> *This heart of mine, could never see*
> *What everybody knows but me*
> *Just trusting you was my great sin*
> *What can I do? You win again . . .*

God, it feels good and by the confused expressions on their faces, I feel certain that I'm shaming them. Who knows, maybe they think that I'm crazy; maybe I am because I don't leave. I stay. I can't walk out the door. I've always accepted a challenge; I've always fought to win; I've always picked up my half of the rope for tug of war.

A few hours later the "friend" is sent away and Rashon makes plane reservations—Chicago to Hawaii. Thank God, we're leaving earlier than planned. Richard is fragile from last night's catharsis that is still unresolved, and he's weary from the burden of having to act out his blackness. That's what sleeping with that "friend" was all about. But I can take it, because I see that this behavior is being encouraged by his family. It keeps Richard tied to the past that they were a part of and which is where they still live. And Richard response is Pavlovian. I understand, which helps deflect my pain. I believe we will overcome this.

Richard and I are on the plane, snorting coke from the huge bottle we're travelling with and arguing. Our fight is silent—we're writing notes back and forth to each other. That's the only way we're

145

communicating. He claims that I have humiliated him, wounded him in some way. He scribbles a melodramatic message on a napkin.

By the time we get to Hana, Richard's severely depressed. I try everything to shake him out of it; my Waylon Jennings imitation, my Sophia Loren imitation, but it's the spider-in-the-window imitation that finally does it.

On Hana, with the help of more cocaine, we get into a long discussion about love and fear that ultimately leads back to Richard's all-consuming pain. Nothing can shake his grim mood. He asks me to leave him alone with Rashon and the coke. I can't compete. His past and his pain, and possibly cocaine, are my competition.

I go back to L.A. and stay at Richard's. Then I start to receive threatening phone calls—a bomb in the house, a bomb car. I never find out who the caller is but I suspect it's "nothing." For me, life has always verged on the surreal and I guess it still does. This phase just has a slightly different texture to it.

After a few days, Richard calls, asking me to come back down to Hana. I am so happy to return to his arms.

Back in Hana and back in love; once again face to face, we begin to heal our wounds, purifying ourselves in our magic fountain that Richard is convinced holds hidden, mystical powers. He dances under its waterfall chanting in his imaginary African language, shaking a piece of bamboo like a rattle. We picnic on the beach in the rain and make love for dessert while being devoured by hordes of biting, red ants. We leap up half-naked. I run into the sea and Richard, tripping over his pants, does a classic belly-flop into the sand. We laugh and laugh.

We take long walks and Richard has daily conferences with the cows in the pastures. "Now, Mr. Very Brown Cow, I would like to ask you just how much fun you really have here in this gigantic meadow that's all your own on this magical island of Maui in the heavenly place of Hana?"

We visit the site for the house. Work is about to begin and we give it our blessings. We feel clean, the bad has disappeared, and we promise that we'll try and hang onto this in L.A.

Back in L.A., Mama and Aunt Dee come for a visit. Too many strong women who love Richard all under one roof. This starts to cause problems. Mama and Aunt Dee soon have Mercy tucked under their very spread-open wings, which undermines any direction coming from me. Mama saves newspapers, compulsively filling her room with high stacks of dated news. What's the point? And the house never seems to be really clean anymore, there's always something frying in the kitchen.

One day I play one of John Prine's albums and tell Mama who he is and what he once meant to me. Big mistake. She delivers this information to Richard the minute he comes home. "Do you know that Big Foot Motherfucker was playin' that damn lynchin' music of her old lover? In your house, son!" Mama's definitely out for some of my blood. Something like this either incites Richard or he laughs at it—sometimes it's both. And I push it until he's forced to defend Mama. He has to. Richard has always liked my connection to country music and has enjoyed it when I play my guitar. But he decides out of principle, he explains, that he doesn't want to hear it because the music was from the hotbeds of racism: Appalachia, the Sun Belt, the old Confederacy.

So old King-and-Queen-rolled-into-one is definitely taking over and with her have come these demons from the past—they've never been too far out of reach anyway.

Some friends and acquaintances of Richard's decide that being chummy with Mama is a smart move. They come out to visit and she holds court. One regular is Lady Java, a high-yellow, voluptuous, legs-for-days transvestite from Watts who's not only Mama's new best friend but is the object of Richard's fantasies as well. Sometimes I feel as though I am in a ghost brothel. Then there's Pam Grier, the actress and ex-girlfriend whom Mama adores and she makes no bones about telling Richard, in front of me, that he should get back with her. So Mama and I lock horns and Richard seems oblivious. Or is he? He can't admit it, but I think Mama and Aunt Dee are driving him nuts.

Since Aunt Dee's and Mama's arrival we've begun a weekly ritual of Sunday gatherings. These usually include assorted children, and ex-wives and girlfriends of Richard's, so these parties are not terribly relaxing. On this particular Sunday, the poolside soiree turns into a late-night gathering around the dining room table. Aunt Dee, Mama and I have just had one of our ongoing battles about food. I think their taste in food is too smelly, greasy and low-rent; they think mine is too bland, expensive, and white. These controversies often end in tense bitter draws. I serve hors d'oeuvres—champagne, Stolichnaya, caviar, and assorted French cheeses to the small group at the table, while Mama and Aunt Dee are in the kitchen preparing dinner—fried catfish and beans. The smell of Peoria and the past seeps out from behind the closed kitchen door.

Cocaine is also being passed among some of the guests. Marvin Gaye is there with his wife Jan, who's got two girlfriends in tow; the actor Calvin Lockhart; Rashon; Jean Hancock, who's Herbie's sister (and who was later killed in a Delta plane crash at Dallas-Ft. Worth); and then there's Richard and myself. Jean is really great. She's one of Richard's ex lovers—who isn't? We've become really close friends. I enjoy meeting Marvin. He's a sweet man in body and in soul. Very quiet, but he doesn't miss a trick and his reticence seems rooted in serenity. Like Richard he's seen it all, but unlike Richard, Marvin seems to have learned from his past and no longer needs to be in constant battle with it. Perhaps his silence is mixed a bit with awe; it's obvious that Richard's stardom and the macho man act that's out tonight in full force are making an impression.

The Tiffany has been repaired and the dimmer's on low; Richard's holding court. Suddenly in the middle of a full-tilt cocaine rap he begins extolling my virtues. At the top of his list is what he thinks is the wonderful trait of stubbornness. "She doesn't back down when she believes in something or thinks she is right. I love it because she won't let me bully her. She makes me see myself and that makes me grow."

The conversation rambles on until Richard initiates a favorite and incendiary topic: Who among the women at the table is a whore? No one says a word. He continues, "Jennifer has impeccable instincts."

Now he directs the absurd question to someone he knows is fool enough to answer. Me. "Come on. Tell us, Jennifer."

Flattered that he has such faith in my judgment, I want to show off. *I'll prove I'm worthy,* I think. I look around the table—there's something odd about the seating arrangement. Marvin's wife Jan sits sandwiched between her girlfriends at one of the long sides of the big dining room table, while Marvin sits at an end. He looks a bit left out in the cold. I remember a saying I once heard: "Beware of a wife with too many girlfriends, for they will always try to destroy the conjugal we." I am reminded of Deboragh and her girlfriends. I look at everyone in turn. By the time my eyes reach Marvin's, the silver tray has reached him. He seems uncomfortable and worried.

Slowly, he shakes his head at me as if to say, "Don't say a word."
Probably good advice.

He takes a line and passes it on. I take a deep breath and a swig
of Stoli. Now I'm high enough to play the jester. I size up the women
and point. "I think she is and . . . her and her."

I've pointed to Jan and her girlfriends. Shit, what have I done?
Maybe she and Marvin are having problems and I'm adding to
them. I feel embarrassed by my behavior, but I don't back down.

There are gasps, sighs, and muted curses. Now I'm nervous. I
look at Richard. There's a slow grin, which tells me that he knows
he's started trouble and that he likes it. "Are you sure, Jennifer?"

"Yeah."

"Well, I'm not, so why don't you apologize to each of the women
you offended."

"Nope. You asked for my opinion and I gave it." Silly girl. Everyone shifts uncomfortably.

"Yes, I asked for your opinion, but I didn't think you'd be fool
enough to give it."

Everyone laughs. Richard calls to Mama to come in from the
kitchen. The silver chalice is filled again and goes around the table
as we all wait for Mama's expertise. She enters the dining room,
bringing the smell of catfish with her. "Mama, Jennifer thinks these
three women are whores. You're the expert, Mama. What d'ya
think?"

She wipes her hands on the towel wrapped around her waist
and looks at every one of us. Finally, she looks at me with an
expression of total contempt. She looks back at Richard. "I think
youse a damn fool."

With that, Mama exits, back to the kitchen and her catfish. She
is smarter than I am.

"Jennifer, apologize." Richard is far from me at the other end of
the long table, which increases the tension.

"No. You wanted to know what I thought and—"

"Jennifer, apologize."

"Richard," I press on, "if you didn't want to know . . ."

"Jennifer."

"What?"

"Shut the fuck up."

"I will not, and don't speak to me that way," I continue, the set-

149

up fool. Now I am in trouble. I have belittled Richard, his standing in the Black Macho Club is threatened.

He picks up the nearest champagne bottle and throws it at me. I see his hand go for it and see it coming. Champagne spills as it hurtles in slow motion down the length of the table catching me on the left side of the head. The force of the impact is substantial. Everyone is stunned and offers sympathetic oohs and aahs. But the rule is: stay out of family fights. I rub my head and retreat to the bedroom, humiliated and angry that I have fallen for the obvious. I overhear Richard, "You see, I told you she was hardheaded."

They all laugh and he is King.

The next morning things get worse. Richard has to get up early to appear in court for a hearing about the New Year's party car-shooting incident. I can't get him up since he came to bed full of vodka and coke, only a couple of hours earlier. I yell and shake him but he sleeps on. I ask Mama for help. She comes in and takes a stab at it, "Get up son. You got court." Nothing. She leaves, telling me, "I always did have trouble getting that boy up." Hearing that, I remember what she used to do when she couldn't wake him. I give him a swift kick in the ass. This works—too well. Not only does he wake up, but he leaps up and comes running after me, cursing all the way. "You white bitch, I'm going to get you for that. You motherfucker . . ."

I'm running through the bathroom and the connecting closets, trying like hell to get to a hallway door and out of there. I don't make it; he's faster, catches me in the shelf-and-drawer section, grabs me by the arm, swings me around, and lands a ferocious blow to my left eye. He keeps pummeling my face until I finally get away.

The damage is done so quickly. I'm blinded by blood but keep running, finding my way into Aunt Dee's and Mama's room while Richard still follows me in mad pursuit. He isn't finished. I barricade myself in their bathroom as Mama holds him back. The instant before I close the door I see Mama holding his arms, telling him to stop. He looks like a car stuck in the mud, its wheels spinning and going nowhere. He keeps crying to her, "But Mama, she kicked me in the ass."

I am terrified. I look in the mirror and can't believe what I see. Blood is streaming down my face in little rivers and my skin looks neon white.

I wait until Richard leaves the house; then I come out of the bathroom and stumble past Mama and Aunt Dee. Having saved me, they are now distant and unconcerned.

Back in our bedroom. I don't know what to do. I'm dazed and frightened and bleeding. I can't call Berry or any of those people. So, I call Jean. "What do I do?" Then someone picks up the extension, which makes me crazy. "If you are listening because you think I'm calling the police, I'm not. Now get the FUCK OFF the phone."

Jean tells me to put some ice on my wounds, get some sleep, and then figure it out. I do that and fall asleep clutching a towel full of ice cubes.

A few hours later, Richard returns. He's relieved, the court hearing went well, the punishment light. The judge has ordered him to pay a fine, have therapy, and donate a certain number of hours to community service. Richard's worried about me and feels contrite. We make love. And I *do* want his love. The sorrow and the tears, the anger and the apologies have added deeper layers to the tenderness and understanding we've shared since the first time. We've been through, and go through, so much together.

Richard decides to lift the towel that's been bandaged around my eye; he sees the wound above my left eye, and looks shocked.

"Richard, what's wrong?"

"Jen, you've gotta go see the doctor. I think you need stitches." Since that first glimpse, I've avoided looking at it, now I, too, am in shock. An open, mean-looking, purple gash above my left eyebrow stares back at me. The rest of my face is swollen and discolored. I panic. "Richard, my face?"

His expression shows me how worried he really is. "I'll call Rashon and have him drive you." Rashon carries me to his car. He is very kind.

The doctor is upset and angry when he sees me. "Did Richard do this to you?"

I decide to be honest; he's known Richard longer than I have. "He hit me."

"He sure did. You need stitches." I count them, eight sutures. The doctor is reassuring, saying that he's pretty good at not leaving scars and that I'm actually lucky because the wound is in an inconspicuous spot right above the eyebrow. I don't feel lucky. Then he says, "Richard shouldn't have done this. You know that, right?"

"Yes. I know that." Do I know that?

But the doctor tells me that there's a good chance I have some facial fractures and makes an appointment for me to have x-rays taken at Valley Presbyterian in the morning. I consider walking out the back door and escaping from Rashon, who's in the outside reception room waiting for me like the KGB. I don't escape.

That night I think about the x-rays as I stare at my face in the mirrors above the bed. I am misshapen, swollen, and turning blue. Richard is lying next to me, frightened and amazed that I even came back. I don't tell him I thought of escaping. He says things like, "Look what I've done to you." It looks as if my face might be mush under the skin. "Richard, what if I need surgery?"

He tries to console me, telling me we'll find the best surgeons available, even if it means going to Switzerland. I lie awake all night and stare at the apparition in the mirrors. I can still feel the impact of the champagne bottle.

I watch Richard sleep. He's coiled up beside me in a fetal position and every now and then he moans, "I'm so sorry, Jennifer."

I remember Hana, making love on Red Ant Beach, and our magic fountain. Now Richard is afraid to touch me for fear of hurting me and I need to be held so badly. Tears run down my face into my hair, still matted with dried blood. Why did he do this? It is my fault, I did kick him. Was it that hard? Hard enough for this? Yes, any kick is too hard. My fault. I tell myself, "Everything will be okay." Thank God, the x-rays reveal no fractures. My heart is a different matter.

During my recuperation I paint a watercolor of our magic fountain and hang it on the wall in the guest room. It feels like a shrine.

The stitches come out, the scar is minimal. I re-enter the world and household life.

April

I feel like an interloper. Mama, Aunt Dee, and Mercy make for a terrible trio. Strange new maids keep coming and going. Mercy even has her own.

Mama doesn't try to hide her feelings; clearly, she hates my ass. I can *hear* her thinking, *White girl taking my son away.* I represent everything that distances Richard from Peoria State of Mind. When I leave a room I can hear them whispering about me. Even Barbara, the cook *I* hired on Michael Childers's recommendation, brings gossip, and starts to badmouth me.

Richard tries to ignore them, but I can feel him being pulled into their web of hate.

Then things get really out of control.

The morning after a late night of coke, vodka, and making love to try and crash through our fears of commitment, the intercom phone rings. It's Barbara; she wants to speak with Richard. I hand him the phone. In his low don't-mess-with-me-voice, he says, "Barbara, please don't disturb us anymore," and hangs up. I ask, "What did she want?" and he says, "I don't know." Two seconds later, it rings again. Barbara, again. "Richard, she wants to speak with you." Now he's angry. "You tell her I said I didn't want to be disturbed, and I mean it."

"Barbara, look, Richard told you he didn't want to be disturbed."

Nerves frayed from the all-nighter, Richard grabs the phone from me and tells her off. "This is *my* lady and *you'll* do as she tells you. Got it?"

The phone rings again. I pick it up and this time it's Mama.

"You tell Richard there's a man out here with a stick."

Lord only knows what this cryptic message is about. I hand Richard the phone feeling confused and a bit scared.

"What are you talking about, Mama? What man with what stick?" He puts the phone down; he's frightened, too. We look at each other. "She says there's some man with a stick." We sit there, bewildered. The next thing I know, as I'm leaning against the headboard, Barbara bursts through the door carrying a huge two-by-four. She raises it high above her head, and with all her weight smashes it across my outstretched legs. This is the "man" with the stick: Whorehouse Punishment! It happens so fast, we can't react. Richard leaps up, and in that instant she's on top of me, large thick hands groping for my neck, huge legs struggling to pin me down. I'm fighting, thrashing wildly, but Barbara is a big girl. She manages to straddle my arms and get her thick fingers around my neck. I don't know . . . what in God's name is going on ? She's strangling me. *Why the fuck isn't Richard coming to my rescue?* I'm choking and gasping for breath, twisting my head I see Richard standing there, by the side of the bed, frozen. No, not frozen. I see something else—he's enjoying this sordid scene. A woman is trying to kill me. Her grip tightens and I fight on, but I'm weakening, feeling that I'm going down for the count. The mind is funny, I am still thinking: *Hey. Interesting. This is about black and white. It's a mini-race-war, right here on this big brass bed. This woman hates me because I'm white. And Richard, the man who loves me, is letting it happen.* His ambivalence is terrifying.

My pleading look finally reaches him, much louder than any scream. *Have mercy, save my life. It's not my fault.* I can feel the hate. I beg him not to judge me by my skin and to have the courage to make that choice. Richard hears me, grabs her, and in one fluid motion throws her off me.

I know that Barbara's relieved, too. I don't think she had murder in her plan. She must have thought Richard would end the attack much earlier. She slinks out of there like a big, mangy animal, stopped in midslaughter. This was Mama's idea and the message is clear: Mama's the boss.

Richard's passivity, his inability to go against Mama makes me feel sorry for him. She's in complete control of him, but she doesn't control me. After this insane incident, I become more determined than ever to help free him from her vise-like grip. Mama and I have locked horns in the past and now we would do battle. I must liberate Richard from his past and us from the ugliness and the double standards of racism. I'll slay the Goliaths one at a time.

I want the beast Barbara out of the house. Later on, when I hobble out to the pool I see that Barbara is out there waiting on company! And, I know that they've all been told what's happened. Talk about the walking wounded! I pay my respects to the guests, *just passing through on my way to the next battle* and do a few jackknifes in the pool. Barbara has been hiding behind Mama so it takes Richard hours and several drinks to find the courage to dismiss her. And when he finally does, he calls her husband into the office, and tells *him* instead of her. I ask Richard, "Do you *really* subscribe to this sensibility?"

"That's *so* white of you, baby. That's his *wife* and *he's* responsible for her."

"If she had murdered me would he go to jail for her too? Bullshit."

Well, here's another aspect of the black macho male mind-set—another piece of the whole myth. I know Richard feels secure in this role but I really believe it's just a role. He will learn, *is* learning how to give up the act, learning to show that he really *does* understand.

Whew! I've experienced a day in the life of a whorehouse.

The next day, Richard's not out of the house two seconds before

I tell Mama that I know she was behind the bandito attack. An argument follows. Richard returns and walks into the middle of a serious fight.

"You're out of line talking to Mama that way."

"Fuck out of line—I get beaten up and you know goddamn well she's accountable!"

This is a fight I can't win. Richard tells me I have to apologize. No can do. Of course I'm the villain and I'm asked to leave the house. I can return only after I've said I'm sorry. When the goddamn cows come home! Thank God I've recently rented an apartment in Beverly Hills. I head over there to sulk.

I can't stand it. Mama's trying to re-create the whorehouse in our home, encouraging Richard's worst behavior.

I buy two delicate finches in a beautiful three-tiered cage. Rashon picks up this magic gift and delivers it to Richard. Hysterical, he calls me. "Bitch, what the fuck kind of voodoo are you doing on me? Sending me two dead birds?"

That damn suffocating valley heat. I apologize to Mama, not meaning one breath of it, and swear to get her out of our lives.

The court case and the divorce are behind him, as well as the settlement with the women who were in the car with Deboragh. I can feel Richard relax and there is a sense that we are quieting down to domestic life.

Richard begins to see the court-appointed therapist, Dr. Cannon, who is a kind and intelligent black man. I join in on a couple of sessions, but the atmosphere seems odd—much too self conscious. On whose part? I watch Dr. Cannon skate around "the movie star." But Richard keeps going, some things start happening and he says that they're getting close to the marrow. Then he starts giving money to the Medical Center in Watts, which Dr. Cannon runs—so much for the marrow. Richard is also going to donate the proceeds from a concert—for the community service part of his punishment. This has the inevitable result. Dr. Cannon kowtows more than ever and the truth becomes harder to find. But we are still in love and still strong.

May

We go to Sammy Davis's house and have a great time. It's very clear and very sweet, how much Richard wants his approval. Sammy is one of the warmest, nicest, and most generous spirits I've ever met. He not only likes me, but encourages Richard to build a life with me, saying, "You've got a good woman here. That's quality."

It's also obvious that Sammy loves Richard the way a father loves a son, and that he's proud of him. Sammy's energy and spirit are so attractive that it's easy to be drawn to him, despite his size, unusual features, and somewhat eccentric appearance.

On our way home, right in the middle of Coldwater Canyon, Richard does a 180-degree turn. I ask, "Where are we going?"

"It's a surprise."

We end up at the Comedy Store on Sunset. I don't know what he has in mind then suddenly, there he is on stage, the audience going nuts. It's the first time I've ever seen Richard perform. I'm nervous.

He begins walking and talking about the first thing he sees, candle wax on the floor. As he starts to relax and talk more openly, ideas start popping and exploding out of his head. He's cooking on steam. He's been away a long time and now he's back home.

I fall in love with him all over again. I am amazed by his guts and the purity of his instincts, his genius as he follows the dangerous, curvy roads of his mind. Candle wax, takes a left and he's an angel, spinning silk wings in thin air. He is in complete control. He moves sensually; he swaggers as he crosses the stage. He looks taller, his hands are sensitive, elegant. Life for Richard is on stage. His words are wise and savvy. And he tells it like it *is*. After all, he knows how bad it can get.

Mitzi Shore, the club's owner, sits next to me, squealing with delight at every outburst from the audience. "Oh, I'm so glad he's back! I do love him so! You're so good for him." I can hear the cash register ringing in her head. I pull a candle closer, sip my vodka-tonic, and begin taking notes on the back of a "reserved table" sign. I write down things he's saying, how the audience is reacting, how far I think he can take a particular idea, how it might be developed. I am having fun.

The following morning we have breakfast by the pool and go over my notes. He loves it, and I start going with him every night, packing a pencil and pad. I love the routine. Every morning, by the pool we work on the ideas—adding, eliminating, discussing. Before the evening's show, Richard goes over his routine and the new material we've included.

He's addressing issues that are new for him, even working on a piece called "Being Sensitive," which is about friendship in love. When he plays his black or uncaring role, I call him "Macho Man," and from this nickname he develops an entire theme that he explores on stage. His growth and his new-found openness are reflected in his work. Such a happy and productive time! I walk into the house and hear him call out from the bedroom, "Jenny Lee, come here quick. I love you."

I feel needed, essential, and fulfilled. It's bringing out all the good in me. We're creating together and he's welcoming me into his world. I see us as a black and white version of John and Yoko, a duet of magic and productivity. It feels as though it will last forever. Richard has finally found his panacea, me.

People look at me as Richard's deliverance; he is the tragic, self-destructive freak no longer, and it's because he is loved. And I have found the love of my life. .

We make plans to have dinner with old friend Warren Beatty but Richard cancels at the last minute. I show up alone at Dominick's, a *very* private, little steak house. Warren is pissed.

"Jennifer—*Richard?* Boy, you *do* like the walking wounded. Michael J. Pollard, now Richard?"

Richard feels insecure about snubbing Warren and sends him a dozen roses, even after I tell him what Warren said.

The Peoria contingent is still in residence, but we're managing to keep a certain distance. We see them more or less in passing. They're still having those silly Sunday afternoon barbecues, shows of family "solidarity." Sammy comes out regularly, so does Ken Norton, with his yellow Excalibur, Ali, and comics from the Comedy Store—Marsha Warfield, Jeff Altman, Gallagher. At one poolside birthday bash Michael Jackson shows up, looking adorable as he sits coyly on the couch in the office, watching me sign checks for the caterers. Among the guests are various exes—ex-girlfriends included—whose jealousy and palpable hostility make me feel unwelcome. Often I try to avoid these shindigs and stay in some distant part of the house, giving the occasional instruction over the intercom. Shelley and Maxine and their respective daughters, Liz

157

and Rain, are usually there. I get along all right with Max, but Shelley is another story. She's a white girl who tries to act black—walks as if she's on heroin and talks like a cross between a female Jack Kerouac and a street pimp . . . embarrassing. Shelley's tried stand-up comedy. Then she joined a circus. It's also very obvious that she's still madly in love with Richard and gets his attention by picking fights with him. Liz and Rain now spend at least one night of the weekend at the house. Liz and I get along. Rain and I don't. Time with "Dad" for them usually amounts to Chinese food at the mall and then back home for about an hour's worth of Atari. I saw Richard hit Liz and Rain only once. He chased them out onto the driveway and smacked their bottoms at Mama's urging. It occurs to me that Mama probably hit Richard pretty regularly.

I get roped into a bizarre excursion with Mama and Aunt Dee and the new, gay, black servant. Mama desperately wants to see Lady Java perform and Richard has asked me to accompany them. So we limo-it over to some funky, all-black, no-name club in another country—downtown Watts. We're treated like visiting dignitaries, immediately escorted to a large, conspicuous center table on the edge of the dance floor. We watch Lady Java weave her magic and cast her spell. A vision in bright, yellow lycra and chiffon, she gyrates and grinds her way through a very seductive quasi-striptease. Mama sits there mesmerized. I think she's in love. Every time Lady Java has come out to the house, she's been dressed to kill with vibes to match. After she leaves, the discussion usually centers on "how she hides it." Richard has secret fantasies about her and now I'm convinced Mama has them, too. She's practically salivating. I imagine the two of them walking off into the sunset together—trapped in a Vonnegut novel. I love watching all this serious eccentricity and feel a bit like a voyeur. Another addiction.

During his "woodshedding" time at the Store, I really get into dressing Richard and introduce him to Armani, Basile, and Complice. He adores the beauty of the new shapes and fabrics and the myriad of Maud Frizon boots and shoes I have specially made for him. When he gestures, his long legs and fingers make a striking image. I talk to him about moving across the stage more, which he does. He looks great, looser and more self-confident. Now onstage he looks like a dancer, gracefully and sensuously gliding back and forth. He loves this new freedom of movement so much that it evolves into a deer impersonation, poetry in motion. I start shopping for myself and develop another addiction: clothes. Rodeo Drive becomes my higher power.

In general Richard seems more satisfied with life. However, the occasional family issue still disturbs him. One afternoon, Richard, Jr. shows up with a head full of pink-foam curlers. He's been booted out of the Navy for questionable behavior and this looked like the proof of the pudding. Richard locks himself in his office and gets roaring drunk, unable to face the fact that his son is gay.

(Eventually, Richard, Jr. becomes a transvestite. He performs to packed houses in Peoria nightclubs, under the name Rainy McNight so as not to embarrass his father.)

My loyalty is still being tested. It is flawless. Richard has arranged a surprise birthday party for Kalilah Ali, Muhammad's ex-wife. During the party, Richard calls Muhammad.

"Hey, listen man, I want to fuck your wife, but I don't want to do it behind your back. I want to make sure it's okay with you." This is crazy. Since Ali and Kalilah are divorced, why ask? And I'm standing right there so he obviously doesn't want to do it behind *my* back either.

Ali replies, there's some laughter and Richard hangs up. That same night, in front of a group of "brothers," he announces to me that actress Jayne Kennedy is my competition.

On the outside I remained unruffled. I think, yes, this shoddy treatment of women is part of the black, male identity crisis. I'm hurt, but I'm torn because I'm keenly aware of the real reasons and causes of these situations. This would be fine if I were writing a thesis, but I'm not. This is part of my life.

June

The Comedy Store is the center of our lives. Since word has gotten out that Richard is putting an act together, every night the audience and backstage has been filled with admirers. John Belushi—always so sweet and always so wacked out—and Chevy Chase are often there. These comics all revere Richard; he's their guru. But I also know they see a degree of menace in him. At one late-night party at Mitzi's, Richard and Chevy are both stoned, sitting on the floor fooling around. When Richard says some things that make Chevy feel really nervous, he leaves. Soon after, the evening starts to deteriorate.

The partying, dope, and late nights are pretty much under control—although the volume does reach the max on a few occasions. But Richard is trying to develop the discipline needed to do his best work and succeeds in moderating his drinking and drug use—for the most part.

We *are* achieving our goal: his career and his psyche are going places. As his career expands so, too, will he. He will heal. In fact, things are going so well that our rare adventures into the abyss seem all the more terrifying.

We leave the Comedy Store a little tipsy on love and energy. But some old grievance is made new again. As we travel along the San Diego Freeway a fight is about to take flight. I naturally find the word and Richard abruptly pulls the steering wheel to the right.

"What are you doing?"

"Trying to kill us."

"Oh . . ."

He takes the new, yellow Mercedes the wrong way down the off ramp. Then he delivers this profound remark, "If we live, then we'll know we're supposed to."

"Okay," I say, shutting my eyes and saying some fast prayers.

No head-on, we don't die. We make it home and it's clear that Richard's angry we've survived. I stop in the kitchen for a snack and a shot of vodka. When I go into the bedroom, Richard is proudly holding up his jacket, his favorite cashmere Armani, now in a thousand shreds.

"Why did you do that?"

"Because we lived."

By the end of the summer, after all those nights at the Store, Richard has an inspired act filled with the lyrical, the poignant, and the irreverent. From "New Year's Eve" to "Things In The Woods," everything's expanding, growing, in forward motion. He's ready to go on the road.

Mama and Aunt Dee finally go home.

August

Richard's words, phrases, and expressions are of an all-wise, all-knowing "I've seen everything," attitude with a hint of sorrow that makes me want to hold him, be tender with him, and fuck him all at once. Sometimes when I try to express my thoughts he'll say, "Is this what you're tryin' to tell me, Mama?" He then puts my words through his truth strainer, giving them back to me in pure simple form. I always know what he means; he depends on that understanding. There is something desperate about the way he needs me, like when he calls my name coming in the front door: "Jenny Leeeee!" It feels good, it feels real, it scares the hell out of me. Each day moves at twice the speed of sound. Richard sticks to the edge, looking for a certain level of emotional chaos, needing to stay slightly off center. It takes a lot of energy to keep up and manage things at the same time. Besides the usual complexity of Richard's life there's been a tour to organize. Twenty-two cities! It's been crazy but fun. Richard's leaving tomorrow. We go out to celebrate my twenty-ninth birthday. He takes me to Chasens, a very chic, old-time Hollywood restaurant and afterwards, he brings me home to a plethora of ribbons and boxes. Treasure after treasure. Magical gifts. Ruby earrings in an enameled, heart-shaped, Battersea box. A perfectly round stone inlaid with the sea and the moon in silver and gold. Bouquets of long-stemmed red roses with love poems tucked into each one.

An endless stream of sweet affection, more than I've ever had in my life.

The bags are packed, the limos are in the driveway. Rashon is here with the new bodyguard and the private jet is waiting. I'm crying all over my new gold satin nightgown and robe. Suddenly, Richard surprises us both and asks me to come. I can't understand why he has kept me dangling till the last minute, but I control my tongue. I pack—literally throwing shoes, boots, and clothes into the suitcases.

The huge crowd at the amazing natural amphitheater in Redrock, Colorado, cheers Richard as he struts across the stage. It's twilight and within minutes lightning begins to flash in the darkening sky and the wind blows fiercely throughout his entire act as if to match his humorous rage. Seconds before the end, it begins to rain. The next stop is in Kansas City, and there I get a little surprise. A doctor shows up one morning at our hotel room. Richard tells me that he's given me the clap. A giant shot of penicillin in each buttock. Then, remorse and confession. It seems that when Richard was in San Carlos trying out the act he had quite a party. He says that it made him realize just how much he really loves me. *Whatever it takes.* Maybe he's learned.

We are uneasy in Kansas City. Richard's been bringing up "the color issue" a lot lately, and we *feel* it here—there's racism in the air. The concert hall is in a rough section of town, the audience is predominantly black, and the atmosphere is tense and somewhat hostile. I think the source is connected to Richard's "crossing over." I'm feeling jumpy and paranoid and say so. Rashon and the new bodyguard feel it, too. Richard is visibly uncomfortable, but he's reluctant to admit it. Instead, he blames me for creating these feelings, while all I've done is simply acknowledge something that he's wishing would just go away. One more show and we're *outta* here. I hate it!

We are sequestered in our hotel, a monolith on the ghostly plains of the midwest. It's three in the morning, the television is burning black and white and all of a sudden Raymond Massey as John Brown rides into frame! It's "Santa Fe Trail." I am proud of my connection to the abolitionist and excited by the movie, half expecting to look out of the window and see him riding against the wind. Richard, however, is in no mood for this and tells me that I'm a "white, honky, bitch, jive, yankee" who knows nothing about the black man's struggle. I am furious. He's not being fair. He's angry because the tension at tonight's concert came from "his people." They've made him paranoid. And this truth is fueling his anger, but he's taking it out on me. I let him know that I think his attitude is bigoted and mean-spirited.

"How come I can't call you nigger, not that I want to or think I should be permitted to, but you can call me those names?"

No answer.

"Is it because I am supposed to feel guilty, or because I'm white, or am I guilty just for being white?"

I do feel, as does any white person who's struggling with racial issues, some of that collective, residual guilt. And Richard is not above using it. He also believes that there is a racist genetic memory that belongs to the entire white race and uses this idea to

162

support his own racism. I love him beyond his color and I try desperately to convince him of this. But whenever we discuss "the color issue" he speaks as if it is my problem, mine alone. I feel that he often uses his blackness as an excuse for his pain and anger and I also believe that he feels a profound sense of shame because he knows better.

The silent treatment until I leave the next day . . . to go back to L.A.

I join Richard in Chicago—civilization! I suggest a visit to the museum, which has a good collection of Impressionist paintings. It's a first for Richard, and I feel as if I am seeing them through his eyes and share his exhilaration.

Steve Martin's in Chicago, too, performing at a giant convention center. Richard's at a smaller but considerably more prestigious hall that he's sold out, getting rave reviews. The local media have been trying to stir up some sort of pseudo-competition between them. Richard wants to check out Steve's show and when we walk into the huge space Steve is in the middle of his King Tut routine. The entire audience is on its feet, going wild.

Right away I realize that Richard will take this personally and I feel bad for him. I am right; he is furious. He believes that he should be playing the larger hall and blames the fact that he isn't on racism.

I tell Richard that his is a class act while Steve's humor is somewhat mediocre. But Richard's in a determined sulk. Later that night, when Steve drops by our suite I sense that he feels eclipsed by Richard's talent while Richard feels outdone by the size of Steve's audience. They cannot connect at all. At one point, Steve wanders into the bedroom and starts counting Richard's shoes. Richard joins him and together they count shoes until Steve says an awkward good-bye.

In a few days, I leave, too.

This time Richard's in Dallas, and when I get there he tells me he's been unfaithful again—with an actress who plays a cocktail waitress on "Dallas." I can't understand this because I know he's in love with me. But I also see that Richard's beginning to show the strain of being on the road. He's drinking more and playing Tarzan—swinging on the vines of his own dark twisted moods. He says he wants to make a movie about his life and asks for my help.

163

I'm happy to hear it. *This* kind of introspection is good for him. Usually, he just refuses to get out of bed, withdrawing from me, from life.

He starts talking about his mother and the whorehouse. "I looked through the keyhole and there she was. My mother was making love with another man." He tells me that after she and Buck had split up, Gertrude had taken him to live on her parents' farm in Springfield, Illinois. One of his happiest childhood memories was getting up at four o'clock in the morning to the smell of coffee and biscuits and going off to work with his grandfather while it was still dark.

"I'd wish you'd known my mother. I took her to Saks and bought her a pocketbook before she came to see me on the 'Merv Griffin Show.' "

Richard also tells me that Gertrude's grandmother was white and that he got to meet her once. He and his grandfather took a trip to the Missouri mountains to visit her. "She was a nice lady," he says.

After one show, Hollywood Henderson, Mr. Dallas Cowboy himself, comes by to visit. He's blitzed out of his skull and seems lost; there are no socks on his swollen, cut-up feet and ankles.

Back to L.A., and then I rejoin Richard in New York. He does a few nights at City Center with Patti LaBelle opening. Even though she doesn't drive, he loves her so much that he gives her a pink Cadillac. We visit Miles Davis in his hospital suite. "When you going to marry the bitch?" he asks in that gravelly voice from hell.

One evening, we stop by Studio 54. My old friend Halston's there, very stoned and very grand, and he greets me coolly. Richard sees this and demands I do something. "Are you going to let him get away with that?"

I know that if I don't do anything, Richard will, so I say, "Hey, Halston, what's up? Richard thinks you're being rude."

He lavishes apologies, saying that he wasn't sure it was me. "Oh, darling, do come sit with us. You know I love you. Go get Richard."

I do but am immediately sorry. Jacqueline Bisset is at Halston's table, dressed in a skin-tight, leopard print, jumpsuit. Real subtle. She and Richard begin flirting like crazy and naturally I get half-insane, have no fun at all, and drink too much. Richard and I start a cold war. By the time we reach the Regency, it's a full-fledged, mostly silent, war. Our exchange is brief.

"Why do you insist on flirting with women in front of me?"

"It's your fucking imagination."

"Oh, yeah, Richard, she was practically fucking the couch and you were almost coming in your pants! In fact what's that spot?"

He runs into the bedroom, slams the door, and bolts it. Shit, what now? I hear some small noises and then some big crashes. I pound on the door but he won't let me in. Finally, he opens it and I rush in, seeing the window is open halfway, furniture's been tossed around, and a mirror is broken.

"What the fuck? . . . Richard!"

"I tried jumping out the window but it wouldn't open far enough. New York—I guess they figure people will try that." I can't believe this.

"So you settled for destroying the room?"

"I'll pay for it."

That old blackism—"He pays the cost to be the boss." I put on a sexy black nightgown and slip into bed beside him, hoping to seduce him back into my arms, my love, and a better state of mind. It works.

So does star power. The hotel management is surprisingly nice about the room and Richard pays more than a pretty penny.

But he's still in a bit of a sulk. He feels pressure too easily and lets it get to him. And often, he sees having to deal with my emotions as another form of pressure. But suicide?

I go to Bendel's for a clothes fix.

October

By the time I return to L.A., I'm having bad cramps and go straight to the doctor. My pregnancy test is negative; he puts in a new IUD. Richard comes home for a quick visit and one night while we're making love, I'm overcome with pain and nausea. I begin to bleed. My first thought is *pregnant*, but that's not possible. I go back to the doctor. He says my IUD is fine and that it's all in my head.

We hightail it over to Hana for a few days R & R. One night I end up in the emergency room after waking up doubled over with cramps. We're both scared. At the hospital, they find nothing wrong, but they don't examine me thoroughly either because it's too painful. At LAX, I'm taken off the plane in a wheelchair, unable to walk. This is getting ridiculous. Back to my doctor. He removes the IUD, gives me more blood tests, and says, "Even though you're down four pints of blood, you're fine," and tells me not to worry. But I am worried and I'm in pain. He seems so damn casual. And he's flirtatious, saying things like, "How's that Panama Canal today?"

Still, I believe this genius of Camden Drive. After all, I'm supposed to have faith in doctors. I deny my instincts and trust him.

A few days later I meet Richard in Washington, D.C. where he's been performing at the Kennedy Center to great critical acclaim. Playing the center is prestigious and it's symbolic of just how far he and his work have come. Richard is interviewed by the *Washington Post*. He loves being taken this seriously.

In our suite at the Watergate we watch Sammy Davis perform on Jerry Lewis's telethon. Richard calls in a donation of one hundred thousand dollars and Sammy and Jerry are visibly shocked. I also think it's a tad excessive but I know that Richard's doing this to show what a good guy he is. He keeps asking me, "Did they like that, Jenny?"

Later in the show, I see Jerry pat his wife on the head, which is really condescending. Now I'm sorry that Richard's given him anything. I return to L.A. My pain has begun again. I see that Jim Jones has just offed a ton of his followers with a batch of nuclear punch and I feel as if I've swallowed some, too. It's raining and I'm frightened.

November

First thing in the morning I go to another doctor who examines me. He says it looks like an ectopic pregnancy, and sends me to the hospital for a sonogram. He meets me there—my right fallopian tube has ruptured and I'm bleeding to death. I've been pregnant in the tube for about six weeks. Six weeks! He says he's as surprised as I am. Jesus—travelling, jogging, making love, an IUD, laxatives! I'm amazed I'm still alive. He needs to operate immediately.

You're down four pints of blood but you're fine. That fuck of a doctor on Camden Drive! Surgery is scheduled for tomorrow morning.

When Richard is told he demands the doctor wait until he can be with me. He cancels concerts and flies all night, making it in time, although there's guilt to deal with. Richard's in trouble with the family. Mama's in the hospital and they can't believe he's visiting me and not her.

The last thing I see is his frightened face as I disappear into the operating room. All I remember is someone knocking over an IV stand. I come to as they're wheeling me out and I hear myself asking, "Am I okay?"

One nurse responds. "Ignore her, she's out of it."

Now I'm yelling, "No I'm not, I just want to know if I'm fucking okay or not!"

I see Richard. He's looking down at me and laughing. "My sweet Irish bitch."

He's beaming, there are tears in his eyes and he's holding flowers. Thank God. I am alive, feisty, and with the man I love. He kisses me and hands me a note.

In this note Richard tells me how deeply he loves me. But the most important part is that he is fighting the racism and fears of commitment that have kept us apart and that he wants to transcend these problems as much as I do. Never has anyone ever written me anything so beautiful and so heartfelt.

In my hospital room I'm given a shot of Demerol and then I pass out. But whispering voices waken me during the night. Richard isn't on the cot next to me. He's in the hall, talking to an orderly.

"Please, I need it. I'm a wreck."

"I'll see what I can do."

I yell for him. "Richard, what are you doing?"

"Jen, quiet. Shsh. My family's so mad at me for being here. I just want a shot to ease the pain." I don't understand. I nod off. Again, I am awakened by whispers.

"Please, just one shot of Demerol." I can't believe it—he's actually trying to score!

Someone finally gives him his shot and he passes out. I am furious. He's selfish and inconsiderate. The focus always has to be on him. I am happy to see him leave the following morning.

Dr. Kezerian says that I'm lucky. I could have, should have, died.

Richard is sad about our "muscle tissue". I think having a child is a big deal and we're not stable enough. Richard's bothered by this and tells me, "You just don't love me enough."

December

A month later we fly to Peoria to keep an appointment with death. Mama is barely hanging on. It's as though she's been waiting for Richard so she could die. Maybe that's why he kept putting the visits off.

It's snowing. The whole family is waiting at the hospital. *Richard has finally come*, are the unspoken words. All their pain looks so studied that I have a hard time believing in it. Perhaps they're really feeling relief. The matriarch who has controlled everybody is now dying—God has her on the mat.

Richard's in her room for about an hour. Then, he calls me in. Shit. Mama is a tremendously proud woman. She doesn't want youth walking in to watch death come and take her. I stand by the bed and feel sorry for her as Richard orders her to say hello to me. She turns her frail head and looks embarrassed. Her lips move but no sound comes out. I don't understand what he's doing. He seems to relish this moment and I wonder if it's payback time.

She mutters something, then reaches for Richard's coat-sleeve and asks him, "Is this warm?"

"Yes, Mama, it's warm."

Mama tells him, "It feels like blue azure."

Then tears are running down Richard's face. I'm relieved when he gently nods his head toward the door, indicating that it's time for me to leave so that they can be alone. I am halfway to the door when Richard calls to me. "Jenny."

I stop in my tracks and look back, confused.

"I love you, Jenny." The air is stinging. I smile sheepishly.

Mama twists her head away. A little more pain for your journey, Mama. Richard has made his point, which is *I'm with her, Mama. And there's not a thing you can do about it 'cause you're dying*.

In some strange way, part of this has been healthy—at least for Richard. That poor, old, mean, stubborn woman.

We go down the street to the hotel after leaving instructions to call us if there's any change. When the call comes in the middle of the night, it's still snowing.

We go back to the hotel and order breakfast. Richard sits, staring out the window. He points to a building and counts fifteen stories up. "I saw a man fall out of that window when I was about nine. No one believed me. I know someone pushed him." Then he tells me that one childhood Christmas he got angry about his gifts and lit a fire in the house. A few years later, he set fire to the fence that surrounded the house of a neighbor who was trying to put his grandmother out of business.

On the way to the airport, we stop by Mama's house. The grieving has begun and much "after death" cooking is going on. It is strange to be back here now that she's gone.

In a few days Richard has to return for the funeral. I have an audition, the first in a long time, and anyway, I don't want to go. He accuses me of having a lover. I have to convince him that I don't. Then I have to convince him that it's okay if I don't go.

"But what will my family think?"

"Who cares? They hate me anyway."

Richard's still mad at me for not attending Mama's funeral, and I didn't get the small role in George Hamilton's *Love at First Bite*.

Some of Richard's performances in L.A. are being filmed for a concert movie and tonight the Long Beach Arena is packed. The air is electric. He's asked me to appear with him in the opening segment as he gets out of the car and walks into the hall. Sweet, but what I'd really like is a credit for my major contribution. Richard gives an inspired performance. Other dates include a benefit show for a charity of Jane Fonda's, which will complete his court-ordered "community service." Backstage, with her husband Tom Hayden very much in tow, Jane flirts openly with Richard. When she leaves, he explodes. "She's a rich, white, rude bitch. Just 'cause I'm doing something for her she thinks she owns me."

Christmas in Hana—thank God! There I read *The Autobiography of Malcolm X*, and for me this is the highlight of the trip. The evolution of Malcolm's outlook into such a profound and global understanding is inspiring. Richard's wanted me to read it to understand our differences and the particular pain and anger of being black. But I also learn from Malcolm that it is possible to transcend narrow-mindedness and the limitations of a collective diseased social consciousness. Now I no longer feel so guilty for being white. We always believed that we can overcome the issue of color and problems connected to it. This is proof—a guide to higher consciousness.

On this trip, our twenty-six foot Harpoon day-sailor arrives and we name it *The Jenny Lee*. We're determined to sail it, although we've been warned that the waters in this area are formidable even for the most seasoned sailors.

The big day arrives—the baptism of the *The Jenny Lee* in Hana Bay. What a nightmare! I used to sail with my father but my skills are definitely rusty, which infuriates Richard as I've assured him I can manage. He's angry about his own ineptness *and* he doesn't know how to swim. We also have an audience: the pressure is on! We set ourselves adrift. The rigging is a mess. The tiller won't steer and the small engine won't start. We're sloshing around the bay, losing our tempers. If I tell him what to do, he screams at me, threatening to burn the boat the first chance he gets. When he tells me what to do, I yell. Finally as Hana Bay and *The Jenny Lee* are about to become one, Richard climbs out of the boat—fully clothed, down to the red leather boots. Through chest-deep water he churns back to shore, barking, "You be captain, motherfucker." I'm left alone on the boat, humiliated and wet. The audience enjoys a good laugh.

When I get back to the bungalow, Richard's well into a bottle of vodka, crying about Mama.

We give up sailing and return to fishing at our favorite spot, a rocky cliff leading down to the sea. One day, a very large fish shows up that Richard swears he knows from a previous expedition. Smart fish! Swimming from rock pool to rock pool, it always gets the bait but never takes the hook. Richard vows not to be outdone by a fish. He goes to the Jeep and gets a spear, walks into the slippery pool—in yet another pair of $800 Maud Frizons—jabs at the water, and curses, "I'll show you motherfucker, take my bait all afternoon!"

Clearly this fish enjoyed fucking with Richard, finally swimming out to sea to giggle with his scaly friends. Richard is obsessed. The day after, he has a new, grander plan. He rigs up four poles with six separate hooks, bait, and weights, which he secures into the ground with iron fishing rod holders. Each hook has been meticulously wrapped with fresh squid. After three hours of preparation, he is finally ready to cast his first pole, to get that fish! "Jenny, watch," Richard says as he stands on the cliff, takes a deep breath and lets the line rip—out it goes and goes and goes, the heaviness of the bait, hooks, and weights breaking the line. The heartbreaking sight of Captain Ahab going down in defeat makes me fall down laughing. Richard turns around, so sad, so forlorn. I couldn't have loved him more.

Christmas in Hana has been good, but Richard's grief over Mama is profound and I fear that our happiness will be difficult to sustain.

L.A. Life begins to percolate.

1979

January

New Year's Eve Richard is furious with me for talking back to him in front of some guests. Macho madness! Dinner at Sammy's house where he tells me how good I am for Richard. I don't ask the obvious. "Yeah, but is he good for me?" He gives me a little black leather purse with a penny in it, telling me, "As long as you have this, you'll never be broke."

Richard does a very bizarre "Merv Griffin Show" where Eartha Kitt, reeking of booze, literally climbs all over him during her number. Richard tells the tale of *The Jenny Lee* and talks about how in love he is.

February

Richard Pryor—Live in Concert opens to rave reviews and long lines at the box office. Richard has finally "crossed over." When his double album *Wanted* is released, it goes gold immediately.

I'm still waiting for a thank you. NADA! Not only nada, but every picture of me inside the album jacket is missing my head! No credit is one thing, but to cut off my head seems overly hostile and sends me into a mild rage.

Offers begin pouring in. Huge deals are proposed for Richard to develop his own projects, write his own contract. He's the flavor of the month, of the year. The pressure is on, and when *California Suite* opens it simply adds to it. There's a glitzy, star-studded, screening-dinner benefit and Army Archer's on his podium outside the theatre, doing his legendary Hollywood greeting of the stars. Army grabs Richard, asks him to say a few words, then shoves the mike under my nose. "And who is this young lady and what does she think?"

I want to kick him in his condescending ass. Instead I mutter, "Richard will be brilliant." Can't go wrong praising "my man."

In the lobby we run into Ray Stark, the film's producer, who introduces us to Governor and Mrs. Reagan. The governor seems genuinely excited about meeting Richard and shakes his hand with warmth and enthusiasm. Despite his politics, I can't help liking him. Mrs. Reagan, on the other hand, retreats slightly as she takes his hand. Richard feels the chill and backs off, too.

Among the people at our table are Ray, Gore Vidal and his companion Howard Austin, Sue Mengers, Marsha Mason, and her husband Neil Simon, who wrote *California Suite* and Mike Mindlin, a writer friend of mine.

The dinner starts off with Ray showering Richard with praise. "You were so brilliant in your concert movie . . . You can do whatever you want to with me . . . I know you are a genius . . . I will tailor-make projects for you."

Then Ray decides to ask me what I think of *California Suite*. Richard gives Ray a look and says, "Ray, do you really want to know what she thinks? 'Cause she tells the truth."

"Of course, I want to know. Come on, tell me what you think, Jennifer."

I take a deep breath and wonder why Richard is encouraging me to be outrageous. I mean, he likes my bluntness until he doesn't like it. But he also likes to stir things up. Am I his conduit? His executioner? Of course I rise to the occasion.

"Well, for starters, I thought all that silly slapstick tennis stuff that Bill, Richard, and their wives do was gratuitous and actually a bit racist. The white people in the film weren't acting so goofy. Don't you think?"

I finish and no one says a word or moves. Then Richard asks Ray, "What's gratuitous?"

Ray is visibly miffed and answers Richard without taking his eyes off me. "Unnecessary."

Richard smiles. "Told ya!"

Now I'm nervous; there's a look in Ray's eyes that tells me he wants a payback. Unfortunately, he's got some ammo. Richard had mentioned earlier that I'd been in *The Sunshine Boys*, which Ray also produced.

"You were in *Sunshine Boys*, right?"

Here it is.

"Right."

"And what did you do?"

"I was Richard Benjamin's wife." I can feel the color rising in my cheeks and pray that he'll back off.

"Oh, yes. That very little part." Then Ray turns to Sue Mengers. "Hey, Sue, did you know that Jennifer was in *The Sunshine Boys*? Hey, Neil, guess what? Remember that little part you added. . . ?"

Richard turns to Ray. "Okay, Ray, now you can stop it. You've made your point." There was such familiarity in the way Richard says this. Some weird fucking camaraderie.

Ray looks at Richard as if to say, *What the fuck are you talking about?* Then he shoots me a look that screams, *Payback's a bitch, dear.* I am being humiliated for having done a small role. The bottom line is that Ray wants me to feel ashamed for not being a star. That's his weapon. I'm completely uptight and miserable.

The evening disintegrates even further when I see that Marsha Mason is overtly flirting with Richard. And I mean *overtly*. Richard is flirting back! Oh boy, this is turning into the gala from Hell. She's so obvious that Neil begins whispering in her ear. She's cocking her head and stretching, her arms high above her head, effecting phony yawns and keeping her eyes on Richard for the entire stretch. If I weren't so angry, I'd be embarrassed for her. Richard's mesmerized, keeping his eyes glued to ol' Marsha, and he's wiggling, too. I'm shaking. The Simons are arguing. Richard and Marsha are posturing. Something about it makes me think, "The two stars at the table *have* to seduce each other." And I'm disappointed—I'd always thought of her as a class act. I ask Richard to cut it out and he insists that he "doesn't know what I'm talking about." I am so furious that I can't tell if the others are aware of what's going on.

Gore probably isn't because he's too busy being larger than life. Before he speaks he looks to see who's listening, sure of his audience, delivering his pronouncements slowly and deliberately. The intellectual elder-statesman loves all this Hollywood stuff. Corpulent, jolly Sue Mengers, the honcho Hollywood agent, is busy hustling, waving at invisible people far across the room, and being kissed by table-hoppers. Ray seems consumed with his success and accepts congratulations as though he's found the cure for Alzheimer's. Poor Neil is unsuccessfully trying to edit the Marsha and Richard B-movie. I've had it. "Richard, this is too degrading. I want to go home."

As we wait for our limousine, the Simons are also waiting for theirs. Marsha uses this last opportunity to wiggle and writhe against a column in the underground garage. Richard and I don't talk the entire way home and then I confront him. "How could you?"

He looks perplexed, shakes his head in disbelief and disgust, and leaves me to deal with this by myself.

I don't sleep a wink. In the morning I jog five miles to diffuse the rage but it doesn't work. Ray calls later in the day to say that Marsha would like to do a project with Richard—probably called *Sit on My Face*. She calls to invite us for dinner. Richard accepts. I refuse to go and he sends her flowers in our place. During the day, he gets together with her and Ray and Neil to discuss the project. It's an interracial love story about a piano teacher and her student—Richard would be the student. I explode again. *We've* been talking about doing a project like this and now Richard acts as if he doesn't know what I'm talking about.

I've begun escaping to my apartment and I'm taking acting classes—trying to resurrect at least a desire for a career. So Richard's been getting mad at me a lot lately for what he sees as my "neglect," and he's started pulling some power plays. His favorite is to cut off my charge accounts and credit cards, which at times has been really embarrassing.

Richard's mood swings are getting worse. I try anything—jokes, imitations—to pull him out of his frightening anger or sulks. Since I know that a lot of these feelings have to do with Mama, I've been getting him gifts that you'd ordinarily get for a child—toys, stuffed animals—and I tuck little love notes into the packages. Often these will brighten him up for a while. Recently I got him a frou-frou doll. I don't know what possessed me to buy it. It's kind of a grotesque little object—blond, a heavily-painted face, and dressed like a whore. But Richard just loves it and maybe that's why; it's a symbol of all the whores he's ever known.

One night I dress up in six different costumes trying to lift his spirits—everything from cowgirl with garter belt, stockings, and cowboy boots to glamour girl, naked under a see-through gown, to his favorite, my imitation of him as the wizard in *The Wizard of Oz*, shuffling around in his oversized shoes. The result is nothing, except that I see how far I'll go to get him to love me. He pouts, I press on. That, of course, is what he adores. Then he finally says, sadly, almost whispering, "My father always said, 'You know a woman loves you when she puts on your shoes.' "

God, if that's as far as we've come . . . but my heart melts.

Ray Stark has been sending scripts almost daily. I read them and give Richard a brief synopsis, along with my opinion. Most are forgettable. Richard says he wants to do something special. After a discussion with Ray he brings up two good ideas. One is *The Toy*, which would be a remake of the French film, *Le Jouet*. The other is based on the story of the "Men of the Bronze," an all-black infantry from World War II. Ray offers me the job of associate producer if I can convince Richard to do *The Toy*. The offer isn't up front and it feels sleazy. I suddenly feel guilty and tell Richard about Ray's proposal. But he surprises me and asks me to stay with the project. He's involved in pre-production on *Family Dreams* and, besides that, he doesn't have much interest in anything other than cocaine. He's been doing a lot lately.

Then, one evening, there's a blow up. Richard is doing a benefit with Muhammad Ali, which entails staging a fight. He dreads it and drinks many glasses of vodka before he even gets dressed. When I suggest that he "cool it," I become the object of his rage. All hell breaks loose. He grabs my diary and my phone book and chucks them into the living room fire. Then he runs into my closets and slashes all my clothes. Not satisfied with murdering my wardrobe, he rips the watch off my wrist and smashes it. Then he comes after the diamond studs, trying to tear them out of my ears. Just as suddenly, he calms down and leaves. I inspect the gashes and rips in my Armanis, Basiles, and my thousand-dollar, worn-once, cracked-ice pants.

A few hours later, I get a phone call from my old friend, Waylon Jennings. "Jesus, Jennifer, how the hell are you?"

"Waylon, how did you get this number?"

"Your man gave it to me. I'm here at this benefit myself. He's just raving about how much he loves you. Damn, I should've known he was with someone like you. He's lookin' good. You're takin' real good care of him, Jen."

Go figure. Music to my bloody ears.

The drugs may be obliterating some hidden pain, but they're exacerbating Richard's highs and lows, which are becoming more extreme, and triggering days of dark mean silent depression. Even his language is changing; it's getting obscure. He's talking more in his "blackisms," and when I don't understand what he's saying, he refuses to tell me what he means. Instead, he dismisses me by saying things like, "Well, you're *white*, baby," and not giving me a chance. I can't stand this withholding. We are making love less and less and I feel more and more like the nurse.

All our fights are so unspecific, the odd remark triggers a battle and at the drop of a hat there's a slap in the face or a punch in the ribs—usually mine—and a smashing of windows. I'm beginning to smash windows, too. At least we're keeping the glass man happy. But what am I doing? Is this some sort of weird exorcism for me too? Richard claims that he's learning from these trips to hell so I try to tolerate them, I try to understand.

Tonight he calls while he's with a hooker. "God, Jenny, I don't know why I'm here."

"Well, why do you think?"

"I guess I'm trying to be macho . . . part of being black, you know." He's laughing nervously, stoned to the tits.

"Richard, why don't you come home?"

"Sometimes, Jenny, it really scares me, how I feel about you. It's easier being here with a stranger and talking about you than actually being with you and loving you the way I do."

"Richard, come home."

"Can I?"

"Yes, Richard. I love you."

A couple of nights later, he calls from Sandy Gallin's house, where he's in a meeting with Cher and Sandy, about a spot on her show. A famous C & W singer is also there, someone I've adored for years. Richard knows that I'm a fan and puts her on the phone. We have a silly non-chat chat. Several hours later, he arrives home blitzed out of his skull, vomiting on the front lawn and moaning about how mortified he is because the C & W star tried to give him a blow job, but he had been far too drunk to "get it up." She literally threw him out of the house.

February

Richard has made the fatal mistake of taking me to Lotty's* house. So whenever he's missing, I know where he is and I drive down the 405 and pick him up. The only problem is, he's spending more and more time there and he's stopped coming home to me.

Lotty's house is a depressing, beige cracker-box bungalow decorated with wall-to-wall rust-colored shag carpeting, imitation Ethan

Allen furniture, and mustard-colored fiberglass drapes that are always drawn. Two black Dobermans are kept behind a chain-link fence in the back. They claw at the patch of dirt yard, always barking.

A badly permed, heavily made-up, bleached-blond valley girl, Lotty is short and thin, and wears baby-blue polyester jogging suits from K mart or Jordache jeans with black satin shirts and black high heels. She has a slight tremor, smokes Merit menthols, and smiles only rarely and then just from the side of her mouth. She serves her guests water and Coca-Cola in green-tinted glasses, acting more like a waitress than a hostess. She's not very bright, either. She breaks the cardinal rule of a good drug dealer; she gets high on her own product; and it is good product. Lotty is also one of the loneliest people I've ever met. She has no personality, identity, or sexuality; she's a blank, white wall upon which her "clients" can write anything. They're her only source of love and affection; when they're whacked out of their skulls, she seduces them.

Coke dealers have an edge; you just don't pay for the dope, you pay for wanting it too. They get paid in cash and in guilt. You snort their "private stash" and pretend that you're not a coke-hound; even if it weren't for the enormous mound of white powder in front of you, you'd be there having this inane conversation. Sure! You might discuss things like the nuclear freeze or the political direction that China is taking. Yeah, a regular bunch of Henry Kissingers with white-walled nasal passages.

Lotty has found a good thing in Richard. I start going nuts, even smashing things. My reactions only strengthen her hold. Night after night I make an absolute fool of myself. One evening I go back and forth at least twenty times, pounding on the door, only the Dobies responding. When Richard finally comes home, we make love and then fight. I get hit in the chest and stabbed in the elbow. I go to the hospital—no stitches required, no cracked ribs.

I'm obsessed and out of control, so how can I make sense out of this uncontrollable situation? I try. And God, the profound humiliation. Richard's even told me to "get lost" in front of this drug diva. And I'm so scared. The good times and the love are worth fighting for, and I *am* fighting, but it all seems to be slipping through our fingers anyway. Everything is conspiring to wreak havoc. Our love is a misguided rocket imploding, erupting, and dissipating in front of my eyes. We're jumping up and down on the inside of each other's souls, breaking our hearts, one piece at a time.

I'm doing my share of drugs, too, but I'm the "healthy" addict. I binge, then I work out, sleep, and generally continue to function. I mean, I'm the "controlled" drug user, watching Richard spin off the map while asking him to stop.

Things are escalating. He's over at Lotty's all the time now and I don't even bother to go after him. I just pray it will find it's own natural end since neither he nor I are able to stop him. Richard has even started bringing Lotty to the house, adding insult to injury. One evening as they're about to leave I say, "Wait a minute, I've got something for you, Lotty . . ." and I give her the damn frou-frou doll. I tell her, "It looks like you." And she's so stupid, she thinks it's a compliment.

And it *does* look like her. The doll is pale, has blond frou-frou hair, and a huge black beauty mark near its mouth. It's dressed in cheap-sexy clothes—a low-cut blue bustier, white pantaloons and high black lace-up boots. I get little satisfaction from this private joke. God, this hurts but what can I do? Richard's disappearing, his appetite for cocaine is increasing, and his behavior is becoming more bizarre and erratic. He is not only enamored with his dope but his dope dealer, unable to tell them apart any longer. Sex between us has cooled, but I have also known for some time that Richard has trouble with the idea that sex and love can be mutually compatible. And I do feel threatened by Lotty even though I know he's not *in* love. He is sleeping with her, practically living at the coke cottage and going off the deep end. I have to let go or I'll go crazy, so I'm trying to stop reacting but Richard keeps turning up the level of pain. He demands a response. He seems to need constant proof of my anguish. "She lets me be who I am," he challenges.

I can't believe it! "Oh, please, you pay her for that shit. You're her fucking john."

"Maybe I like the way she makes me feel. Maybe I like being her john."

"Maybe you like being a 'john,' period." Coke can make sex supernatural or impossible. I figure that the two of them must be getting into some high-tech kink.

Still losing ground. Richard's stoned and taking a bubble bath. While he's in the tub, he shaves off half his mustache. He's acting so weird; it's beyond the mere high. "What are you doing?" I ask. Now he's dressing, putting on this major happy act, singing to himself, being overly jolly.

"I'm going out."

"To Lotty's?"

"Maybe, maybe not."

Now he's dressed: red Adidas jogging suit, silver Nikes, and top hat. Top hat? What a sight! And with only half a moustache! I guess he is going jogging-over to Lotty's. God, the *last* thing he needs is to get any higher.

I can feel the iron hand of Mama pulling him into the grave. Richard is completely out of control. Time to do something. I call Uncle Dicky and Dr. Cannon.

I talk to Richard about getting help. Thank God, he says he needs it. He'll enter the hospital under the Doctor's care for the time-honored Hollywood euphemistic condition, "exhaustion."

But the night he's supposed to go in he changes his mind. Uncle Dicky's here and he tries his best, but Richard won't be convinced. Time for a new tactic. I put on my sexiest gold ankle strap shoes, silk gypsy skirt, skinny halter top, and seduce him into going. Me, the angel dominatrix—I make tender but raunchy love with him, telling him how he has to be a "good boy," and do what I say. He's high and just loves being submissive.

February 16

In the hospital, Richard's kept sedated, and has daily sessions with Dr. Cannon dealing with his compulsive behavior. Every day I arrive with a gourmet dinner and afterward, we make love in the hospital bed—which I like! Nothing like forbidden sex.

I also like the fact that Richard's in the hospital. He's safe and I know where he is. The mood elevators he's taking have him on the top floor. Meanwhile, I've kept the whole matter a secret. Mostly, this means taking care of the ex-wives. One night, an especially mad ex-wife calls demanding to know where Richard is. "I can't tell you, but tell me what you need. I'll take care of it."

"Bitch, you tell me where the fuck Richard is or I'll blow your motherfucking brains out." That silly, tough act. I hand the phone to Uncle Dicky.

After Richard's release from the hospital, we come straight to

Hana—Dr. Cannon's orders—so he can finish recuperating. Is this the only place where we can be sane and happy together?

Dr. Cannon has also suggested that we take a trip to Africa and become more a part of the world. Good idea! We decide to go to Kenya. I return to L.A. early in order to plan the trip. Richard stays in Hana reading *Origins* by Richard Leakey. When he gets back to L.A, he's excited, full of hope, and being very loving. Before we can leave, though, Richard has one last obligation to fulfill—"The Barbara Walters Show."

April 7

Everything is ready. Barbara's producer has called to ask about the color scheme of the house so Barbara can "dress to match." The crew arrives at nine A.M. Barbara comes later with her hair and make-up people. She seems very excited, almost nervous. I like her. Richard is wired and is drinking in order to relax. Liz and Rain are here; they'll be in a shot or two. And I'll be in a couple of shots for the opening segment.

When the actual interview begins, Richard's drunk and far too candid. He also announces to the world that his only marriage was to Deboragh. Of course, Richard has been married many times before but not to Maxine, Elizabeth's mother. Both Lizzy and Rain are devastated by the statement. Throughout the taping, Richard is his most iconoclastic self. Barbara swoons as he flirts with her—raving about her "robin's-egg-blue eyes," and saying, "You should always only wear that color."

Everybody seems to have enjoyed themselves and agrees that it's a good interview. While they pack up, I'm outside talking to one of the guys on the crew, and Richard sees us. He walks right over and accuses me of flirting. They all see the monster coming and make major tracks to get the hell out of there—in the nick of fucking time. Richard starts his interior house demolition, while Rain and Elizabeth, looking frightened and helpless, watch. This rampage seems to last forever. Our feet get cut on shards of broken glass—the good Doctor to the rescue.

The next morning Richard takes me to a Rolls-Royce dealer and tells me to pick out one as a make-up present for his behavior. I tell him it won't work. I just want to go on our trip.

But before we go, I ask Richard to get the damn frou-frou doll back from Lotty. As much as I can't stand the thing, I also don't want any part of Richard to remain in that coke-cottage. I want it to be a clean break. He agrees and sends a friend over to pick it up.

Easter Sunday

On the long flight to Africa, we decide to make a lot of changes, beginning with a new, clean-freak maid. We will create a civilized life together; the bad is behind us; our love is worth saving and the future is waiting.

We get a connecting flight out of Nairobi and late in the afternoon we arrive in the Mombasa Airport. We've arranged to have a driver meet us there who will take us to the house we've rented for a week.

The "Mercedes-with-a-driver" turns out to be an unaircondi-tioned Audi driven by the perplexed-looking "Lawrence," who speaks little English. We improvise.

In blistering heat, we ride through the countryside, the small villages, and the city of Mombasa. Seemingly endless stalls line the streets selling food, fabric, and "high fashion" shoes. The side-walks spill over with people, weaving in and out—full-bodied women and lean men sway sensually, gangly children run about, all in varying tones and shades of brown and black. The women wear colorful fabrics wrapped around their hips and carry baskets on their heads. Many have babies on their backs. The men wear shorts or pieces of cloth wrapped like sarongs, and some add ill-fitting sports jackets to the ensemble. Some of the young girls add mildly disturbing versions of Western-style platform shoes to their outfits. Home for these people is in the mud huts along the road, or in the uniformly packed-and-stacked government-owned buildings that bookend the city, or in the small rooms above the shops with the ever-present colorful fabrics flying from cracked balconies.

We take a jammed ferry across a swollen, muddy river and finally we're on the narrow dirt road leading to the place we'll call home. A white, elderly, very obviously alcoholic lady with an English accent greets us—think of any Tennessee Williams play! She speaks halt-ingly, weighs about four and a half pounds, and looks like a wind-blown sand dune—she's definitely been here a little too long. We follow her shaky lead to our "complex of rooms." Wait! We'd rented a house! Worse yet, these rooms look like they're from a horror movie set—run-down, dark, smelling of mildew and ammonia. The doors have new locks, but they'll never do! I'm already having visions of being macheted in my sleep by one of the men who'd been peering at us from behind the trees. To top it off, the Indian Ocean—"right outside your door"—is so far away it looks like a blue dot on a map. "Oh," says the Concierge from Hell, "sometimes the beach is bathable but when it's not you can use the pool at the Leopard Beach Motel."

Then Richard decides he absolutely must use the bathroom. I go to the car. Two minutes later, he comes running down the road and jumps in. "There was a giant lizard in the toilet staring back at me!"

We hightail it out of there without saying good-bye and without knowing where we're going.

Although there are many hotels along the coast, they all look alike. In our jet lag and paranoia, we are certain that the wrong choice could mean death. Finally, we leave it to Lawrence, who's growing wary of us.

Three and a half days after leaving LAX we go to sleep, only to be awakened a few hours later by the mad buzzing of flies. We go downstairs for a drink and sit by the edge of the Indian Ocean, holding hands under the palm trees and staring at the shadows they cast in the sand. Richard kisses my toes and it's all worth it. Despite the bad beginning, we're happy and in love.

But at breakfast, Richard picks a fight, two fights, and then stalks away. After about fifteen minutes Richard returns, refusing to speak to me. He orders another omelet, eats, and then takes me back to the room, telling me that he wants to fly to Nairobi. Alone. At this point, I honestly couldn't give a fuck. Twenty minutes later he calls from the lobby to ask what I'm doing. I join him and his profound sulk. The flights are all booked. He takes the room key, saying that he'll be right back. I wait for him for over an hour, then go to the room, where I find him lying on the bed. I ask him to please stop whatever it is he's doing and just let us love each other. Says Richard, "I don't love you. I love Deboragh."

"Do you mean it?"

"With all my heart!"

I try not to react and tell him I'm going to the beach. Then he threatens to hit me. "I don't love Deboragh, I was just saying that."

Well, he's finally got my attention now and I decide to turn the fucking tables. "I'm taking the night train to Nairobi. When you're through sulking, you can join me there."

I start packing my suitcase. Every time I put something in it, he dumps it on the floor. This mean slapstick routine continues until I figure out that all I really need is my pocketbook. As I'm walking out the door, he rips the bag off my shoulder and empties it onto the floor. We both dive for it and end up wrestling over the contents. He gets hold of my passport and starts ripping it page by page while I futilely try and rescue it. I go into my full-tilt stubborn mode. "Fuck it! I'll go to the U.S. Embassy and get a new one!"

As I start out the door, Richard flings himself at my feet and grabs my ankles, holding on for dear life. "Please, don't leave me, I love you so much."

When I look down at him, my heart melts. I'm his once again, and all else is forgotten. "That's all you need to say. I don't want to go either."

We make love and go have a nice dinner. But, as usual, things are okay only for a short time. By breakfast we are quarrelling. Then through lunch, then through dinner. His moodiness is unbearable.

Finally, we leave Mombasa for Nairobi, driving the car ourselves. On the way, we stop for lunch, drink in the scenery, and otherwise enjoy one another's company.

We check into the Nairobi Hilton, which doesn't make me happy. I want something with some charm, while Richard demands immediate comfort and sleep—which he does for endless hours, for days. I hit the streets, wandering through open-air markets, buying colorful fabrics and straw bags, and sitting in the cafes sipping espresso and eating pastry. Nairobi is a sophisticated city, with a very European feel to it. There are lots of mixed-race groups. And, everywhere there are people in love—kissing and hugging one another.

But why am I alone? Well, I mustn't feel sorry for myself, if I have to be alone, why not here? I consider myself lucky. Lucky and alone.

In the afternoons, I check in on Richard; usually he's still sleeping. I toss some of the fabulous pastry at him and take off. I don't want to sulk with him. He says he's afraid of being recognized. So far though, only two people have—a couple of exiles from Uganda who'd seen him in *Silver Streak*. I really think that he's just intimidated by the newness and blackness of it all.

I manage to drag Richard to the Leakey Museum, where we see the sorts of things we'd read about. It's amazing for both of us, but Richard's real epiphany occurs when we get back to the hotel. We've just returned from the museum, he's looking around and suddenly, he stops.

"Jennifer, there are no niggers here." I'm not sure what he means. I'm standing there, too, looking around the hotel lobby. It's full of people, mostly black, who are milling about. He tells me again.

"There are no niggers. They have so much self-respect." I understand. He finally got it. "Jenny, black people run this country."

In general, Richard's mood is improving and we're getting along much better. So we're going to go on to Treetops Lodge in the Aberdare National Park. We drive a couple of hours outside Nairobi, where we're met by a guide who takes us by Range Rover to another summit. From here we walk to Treetops. It's amazing, a hotel perched high in the branches of a group of Cape Chestnuts. The accommodations are tiny cabins—it's like being on a ship in the trees. Monkeys are climbing everywhere, the cabin windows are covered with wire mesh to keep them from pilfering your luggage. Their inquisitive, adorable faces peer through the screens at you. The big event, though, is at sunset, when the elephants, rhino, buffalo, and gazelles come to the pool below us to drink and hang out. The photo freaks go ape.

The rooftop of the lodge is the best; you can play with the primates who swarm the visitors. I love it, though Richard can't wait to leave. He finds it all much too confining and unprivate. I think he's mad 'cause he can't sleep as much as he wants! He gets testy when one smelly tourist asks to use our shower. We have one of the few on board. "No way!" he says. Good thing we're just here overnight.

We go back to Nairobi and get ready for our final road trip. The night before leaving for the Maasai Mara Reserve, we have dinner at the Red Bull Inn. The owner, an American exile pseudo-hippie, asks Richard if he knows Gordon Parks, Sr. He explains that he'd become friends with Gordon, Jr. when he came here to make a documentary; during filming, Gordon, Jr. was killed in a plane crash. The restauranteur had been photographed with Gordon, Jr. the week before his death and wanted Richard to deliver this very special "last" photograph to Gordon, Sr. It's a black-and-white snapshot, faded and out of focus (as if prophesizing tragedy).

Richard has never given it to Gordon, saying that it's just too damn sad.

We start out bright and early for the Keekerook Lodge, northwest of Nairobi, in the very heart of Maasai territory. The lodge is said to have good food, good service, and comfortable accommodations. We are given a map and directions and are told that it'll be about a two- to-three-hour drive. We set off in our un-airconditioned Audi, happy, looking forward to this new adventure. But, we get lost before we're out of the Nairobi city limits. I'm trying to read the map and am giving very confusing directions. Making matters worse is the fact that the steering wheel's on the right side of the car. In no time, the Travelling Fighters are at it again.

Eventually, we find the right road and drive out of civilization . . . and drive and drive. Four hours later, there's still no sign of anything except more miles of rough road. I'm very nervous and not just because we seem to be going nowhere. Richard's driving fast and recklessly. When I ask him to slow down, he drives even faster. Then, on one stretch of macadam, we see an old black man, wrapped in a red blanket, standing by the side of the road, raising and lowering his arms in a slow, authoritative rhythm. No way we wouldn't stop for an old Maasai tribesman, his demeanor ancient, domestic, and humble. Before we know what's happening, he climbs into the back seat with complete alacrity. He has neither fear nor self-consciousness; it's as though we've been sent to pick him up and he motions for us to continue down the road. We can't decipher the sounds he is making, but through his looks and gestures we somehow understand everything. A thick, blasting, musty aroma has filled the car and after a few moments I recognize the smell. This man is wrapped in layers of time; it's the odor of centuries, of eternity itself. A mile or so later he motions for us to stop, climbs out of the car and disappears into some thick green terrain, leaving behind a scent . . . something I know will linger in my soul.

We drive on, growing more nervous with each mile. We don't say a word but we can hear each other thinking "gas" and "nighttime." Finally, we come to a checkpoint where a Maasai dressed in camouflage gear stands in front of the wood-slatted gate. Holding a clipboard, he walks up to the car and points to a space on the paper. He is distant, aloof. I sign. He swings open the gate.

Suddenly, it's as if we've driven onto a movie set. A vast space of flat, green land, filled with sculpted trees and moving shadows, rolls out before us. Even the clouds seem bigger, closer, and faster moving. I remember the line, "I had a farm in Africa, at the foot of the Ngong Hills."

I look at Richard. He looks at me. We're here together and yet somehow all alone. The rigors and awesome beauty of this land is almost shrill in its intensity. Richard grabs my arm. "We're in the jungle, Jenny."

Then, out of nowhere, galloping giraffes, ambling elephants, leaping gazelle, hundreds of wildebeests, and swooping birds. I'm looking for the Assistant Director who I *know* is somewhere behind this backdrop, shouting into a megaphone, ". . . okay! Now the rhinos!"

We are stunned by the sight of God and tired from all our driving. Still, neither of us dares ask the obvious, "Where the fuck is Keeker-ook?"

Yes, we're on the reserve, but there's over seven hundred square miles of it! The sun's about to set and so's the gas tank. Our silence tells all. Are we lost? True panic is about to set in when we come to a fork in the road. We see another car—only the second one we've seen since we started out—then we see the smallest sign in the world. It says KEEKEROOK and has a painted red arrow pointing the way. The very nice Indian couple in the other car tells us—yes—we're going in the right direction. The lodge is about an hour away. Thank God. But driving in Africa is like driving in Texas—an hour usually means three. They also tell us that we're lucky; within a couple of miles there's a pride of lions who've just eaten and are relaxing by the side of the road. Richard perks up. I just want to get to the lodge and a drink.

Three young Maasai boys are also at this intersection; I give them each a shilling and take their picture. The oldest one, obviously the leader, begins to imitate Richard, saying "One shilling, one shilling, one shilling." We all laugh. As I give him one of the photographs, he admires my diamond and ruby ring, a gift from Richard. One of the younger ones looks at it and begins tugging at my finger, trying to pull it off. Funny, until I want my hand back! Richard thinks this entire exchange is brilliant and takes a picture.

*   *   *

We keep on driving, until suddenly we hear a loud bang. Flat tire! My first thought, *The Lions!* Richard opens the trunk and starts pulling out tools and the spare. This is a frightening thought—the only thing I've ever seen him change is his clothes. Then, the invisible A.D. yells, "Bring on the Maasai!" Suddenly, in the distance, a sea of red blankets is moving towards us. I remember a William Burroughs line, "Paranoia is knowing the facts." Richard tries to keep his cool. "I'm sure they're friendly."

That's so stupid I think. Well Richard, they had better be, 'cause there sure are a lot of them."

He looks at them. "I see your point."

He quickly packs up and we drive down the road a few miles. Since I know that there are lions around here, I suggest that we travel the rest of the way to Keekerook on the rim of the tire. It's a stupid idea, especially since we don't have a clue as to how far it is.

We find a flat piece of road and again Richard opens the trunk and arranges the tools. I'm really nervous, about everything, though the lions definitely top the list. Richard suggests that I act as lookout and watch the nearby herd of gazelle. If they start to run, then the lions must be coming. I keep my eyes glued to—epoxied to—these dainty little antelope. Every time one twitches or looks skyward, I scream, "Richard, one moved!"

At the same time I keep looking over my shoulder to make sure that the wandering sea of red blankets isn't bearing down on us. I'm a complete wreck. Richard calmly displays a manly talent, surprising us both by changing the first tire of his life. Richard's proud and I'm relieved. Now all we have to do is . . . Just get to the fucking lodge.

We're back on the road not five minutes when we come up on the pride of lions. I hope that the A.D. has the animal handler nearby. Richard's elated; I'm not. "Jenny, my God, look at them."

They are magnificent. About a half-dozen large, lethargic *bad-*looking beasts are lolling on the grass as if they've just enjoyed some enormous feast. Some are sleeping, some are just hanging out; it's clear to me that they just want to be left alone. Richard doesn't see it this way. As we get closer, he slows the car down to a crawl. When we are smack dab in front of them he stops the car completely. I can't believe it. "Richard, don't you think this is a tad close?" He's already busy getting the camera ready. "No, Jenny. This is great."

Then he rolls down the window.

"Richard, I don't really think this is a hot idea."

He's begun taking pictures. "Ssshh Jenny! You'll disturb them."

"No, Richard, I think *you're* doing a good enough job of that." Then I think, just hang on, it'll be over in a few minutes. Suddenly, I see him reach for the handle; I grab his T-shirt. "Richard, what the hell are you doing?" He jerks his arm free and continues to open the door. "I'm going to get a better picture." In a shouting whisper I tell him, "That's absurd! You're already so close. You're going to really piss them off."

The door is open. He pivots his body around and slowly places his legs, one at a time, on the ground.

Loudly I hiss, "Richard, what in God's name?"

"Ssshh, bitch, I'm getting out. You blind?"

Oh, no. "No . . ."

Disturbed by our conversation, a lion lifts its gigantic head. As Richard begins to stand, the lion gives him a look that says "What is this stupid motherfucker doing?"

One last shot at saving our lives—I grab his shorts. "Please, don't do this Richard."

Again he jerks himself free, looking at me with contempt. Then, as he sees the terror in my eyes, his hostility turns to pleasure. He is enjoying my fear—I think that maybe he really *is* nuts. In fact, it suddenly occurs to me that my fear may be motivating him. I can't say a word. Instead I pull the keys out of the ignition. Richard's smile becomes even more sadistic since it's obvious that this pathetic attempt to do something can't do anything. My only recourse is to pray and to let him act out whatever madness he has in his mind. I can't control him. I look away for several seconds and when I turn back, Richard's standing some five feet away from the beasts—snapping away, bending, leaning in, and testing the gods yet one more time. As he moves even closer to the animals, one looks directly at him and stretches out a huge paw, as if to say, "You can get hurt!"

Richard looks back at me, grinning devilishly. My terror fuels him, gives him courage to press on. Suddenly, in unison—where's that animal handler?—all the other lions awake to Richard's presence. They look perplexed and bothered. I'm praying faster! Then, in one

188

quick fluid motion, a lion stands up. Richard is finally scared. He races back to the car, dives in, rolls up the window, steps on the gas, and we're outta there.

Without even thinking, I box his ears. I am so furious that he's put our lives in such danger. He can do it with his own, but he doesn't have the right to do it with mine! I scream at him all the rest of the way to Keekerook. He gloats, says it made him feel like a man.

"I go out on my soil. *My* soil, Jenny, and let my ancestors off my back. This is my motherfucking country Jenny and I brought them all home. I am an African Man."

Oh, please! I want to kill him.

"You were almost a fucking dead African man."

We pass through two more checkpoints, each manned by Maasai tribesmen dressed in camouflage. (Maasai are easily recognizable with their long, twisted earlobes.) At another checkpoint, a tribeswoman walks up to my side of the car and stares at me. Wrapped in that thin red fabric, she's tall and lean with arms and legs for days. Her twisted and pulled earlobes hang down to her shoulders and her braided hair is coated with red clay. Colorful beads adorn her ears, head, neck, arms, and wrists. I think she is the ultimate in chic. She takes the sunglasses off my face and tries them on. She is mesmerized by me. "Jenny, she wants to take you home." Men! Thinking about threesomes, even in the middle of the bush.

Richard raves on and on about his ancestors and his achievements until we finally get to Keekerook and get that much-needed drink. Then the manager of the lodge approaches him. Not only is it extremely dangerous to get out of a vehicle on the reserve, it's also illegal. But *nothing* can dampen Richard's glorious sense of male accomplishment. Even in the shower he's singing, "Oh, yes, I'm a magic man for what I did . . . I'm the best there is for what I did . . . ho, ho, ho. I'm black and I'm brave, oh yes I am."

Over the next few days, a guide drives us around in a Range Rover, where we watch cheetahs, wildebeests, monkeys, giraffes, water buffalo, elephants, hippos, jackals, and secretary birds. Richard's favorite moment is seeing a lion attack and devour a Cape buffalo. And always, there's the elegant, majestic presence of the Maasai men and women.

This morning at breakfast, just when I'm counting my blessings,

Richard orders a martini. Trouble ahead. Then the poor waiter brings him sausage with his eggs. Richard detests "pig." Instead of sending it back or pushing it to one side—my stupid suggestion—he decides to "show me" by wolfing it down, then vomiting it back onto his plate. Charming and very attractive, I must say. I guess things have been going too smoothly. Serenity—too frightening a concept for him. Richard can't stand it, so he's off looking for his demons. Maybe he really is possessed!

I dodge his mood swings and manage to enjoy the rest of our stay, which includes sunsets, great food, feeding monkeys by the pool. And, after our wild fights, making love, which is as eternal and full of promise as the land we are in. When our stay is over, we leave Keekerook and the reserve almost uneventfully. But first, Richard has to roll down the car window, to bid farewell to the sixty-foot spitting cobra slithering across the road.

Back in Nairobi, we purchase a ton of African art and ship it home. But leaving Kenya is not as easy as entering.

We are scheduled to take a 747 night-flight to London and then Concorde-it to New York. A few minutes after we board, a stewardess announces that the fuel tanks on our plane don't hold enough to make the trip to London. "You know, the good ones with the Rolls-Royce engines, they're all in London. But with the help of God, we'll get you there."

Then a mechanical problem occurs—something about fuel spewing out of the tanks in torrents, drenching the wings.

"Everybody off until we know what's going on and have it remedied." In the lounge we have cocktails and naps. We notice that, for some reason, there's an abundance of gun-toting soldiers in the airport. We've been growing more paranoid by the minute anyway. This only adds to the tension.

Back on the plane, Miss Doomsday Stewardess is entertaining us with horror stories. There's one about a co-worker of hers who'd been walking in Nairobi one night when two men accosted her. They chopped off her finger in order to get her big diamond engagement ring (I wonder if the fiancé married the girl with nine fingers?). Miss Doomsday is going on and on. I want to kill her, or at least tell her to shut up. Then, as the doors are closing, she tells us the fuel tanks have been repaired and that we're on our way to Rome. Rome? ". . . to refuel. Rome is beautiful this time of year. Have you been?"

BOOM! SLAM! BAM! The doors close, my heart sinks, and the engines rev as we begin traveling down the runway in what I'm now convinced is Death Plane. I know Richard's feeling the same but he's keeping quiet. We're picking up speed, moving faster, faster down the runway. I start hyperventilating. I look at Richard and manage to say, "I want to get off this plane. It's going to crash."

That's all he needs to hear. He looks at me, stunned, as though at this moment I am imbued with psychic powers. He raises his hands as if he's asking for the check.

"Stewardess?"

"Yes, Mr. Pyror. Can I help you?"

"Yes. You see my wife is not feeling very well and we would like to get off the plane."

"I'm afraid that won't be possible. We're about to take off," she says in her clipped English accent.

I believe this premonition—or my first panic attack—means inevitable death. I imagine me and everybody else on board hurling towards the oblivion below, falling amid a storm of clothes and shoes spilling out of the broken luggage. I'm in a full-tilt panic, sweating like crazy and now Richard has "contact" paranoia.

"Well, then I would like to speak to someone in charge."

"What's wrong with your wife?"

"She has an infection, she has some stomach problems."

By now everyone in the first class section is staring at us. They are unruffled.

The stewardess tells Richard that we have to wait until we get to Rome. He won't accept this and scrambles over me, in search of someone in charge. Now I'm beginning to feel a little embarrassed by starting this panic. I turn and see Richard talking to the "honcho" steward. I motion for him to come back and take his seat. He gives me a cold hard look that says, "Bitch, you started this shit. Don't you dare back out on me now."

I know him well enough to know *he* won't back down. He disappears up the stairs, in the direction of the cockpit.

We continue to taxi down the runway. I'm trembling. Finally Richard reappears, sits next to me, and says in sotto voice, "Pretend you're very sick."

Christ, I don't have to pretend.

"Richard, what did you do?"

"I told them I had a bomb."

The plane suddenly does a 180-degree turn.

"YOU WHAT?"

"They didn't believe me, but they weren't quite sure. Anyway, I don't know what they're going to do."

To think I had started all this! All eyes are on us. You could hear a pin drop.

"I told them if they didn't believe me, then they can believe I am a very rich black man who would sue their white asses off them and their fucking airline. I'll see to it they'd never fly again."

Now I am really terrified. The plane comes to an abrupt stop in the middle of the tarmac. The captain himself escorts us off the plane. We climb down the long ladder; uniformed soldiers are at the bottom ready for us. When we get inside there are all sorts of suits standing around, waiting to talk to Richard. I excuse myself, go into the bathroom, stick my whole hand down my throat and begin wretching and gagging so violently they could hear me in Dripping Springs. In the meantime, Richard is telling them some fantastic tale of chronic illness, medicine left in some hotel room. Suddenly, everybody has become very helpful, although I see some skeptical faces among the believers . . . . Narrow escape!

Some quick arrangements are made and we're driven to the Norfolk Hotel, back in Nairobi. At some point during the ride, Richard becomes convinced that the driver is a spy and that the car, that *everything* is bugged. He won't let me talk until we get to our room and even then I'm only permitted to whisper. The first words out of my mouth are, "Richard, I wish you wouldn't drink so much."

He hits the ceiling. "Bitch, I got you off that fucking plane." I apologize, but he's mad.

We search and search—of course, we don't find any bugs—but he stays paranoid about it . . . all night. And he stays mad at me . . . all night. I whisper "I'm sorry" until dawn.

And when Richard wants to punish there's no one better. He can wear me down to the point where I can truly believe the bad weather is my fault. And he stays mad, for days until I've expressed the proper submissiveness, proving my endless love and devotion. Sometimes all this love and devotion is a hair shirt.

The following evening we check through customs. We answer all of their questions. We do not carry any of the local currency, as it's against the law. We're especially careful because we're still being watched. When we get to our seats Richard takes off one of his shoes and hands it to me. Stuck inside is a wad of Kenyan money.

May

Back in New York City at the Regency Hotel, Richard and I stuff ourselves with good old American junk food and watch movies. After planning and canceling the trip several times, Richard finally accompanies me back home to Cropseyville to meet the family. In the Albany airport, a woman practically knocks me down trying to get to him. "I'm Rose, I'm so glad to meet you, Richard." We are amazed at her rudeness, in contrast to the courtesy we'd experienced from women in Africa. They would never speak to Richard without addressing me as well. There I felt like a person, here I am an accessory. Richard tells her, "You're rude, Rose. This is my lady, Jennifer." Africa has left its mark.

On our way to the house from the airport, Richard looks slightly alarmed. He's worried about being in "red-neck country," but our house is safe. My family is not simply a bunch of "white liberals," they put their money where their mouths are. And there is absolutely no sense of awkwardness as it relates to Richard's color—I know that Richard feels this too. I love my family for that.

We eat Yvonne's salty quiche as my father and Richard tell stories and laugh. Richard is considering developing a project on Attica and they start talking about problems in the prison system. Harry tells Richard, "The men in the National Guard who have been called out to man the prisons relate better to the prisoners than do the career corrections officers." Richard replies, "Well, that makes sense. Prisoners are in for three-to-five, five-to-seven, seven-to-fifteen. They get out, but those corrections officers are in there for life. What do you think it would do to someone, looking up a guy's asshole day in and day out?" Dad gets that slow grin on his face, finishes chewing, and says, "They probably get tunnel vision!" They both crack up. They seem to genuinely like each other and I have to do little to help conversation along. They are at ease, sharing their similar sense of irreverent humor. I watch Richard smoke his Marlboros and Harry suck on his pipe and think that they are both handsome men, charismatic and sensual, real ladies' men. Each is in control, each commands attention, each a King. I am enjoying this and see that my being with Richard is no accident.

Though I've brought men home before, Dad knows this is serious and is giving it the appropriate respect. No one acts surprised by Richard. In fact, my family expects the outrageous from me, they accept it and even celebrate it. After all, I am my father's daughter. Yvonne seems slightly thrown by Richard and very eager to please. Her children, K.K. and Caroline, are definitely impressed by his celebrity. Richard is not thrilled with K.K. and later on tells me, "God, that skinny little bitch tortures your brother, ya know! I don't know how he takes it."

Unfortunately, this is true. The teasing is part of a subtle and cruel flirtation that K.K. has going on here. In fact, she started as soon as they moved in. Even though they're not related by blood, K.K. and Byron are "step" brother and sister.

Byron is awed by Richard and gives him a treasured beaded antique Indian pouch as a memento of this meeting. Richard is grateful, but I can see that he doesn't fully understand how significant his visit is. Byron is an unusual young man. He's very sensitive and seems wounded and lost much of the time. I worry that his struggle is sometimes too much for him. He's talented and creative and if he identifies with Richard, that's good. He needs to see that others even more alone in the world than himself have survived the pain: survived and triumphed.

Being back home has a way of bringing me right back to my childhood as if my adult life had never existed. Richard takes a seemingly endless nap in my old bedroom, which provokes Yvonne to comment, "He likes to sleep, huh?" After I get him up, Harry takes him for a long walk in the pasture, while Byron and I tag along behind. I watch them walking, talking, and laughing, and I am again moved by how alike they are.

Richard asks my father how he'd feel about our having children, which is funny, since I've decided that I don't want any. Then it occurs to me that he's testing my Dad, who gently tells him, "Richard, I care about Jennifer's happiness and well-being." Aah. He does not disappoint. He means it. If having children is what I want and the relationship is stable, why not? Harry says this in a fatherly tone and I can see that Richard appreciates it and that he respects Harry for his honesty, acceptance, and love. I know I do!

We are back in L.A., where it becomes clear to us that Richard's outspoken position on racist buzz-words—i.e. the fact that he is dropping the word "nigger" from his vocabulary—is a source of confusion and even anger in the black community. He's told *Jet* magazine: "The word is really like a branding iron and when you . . . examine it you see it's nothing. If I can do something to help get its usage stopped, I'd appreciate that." There is much comment on this from the media, his fellow comics, and even his close friends. Paul Mooney and David Banks tell him that the talk is that he's jumping ship. It seems that some fear they are losing Richard as their strident black voice and they want to remind him that despite his ever-increasing celebrity, he still belongs to his brothers and sisters—to the streets. Some of his comments about our relationship, which he made in the Barbara Walters interview, were also excerpted in the *Jet* article. These have caused even more anger. "We went through the racism together. We went through a lot of stuff together and found out that we really have souls and we are people." Richard has said time and again that the soul has no color, that love is love no matter what boundaries it crosses. But I am shocked to find that a lot of black people are angry about our relationship, and that sometimes he is asked, "Why don't you like black girls?" I'm sure that there are some pissed-off white people too, but we haven't heard from them.

Richard is hurt and confused by all of this and he's feeling more vulnerable than ever. A stranger at the gate put him absolutely on edge. I have had an alarm system installed and have mega-lights put up all around the grounds, which now resembles a compound. He has gotten some wacko letters filled with veiled threats and I see the terror in his eyes when a too-ardent fan approaches. I feel his fear and I have it, too. No one says it, but we think: *Richard could be killed*. His paranoia is making him retreat from his new outspoken position. He has simply dropped the subject, saying that the idea of giving up racism "frightens some people and that it's not for everybody," adding that "you can piss people off really easily." So, he no longer discusses it. After a bold emergence as a leader, it's a queasy and furtive withdrawal.

Lately, I've been on the receiving end of Richard's paranoia. If I even slightly challenge him, he demands that I give him back "his" rings. Or he'll simply grab the chain off my neck or snap the band to my watch. He teaches me the true meaning of "give and take." Impulsive and cruel. He's got to reestablish his power somehow.

Being back in L.A. has also reestablished our use of the "white lady." We're just recreational users, going easy during the week and saving our big all-nighters for the weekends. Good old Joe has been supplying us, or I'll pick up a packet from a friend, but we're not buying in any quantity. Coke is all over this town and we're making an effort to keep ourselves under control.

May 9

The decision to hire a new housekeeper keeps getting put off. I am determined to press the issue, especially since Mercy has come upstairs to Richard, complaining, "I no more want to wash Jennifer's underwear. A real lady does this herself." Richard looks at me as though this is reasonable. I am in a state of disbelief. Fuming, I tell her, "Well, in my house, people's cotton drawers get put in the washing machine. So, Mercy, you can continue to *wash my underwear.*" Since then, we've been locking horns over everything. Then, one morning I'm sitting in the bedroom nursing the frayed nerves of an all-nighter. Mercy brings in Richard's breakfast tray and while placing it on his lap makes an ill-timed, off-side remark to me. I pick up the gauntlet. "You know, Mercy, I know about you and Mr. Pryor rolling around on the floor, kissing during *Greased Lightning.*"

That's all I need to say. The tray goes flying—eggs, bacon, toast, and milk drip from the ceiling and cling to the walls. I look at Richard. "Well, you said you were going to fire her."

He looks as if he wants to kill me. In a voice filled with contempt, he calmly says, "I lied."

That's it! I walk over to the window and with systemic madness begin punching out the small leaded-glass panes. Crash! Crack! Pow! Richard begins running down the hall. I follow furiously behind him, dripping blood on the yolk-splattered carpet. He yells to Mercy to call the police. We all end up in the upstairs office screaming at one another. It's a familiar scene but Mercy overplays her hand. "Mr. Pryor I call the police. They be here any minute."

Richard is just as shocked as I am. Bad judgment call. I pick up the phone, call the accountants, and arrange for Mercy to be fired and given two weeks' severance pay. Richard picks up the extension and says, "Who's the boss here? That's right, make it a month's." (This is funny. Obviously, the accountant has said, "You, Mr. Pryor," which is all that Richard needed to hear.)

In fifteen minutes, Mercy is gone. Twenty minutes later, the police arrive and I greet them with a bloody towel wrapped around my hand. I tell them that we've had only a "small domestic squabble," but these fellows are all business and they won't leave until they're sure that Mr. Pryor is all right. I can't believe it! Then I have to beg Richard to come downstairs and prove that he's in one piece. I drive myself to the hospital where I get five stitches in my hand. When they ask what happened, I tell the partial truth—I don't have to protect Richard. "Lost my temper and crashed through a plate glass window." When I get home, Richard gives me a "whipping" with his African shillelagh, then we make great love. Oh, yeah!

May 11

Richard does "The Johnny Carson Show," talks all about Africa, his new outlook, and gives the shillelagh to Johnny. Thank God! Good help *is* hard to find and after an arduous search, I hire Carmen, a sweet young El Salvadoran who's been working at the house on weekends.

Richard's been sending me flowers.

We visit Sammy and Alto. They invite us to go with them to the SHARE benefit and rope Richard into performing.

May 19

It's a theme benefit so we all dress up in Beverly Hills-style cowboy garb. I should feel ashamed. Sammy does a little tap dance wearing six-shooters and a cowboy hat, which looks as if it will swallow him up. Richard does a routine all about the word "fuck," and everybody loves it. Alto performs as well and she kicks up her legs with the best of them. She does seem awfully large for Sammy. The audience, a sea of bolo ties and suede fringe, cheers and applauds.

May 29

"The Barbara Walters Show" airs. Richard is happy and I'm relieved.

May 30

Richard has a terrible nose bleed. He gets into an angry snit with me and leaves with David Banks. When he returns, he smashes the shutters in the bedroom and asks David to please take me out—he's afraid he'll beat me up. I return and all is well again.

Flowers from Richard.

June 2

We go to some sort of promotion on the Paramount lot where Richard performs. At the end of the evening, we sit in a trailer with Don Simpson and get stoned. Suddenly, Don and I are in a horrible fight—over what, I've no idea. We're all cranked, so there's no telling. But Richard decides that our anger is a cover-up for something equally intense—like sexual attraction. Maybe, but it feels more like some sort of competition, Don's so damn arrogant. I've heard a rumor that he likes to get women coked up enough to play slave in the bedroom. This town goes from bad to worse.

June 4

Barbara Walters calls and asks how we liked the show. Then she asks a very sweet question. "What did your father think?" She says that she'd love to have a cup of tea with me some time. Even if she doesn't mean it, I like her.

June 5

When Richard arrives I'm in a bitchy mood and throw a bottle. Very dumb! He destroys some things and sulks. Our m.o. now is that I say something, which produces a morbid sulk and then, we're off to the races! But tonight we settle down to watch a horror movie; it's full of crypts and blowing dead leaves. We're all alone in this empty, eerily-silent house. Then I make a comment about his latest bout of destruction and we're in one more minor argument. I leave the bedroom in a mild huff. As I'm walking towards the kitchen, I hear a gunshot. My heart stops. I take two more steps and hear another. I know that there are six bullets in the .357 that Richard keeps by the bed; now four are left. I switch on the lamp in the back hallway, turn around, and see him walking slowly and deliberately towards me, not making a sound. He stops on the edge of the pink carpet, a few feet from me. Both hands are behind his back. He glares at me with eyes that look like two black holes. BAM! He pulls the trigger and the bullet hits the stucco wall behind him. Three bullets left. As he brings the hand with the gun around, he doesn't take his eyes off me. Then, slowly, the other one cradles the hand that holds the gun. Carefully, he aims the weapon straight at my forehead and cocks the trigger. He wears that .357 like a kidskin glove. I don't even breathe. Then in a deep, faraway voice he says, "Get out, bitch."

No problem.

I head out the back door, sit on the step, and light a cigarette. I think about what just didn't happen. I know Richard could have pulled that trigger. Twenty minutes later, I walk bravely back into the bedroom and confront him. "What the hell was that all about?"

"Oh, Jenny, I just wanted to scare you." Where have I heard this before?

"I'm so glad you didn't make me shoot you. I would've had to kill myself then." As though the *worst* thing that would have happened would have been his suicide, which would have been my fault too. I notice the frou-frou doll has a bullet hole in her foot. I take the gun and empty the chamber, keeping the remaining three bullets as a souvenir.

Shortly after the Barbara Walters show airs, we get a letter from two teenage girls who used to live here. They write that a previous owner's wife had turned up missing, the body never found. It's assumed she's buried on the property—have we come across it yet? Habeas Corpus Phobia sets in, fueling our not so rational coke-induced paranoia. It gets worse when I ask the handyman to tear down a small doll house that's on the front lawn. He looks it over and tells me, "I don't know why anyone would want to pour a solid two-foot foundation for a flimsy little plywood nothing." It is left standing, haunting us, particularly during long nights of drug use. But even some of the staff have heard "things that go bump in the night" during the day. I remember what Deboragh had said about the house.

June 7

I spend the day with Richard on the set of *In God We Trust*, which is directed by, and stars, Marty Feldman. It's an unprofessional set and Loretta, Marty's wife, treats some of the actors so badly, it's actually painful to watch. Two days work and Richard makes $50,000. Not bad!

June 8

Richard brings the Feldmans home with him. We're all sitting on the bedroom floor, drinking and doing coke, when Richard tells Loretta what I'd said about how she'd treated those actors. After a huge fight, the Feldmans leave and Richard sends flowers the next day. Loretta is a piece of work, in the overstated tradition of Tallulah Bankhead.

June 15

Lunch with Thelma Houston. Richard makes an off-side hostile remark and I spit in his face. The gun episode still festers. Richard is shocked and asks, "Why did you do that?" I tell him, "Six guesses and the first three don't count." This is completely lost on him and his righteous indignation!

June 18

Richard goes off to Hana for some time alone before the on-slaught of work on *Family Dreams*. He begins taking flying lessons that I figure is a fast, easy way to die.

I find out through Louisa, my friend and spy at Hana Ranch Hotel, that Richard is sleeping with an overweight and blond hippie by the name of Starlight*. He met her when she was babysitting for Sidney's Poitier's and Joanna Shimkus's children. By now, I am accustomed to other women, but not in Hana.

June 21

Hana. We have dinner with the Poitiers—who I think are uptight. Joanna tells me that she had children only after she'd "had a career." Message to my statement that I don't want any kids? A woman isn't complete unless she has children?

I meet Starlight. She wears great big muu muus and flowers behind her ears—a real passive-aggressive type who smiles sweetly. I tell her that it's over! She gives me the kind of "gotcha" smile that a vampire might after drinking your blood—or sucking your man's cock!

July 2

During this damage-control trip to Hana, we receive a call from Raul telling us that Ginger, Richard's miniature horse, is dead. Carmen had let her out to run in the orange grove but had forgotten that the Great Dane was out there too. Just like the Cape buffalo was eaten by the lion in the wild, Ginger had met her fate. Richard is very upset about this, but somehow I don't fully believe his grief. He liked the idea of Ginger better than Ginger herself. Ginger's appeal was that she was so unusual—he'd parade her out for company, but that was about it. Still, I feel horribly responsible. Richard agrees. It's all my fault.

July 8

Back to L.A. where I try out a few more cooks and maids. One refuses to wear shoes. Another one, when I ask her to please set the table, snaps, "I'll do it if I have the time." I settle on Dora, but *her* problem is that she doesn't speak English. I send her to Berlitz, but all she does is cry for her family in Peru. Who's the boss here, anyway?

New rule: Any violence or nasty behavior—no sleeping together. I think he's getting the idea—yeah, in my dreams!

Work on *Family Dreams*. One afternoon Roger Simon, the original writer, is ambushed by Richard and his cronies in a feeding frenzy of racist verbal abuse. He didn't deserve that. After an endless parade of writers and rewrites, Richard and I begin redoing the final shooting script. We are back in productive-land; working together is the kind of positive communication that we need. But when I ask for credit, I am told, "You've got a part in the movie. Go to the guild if you want credit."

We have a fight over this and he hits me on the left forearm with some new stick he's got. Off to the hospital for x-rays. I tell them I was "hit accidentally with a baseball bat." God, this is such a huge issue for Richard. What's wrong with giving me credit for the work I do? I've earned it. I've made some solid contributions to his career—beyond nursing him or loving him. Perhaps he feels that his creativity is being threatened; sharing his life is hard enough, sharing credit would be too much. Too intimate? Well, someday, I'll get mine when our relationship is all sorted out.

August 31

My birthday rolls around again and at dinner Richard gives me a diamond heart necklace in a music box. We return home to champagne and cocaine. Richard prefers cognac with his coke and drinks and snorts away. I am high enough to tease him. As he stretches out on the bed, I begin to play with the toes of one of his beautiful bare feet. He doesn't think this is funny and warns me, shaking his new stick, "Do that again, bitch, and you're in trouble."

It's my birthday, what could he do? Giggling, I ask, "What will you do?" assuming that the worst would be a whack with the stick. I tweak his big toe again.

Up in the air, flying off the bed, he's coming after me, cognac bottle in hand. He's got me, I'm backed up against the wall; he smashes me over the head with the half-filled bottle. I plant my feet on the ground and my hands turn into fists, as I try to fight back, but his rage and his bottle overcome me. All I can do is try to shield myself, trying to break the blows with my hands as he's hitting me on the head and on my face, again and again. I slide down the wall screaming, "Enough!" begging him to stop. He finally does and now I can feel the warm trickle of blood running down my forehead, into my eyes. I stumble into the bathroom, grab a towel and drive myself to Valley Presbyterian, where they are getting to know me pretty well. The doctor takes one look and demands to know, "Who did this to you?"

"None of your goddamned business, just stitch me up." Ever the cowgirl!

I decide to lie. "I fell down the stairs."

The young doctor is angry. He sutures my right temple while he delivers a lecture, which I ignore. "You better figure out why you let someone do this to you. Nobody has a right to do this to another human being . . ." Yeah, "real-life" drama-show dialogue.

When I return to the house, five stitches later, Richard's cooking breakfast and telling Rashon how I'd deserved the "whipping" I'd gotten. "Mama, I was just telling 'Shon how you provoked me."

I couldn't disagree more. "Yeah. Well, Richard, I'm sure the prisons are full of guys who say, 'The bitch made me do it.' "

The next thing I know he walks over to the table, picks up the family-size bottle of Worcestershire sauce and smashes me on the head. He grabs me by the hair, pulls me off the chair and onto the floor, and drags me around the kitchen, demanding an apology. "I'm sorry!" Rashon just sits and eats his eggs.

Several hours later, I wake up in the guest room and make the grim mistake of looking in the mirror. I don't recognize this person. I am lost; there is a mound of contorted flesh and discolored skin. The whites of my eyes are completely red. *Where am I? Who am I? Why?*

Richard is sorry. I will heal. Somehow we will find our way back to love. I believe this. He is sorry. Everything will be okay.

Jean Hancock has written a sweet birthday poem for me and she had it framed. I need comfort and go to find it, but I forgot that Richard is jealous of Jean and that he's smashed the frame. But I can still read it and I especially like the last verse:

> *I wish you happy birthday*
> *The best your life can be*
> *We pray and love for Richard*
> *And now for Jenny Lee.*

September 7

This last beating has taken something out of me. Besides the physical pain, I feel incredibly lonely.

Richard arrives home at 7:30 A.M. He's in a great mood, except for the fact that somebody tried to give him a blow job last night and it didn't work. I guess we're going to Maui, although I don't feel up to it.

September 12

Richard leaves without me. I go see a shrink whom I've no faith in.

September 14

Waylon calls. He talks about his four-month-old boy and tells me how much he really likes Richard. I really like Waylon. God, if he only knew that I'm sitting here all black and blue.

September 17

Fly to Hana, our private hospital, with red eyes, bulbous head, and broken heart. When anyone asks, I say "roller-skating accident."

September 18

Go to check on the house. It's looking great, but I'm told that someone's been stealing lumber. Richard carves our initials in a tree. Nice gesture, but somehow it just makes me feel more depressed. The house is lovely, but I can't conceive of us in it like this. What do I do?

September 21

What is the point? We don't really communicate. Our routine is to have a fit, walk away, go to sleep. I run, check on things, shop, run some more. I feel totally listless, but still I jog. Richard's out flying this morning and I go to the hospital to have the last two stitches removed. Now Richard's accusing me of trying to come between him and his relationships with everyone—including his family and Rashon. Then he says that I can't come between him and Rashon because Rashon's known him longer than me. Christ! That's an either/or situation if I've ever heard one! Either Richard's complaining about my neglect or about my interference. Perhaps I should go home. Richard feels it's an intrusion if I express myself and generally treats me terribly. We don't make love much anymore and I'm continually apologizing for everything or hating myself for taking so much. I've let him get away with beating me up, physically and emotionally, and it's damaged me in more ways than one. Although I can't imagine the end, I think it may be near.

September 24

Oz Scott, the director of *Family Dreams*, is here with his "lovely wife" for a project pow-wow. After dinner last night Richard decides to divulge the true nature of my red, black, and blue souvenirs. "Just tell them the truth, I beat you up. I beat her up."

And for dessert, he flirts madly with Oz's wife, who eats it up. The weird thing is that it doesn't seem to bother Oz; I suppose he sees it as part of his job. I've never really understood the terrible insecurity that drives men like Richard to compulsively seek sexual conquest. And all I seem to do is react and think it's because of me, trying to control it, trying to make him love me enough so he doesn't have to look elsewhere. After they leave, I beat Richard up and he lets me. I wish that I had the strength of ten men. Naturally, he won't speak to me now and I hate myself.

October 1

I have a dream—I'm receiving a standing ovation for being with Richard! Then I remember the "Award" he once gave me, a framed certificate, "For Love and Understanding."

Finally, he admits to me "If I had been beaten up the way I beat you up, I'd want to beat somebody up." We make good love and I make plans to go back to L.A. Richard will stay in Hana.

October 8

Hire Dina to help Dora—a maid for the maid! Richard has begun work on *Family Dreams* in Seattle. He's not only the star, he's also the executive producer. Days go by without a phone call, which is strange and anxiety-provoking. I am trying to exorcise all my feelings in acting class. I can feel my anger becoming dangerous and I've got to control it somehow.

I try talking to Berry Perkins about it but it's just making me feel worse. She's upset too, feeling neglected because Tony's been in London. We both cry and talk about getting on a plane and taking off.

October 13

I spend a small fortune at hip-expensive Maxfield Blues, score a couple of grams of coke, go to Universal to see Richard's first rushes, and on the way home get a porno magazine—for the ads. Then I call a hooker. She's got a broken leg, so I have to call another. So the hooker with the two good legs arrives and we proceed to have a totally and completely drug-crazed, decadent, debauched night. Before she leaves, I give her the frou-frou doll, telling her "It looks like you."

I feel liberated. First of all, I have acted out my own fantasies; I've never been alone with a girl before, it's always been with a man and at his request. Now I know how a man feels—the power of paying for someone and then sending them on their way. Richard won't like it, but because I was with a girl and not a guy he can't really feel threatened.

I call Richard and tell him everything.

October 15

I am summoned to Seattle. When I walk into the trailer, I see the pain in Richard's eyes and I know that I put it there. I have lived in a state of surreal denial for both of us for so long, holding on to normalcy amid the madness. His window to reality has turned into his mirror image and now all he can see is the abyss. I am in full-tilt guilt, once more lost in his pain, forgetting my own pain, or why

I'd done what I had, as I genuflect and whisper mea culpas like a thousand nuns.

I fly back and forth between Seattle and L.A. We cling to misery, not knowing what to do or how to let go. When I return to L.A. I go to my apartment and try to connect with old friends and routines. I tell no one what's really going on.

He's rented a beautiful house on a lake. It begins to look like a good place for a murder. I find out that on the nights he's supposed to be playing poker with some of the guys, he's been carrying on an affair with the tiny Polynesian actress he has asked me to coach. Richard has even come on to the housekeeper. During one fight over his new "lei," he stabs me in the knee and kicks me in the back. I have to stop at the hospital on the way to the airport.

Whenever I come here, all it does is rain. Go see *Apocalypse Now*—heads stuck in the dirt remind me of me. Marlon—brilliant, manipulative, psychotic—reminds me of Richard. Mayhem rules. Put an egg in the microwave and it blew up in my face. Cicely and Richard aren't getting along. She's puritanical and judgmental that goads him on to greater extremes. He's drinking and drugging and he's fighting with everybody; he's attacked a production manager with a two-by-four; he's even punched out Oz. A grip loses his legs in a freak accident. Someone has put a curse on this film. *Family Dreams* is a nightmare.

Despite it all, I look forward to my small part in the film. My last and most recent accomplishment, a song I co-wrote with Paul Jabara, "My Man Ain't Man Enough For Me," is being used on the soundtrack of *Honky Tonk Freeway*.

October 30

Today, in between takes for our last scene, Cicely walks over to me, bends down, and picks some lint off my skirt. This is a bit odd because she's mostly treated me disdainfully—I find this display of cautious respect utterly condescending. At 1:30 P.M., Richard shows up drunk, interrupting an otherwise smooth work experience. Thanks.

November 5

"Berserk Angel," a terrible article written by William Brashler about Richard's violence, appears in *Playboy*.

November 8

Richard comes home tonight drunk, which is not unusual, drinks some more, snorts some coke, throws his dinner into the sink, showers, dresses, and leaves. First he kisses me and seems to love the fact that I'm mad. All it does here is rain and I want to go home.

We make it to dry L.A. When Richard walks into the bedroom he immediately asks, "What's missing?"

My heart does cartwheels. I forgot to tell him about the frou-frou doll. "I gave the frou-frou doll to the frou-frou girl."

He gives me a horrified look. In an almost inaudible, menacing tone he tells me, "You gave my doll away? Get it back!"

I promise to find the damn doll. Despite it all, I think we're on the mend.

But new trouble arrives on a beautiful fall evening. Richard has called, begging me not to go anywhere, telling me he'll be home soon with a wonderful surprise. "Something you'll love."

I have to go out but the minute I walk into the house I know something is terribly wrong. It is ominously quiet . . . . the air is thick and still. I smell something strange. As I walk towards the bedroom, the smell gets stronger. I reach the bedroom and I can't believe my eyes. The pale pink, down comforter is ablaze in a horrible ring of fire and next to it stands Richard. He is transfixed, mesmerized by the flames. Pushing him out of the way, I grab a corner of the cover, drag it into the bathroom and shove it into the tub, turning on the faucets full force. The room fills with smoke as the mattress smolders, spitting and puffing. The horrible foul odor permeates the entire house. Rashon arrives and expertly removes it from the house. I am glad Richard is safe but I need to know what happened.

"I was just trying to light the pipe the way you're supposed to." He seems amazingly unruffled. "You see, Jenny, I guess the cotton swab was just too wet with the rum you're supposed to put on it . . . cause when I lit it, it dropped on the blanket and then . . ."

"Never mind, Richard. Why didn't you try and put it out?"

"I didn't know what to do, all I could do was watch. It's a good thing you came in when you did, Jenny."

The next month is full-tilt freebase. The dreaded pipe. The "devil's glass dick" has taken its place in our lives.

In the beginning, I am his partner in this painful pleasure. I even crawl around on the floor with him sometimes, looking for remnants of the baseballs and occasionally smoking bits of the carpet or fragments of plaster. But the drug excites me, which annoys Richard as I intrude on his fragile state of oblivion by wanting to make love. All he ever wants is to smoke more. He begins to pass me the pipe begrudgingly; less for me means more for him. This demon drug gives too much bliss to be wasted on someone who doesn't *really* appreciate it.

The devil has moved in. High on this stuff one night, I look out the window and see caped dwarfs and goblins wearing pointed hats and skull caps creeping out of the hedges. There is a veritable army of denizens of the dark, all coming after me like the zombies in *Night of the Living Dead*. Terrified, I call the police. When they arrive I take full advantage of their visit and lead them around the grounds in a frenzied search for my hedge people—actually grabbing the flashlight out of one of the officers' hands, sticking it into and under the bushes. But my dark creatures have disappeared and so, obviously, has my mind. I've never called the police before, even when I should have.

Freebase has a hold on my imagination and is having a field day. I can no longer function. After basing for two or three days straight, I pass out for the same amount of time and wake up in a soporific haze with new strands of gray hair that I have the housekeeper pluck out. My thin body has become "camp-like" and my nails are chipped and filled with dirt. The worst part is I don't care. Freebase is stealing the last of my pride and, it seems, my vanity.

I have stopped basing. This stuff is much too serious. I snort and Richard smokes. He is developing a conspiratorial and symbiotic relationship with this drug.

Every day gets crazier and more dangerous. Richard gets high and interrogates me. "You bought that doll for her, didn't you? Where did you really meet that hooker? Are you still seeing her?"

Obediently, I answer the questions over and over again; I am patient. As the drug use increases so does Richard's paranoia about the hooker. Drugs consume Richard and guilt consumes me.

One morning before he leaves, he actually tells me that if I could just find the right word, everything would be all right. This is not sane, there is no "word" but I search for it anyway.

Daily interrogations continue. Richard sleeps all day, wakes up, and sends Tommy, our well-connected driver, to pick up prepared base from Joe, paying outrageous sums of money for the drug and its delivery. Slowly, Rashon becomes drug-fetcher and then chief gourmet chef of the mad potion—anytime, day or night. It's looking like a real-life remake of *The Servant* in slow motion. Rashon takes more and more control as I begin to look in from the outside.

December 15

Joe, Jean Hancock, Richard, and I smoke until the base is gone. Jean leaves and returns with several packets, giving me one to snort. I retreat to the bedroom. Meanwhile, Jean had told Richard that she had a "special" packet just for him. But she can't find it, and then recalls the one she'd slipped to me. I'm snorting in the bedroom, playing my guitar. I keep dozing off, assuming it's simply bad dope. I'm on the nod and miss the knock at the door. Suddenly, Richard bursts into the room, ripping the door off its hinges to get to his "special" packet. Pieces of wood fly. In a rage, he throws me off the bed, demanding his secret powder.

Richard has learned to cook it. If he's not smoking, he's bent over the stove, a regular Julia Child. He is now getting the powder from Sophia*, an old friend of Richard's and Jean's. She lives in the Valley, in a run-down estate. She deals to the hip elite; jazz musicians and their wives. Sophia will voice her concern over Richard's freebasing but keeps her palm out—waiting for the cash. She plays the role of a heavy-set European earth mother, and supplies her "primo shit" in a homey setting of animals and kids. She even keeps a pot of soup boiling on the stove. A year ago, while Sophia and her husband were sucking on the devil's glass dick, her baby daughter fell into the pool and drowned. Sophia made an altar to the dead child and invests in future karma with Buddhist chants. She dispenses the following advice, "Chant and everything will be bliss. Look at Tina Turner, I got her to chant when Ike was trying to kill her and now everything is fine."

Things get even stranger. One day I walk in on Richard while his head is entangled in the legs of a hooker. I smash the chess

210

set. But somehow this episode ends humorously: Richard and the hooker move to the guest room and lock the doors. I go around to the outside, smash a few windows, and begin yelling. When he comes to the windows he begins yelling too—in pseudo-Italian. I follow his lead and we fall over laughing—Marcello Mastroianni and Sophia Loren in *Divorce Interracial Style*.

We are screechingly paranoid. One night we walk through the house clutching each other, and look up to see the orange face of the devil himself staring down at us from the office. In a grand gesture of resolution, Richard asks me to flush my stash down the toilet and throws his pipe away. The next day, he buys a new and bigger one.

He's supposed to do a small part, the Pharaoh, in *Wholly Moses*, which is being produced by an acquaintance of mine, Freddie Fields. Richard keeps putting it off, blaming me for his agreeing to do it. "I said I'd do this because he's a friend of yours. He used you to get to me, he was smart and you betrayed me."

December 21

Richard cancels again; I apologize again. Finally, I suggest he do this cameo when he returns from Christmas in Hana. Richard has decided that he'll "kick" while we are there.

I go on ahead with Rain and Elizabeth but Richard stays behind for a few extra days of drugs.

Christmas Day

Finally, he joins us on today, which has been awful. Richard tells me that he's considering having his Polynesian lover come to Hana. Over my dead body! (I'm sure that could be arranged!)

1980

New Year's Day

Big hotel party, get a bit tipsy, Richard and I go to sleep around 10:30, the kids stay up till about 1:00—everyone has fun. I love Richard so much. I resolve to love Richard, to help him find peace, growth, and happiness—*And all this for me too!*

A hurricane suddenly hits the island, knocking out electricity, telephone lines, washing out roads, and otherwise crippling Hana. We rough it and love it. The pioneer spirit brings us closer together. I cook our meals over a bunsen burner and we make love by candlelight. No deal-makers or drug dealers can get to us! But there's a bad dynamic going on between Rain and her father. She's good at manipulation and gets more attention than Elizabeth. One evening, I tell him that I feel the relationship is a deeply troubled one, which causes a minor outburst I happen to capture with the SX-70 that's in my lap: Richard in motion, rushing towards me, one arm slightly raised.

January 4

What a beautiful day! We all wake up happy and set off for the beach and swim, snorkel, and boogie-board. Richard wades out too far and almost doesn't get back. Fortunately, Helena, an old friend from New York, is there and she rescues him. Richard writes I LOVE YOU in the sand. The tide washes it away.

January 11

Ann-Margret and her husband Roger Smith are here. It's raining and we go for a picnic in the pasture overlooking the sea. Roger's a character, asking about the "magic mushrooms" that grow in Hana. Ann tells us how Roger took her up in a plane one day and threatened to crash it if she didn't agree to stay with him.

I fly with the kids to Honolulu and get them on their plane home. I shop, have dinner at Rex's, and feel good being away. Richard calls, furious, wondering why I hadn't phoned him yet. I get back to Hana and he is happy to see me. Richard fishes, fishes, fishes, and I go to the beach, beach, beach.

January 15

Richard's paranoid and in a bad humor. He's been clean for several weeks but last night, our last night here, he had a dream about freebase. I suggest that this is a pretty good indication that he's craving the drug. He hits me across the legs with a leather belt. We are now on our way back to L.A. God help us.

January 19

Tommy meets us at LAX in a white stretch. As we head towards the freeway, Richard instructs him to take us to Joe's. I can't believe it—just off the plane! I tell him, "Not me."

"You're coming," he says.

"No, Richard. I am not."

He tells Tommy to stop. My bags and I are put out at a Texaco station, leaving me to call for another car. He returns home a few hours later, high on base, with an evening's supply.

January 24

Richard was out all night. He calls this morning to say he's at someone's "magic" place, someone he's been with before. I hang up on him. He calls back to tell me that he's at my apartment—I forgot I'd given him a key. I call a car to get him. When he gets home, I put him to bed, give him aspirin and vitamins. The dogs run away—who can blame them!

January 26

Hire a new housekeeper, Litia*.

January 27

Richard's a horror: hitting, throwing things, taking my rings, accusing me of sneakiness regarding *Wholly Moses*.

January 28

Finally he does his cameo and comes home worse than ever. I ask what's wrong and he goes crazy. This has nothing to do with me, but I've got no room for error.

Richard is smoking around the clock again. He starts filming *Stir Crazy* in a month—he'll *have* to stop then. Meanwhile, he's obsessed with the doll again, asking me the same questions over and over. Aunt Dee and Uncle Dicky are here for another endless visit.

February 3

Richard's locked himself in the bedroom. I watch *Norma Rae* and her painful struggle. Her courage to stand up to trouble and to accept herself are inspiring. In the end, her bitterness is replaced by self-esteem and the joy of winning.

February 7

I come home to find Litia and Richard freebasing at the kitchen counter, and immediately confront her, "Did you fuck him, too?" All hell breaks loose. She cries, Richard hits me, I fire her. She leaves, then he demands that I rehire her, saying, "Holmes, this is my house. She comes back." Then he locks all the doors.

Richard has tried to give it up—smashing the pipe has become a daily ritual, as well as buying a bigger and better one the next day. I feel emotionally obsolete, as I have become his excuse for getting high. He says that I have deserted him and that the pipe gives him the friendship, love, and understanding that once came from me. It's all because I slept with that damn hooker.

February 10

Drive Aunt Dee around, go to Sophia's, and fix tacos and enchiladas for dinner. Richard begins yelling uncontrollably and begins his interrogation. I tell him I'm leaving and he demands that I give him back all my jewelry before I do. Really punk. I move out—at 2:30 A.M.

February 11

I go to see him and he's at the kitchen table with Uncle Dicky and a "Stepin Fetchit" from Richard's Berkeley days, holding court and freebasing. When I step through the door a giant-size bottle of rum comes hurling through the air at me. I leave.

Valentine's Day

I send Richard a poem to tell him I want to stop our silly games and that I still love him.

Go see a Brazilian psychic in the valley, a friend of Sophia's, who tells me to be patient and strong. What the hell does that mean for forty dollars? Then Sophia offers me a job as a drug dealer. Thanks, but no thanks. I take them, that's bad enough! God, what a vulture.

I miss Richard terribly. We speak on the telephone but he's a million miles away. He tells me, "Find the doll." I can't believe it—my life is in the hands of that fucking frou-frou doll!

As if things aren't bad enough, Harry sends Byron to visit, hoping that I might be able to control him, fix him. God, I can't even help myself! And I can't tell Harry the trouble *I'm* in.

February 21

Byron's been here a few days. One night, I hear a wailing sound floating down the street. It's a voice like Otis Redding's, a haunting, moving voice, and as it gets closer to my apartment, I hear the backup harmony of police sirens. That lonesome voice is now out on my front porch. I open the door to see Byron. The LAPD is right behind him, wanting to know what the hell is going on! I tell them he's my brother and drag him inside. They look worried. "You know miss, if he's on dust you could be in danger."

I dismiss the thought. But they have a point—Byron, when drunk, becomes violent. He cranks up the stereo blasting the music of his idol, Jim Morrison, and then begins carving into his chest and stomach with a fork. I stand there helpless, pleading with him to stop. In the middle of all this Richard calls, and I ask him to talk to Byron. I hand Byron the phone—he tells Richard that he wants to kill himself. There is a long pause. When Byron hangs up there is an odd smirk on his face. "Byron, what did he say?"

He told me, "If you want to kill yourself, go ahead and do it."

I send Richard a telegram telling him to leave his drugs at home and meet me at the Beverly Hills Hotel for a night of love. I go to the hotel and wait for him to show up. No Richard. Watch *How to Steal a Million* and fall asleep.

Byron comes into my room one morning and as I try to put my

legs on the floor I fall down. He says, "You've got no circulation in your legs. Taking something, Jen?"

February 25

I realize that I'm taking something every day—coke, Quaaludes—so I decide to go to an AA meeting with Bobby Neuwirth. At the Camden Drive meeting there are lots of familiar faces and lots of cheer and missionary zeal. Get a modelling job and start going on interviews again.

During an argument with Byron, I yell and point my finger at him and he knocks me down. When Richard calls, I tell him and he says, "Good for him."

I've tried to get work for Byron but he doesn't have the desire—I guess I should talk. I've even arranged for him to meet with Ray Manzarek, one of the Doors who's now a producer. I thought that if Ray heard some of Byron's lyrics, maybe he'd give Byron some direction, or at the very least, some encouragement. Byron doesn't keep the appointment.

February 29

Byron leaves. Thank God, because I just can't handle it. I continue going to meetings and am amazed by who I see there. It's a big social club! There's lots of gossip; that's nothing new, but I expected AA to be free of some of the usual Hollywood low-consciousness bullshit.

Now Richard's calling at the weirdest hours, asking things like, "What did you do the day before? Where did you go? Did you see the hooker?" He says that he loves me but that things are now out of his hands. What does this mean?

March 7

Richard asks me to come out to say hi and gives me a set of specific instructions on what to wear—a black skirt and blouse with stockings, a garter belt, and high heels. And what time to arrive—at exactly nine o'clock. And also what to do—flash your headlights, leave the car just inside the gate, walk to the front door and wait for him to open it.

A litany of mysterious instructions. There is clearly something erotic in Richard's based-out mind and he doesn't want Aunt Dee to know I'm coming. A vision in black silk matte jersey, I go to the Friday night Rodeo Drive AA meeting and from there out to Richard's. At the appointed hour, I blink my lights and the gate opens. I park, get out, hold my breath, and walk to the front door. When I step inside I see Richard standing in the dim light, looking like a Mel Brooks caricature of the Gestapo, complete with some absurd makeshift S & M get-up—it is almost sweet. His beard and moustache are shaved to points, he grips a riding crop in a gloved hand, and speaks in a chilling German accent. "My darlink. Kum ing ze beddroom."

Oh, my poor love. With drugs you can become anything, you can fuck a radiator and send it flowers.

We engage in *Cabaret*-like sexual escapades, mostly with me in submissive skits or positions. At dawn I leave the cloud of freebase in his dirty bedroom. It's like hell in there.

Richard's been calling at all hours and in the middle of the night. Sometimes he peers into my windows, checking to see if I'm alone. He's having my apartment watched by a number of different people. His preoccupation with the doll has intensified; if I find the doll, everything will be fine. I try to locate the hooker, but she's moved. What can I do? He's obsessed with the doll and I'm obsessed with him. I hold on by going to meetings and praying. I do a couple of modelling jobs, but these do very little for my self-esteem.

March 16

Visit Richard—God, he looks bad. Long, dirty fingernails, bloated body, and mad eyes. Thank God he leaves tomorrow to start *Stir Crazy*. He'll have to quit then, otherwise how the hell will he get through it?

I escape to the movies; get a ticket for jay walking in Westwood! Paul Jabara calls with a demo of Beverly D'Angelo singing "My Man Ain't Man Enough For Me." The search for the doll is interrupted by Richard's departure.

March 20

Richard calls from Tucson and asks if I can love him now that I no longer do drugs. I tell him yes, although I don't tell him that I now know I'm not the reason *he* is doing drugs. I truly thought it was all my fault but I found out in AA that, as they say, "I didn't cause it, I can't control it, and I sure as hell can't cure it." This is a major relief. But there's still my addiction to him, and guilt over the damn doll.

March 22

I go to Tucson. Richard has not stopped smoking—he is smoking astronomical amounts when he wakes up in the morning, in the car on the way to work. He even cooks in his trailer between takes. He's also becoming less and less concerned about who knows. He's got Rashon going on buying trips to L.A. to keep him supplied. The set is really tense. It's Sidney Poitier (who's directing) and Gene Wilder against Richard and Rashon, with poor Hannah Weinstein, the producer, in the middle. Richard is out of control and has isolated himself from everyone, and Sidney and Gene are clearly upset by this. They are staying in a beautiful hotel in town, while Richard has rented a house high in the hills, with orange shag carpeting, thin brown bedspreads, and flimsy furniture from Sears. Coyotes howl. The nearest 7-eleven is twenty minutes down the winding road. It's a good highway for dumping bodies.

March 24

They've been filming at Arizona State Penitentiary. Richard has snuck in some coke for the inmates, forever playing the role of "Crazy Nigger." While I'm with him, talking to some of the prisoners, I can feel the fear beneath Richard's hip facade. The inmates, who divide themselves into three groups—whites, Hispanics, and blacks—sense it too and I suspect that they are laughing at him, not with him. Never before have I felt like such a white arm-piece.

March 31

All I talk about is Richard—I've become so damn boring. Richard calls and demands the code to my answering service so he can get my messages. I refuse, he gets angry and crazed, and *I'm* feeling nuts.

April 4

Tucson. I read sections of AA's "Big Book" to Richard as he sits on the edge of the bed staring into his pile of cocaine and sucking his pipe. He nods, agreeing with everything I read, then loads his pipe and breathes the mad potion deep into his lungs. At the rodeo set, he looks pathetic, dressed up in his clown costume, sweltering in the Arizona heat, based out of his skull. I stand several feet away from him, talking to Tyne Daly—who's exceptionally nice and who obviously knows her way around the interracial relationship block—and her husband, Georg Sandford Brown. Then I start hearing what could be a double boiler. The loud gurgling sound is coming from Richard's chest. He stares back at me from behind his big red nose, his red wig, and the yellow hat with a daisy stuck in it. I think of one of John's songs: "I got stuck in the ice—without my clothes/Naked as the eyes of a clown."

April 5

Lunch with Hannah at the Arizona Inn. She says everyone is worried that Richard won't be able to finish the picture because he's in bad shape—and he just doesn't seem to care. When I try to talk to him about it he throws a glass of milk at me and tells me he's given my jewelry to the Polynesian actress. Second-hand love and second-hand jewels. Well, good riddance. I don't want the damn things. No more emotional blackmail.

April 12

Back in L.A. Richard sends Joe to my apartment to spy on me. I talk to my AA sponsor about Richard's never-ending interrogation about the hooker and the doll. She suggests I tell him, "It's my body, I can do with it what I fucking want to. Now leave me the fuck alone." After more insane phone calls and threats, "No doll . . . where is the doll . . . we are not together," blah-blah-blah, I deliver my little speech and take the phone off the hook. A few hours later, I hear someone trying to get in through my living room window. I scream, "Who the hell is there?"

"The police."

I open the door and sure enough, the Beverly Hills cops.

"Richard was worried, he thought you might have killed yourself 'cause you had your phone off the hook for so long. He asked us to break in to see." I can't believe my ears. Even the police jump for him.

"I'M VERY MUCH ALIVE. THANK YOU!"

"Yeah, well, you look it. Oh, by the way, will you please call him? He's expecting to hear from you." Jesus, they take messages too!

"I'll call him, anything else?"

When I call Richard, he tells me to go look in my garage and says he'll hang on. I discover that my car, the Porsche he'd given me, is gone.

"Why, Richard?"

"Because of the way you spoke to me."

April 20

This fucking AA. I like the information, I loathe the politics. They're all such busy bodies.

April 23

In Tucson. I don't go to the set with Richard today because he's working with Diahnne Abbott and doesn't want me there! Pretty obvious! I find lots of phone numbers on scraps of paper lying around the bedroom—pretty obvious.

April 24

A bad scene. Richard's put the word out that he wants to score and a serious group of leather-jacketed, motorcycle-riding thugs show up on the set. He brings one into the trailer and thinks nothing of leaving him alone with me. I go outside and wait for the deal to be done. It just so happens the State Police and Federal Narcotics agents are doing the same. They follow us back to the house but Richard doesn't care. Several times along the way he stops and shops—looking for a new pipe. The phone rings all night with offers of "primo shit." Dealers are crawling out of the woodwork. I am awakened by the smell of cigarette smoke and the crunch of gravel under someone's feet outside our bedroom window. I shake with fear as I pray it's the good guys, the narcs. Richard tells me not to worry. "My shotgun's loaded."

"Oh, boy. Now I really feel safe."

The next morning Dick, our sweet, elderly driver tells us that there's been trouble on the set and that he's been questioned. Apparently, all of Richard's activities have been monitored by the narco-agents. They, along with the State Police, are now swarming all over the set. Richard decides that the best approach is the direct one. Dragging me along with him as the entire cast and crew look on, he walks up to a couple of these narco-agents and apologizes. "Yeah, I hear you're mad at me. Gee, sorry man, that won't happen again, guys!"

They were surprised and definitely pissed. They warn him, "Yeah, big guy, don't insult us like that again or next time we'll be forced to do something about it. We suggest you don't buy anymore dope while you're here. And don't try leaving the state with any or you'll be picked up."

Jesus! I know it's because if they bust Richard, the picture will be shut down at great expense.

One night Rashon tells Richard a story about a white girl we all know who'd been beaten within an inch of her life by her black lover. As they suck on the pipe, they recite the details of the beating over and over. Their freebase-soaked brains are obviously fascinated by it. "That's what happens when you mess with a brother, Jen."

Rashon is now in control—courier, cook, and confidant. He dresses almost entirely in African gear and his rap is getting pretty strange. "When the revolution comes, they'll be chopping off babies' heads and sticking 'em on top o'parking meters!"

Thank you for sharing!

April 26

Last day of shooting in Tucson. Richard shows up for work smashed out of his skull and I end up talking to Gene about the trouble. As we all get into the car to go to the airport, Richard decides he wants to go back to the house for his dope. I tell him, "But I threw your pipe in the garbage, Richard."

"I'll find it and I've hidden my dope."

Nothing matters except that smoke. The driver turns around. I get out and catch a cab to the airport. Everybody on the plane places bets on Richard getting busted. I dislike them all for their superior attitudes. There is pity and judgment in their eyes. Gene comes over, sits next to me and begins another discussion about "Poor Richard." Suddenly, there he is, standing in front of us, high as a kite.

"Get the fuck out of my seat, Gene."

"Oh. Hi, Richard."

As nuts as Richard appears, in the midst of this unfeeling hypocrisy, he seems almost sane—for about five seconds!

Back in L.A., Gwen, my actress friend from AA, advises me to "surrender, let go of Richard before he kills you." But I *know* she loves the drama of it all.

April 28

Back to my apartment where a beautiful bouquet of roses is waiting for me. Then every hour some sort of wonderful flower arrangement arrives. What's up? Richard says he's going to get straight, but I know now that he's a junkie. Addicted to base.

April 30

It's nearing the end of filming and Richard has a fight with someone on the crew—something about "watermelon"—so he walks off the set, quits the picture. On the way home, he stops at Sophia's to pick up a huge batch of dope; he's been buying in bulk for a while now. He enters his familiar dimension of dementia and calls me. I'm a "Stand By Your Man" kind of woman . . . right? I go running out to the house, to be by his stoned side . . . right? Wrong! My AA friends tell me that I'm really "dealing with the pipe and the bottle, not Richard." They believe that I'm in danger and don't want me anywhere near him.

When I walk into the bedroom, I see that the antique child's desk holds a giant mound of pure cocaine. Richard's sitting on the edge of the bed staring into it. He's been tearing through it, cooking up a storm, Not only is he stoned, he's also severely depressed about quitting the picture. I try to talk to him, but it's useless. I give up and go to sleep, leaving him puffing away. Right before dawn, I'm awakened by Richard, who's stealthily replacing my handbag on the bedside table. He has obviously been up all night. I ask, "What are you doing?"

"Just checking." Oh, Lord. High-tech paranoia.

"And when did you get that license plate on your car?" Now this is getting scary.

"What? Richard, what the fuck are you talking about? Christ, I'm leaving. This is just too absurd."

"Oh no you're not." I don't know what he's talking about.

"I'm not what?"

One look at him and I *know* the answer! I get up but he's faster and reaches the door before me, bolts it, spins around, and looks straight into my eyes with his glazed mad ones.

"My career is over. I'm going down and you're coming with me." I don't need to hear anymore, but he tells me anyway.

"I'm going to kill you and then myself." Oh, God, I think, *Hollywood Babylon II*.

I'm scared, scared, scared. I have to think fast, not panic, but how? He's got my arm, he's pulling me.

"I want you to see something." He's trying to get me into the bathroom. Something tells me that if I go in there I will die, amidst all those mirrors and beautiful bottles of cologne. It's soundproof, no one will hear me. He might have a gun in there; they're all over the house.

"You're going to die this morning Jenny Lee, do you hear me? This morning Jenny Lee, you are going to die." God, this is too real, or too unreal. Weak and dizzy with fear, I fall on my knees.

"Please don't hurt Jenny Lee. I beg of you, please don't hurt me, Richard." Then I see the familiar smirk, a pause, and I make a break for it. I get to the far side of the bed, but he lunges and grabs me by the throat. I jerk free and run towards the door, screaming bloody murder. He catches me again, this time getting a tighter

223

grip on my neck; he's choking me, his nails are cutting into my flesh. I know that Aunt Dee and the housekeeper are out there somewhere. Why the hell aren't they coming to help me? Then there it is: a frozen moment. No one, nothing moves. The air is thick and still. I hang onto one thought: survival. Then, still clutching my throat, he slowly walks me back to the bed, beside the dwindled mound of coke, and sits us down. It's all in slow motion. He's watching his reflection in the huge wall of mirrors behind the bed as he pins me up against the brass bedposts. There's not a second's worth of space between us; he says if I move, he'll break my neck. I don't even breathe. *Concentrate. Survive.* I look at him watching himself in the mirror and I wonder what he sees. He looks like the devil to me, but I also see his fear and then I know that this is how death sometimes happens—at the hands of fear. Rage has its own agenda, its own momentum, and its own form of control. Then fear turns to panic and Richard is terrified—he knows how close he is to killing me. But he can't let go. This monstrous fear contains my death. I grab my tiny cross that dangles at the end of a long gold chain. I look out the window, past the bushes and the breaking daylight, right up into the sky and tell God with silent desperate words that I am putting my life in his hands, that I trust he doesn't want me to die and that he'll help me find a way not to. "Turn it over to God." It comes ringing back to me—a loud undeniable truth. He's in charge; I just have to submit. I have no choice; I just do it. All at once, I *know.* I have to calm Richard down, make that terror and fear go away, make him feel safe, and lead him away from this insane act of murder. I tell him I love him, that we are going to be happy, that we will find the answers to all our haunting questions. I tell him that we will have babies and that we will lead a nice life. And, I tell him that as long as we love each other we will find a way to make sense of it all, we'll find a way out of this mess and into the light. I ask him to believe me and to trust that I know this to be the truth. I ask him to follow me. God helps me. Suddenly Richard switches back to the person I know. He stands and says, yes, he also knows that everything will be all right, that everything will be fine. Slowly, I stand, and with as little movement as possible, I walk to the center of the room trying not to disturb this new state of calm. I pick up my blue pants and carefully slide them onto my legs, still talking. Even more slowly, I begin walking to the door. When I'm halfway there, Richard lunges at me, but this time I'm faster. Quickly, I undo the lock, throw open the door, and escape. I run, leaving my death behind. When I reach the end of the long hallway, I look back and see Richard standing at the bedroom door. "Jenny, I was only kidding . . . can you bring me something to eat?"

Now that was nuts but do you want to hear something crazier? I go tell the housekeeper to heat up some food and bring it to Richard! I go back to get my pocketbook and say good-bye. I know the madness is all over for now. Richard is wiped out from his long night of drugs and this morning of close death. He looks so broken. Freebase is killing the man I love and it has almost killed me, too.

I thank God that I was sober. If I hadn't been, I probably wouldn't have found the right words. I probably would have cussed him out and assured my death. I know that the housekeeper and Aunt Dee must have heard my screams. But they're all so in awe of Richard—the phenomenon of money, the fame, and the power. Does it also include a license to kill? Apparently it does!

Afterward, I go straight to an AA meeting, where I run into Gwen. She sees the hand marks on my neck and pleads with me to stop seeing Richard.

A couple of days later, Richard calls and asks me to come see him. I refuse. The next time he calls Jim Brown is at his side and Richard puts Jim on the phone.

"Don't worry, Jen, he's calmed down now. He won't hurt you."

"Jim, Richard is just plain nuts when he smokes that stuff. If he'd stop—"

"He has, Jen. He's not smoking, I promise you. Please see him. He needs you, he loves you so much. Come on." Then Richard gets on the phone.

"I'm sorry you're afraid of me. Please forgive me and come down to the set and pick me up, later this afternoon. I love you. Please, Jenny Lee!"

Richard's problems with the film have been ironed out and he's back at work. I promise to see him the next day.

Richard is high when I get to the set. And his paranoia has reached such enormous proportions that it's almost funny, if only it weren't so scary! He's always on the lookout, peering out from behind the curtains of the mobile home. He whispers, "They're out there, Jenny."

Together, we drive back to the house, have an early dinner, and go to bed. An hour or so later, there's a huge bang. Instead of investigating the sound, Richard grabs two guns, cocks the triggers, and lies back down, cradling them in his arms, waiting for the intruder. It's just a noise. I hold him all through the night; my hands are on the guns, too. I'm afraid that at any moment he will turn around and shoot me. *What am I doing here?*

May 4

The hunt for the doll escalates. Richard is now so completely convinced that his sanity depends on finding it that he's been on the prowl, stalking me. Things have gotten so bad that I've got the Beverly Hills police regularly checking on my apartment—at all hours of the day and night. They feel like my own private bodyguards.

Thank God for AA. My mind *is* my own, despite everything. Gwen says that obsession is an insane desire to win. I don't know about winning but I certainly can't let go of Richard. AA's concept of "surrender" has me baffled—I see myself on my knees all bloody and ragged, waving a white flag.

Tommy's heard that Richard's been giving top dollar to anyone who can get information about me. Of course, all Richard's getting are a lot of bizarre fabrications, which he believes, and confronts me with. I tell him that it's all madness, all lies, but I can't get through to him. He'll say, "Listen, you can tell me, Mama. You were broke, right? Once when I was broke I fucked an old lady for her welfare check." His stoned voice, trying to sound casual, tells me, "And the pussy was good!" Jim Brown has been recruited to hunt for the frou-frou doll. Crazy, dangerous, and embarrassing!

Tommy has me meet him on the street in front of the Wonder Bread factory in Beverly Hills—he's got something to tell me. As I sit and smell the white bread, Tommy says he's heard "on the street" that Richard had tried to arrange a hit on me. Since the Mafia doesn't get involved in domestic squabbles, Richard went to some thugs to "break my legs and work me over" instead. I can't believe what I'm hearing.

May 6

I'm sleeping in the hallway of my apartment because it has no windows. Richard calls and reads me a passage from the Bible, "The rivers will flow with the blood of your brothers and sisters." I panic and call my father for help. Harry calls the set but instead of getting Richard, Hannah takes the call and says that he's busy. But Harry refuses to get off until he talks to Richard. Harry finally gets Richard and tells him that if these threats continue he'll have to fly out and take care of everything. Dad does it! Richard apologizes and agrees to back off. I feel safe—for about two-and-a-half minutes.

May 12

Richard appears at my door at four A.M. wearing his pajamas and slippers. He comes in, checks the shower, all my closets, even the pantry, looking to see if anybody is here. He looks like a lost ghost. He finishes his sulking, and without saying a word, simply walks out the door. I pray that Uncle Dicky returns soon.

May 14

Hannah Weinstein has hired two detectives for Richard. They've flown in from New York to help track down Richard Pryor's frou-frou doll. Unreal! They've questioned Tommy and now they want to question me, too. I refuse, I've told them everything on the phone, but Tommy convinces me, and like a fool, I agree.

Tommy picks me up for this interrogation. We head out toward his office and on the way we meet the detectives at the Mobil station, so they can follow us. Amazing—real cloak-and-dagger stuff. At least I feel safe with Tommy—I'd never meet them alone! Once there, they ask me the same old tired questions about the goddamn hooker and the goddamn doll. I tell these two mooks the whole sordid and silly tale—sure that they're getting off on it—and I tell them that I go to AA. They tell me that they do, too. Then they mention that "Richard thinks that diamonds are involved." Oh, yikes! I'll pray for us all! That's the end of it. They're meeting with Richard this evening to tell him what they've learned—which is nothing new.

May 17

Apparently, something is lost in the translation. The mooks call me this morning and say, " Mr. Pryor knows about Judy." Richard calls and says, "I'll always love you." *What the fuck is going on*? Tommy clears it up for me: The mooks go back to Richard and figure they'd better give him his money's worth so they tell him that I've been involved in porno movies, that I am a madam(!), and that I am having an affair with Tommy! Richard believes every lie he pays for. At this point, I can't help laughing at it all, but Tommy is fuming. "They're soaking Richard and making trouble."

"Tommy, it's no big deal. It's too insane!"

But he's mad and tells me, "I'll take care of them, Jen."

When the detectives get back to New York, they're met at a train station and their legs are broken.

May 18

The doll is dead! Unbelievable! Sammy Davis's off-duty LAPD person tracked it down. He's found the hooker's boyfriend and located her through him. Apparently, she left town when all this trouble started and now lives somewhere in the San Francisco area, terrified. The detective actually spoke with her and it seems the doll was eaten by a dog. THE DOLL IS DEAD! I feel like dancing! But now, something even worse is happening. Richard is *not* okay; he has *not* been "cured." The doll had become his hope for sanity, his one conduit to reality. Now he has none. He has no more excuses. And he seems to have no hope. I'm sure that he's headed for deeper water.

May 20

Richard calls me and tells me to call the ex-girlfriend—in Hana. Too much! I can't believe it all! After all the stalking and craziness about that doll, now he's down to flaunting women in my face. And I keep going back for more! Jen! Resurrect thyself!

I take a Quaalude and make the fatal mistake of mentioning it in AA. They tell me I have to raise my hand again—the old thirty-day ritual. "How 'bout if I raise my hand to wave fucking good-bye?"

May 23

This morning Richard calls and we actually have a nice talk—some how the madness is taking a break. He tells me that after that abusive phone call in the middle of the night that he spent the rest of it outside my window. Jesus—the wonder of drugs!

May 27

See Lena, the psychic, who tells me she sees trouble for Richard—well, what else is new? Tells me to pray a lot. I have been! Talk to Harry, who says that Byron's in real trouble. I say that Byron needs AA. Harry can't respond, he just sounds so sad.

May 28

Richard calls to tell me that if I even try to call him, he'll have me hurt.

May 30

Go to a "round-up" in Palm Springs with Gwen and her friend Allan—a million sober control-freaks under one roof. It's good to be out of town, however, and it'll be even better to get out of Palm Springs!

June 3

Richard's flown off somewhere. I have a long talk with Jim Brown—about everything. Jim assures me that Richard is aware of his problem and has decided to do something about it. Jim also says, "Richard adores you. Don't be afraid."

Easy for him to say.

June 7

It's Saturday, and I feel brave, so I go visit Richard. Rashon is there and they're both whacked out of their skulls. Richard tells me that one night, he saw himself as the embodiment of the devil:

skeletal, half-nude, orange, walking through a wall. He asked the apparition if it really was himself he was seeing.

"Yes, I am you," said the devil. And he left—through the wall.

We make love and share an empty and bizarre non-intimacy. I go straight home, write a song, and read it to him over the phone:

> *The way you made love to me was a pity*
> *A shame and a disgrace*
> *Your ice cold heart chills my soul*
> *Your woman is freebase.*

I can *feel* him hear it. In fact, I think I have given him ideas, because after a long silence, he remarks, "I'm going to do something about it, Jenny." Now I am really worried. What does he mean? Please God, help him.

June 9

I am on my knees and my hands are grasping his as he sits on the edge of the bed, staring into space. Richard looks worse than I've ever seen him. Somehow, I know that an ending is near but I don't know what kind. His face is sunken and a strange yellow hue, his stomach is bloated and his eyes are a deep desperate black. I am trying to get through to him. I tell him that I love him and that these days will soon be over. I've had to wait all afternoon to see him. I've been sitting in the atrium watching the large goldfish swimming, in slow motion, in a small pond with a sputtering fountain. He has been locked in his bedroom with his newest bodyguard, who's a needy family friend from Peoria, and his pipe. The house is eerily quiet. Aunt Dee is still there, she gives orders to the housekeeper and pretends that she is in control, that someone's in control, and that everything is fine. She's still saying "You know Richard." I know Richard feels protected by Aunt Dee; she has her hand out less and is more concerned than most.

Since Saturday night Richard's decline has been dramatic. He is sinking and no one will listen to me except Jim, but that's all he does—listen. He was well-intentioned, but now I'm afraid he might also believe Richard when he tells him that I am the problem, that I am the reason that he's doing drugs and in the shape he's in, and that, anyway, he has it all under control. No one can challenge Richard and his insane world. It's protected by centurions who are just as mad! Intimidated and impressed, they have left him all alone with his pipe and his own destruction. His power, his money, and his celebrity have given him a way to exonerate his behavior and they've also isolated him. He's actually permitted, even encouraged, to take this slow walk to death. Because this is what Richard says he wants to do, no one will stop him. I've asked for help, but I can't get any. Dr. Cannon, Richard's family, and his friends all insist that he's fine. They all know better but they are cowards, afraid of losing their connection to Richard's power. Too awed to stop this person, whom they claim they love. But how could they? He's disintegrating right before my eyes and no one is willing to acknowledge it.

"Richard, it's time to get help—this is out of control. You belong in a hospital and I'm going back East for a while."

He just sits there and mumbles something I can't really understand, something about a plane ticket. I continue, "Richard, it's time to get help."

Whispering he says, "I've made up my mind, Jenny."

"What are you talking about?"

"Jenny, I know what I have to do."

"Richard, please tell me what you're talking about."

He continues, "I've brought shame to my family."

"Richard . . ."

"I've hurt them badly. They're after me now, anyway. They're coming to get me."

Now I am beginning to panic. I know I am witnessing drug psychosis. I'm back on my knees. "Who's coming after you? Please, Richard, you're talking crazy. It's that shit you're smoking."

"It's no use, Jenny. I know what I have to do. There's no way out now."

"Richard, you're talking about hurting yourself, aren't you? Please, Richard, you don't have to do this . . . it's not too late!" I'm crying and beg him, "Richard . . . please."

"Jenny . . . I'm going to do it . . . now you had better leave or you are going to get hurt, too."

I spring to my feet and back off. I have learned not to take his threats lightly. I am standing at the foot of the bed. "Richard . . ."

Now I am terrified that he is going to do something to me as well.

The look in his eyes is chilling. "It's too late . . . I've decided. You better go, Jenny, or you'll get hurt, too."

I know he's not just being dramatic; I know he means business. I run into the kitchen where Aunt Dee is sitting with Richard's stoned bodyguard. I am frantic.

"Please, help. Richard is going to do something to himself. He just told me. He's going to hurt himself. He's out of his mind on that stuff."

They laugh at me. Imperiously, Aunt Dee looks up from her cup of coffee with contempt.

I hate her. I run out of the house, jump into my car and drive like lightning out of the valley, over Coldwater Canyon, and down into Beverly Hills, to my apartment and my phone. I don't know how he's going to do it. I think of all the guns. I talk to myself the entire way back. It is the fastest but longest drive of my life. I *know* he is going to do something. I have to call Jim Brown. He might just think I'm paranoid; he's told me that everything's under control and that Richard has promised to check into the hospital in a week. But now it's too late. There is no one else to call. The housekeeper answers the phone.

"He's rollerskating."

"It's important." He finally gets on the phone.

"Jim, Richard's going to do something. He's going to hurt himself."

"Now, just calm down." He's about to do nothing of the sort. Why is he talking to me as if *I'm* the person who's lost it? Why won't anyone fucking listen to me?

"Nothing's going to happen, Jennifer. I'll call him later and talk . . ." I slam the phone down and call the house. Raul's "Hello" is interrupted by a haunting scream. Oh God, it's Richard.

"It's Richard!," The bodyguard shouts. Then the phone drops. I hear screams and chaos in the distance, Aunt Dee screaming. I hang onto the receiver for dear life. Then I hear the bodyguard pick it up and more yelling, "It's Richard! It's Richard. He's burning! Get a blanket!"

The phone drops again. I leap into my car and speed out to Valley Presbyterian. Raul is in the lobby.

"Where's Richard?"

"They just left here, they took him to Sherman Oaks Burn Center."

"Raul . . . ?"

"He was burning, Jennifer. He was running down the road, burning."

Shit! I know what he's done. I knew he was going to try to kill himself, I just didn't know how. He lit himself on fire. He did it with the 151-proof rum that he uses for smoking base. Jesus! The motherfucker must have poured it all over himself and lit up. Fucking self-immolation! *How could he do this*?

This is the moment when I realize, finally, that Richard *is* crazy.

"God, Raul, what has he done? Come with me to the hospital."

"I can't. I have to go back to the house and clean up before the police get there."

In a daze I head over to Sherman Oaks. When I get there I run into the emergency room. They're all there—Aunt Dee, the bodyguard, and Richard's cousin, Denise. Somehow, I have to speak to Richard's doctors and tell them what he's been doing, what's in his system. I'm afraid that they might give him painkillers that could cause an overdose. I grab an orderly. "Where are Richard's doctors? I have to tell them something."

Aunt Dee looks as if she wants to kill me. "There's no need to say anything, Jennifer. We don't want the police involved."

The paranoid ghetto mind set is so strong, it still has a grip from the days of running a whore house.

A doctor comes and takes me into a private room. "What is it you want to tell me?"

"You should know that Richard has been freebasing cocaine and drinking a lot of vodka over a long period of time; continuously for the past few days. He was in real bad shape. He did this to himself."

"Thank you for telling me. Now you sit tight and we'll take care of him. He's in the right place."

That piece of information helps keep Richard alive, but it puts the final nail in my coffin. I am completely ostracized by the family and by Richard.

I call Jim at the Reseda Rollerrink. "Richard burned himself. I just wanted to let you know." Click.

The sad vigil begins. Every day I go out to the Sherman Oaks Burn Center and overhear tales about the latest skin grafts and other excruciating details of Richard's condition. I envision him lying in some hospital bed, looking like steak tartare, teetering on the edge of death. I am not allowed into the sanctity of the VIP waiting room. I am an outcast because, after all, I'm the reason that Richard is here—that's the party line! I know it's Richard still giving the orders to his group of loyal followers. I also know that this is one of Richard's classic tricks; he gets everyone to behave the way he wants them to and then he does what he damn well pleases. And to hell with all of them. So I stay in the hallway adjacent to the waiting room, where I can overhear the news, and sometimes the head nurse will stop and speak with me. Even Jim Brown won't acknowledge me; he could jeopardize his position with the family. It's beyond humiliation, but somehow I don't give a fuck because I still love this man.

Everyone has their fifteen minutes of fame—Aunt Dee, Uncle Dicky, his daughter Denise, Aunt Mexine, Shelley, Deboragh, and all of Richard's kids. They huddle together exchanging war stories, jokes, and sharing their constant fear of Richard's keloiding skin. Aunt Dee always dresses in her finest and gets her hair done before coming to the hospital. All the mothers and all the children pose willingly for *Jet* and *Ebony* and answer questions for the local newscasters. Aaah, reflected glory at its best—or its worst. What a scene! Almost daily Deboragh is summoned to Richard's bedside and everyone assumes this means that they're getting back together. Not me! But I'm also sure that this is where Richard has decided it's over for us. My friends keep asking if I have seen him and with the color rising in my cheeks, I tell them that he simply doesn't want me to see him in this condition. Liz Smith of the *Daily News* accepts this, prints it in her column, and says that I am standing by my man.

One morning, the sweet black head nurse pulls me aside and says, "I want to talk to you."

She takes me into her office and sits me down. "Hospitals are a great place to punish someone. I know you're Richard's lady and you've had some problems; he's talked about you. But honey, he's not going to see you. I don't know why, that's not my business but seeing you here every day, looking so sad and treated so badly, is not going to make him better, and frankly, I can't stand to see it."

She is indeed an angel. I have stopped going there and instead I keep in touch with her by phone. She brings Richard notes and gifts from me, keeps me informed about his progress.

"Today he told me that you hurt him badly. He loves you very much, but will not see you."

It's funny. Even though he is using this place to punish me, and I hate him for it, how can I be angry at him? In fact, I'm amazed by his ability to keep manipulating things, despite the pain and his critical condition. Because of Richard's general debilitation at the time of the fire, there are many other complications including pneumonia and a kidney condition requiring dialysis. What an incredible will!

Jim Brown is running interference at the hospital which has become quite a circus. Everyone wants to see Richard—Elliott Gould, Sidney Poitier, Rosalind Cash, Stan Shaw, Sammy Davis, and Redd Foxx; there's even been a phone call from Teddy Kennedy. Marlon Brando arranges for an HBO hook-up so he and Richard can watch the Roberto Duran and Sugar Ray Leonard welterweight fight on June 21st. There is an outpouring of love and good wishes from his public. Richard's received over thirty thousand pieces of mail. Jim has also had to run interference back at Richard's home. It seems that a few family members and "close friends" have been helping themselves to some of his belongings.

One really tragicomic event that has come out of this is a telethon called, "Skin for a Friend," which Redd Foxx is producing in order to raise money for Richard's very expensive hospital stay and plastic surgery. Talk about a comedy of errors! From start to finish it's an embarrassing disaster. They can't get national air time, so it'll only be shown locally; therefore, many celebrities drop out. Even Foxx himself exits leaving Altovise Davis and Leon Kennedy to fill in as hosts. They get a group of tragic burn victims in close-up so everyone can see their horrifying agony. A "one-of-a-kind" paint-by-numbers portrait of Richard, bearing a bizarre resemblance to Abe Lincoln, is auctioned off. Financially its a big mess and Richard has to send in his accountants to straighten it out. Eventually all monies raised are donated to the Sherman Oaks Burn Center. Shortly afterward, his one million dollar Screen Actors Guild insurance policy comes through to cover all medical expenses.

My friend Peter Lester calls, asking me all about freebase, how it's done, what it feels like. Of course, he segues into questioning me about what *really* went down with Richard. I skillfully avoid saying how it actually happened. I must protect Richard. At the end of our conversation, Peter tells me he's had his tape recorder on the whole time. Maybe he learned this sneaky tactic from Andy Warhol? Peter's article runs in *People* magazine, without my name and without the truth. I am committed to keeping this secret that makes me feel even more isolated and lonely. What Richard has done is so sadly horrific; it's a wicked, shameful secret that I must hide for him and for myself. I am also nervous about all the drug dealers and their fears of being busted. But one of the hardest things about this whole ordeal is that people ask such insensitive questions; their lack of manners and tact is truly unbelievable. It has taken me quite a while to learn to say, "None of your goddamn business." And it never lets up. In Hollywood, gossip is currency—gossip is gold.

Richard has decided to sue David Franklin. Among other things, he is questioning where his salary for *Stir Crazy* has gone. I know it's lining the walls of Richard's damaged lungs. I also hear that Richard's been doing dope in the hospital. Jesus!

Re-entry is difficult. For so long now, I've been out of touch with my own life and with many of my friends. Paul Jabara won an Oscar last April for "Last Dance," a song that Donna Summer sang in *Thank God It's Friday*, and I haven't even called to congratulate him.

June 14

There's a party at Paul Schrader's house being given by Paul Jasmin and the infamous blond cocaine dealer, utterly cool Super Dyke. She's known for her systematic seduction of the hottest heterosexual women in Hollywood. The hippest people are there, all looking at me—or at least I think they are—as though *I'd* burned up. I decide to get drunk and the last thing I remember is saying a slurred hello to Richard Gere before I leave.

July 3

I visit Freida*, an old girlfriend from New York, with my gay buddy Marcel*. Freida is still searching for a career. Her married sex-life isn't so hot either.

The three of us sit at the candlelit kitchen table, drop some 'ludes, and talk about sex. Marcel pipes up. "If I were straight, I'd make love with Jennifer. She's sexy."

Frieda agrees. "You're right. Jennifer's sexy. I'd like to make it with her!"

We all giggle. I decide to stay the night. Freida and I share her oversized bed. A few minutes after we shut off the lights, I feel my old friend fumbling beneath my T-shirt. Next thing I know, she's giving me head! She's strangely matter-of-fact about the whole business, and has only her own pleasure in mind. The next morning, Frieda is acting like the fucking Queen of England, as if she doesn't know me, as if the entire scene hadn't even happened! I'm furious. Talk about denial. I am more isolated than ever.

July 23

After several weeks of excruciating silence, Richard called last night to tell me that he's being released tomorrow, and asks me to come visit him. I agree, and when I arrive I'm shocked and truly saddened at what I see. The fire has not only burned his skin but his soul and spirit as well. He is emaciated, frail, and his smile is bitter. He's sporting maroon velvet slippers with gold embroidery—the kind aging movie stars wear. To turn in his chair, he has to move his entire body. I feel like a puppy dog, waiting for a sign of affection that never comes. I don't know why I'm here. He looks at me and says, "Gained some weight, Jenny?"

So sweet. "Yes, lots of Big Macs—good for the blues."

We walk up the hall hand in hand; rather, I walk and Richard shuffles. When we get to the door he says, "Thank you for coming. It was good for me."

A brush off with razor-wire.

July 29

Richard calls to say that he's in better shape; in fact, he'll stop by this afternoon. I am upstairs talking to my neighbor when he and Rashon finally show up in the new yellow Corniche. I can see from the window that Richard's acting really strange. When I go downstairs to greet him, paranoia flashes like lightning across his contorted face. He turns on his heels and leaves. Emblazoned on the back of his black satin jacket are the words *Up in Smoke*—the new Cheech and Chong movie. It gives me the creeps. Does *he* think it's funny? He looks mean. . . . I know I won't see him for a very long time.

I am going on lots of interviews for commercials but I'm not getting any work. Of course not! I'm a fucking basket case! In fact, I should probably be weaving a few. But I have signed with Entertainment Company for songwriting.

August 5

Still no word from Richard. I hear from Maxine that the male nurse he bonded with in the hospital is living with him to help keep him off the pipe. I also hear he's back with Deboragh. The speculation about how he "did it" won't let up and I still haven't told anyone! He does an interview with Barbara Walters and he looks so fucking bad—almost bald, scarred, and discolored, like a low-rent junkie! During the interview he tells her "how it really happened"—which means he gives her the phony story put forth by David Franklin about malfunctioning lighters, lighter fluid, and rum. He talks of being a changed man, full of resolutions. Full of shit! I think he's beginning to believe it himself. Too bad he can't keep his lies straight—saying in one interview that the rum spilled all over the place as he and his buddy lit cigarettes. The truth is eating *me* alive, I can only imagine what it's doing to him.

August 15

A friend calls to tell me, "Cut out the article about Dorothy Stratton's murder and tape it to your phone." Poor girl, she couldn't let go . . . .

September 11

Party at John Schlesinger's. George Christy, among others, asks me about Richard. My new stock answer is "If you can't stand the heat get out of the kitchen, no pun intended." Rude people! I hope Richard doesn't read *Hollywood Reporter* 'cause in today's column George quotes me! All the gay boys ask about the size of Richard's cock and if it has any burns on it.

Freida calls and asks me to come see the new chairs she bought at Robert Mulligan's on Melrose. Somehow, I *know* that these have to be the cottage chairs I sold him last week. Sure enough, she's got 'em, having paid triple the price I sold them for (and four times the amount I bought them for). Freida is now having an affair with the hetero-seducing Super-Dyke. I watch them flirt with each other at a party, as Frieda's nose drips cocaine residue into the vegetarian tacos.

September 23

I move into Barbara Steele's very well-arranged chaos on Lasky Drive. Full circle. She's been through hell, too; her ex-husband Jim Poe recently died when he'd OD'd on Quaaludes and cocaine during a mudslide that ripped through his house on Malibu Hill. Barbara's working for a director-producer on whom she has a wild crush. She's definitely pulling it together but, unfortunately, the boss is married! Somehow this fits her alluring disorder.

September 29

Trying to jog my blues away at the nearby Beverly Hills High School track but the only things going are the Big Macs. Go see *Ordinary People*. Mary Tyler Moore is cold and cruel to Timothy Hutton and it reminds me of how Yvonne treats Byron. He doesn't get the nurturing and understanding he needs, just browbeating and name-calling instead.

October 22

I can't get an acting job to save my life but I must work. Read an ad in the *Hollywood Reporter*: Take Care of World-Renowned Celebrity—Home and Business." Well, God knows I can manage that! Guess what? The celebrity turns out to be Trini Lopez, who I don't think has had a hit since "Lemon Tree Very Pretty." Naturally I get the job—I have great credentials in this "taking care of star" area. But it's all just too sad. He has me doing things like writing fake fan mail to radio stations all over America and taking his white vinyl boots to the shoemaker. I quit after two days. I begin reading scripts and writing synopses for Barry Beckerman. I won't get rich but it's good therapy and discipline. Sophia calls again and offers me a job as a drug dealer, which I consider for about half a second.

A small party at Paul Schrader's house and I allow myself to be seduced by the mighty, the hip, Super Dyke. This legend does not disappoint, giving me a first—she actually blows coke up my ass through a silver straw. She demands passivity—shades of Max Schell! I can appreciate the extreme experience but dyke-age is definitely not for me!

November 9

Meet Treat Williams at Barry Beckerman's. He is a real treat—sweet and smart and stoned!

November 11

Bobby Neuwirth calls. He and the rest of the folks at AA hate that I've left the fold, but I can't take it anymore. Their big emphasis is on how many days they've not ingested a substance. At meetings they ask, "How much time ya got?"

And I tell the truth, "Twelve hours. I took half a Quaalude last night."

The horrified expressions on the virtuous faces are more than I can stand. It's easier not to go. This sober singles' bar of the eighties cannot accept anything less than strict adherence to the rules—moderation is a word they don't even know how to spell! A half a Quaalude doesn't lead me to death and no longer leads me to five more. I suppose that if individuals are making choices, this threatens the group concept. I hate "groupness".

November 19

Barbara's casting "The Winds of War" with her boss Dan Curtis. She roams the apartment at three in the morning and I have to get up and keep her company and give her my undivided attention. She's draining.

November 21

Dinner at Barry Beckerman's with Treat Williams. When I get home, there's a message from Richard, who's in Hana. I run out to get cigarettes before I call and run into Georg Sandford Brown. He questions me about Richard and I refuse to answer. When I talk to Richard, I am flooded with love, but he tangos on my heart, mentions other women, and I hang up.

November 22

I am in agony over him; he calls again and endless discussion goes nowhere. I can't do this anymore! I need my AA pal Linda Kramer. She's so smart about Alanon issues—a real genius in the "relationship area." LTK is petite, attractive, well-dressed and has a gray, toy poodle named Gumdrop that she dotes on. (Gumdrop was kidnapped and held for an $8,000 ransom, which LTK paid.) She shops at Neiman Marcus, drives a white Mercedes 450 SL with "LTK" on the license plates and looks every bit the typical Beverly Hills divorcee–JAP. But she has a wonderfully twisted mind, a loving soul, and a completely original sense of humor. And she dispenses great advice. "What comes naturally for men, women have to learn" is one of her maxims.

I call her and she tells me, "You have given away all your power. I'll help you, but lord only knows why you want this man back!" Music to my obsessed ears.

"He's sick. It'll be easy, junkies are always easy." She teaches me the true value of my answering machine. And then she gives me some basic rules: "Don't answer the phone, but if you must, don't stay on more than three minutes. And you get off the phone first. If you stay on the phone with a man too long, they don't need to see you. Cuts into the desire. Don't tell him you love him. Don't give him any information about your life. And keep things light, no heavy relationship talk." This is definitely news to me and makes love seem a bit clinical. "Your way isn't working. If this way doesn't work you can always go back to your old way." I've always thought that love is enough. I don't want to play games. But LTK says that these aren't games, rather they are rules that you've got to follow because this is just the way things are between men and women.

"Men hate it if you don't have the power," she continues. "You've got to be smarter. And never, ever, express neediness." I have a lot to learn.

Then she explains the "dangling carrot" concept. "They reel you in, they throw you out. You can never get your balance. You get hooked on abandonment." Bingo! Disorientation leads to love—it certainly leads to obsession. This m.o. will be tough. I see the light at the end of the tunnel (or is that the light of an oncoming train?!).

I understand that this is designed to get my "power" back, but I am inept at even getting off the phone. LTK gives me some magical phrases: "Tell him, you've got a cake in the oven, someone's at the door; don't even say things like, 'talk to you later.' "

Right—cake's in the oven—is she for real? However, I will do what she says, because I've been giving new meaning to the phrase "on the floor."

November 23

Richard wants me to come down to Hana for Thanksgiving but I have made plans to go to Cropseyville. He wants me to change them; I refuse, telling him I'll see him when I return. He's shocked! So am I.

November 25

Fly East with Barbara, who'll stay in New York while I go on to Cropseyville. She's making me nuts, too, telling me that I must "nevah" go back with RP. She gets mad when I talk to him but I tell her, "I gotta do what I gotta do."

November 27

Speak to Richard who tells me he thought I burned up in the big hotel fire in Las Vegas.

November 29

God, coming home is always a drama. I don't know what I'm looking for on these excursions. I have a huge fight with Georgia. Richard calls and I get off the phone after three minutes. This is easy because he's angry that I'm not with him. He wants what he wants, when he wants it.

December 8

John Lennon was shot and killed today; the world weeps. I have sushi on Mulholland with a friend and drink a lot of saki.

December 11

Richard's in town to do Johnny Carson. It's an embarrassment; he talks about dating again. He has asked me to return to Hana with him. This is not a great way to begin, but what the hell, I can't wait to see him.

December 13

I'm waiting for Richard in the VIP lounge of United Airlines, feeling like a nervous school girl when he walks in wearing head-to-toe black Issey Miyake, looking bone thin and weary. Things are awkward as we embrace, but I am sure of one thing. I love him desperately.

We neck all the way to Honolulu, happy to be back in each other's arms. Jan-Michael Vincent is on the plane with his girlfriend. He's charmingly drunk and looks like the California surfer that he is—too much sun. He sweetly asks for Richard's autograph. Richard soaks up the adulation.

Norman picks us up in the old Silver Cloud and it's as if none of the hell we've been through has transpired. Norman is truly happy to see us. We're spending the night in Honolulu, and on the way to the Colony Surf Hotel, the Doobie Brothers song "What a Fool Believes" plays on the radio. Richard says, "This is the song I listened to day in and day out thinking of you."

We make love almost immediately. While there is an almost mist-like quality to our love-making, a little cruelty invades the gentleness. A mix-master of love—a high-powered, electric, love-hate thing. And there is Richard's burned body, which I haven't seen since the fire. It is a shock to touch the raised twisted bumps, edges, and strips of grafted skin. His attitude is even stranger, his scars like a badge of honor, or worse, a weapon. He shows them off as if to say, "See what you did to me!"

He looks into the mirror. "I'm a forty-year-old burned-up nigger Jenny, and they love me." I feel my hair shirt. Richard decides to take a nap and asks me to give him a massage as he sails off to sleep. I pour the oil into my hands and rub his "in relief" skin. He should sleep in a stretch vest to keep the new skin from shrinking but he hates it and refuses to wear it. He doesn't seem to care about how disfigured he is. It makes me sad.

Despite all these subterranean feelings and unspoken resentments, it is a spectacular afternoon. He's sleeping as I look out the huge, open glass doors to the sea. It sparkles like a field of diamonds, a soft breeze is blowing, and the air is full of love.

We have dinner in the hotel dining room and see Mike Douglas, the former talk show host, and Jack Lord from "Hawaii Five-O." Everyone treats Richard as if he is the mythical salamander who has survived the fire.

Throughout the night I hear him scratch his skin grafts with his fingernails, which causes them to bleed. The terrible noise keeps me awake.

December 15

Hana. The house is finished, and it's exquisite. Very *House and Gardens*. Japanese Shoji doors separate large airy rooms; white linen-covered couches, bamboo and wicker furniture, and exotic foliage in huge woven baskets are everywhere, and a dramatic deck wraps around the house, where two white Samoyeds, Boyfriend and Girlfriend, play. To complete this picture of perfection, Okima*, the very young and very beautiful Japanese housekeeper, moves silently through the house, taking care of everything. She bathes Richard in the huge Jacuzzi and massages him with his special emollients. Naturally, I think she's been to bed with Richard, but when I ask, he says I'm crazy for even thinking such a thing. Right, like where could I ever get such an idea? Okima is a major sweety pie who's also a wonderful cook and serves the meals with rapid little smiles and offers respectful tiny headbows as she backs barefoot out of the room. I cannot compete with this subservient perfection and it's hard to imagine that she doesn't just as willingly suck his cock. What most enrages me is the lie—I'd sleep with her

244

too if I were in Richard's position. This is definitely Richard's turf, which provides a shield for him that is difficult to penetrate. His life, his things, his, his, his . . . I feel like a subplot in a Richard movie, or more accurate, like one of the talented and beautiful female stars in an Elvis Presley movie—present, but conspicuously superfluous. Our love and memories are no match. He says he feels me all through the house. But what was once our house is now his house and I'm aware of my place. It's good to be back and see friends at the Hana Ranch Hotel but I am also happy to leave a few days later. Not one word has been said about all the past madness; swept under the rug till the rug turns into a monster.

December 18

Speak to Maxine, my informant, and she tells me Deboragh and the children will spend Christmas in Hana. Merry agony! I take advantage of LTK's offer and call her answering machine a million times. "LTK, this is Jennifer, I'm calling you instead of Richard. I'm flipping out, I'm crazed with jealousy, and I am frightened."

December 20

Richard calls, I pick up the damn phone by mistake, he says he loves me.

December 21

Party at Beverly D'Angelo's house. Richard has not called today.

December 22

Spend the day with Teo, which is really nice. I need to talk to and feel close to something other than my own pain and solitude. We end up making love, a safari of sorts. Richard calls twice, *with Deboragh there*, and says, "I'm in love with two women, I don't know what to do." I know what to do! "Gee, Richard I just slept with someone and thought of you. Guess that means I'm in love with you!"

A little of his own fucking medicine.

245

December 23

LTK calls this the dance of death, the old two-step. I'm surprised when Richard calls today and says, "All of this is too damn painful. It's best if we stop right now."

I agree. Fine and good-bye. A blue Christmas; fucking agony.

December 27

Party at Paul Jabara's house. Paul's friend Neal falls over the railing. What a drama—emergency room and the whole nine yards. See David Geffen there and we talk about John and Yoko. He says the new album will gross about $12-$14 million. He also says that Richard's star won't last because he's not honest. Food for thought.

New Year's Eve

Go to a few terrible parties and back home to my lonesome bed.

1981

New Year's Day

Richard calls. The deep, faraway voice coming over my red phone sounds bluer than blue. "Hello," the-love-of-my-life-voice says, "I just wanted to say I love you." He continues about how he's so sad because he's so torn between two women. It's all blah, blah, blah, but against LTK's instructions, I call him back to tell him, "I love you, too."

This evening, around midnight, the phone rings. "This is a friend of Richard's . . ."

"Who is this?" I know it's Deboragh.

"It doesn't matter. I have something important to tell you. Richard is very, very much in love with you. If you care anything at all for him, you will be with him. He doesn't want to live without you."

Click. She's gone. I'm baffled. Deboragh's a majordomo at the love game, how could she make as sincere a call as that? Boy, that bastard's got us both going.

January 2

Dinner party at John's and Michael's. Paul Jasmin, Helmut Newton, Warren Beatty, Robert Towne, Beverly D'Angelo, Michael and Marysa Maslansky, and Ray Sharkey are there. Ray looks like a hundred miles of bad road that I could use! We neck in the kitchen and decide to leave together. After a stop at Ray Lafaro's house, we end up at his place in Venice where he makes love to me—I should say "fucks me"—with his sunglasses on. Like he's fucking Jack Kerouac or something! This boy tries too hard! Leave a note in the A.M. and make my getaway!

January 4

Ray Sharkey drops by, we kiss, talk, and then good-bye. Richard calls, furious. "Someone" told him that I'm seeing someone else. Richard better make a move. This is getting tired.

January 7

Back down to Hana. We have a few blissful days of love-making, long walks, afternoon naps, and at-home movie watching.

January 12

Richard asks me to help him with some writing. A book's in the works about his life. Robbie Lantz, his agent, has been negotiating with Random House. It will open with "The Fire." As I'm taping him and taking notes, I hear him talking as if he were the victim of some abstract phenomenon. The truth is missing and I tell him that.

"Richard, you did not go through the burning bush. Have you forgotten that you did this to yourself? I think you'd better call a spade a spade. Remember, I was there! If you're not going to be truthful with yourself, you have to be with me." He just stares at me with eyes like black holes. I know he hates me knowing the truth.

We stop work. He struggles with this for a few days and ultimately begins to expose his demons and his inner storms in the process; we are falling in love again. I see hope. He does not receive the million-dollar advance, telling Robbie Lantz, "Jennifer says my not getting the advance is an excuse to stop writing because I'm getting too close to the truth."

Time to leave.

January 23

Back to Hana. We make friends with Bill Dana and his new wife Evelyn, who live on the gold coast of Hana. Bill is sweet and kind but a bit obsequious, which makes Richard uncomfortable.

February 2

Aunt Mexine dies of a heart attack—they all die of heart attacks—and this echoes the pain leftover from Mama's death. I feel terrible that I hadn't spoken with her recently. A grifter, but the one in the family I felt almost comfortable with.

February 4

Boy, do I need Alanon. Richard's told me Deboragh's coming down this weekend. I don't react but it hurts like a motherfucker.

February 14

Back to Hana. Richard says he wants me to work with Howard Koch on Richard's upcoming project—*Some Kind of Hero*. Back to L.A. Richard is needed for reshoots on *Family Dreams*. Michael Schultz is directing these—he has the most amazing blue eyes!

February 20

Meet with Howard Koch. A nice enough man, but he can't help treating me like "the girlfriend" . . . condescending and patronizing.

Richard's at the house in Northridge. I convince him to get away from the ghosts of Freebase Past, and move him into L'Ermitage in Beverly Hills. Once again, I'm riding shotgun on Richard's life.

February 22

Again I'm lonely and depressed. All wrapped up in Richard and his life; with me as a subplot. He ignores my life. I hardly seem to have one. Trying to create a life, I'm going on interviews, but not getting jobs. And Richard doesn't even *ask* about what I'm doing. But, I do allow this. I'm almost afraid to be without him. I wonder if love and fear go hand in hand. Richard needs a new secretary; I finally hire a girl named Lauren. In the past, every employee I've hired has been manipulated by Richard into some kind of power struggle with me. Lauren handles this dynamic better than most.

During reshoots, Richard takes up with a Filipino flame, who begins calling in the middle of the night.

March 1

We break up. Richard goes back to Hana.

March 4

Go to Chastity Bono's birthday party. What a joke—what a house! It's a major Egyptian fantasy. Cher believes that she was Egyptian in another life.

March 12

Dinner at the Maslansky's. Michael tells me that Richard's agreed to present at the Academy Awards only if his co-presenter is Jane Seymour. Thank you for sharing, Michael.

March 13

Spend the evening with Chris Wilding, Liz Taylor's son, and Al-lene Getty. They're a cute couple and very much in love.

March 19

Richard calls, I tell him I'm through.

March 22

Byron's here. I take him shopping and buy him some clothes, but I'm too engrossed in my own problems to help him with his.

March 31

I watch the Awards, Richard presents, his date is the Filipino extra.

April 1

Drive Byron to the airport; he's headed to college in Colorado. My heart breaks for him.

Barbara's back from Europe, roaming the halls in the middle of the night. She says that all over Europe the TVs in her rooms glowed green in the middle of the night, as if someone were trying to communicate with her. Yeah!

April 8

Byron calls. I try to talk him into going to AA.

I hear Richard met Margot Kidder at the Awards. They're dating, and guess what? She's starring in *Some Kind of Hero!* Then Richard calls to tell me Margot wants him to drop me—ha! I hear tons of gossip, turn my answering machine on, and leave it on. Time to get myself a boyfriend!

Beverly D'Angelo and I get together with David Geffen for a threesome at his house off Benedict Cannon. David's bedroom is very masculine, very Ralph Lauren, filled with dark mahogany furniture and upholstered chairs, quilts, drapes, and pillows in dark-toned fabrics. A big dish of coke sits on the bedside table and Bev and I dip into it every few minutes. David doesn't touch either of us and doesn't seem terribly excited watching as Bev and I tango naked in his large four-poster bed. He just leans up against the backboard in his white jockey briefs, watching. This old edge is getting a bit tiresome.

April 18

Another fight with Richard. Party at Anthony Getty's, where I meet Timothy Leary. I ask Timothy if he's ever ended a relationship from his head as opposed to his heart; he says he'd never even try something that insane! A little bohemian validation!

May 8

With Richard Perry's help, I organize a table at the Roxy— Jimmy Cliff is playing. Good old Beverly D'Angelo, Don Boyd, who produced *Honky Tonk Freeway*, and myself all go. To my amazement, I spot him—my new boyfriend—while we are waiting to get in. Tall, dark-haired, and well-built. He begins eyeing Bev in her skin-tight black jumpsuit—God, Bev can look so cheap sometimes—but finally, I catch his eye. He looks me up and down. I'm wearing skin-tight purple leather pants, a Kansai T-shirt, and white cowboy boots. Guess I can look pretty cheap, too! I give him my best come-hither look. When we're inside he sashays over to me as I'm dancing to the sexy rhythm of "The Harder They Come." He stands behind me and whispers in my ear, "Give me your number." Lord—complete with sensual South American accent! This is *too* good.

May 10

It turns out we had kind of a close call that night. Margot Kidder's friendly with Bev, and told her that she and Richard were driving around that night and that they almost came to the Roxy. That would have been pretty!

May 11

I sleep with the Venezuelan, who's a great lover—a USC boy. My first younger man—no problem with that!

Richard calls and invites me to the set for lunch. The second I walk in he says, "I know you're seeing someone."

I can't believe it. So I tell him. "Yep, a darling student at USC from Venezuela."

Then, "Well, I bluffed, Jen. I didn't know anything but I'm glad I know now."

I get furious. "Well, big shot, you've been seeing Margot all over town. So what's the big deal?" A little of his own medicine.

We call it a draw and make love in his trailer.

May 18

I have been having delicious rendezvous with my young lover, usually in the mornings *and* in the afternoons. Richard calls, says he desperately needs to talk to me, and sends a driver to bring me to the set. I wait for him in the trailer wondering what this latest drama is. Suddenly he comes in, puts his hands on his hips, and says, "Okay, Jenny Lee, enough of this shit—will you marry me, goddamn it?"

I don't answer because I feel a trap, a set-up. We make love and then he takes me outside and introduces me to Michael Pressman, the director, and says, "I'm going to marry her!"

Nothing is real with Richard till it happens. And I realize, this is probably for Margot's benefit—I have heard that they actually made love during one of their love scenes. Nothing surprises me. Now I am spending more time at the hotel with Richard, and meeting Diego* afterwards. Diego isn't happy but then he's a little rascal too. He sometimes sees an ex-girlfriend of Bev's husband, Lorenzo. Small fucking world!

May 24

Go to the races with Richard, Howard Koch, Sr., and Ray Sharkey! Shit. I have to tell Richard about Ray. I downplay it, "We've met before."

Ray's on heroin and during lunch he nods out into his chicken salad. Very embarrassing, especially in our exalted VIP area. Richard keeps nudging him, "Hey, Ray, what'd ya think of number five in the sixth?"

Funny, but not very.

May 30

I've called and called but Richard's had a block on the phone at L'Hermitage for the last two days. I hear through the old grapevine that he's holed up with a new pet. "Somebody" (not me) isn't very happy, sneaking into his room and slitting all his silk Armani shirts! (Wonder who?)

July 14

Richard and I are invited to Burt Reynolds' house to see the movie he's directed, *Sharkey's Machine*, starring himself and Rachel Ward. Dinah Shore is there. I haven't seen her since I danced on her show with Paul Jabara. Before dinner, we all watch this endless rough-cut in Burt's screening room. During dinner, Richard asks Burt, "How was it working with Rachel Ward?"

Burt begins rolling his eyes way back in his head and smirking, shifting in his chair like macho man. I want to scream! *We got it Burt—you slept with her, right?* Finally, Don Juan speaks, "Richard, she's truly incredible."

It's beyond clear what he's referring to! What a creep. There's sweet Dinah, sitting next to him, listening attentively and pretending not to feel hurt. I can't stand it. The male servant fills our wine glasses and Burt makes some inane, meaningless toast. I decide to make one, too. I hold my glass up, look straight at Dinah and say, "This is to you and for you. I think you're a great woman."

She is surprised . . . "Well, Jennifer, that's very nice. Thank you!"

Burt knows exactly what I'm doing, and blurts out, "What she really means to say is, I'm an asshole."

I don't say anything and he excuses himself from the table. Richard takes this opportunity to ask Dinah if she has black blood in her, explaining that he's heard the rumor for years. She graciously answers that it is definitely a possibility, adding that at one point in her career she had problems with certain clubs because of it.

Burt returns with a rather different demeanor; he seems high, less macho.

Four days later, we go back to Burt's house for dinner. Dinah is there as well as Dani Janssen (widow of David) and her fiancé, Hal Needam (he was the stunt coordinator on *Rape Squad* but I am too embarrassed to remind him of it—I'm sure he wants to forget too). Plenty of tension in the air and Burt is taking some not so subtle shots at Dinah. Poor baby—I think she genuinely loves him. I know the feeling. It occurs to me, especially listening to Dani talk about her recent purchases at the well-known "Trashy Lingerie" on LaCienega, that Dani has all the characteristics of a golddigger. I go to the bathroom after dinner and Dinah comes in. She tells me, "Burt and I are really worried about Dani marrying Hal." I think, but don't say, maybe you should worry about how Burt treats you. But then, who am I to talk?

Some Kind of Hero wraps and Richard goes back to Hana.

Barbara, who's been in Italy, calls and asks me to meet her there. I think this is a good plan, especially since Richard has dropped the subject of marriage. When I mention this to him, he asks me to wait until *he* decides. Incredible selfishness.

July 21

I fly to Hana to try and figure all this out. My friend Maria Smith and her baby son, Luke, have come along with me. When we arrive Richard takes one look at Maria, whom he's met before, and says, "You're sexy."

This trip does not go well at all. We start fighting right away. Maria's staying at the hotel and I call her at least 75 times in one hour, telling her to pack. She keeps going to the front desk to retrieve her laundry, then drops it off again when I call back to tell her we're staying. The hotel people think she's nuts until they find out she's with us.

Back in L.A., I make plans to join Barbara in Europe. When I tell Richard, he freaks out. "Please, let's figure it out."

"No Richard, I'm leaving."

He begs me. "Well, you have to come down for the house blessing this weekend." I go back to Hana.

August 9

The house swarms with Hana-ites. Boy, can they eat and drink! Gregg and Michel, Deboragh's friends from the hotel, have arranged everything—right down to the guest list—and it feels like one of Mama's picnics by the pool: all fans and sycophants. Henry, the sweet man who owns the gas station, is also the local minister and he performs the actual blessing wishing us health and happiness in our new abode. Hope it takes! He also asks, "When are you two getting married?"

I try to be a good hostess to the guests and to the dirty hippies who crash the party. My beautiful headband of flowers wilts miserably, and I look like a rumpled wood nymph. Okima gets drunk —what's up? Richard smokes one of those powerful Hawaiian joints and gets hugely paranoid when he sees me talking to a landscaping guy about a papaya orchard. He thinks I'm telling him where to meet later! After most of the guests leave I hold Richard's head in my lap, trying to comfort him. I know grass paranoia, that's why I hate it. He keeps saying, I'm sweet to help him. Why does this surprise him? Then he proposes again. "Jen, let's get married next week. You are so kind to try and make me feel safe."

Wow! My first feeling is surprise at *not* experiencing a great surge of joy. I've missed Diego and now wonder if I should marry Richard when I have feelings for someone else. I don't have a lot of faith in Richard's ability to stay married, but after all, isn't this what I wanted? Maybe it could work. Maybe I don't really want to be in a traditional marriage, and I know this would be anything but that! Maybe things will change for us if we do get married; not likely, but one *can* hope!

August 12

We go to the hospital for blood tests—yikes—this is really happening! Today Richard begins freaking out. I suggest that I leave so we both can think it over. He says he doesn't want me out of his sight. I am filled with second thoughts. Every time he voices concern, or even *looks* concerned, I offer to leave. Isn't this what I wanted? As Willie Nelson says, "Careful what you're dreamin', soon your dreams will be dreamin' you."

I go call Diego from a pay phone in the park near by. "When are you coming back? I miss you." I can't bear to tell him. "Not for a while." I don't have the nerve to tell my sweet young lover that I am getting married in four days. He'll have to read about it in *Time*. He doesn't understand what I'm doing with Richard anyway. I put Diego's favorite song, the Stones' "No Expectations," in the tape deck and drive to the beach. I long to be in his arms.

Richard can't tell anything is wrong. And he wants to keep everything a secret, a tad insulting. He says that this way "we can see if things work out." Whatever the fuck *that* means. There's no time for any of my family to get here and he keeps saying that it's not a big deal. Well, maybe it's not a big deal for him 'cause he's done it so many times before, but it is for me. He's also terrified of what his family will think—Jesus!

Speak to Maria and give her the news, including this secrecy bullshit. She has a good idea. "I'm going to dinner at Elaine's tonight. I'll take care of it."

Maria calls; she's dropped the news at a big table full of bi-coastal, bisexual movers and shakers. Now L.A. and New York are buzzing: "Jennifer and Richard are getting married."

Richard flips out. "How the hell did this happen?!"

"Gee, Richard no idea. Maybe Maria knows."

I also call Barbara to tell her that I won't be meeting her in Italy, that I'm getting married instead. She flips. "Noooooooooo—you can't do this. You make the best husband!" Lord.

August 15

Go to Honolulu with Louisa and Carol, who'll be my bridesmaids, to shop for my dress and get other essentials for the wedding. We fly over in the helicopter that does scenic tours, which Richard has leased for the day. We put on earphones and listen to the sound-track of *Superman* as the pilot dips and soars into and out of hidden lush valleys and between the mountain peaks with their cascading waterfalls. Amazing!

Back at the hacienda, good old Skip Brittenham, Richard's law-yer, is ready and waiting for me, with pen in hand, to sign the proverbial pre-nuptial. It's been looked over by my lawyer in Beverly Hills, so it's all very kosher. Skip is so eager and so desperate to get my signature—on the fucking eve of my wedding—it all feels rather crass and vulgar. He's also brought our wedding rings. How's that for a mixed bag of messages from the messenger? In his defense, I must say that he does seem a bit nervous. "Well, this is unpleasant Jenny, but let's just dispense with it as quickly as possible. I'm sure we'll never have to use it."

August 16
My Wedding Day—Hana, Maui.

I wake up on this crisp clear Sunday morning, a mass of frayed nerves. I dive into the freezing cold pool and swim for several minutes, trying to ready my mind for the day, for the ceremony. Louisa picks me up and we meet Carol at Mass, where I take communion. Back at the house, I put on the white, knee-length, silk-matte jersey with a slit up the side—white sequins spilling down one shoulder—that I found in Honolulu. Richard is beautiful in white slacks and matching silk shirt. When my bridesmaids and Henry the minister are in place, we begin. Harry Hasegawa, who owns the general store, gives me away and reads a sweet message from my father:

> As father of the bride, let this message instruct all who hear, that I make this gift with fullness of heart. I now relinquish to Richard my role as nurturer and protector of my beloved daughter so that he and she may know in largest measure the spiritual enrichment, reciprocal fulfillment and lasting happiness that the holy state of wedded unity may open unto them.

Touching and lovely—Harry still holds fast to the romantic ideal.

It *is* an unbelievably beautiful ceremony. We stand facing the sea with the hills behind us and God on our side. I cry. Richard cries. Everybody cries.

The reception is lively, with lots of champagne and food. Okima gets drunk and seems very sad. I mean, is she in love with Richard or what? Carol sings beautiful Hawaiian love songs. Bill Dana tells some bad jokes and Skip gets tipsy along with everyone else.

Finally we are all alone, married and all alone. I put my new wedding-night nightgown on and expect to make glorious love. Richard just rolls over, turns the light out and tells me, "Good night."

Fuck. I can't believe it. Good-night? On my wedding night!

"Richard? Why the hell are you giving me the freeze on this night of all nights?"

"Turn the fucking light out, bitch!"

He picks up a glass from the nightstand and hurls it at me, missing my head by a hair's breadth. It hits the wall with such force that a triangle of glass remains stuck in the wood. Full of champagne and determination, I continue. "I can't believe you just did that!"

He jumps out of bed, runs toward me, grabs me by the neck, smashes my head against the wall, then throws me onto the floor. "Believe this, bitch. I'll fucking kill you." I run outside and fall weeping on the ground, crying into the wet grass in my torn white wedding nightgown. Sad and hurt, I rip the nightgown into a million shreds, then stuff it into a garbage can. I put on a T-shirt and cry myself to sleep on the couch in the dining room.

August 17

It's morning and I hear Richard on the phone asking Skip if he can get the marriage annulled.

We patch things up but the first blood has been spilled on our clean state of matrimony. I fear trouble ahead, but thank God we're staying in Hana for a couple of more weeks before going back to L.A., where Richard's going to start work on a new concert movie that he's already nervous about.

Margot Kidder's been sending telegrams. "Who do you think you are? Henry the Eighth?" Yeah, and she's Dorothy Parker. Such wit!

There are more serious domestic issues to deal with. Okima, the perfect housekeeper, is behaving strangely. I find a bottle of vodka next to the Mr. Clean in her bucket. She mops the floor and cries. I've tried talking to her about what's troubling her, but can't get through. I know it's heartbreak, I know she's in love with Richard. She keeps saying, "Mr. Pryor doesn't need me anymore."

I try to reassure her but it's no use. She's so distraught, she's even tried to run away. Louisa found her down at the airport, trying to hitch a ride to Honolulu.

August 18

This morning Okima comes to work with a black eye. I decide to try and have a talk with her husband about the obvious battering—something ironic about this. I get nowhere. We suggest she take some time off. A week's holiday in Honolulu is agreed on, which leaves me as chief cook and bottle washer. Yikes! I want to cook everything Richard loves. My first dish is his favorite, oxtails and beans. I begin early in the afternoon and when evening rolls around, Richard is wondering where dinner is.

"Baby, you can tell they're done if you mash 'em."

Great idea, why didn't he tell me sooner! I grab the potato masher and go at them. Richard emerges from the bedroom again. "Mama, what are you doing?"

"Mashing the beans, like you said."

He doubles over in laughter. "I didn't mean all of them. Just one to see if they're done."

I never was a cook.

August 22

People are coming by—Stan Shaw, Pat Morita, the mayor of Honolulu, one of the state senators. Connie and Willie Nelson are on their way here to buy some land. Willie's lawyer and Skip have arranged a meeting with Richard. I am nervous, for obvious reasons.

August 26

On our way to the hotel to meet Connie and Willie, I say, "Richard, I have to tell you something."

"Talk to me, Baby."

"Uh. . . . Do you remember I told you I worked on Willie's First Annual Fourth of July picnic at Dripping Springs, Texas?"

"Yeah?"

"Well. . . . Willie was a lover of mine."

"Shit, Jennifer, did his wife know?"

"No, I don't think so. She was pregnant at the time. Do you think I'm awful?"

"No, I don't think you're awful. I love you and your honesty." Richard can really surprise me.

Connie and Willie sit in rattan chairs waiting for us. As we approach I can see right away they recognize me and I thank God I've told Richard. It's a surprisingly warm greeting on everyone's part. I drive back with Connie in their rent-a-car, while Richard and Willie take the jeep. Connie tells me about the affair that Amy Irving and Willie had. "I told Willie I'd sue him for every penny he's got if he didn't stop seeing that little tart."

259

I like Connie. Tall, big-boned, with white platinum hair, she's one tough Mama. She wears an abundance of turquoise rocks on her hands, wrists, and around her neck, a pink windbreaker, jeans, and Nikes. No fashion victim she!

They spend the afternoon with us. Generally, it's pretty relaxing, though some tension does develop between Willie's and Richard's egos.

August 23

Richard doesn't want to go back to work, he thinks it's too soon. He's been threatening suicide and somehow I think it should be taken seriously; we've got guns here, too. I beg him to tell Ray Stark and Guy McElwaine, who are producing the film, that they should postpone it. Deaf ears!

August 31

It's my birthday and Louisa and Carol come over with a gardenia bush, which we plant at the foot of the outside stairs. We get drunk, I play guitar, and we all sing country songs, ending with tears during "Amazing Grace." I can't blow out the trick candles on the birthday cake and Okima starts yelling, "Mr. Pryor! Fiya! Fiya!" I'm feeling sad since I'll be leaving in a couple of days to take care of business and prepare the house that Lauren has rented for us in Trousdale.

September 2: L.A.

I like the new house. No demon memories, no ghosts, no imprint of anyone's personality. Just new and well-decorated. It's not far from the Comedy Store, where Richard will be woodshedding for the film. Lauren has also hired a new housekeeper, heavy-set, black, and very familiar. "Hello, Jennifer. How are you?" she says on our first meeting. Call Lauren. "Do you think it's asking too much if she calls me Mrs. Pryor?" Somebody respect me!

September 8

Richard's home and already things are shaky. I try to talk to him about it but all he says is, "The minute we got married you changed."

I do feel less of a need to kowtow. Since, it seems, my personal life is falling into place, I can focus on other areas, like neglected friends and work. I tell Richard. "Yeah, I need some of my life back." He resents this, saying, "You are my conduit to reality."

He doesn't know how much pressure this is for me. Or if he knows, he doesn't care. And he's asked me for my "dowry" so many times that it's no longer funny. I think he's seen *The Quiet Man* once too often.

September 10

Dinner with Henry Winkler and his wife, Universal's Tom Mount, and Burt Reynolds at some restaurant in Santa Monica. In the middle of it, Tom gets a call from Muhammad Ali, who insists on coming over. He walks into our private dining room, sits down, and devours everyone's uneaten desserts, punctuating his bites with that strange slurred speech.

September 15

Go to Sammy and Altovise Davis's for a dinner that Sammy has cooked himself. During the meal, Richard blurts out, "I'm not ready. I'm going to fuck up. I want to go back to Hana." Sammy is so supportive and says, "Go away with your wife before it's too late. Go away with your life before it takes you away."

Amazingly, Richard agrees. "We'll go back to Hana and live a healthy and healing life together until I'm ready to face this."

This morning Richard talks to Skip and Guy about postponing the film. Impossible. They are planning a tour for Richard as well. Do they want blood? They tell him, "It's your time, don't blow it."

Skip is also thrilled with the deal he's gotten for Richard to do *Superman III*. "Four million plus a percentage of the gross. Your picture on the billboard will be the same size as Chris Reeves's." When I ask Richard about our return to Hana for a healthy, healing life, I get a belt in the mouth.

Visit Barbara who claims to be devastated by my marriage and is unable to get out of bed. Dykedom? Nah, just weird dependency. Richard goes to the Hearns and Leonard fight in Vegas.

September 17

I buy what I think is a beautiful gift for Richard. It's a pre-Civil War cigarette and match holder, with a small black child sitting on top of two yellow haystacks smoking a corncob pipe. Right before Michael Pressman shows up for dinner, I give it to Richard. He takes one look at it and screams, "I fucking hate it!"

Shocked, I ask, "Hate it? How can you hate it?"

"It's fucking racist."

"It's fucking black art; it may have been racist but it's not now. This is an artistic documentation of those times." Now I'm on a roll. "Open your eyes."

"I'll open your eyes, bitch."

With that, the pre-Civil War object goes sailing through the plate glass window in the bedroom, shattering it into a million pieces. I'm out of there, having already filled this month's quota of beatings. I drive around, punishing him by leaving him alone with his dinner guest. When I return, Richard's discussing the gory details of the fight with Michael Pressman; he loves to discuss our problems with anyone who'll listen. After dinner, the doorbell rings and in walks James Anderson, Richard's new bodyguard. Richard stands up from the table, gets a jacket, and walks to the door without a word.

"Where are you going?"

"Out."

"Out?"

"The Store." At one point, I was asked to associate produce the film but somehow this idea has gotten lost in the shuffle. I feel that Richard wants to distance himself from me. He's back on the "party circuit" too. Our new pattern is he comes home late, slaps me a few times and I leave.

September 19

Mick Jagger comes to the house this afternoon to ask Richard to open for the Stones' HBO special. What a punk. Mick gives me a cursory handshake and doesn't even look me in the eye. His

chauvinism is palpable, his manners non-existent. His general attitude sucks, as does that of his bodyguard, who stands outside like
a giant black Mr. Clean. How boring! He offers Richard $50,000 to
do the special. Richard tells him no and good-bye.

September 21

For the past three days, Richard has shown up at dawn. I work
out at the gym, have almost daily massages, and try to reroute this
misery. It's becoming increasingly clear that I will not be able to do
this myself. I need help. The pain is too deep, the hurt too intense.

September 23

At dinner I try talking to Richard about my heartbreak. "Richard,
what is it you really want?"

Looking down at his hand he says, "What I *really* want to do is
slit your fucking throat with this steak knife."

I look at the curved, shining steel blade, then into Richard's black
eyes. I imagine my blood splattering from my throat on the glass-
top table, my head dangling over my limp body. I shiver in terror.

September 24

Connie and Willie arrive for a two day visit. I wish they were
staying at a hotel, this house is just too damn small and our problems too damn big for company. Richard and I meet Burt Reynolds
and Sally Fields for dinner at a Chinese restaurant in Beverly Hills
before the premiere of *Paternity*—Burt's new film with Beverly
D'Angelo. Sally is very arch, self-conscious, monosyllabic. She
looks as if she's in physical pain when she talks to us. It stems, I
think, from her relationship with Burt. They don't seem to connect
at all; Burt even makes some remark about trying to get her back.
We go to Mann's Chinese for the opening and see Army Archer
and a huge crowd. Burt's been acting nervous about the film but
now he seems to be in his glory. That is, until the movie begins. It's
a major piece of shit. On the way out Richard confesses his undying
devotion to Arlene Dahl who *is* a vision with her thick red mane,
large breasts, and oldtime moviestar demeanor. Richard adored
her in *My Wild Irish Rose*.

We go get Connie and Willie and head over to the Comedy Store where we're greeted by parazzi, who, we later find out, had been arranged for by Burt. Richard asks Willie, Burt, and Robin Williams, who happens to be at the Store, to come on stage. They all pile on. Willie sings, Burt tells an old, tired joke about Mae West, and Robin improvises brilliantly. The audience can't believe their luck. Afterward, we have drinks in the back room and the photographers descend. As we all stand in line, one comes forward, takes my arm and says, "Darling, would you mind terribly?" He then pulls me out of this star-studded lineup. At this moment I have no identity. I realize that I *have* traded myself for a walk-on part in Richard's movie, and that I am only recognizable by the glory I reflect. It's glare is blinding, its heat burns.

We pile into the limo and head for our house. Robin and his wife, Valerie, follow behind in their car. Richard and I begin arguing about nothing. Then he says to the driver, "Stop the car."

Connie, Willie, Burt, and Sally look confused and slightly amused. I know what he intends to do; I decide to beat him to the punch. "You think you're going to get out and cause a scene Richard? Well, allow me, motherfucker."

I throw open the door, make a grand exit, and begin marching up the road in the middle of Trousdale Estates, cursing under my breath. Robin pulls up alongside me and shouts to get in. Richard who's now in Robin's car, pleads. "Please get in, Jennifer, before the police show up."

I refuse, even though my feet are killing me (Charles Jourdan), and keep on walking until the police do show up. Robin talks them out of giving us a summons and I want to laugh at his syntax and sweetness. Instead, I hold onto my righteous indignation as I climb into the car. Connie and Willie are waiting on the front steps of the house. Burt and Sally have dropped them off and hightailed it to safer ground. Ray Charles could see the kind of night we're in for. I go hide out in the bedroom to avoid the inevitable scene. Robin comes in to talk to me. We cover love, rage, loneliness, and fear of intimacy before Connie comes knocking at the door, telling us in her sweet Texas drawl, "Richard is goin' crazy. He's throwin' dishes in the kitchen and I think he's real upset you're in here talkin' so long to Jennifer, Robin. I think y'all better come on out."

Sure enough, Richard's plowing through the dishes, swearing in between primal sobs. When he sees us he stops, takes off his diamond-studded watch, and hands it to Robin. "What's this for, Richard?"

"So you can tell time, motherfucker. How long you been talking to my wife!"

The evening wears on. Richard flirts with Valerie. At one point she's on the couch while Richard sits beside her and puts her white leather Adidas-clad feet on his lap. Once again, I retreat to the bedroom.

September 25

Connie and Willie go off to a Miles Davis concert. When we get home we see that a very drunk Okima has her hand up the back of Connie's blouse, leaning on her shoulder and cooing, "I wuv her so much."

Things are getting more surreal by the minute. I peel her off Connie, who seems to find this whole episode rather amusing. What a good sport. She pats Okima's hand and tells her, "Yes, honey, I know how ya feel." Maybe she even likes it. I pour smitten, drunk Okima into bed. This morning, she's missing. Great! What do I tell her husband? "Oh listen, Chris, by the way I lost your wife." Why did I insist on bringing her to Los Angeles with us?

Connie, Willie, Richard, and I drive to the beach for a hamburger. The ride out is fine and the meal is good. But tension sets in on the way back when Connie begins talking about how she helped Willie create his hallmark concept album, *Redheaded Stranger*. Naturally, I ask if she got credit and her answer is a booming "No!" which echoes in the great yellow Rolls. She shows me a clipping from the *Austin Statesman* entitled "The Redheaded Stranger Sings in Connie's Life!" The tension in the car worsens.

September 27

Thank God they're gone. On top of everything else I had to spend their whole visit avoiding being alone with Willie because of Richard's jealousy. This was no easy thing to do.

September 29

Okima returns and she and Richard have what amounts to a lovers' quarrel. I'm sending her back on the first plane to Hana! This marriage is a mess—what to do? Richard Rush comes to dinner to discuss a project with Richard, but I've locked myself in the bedroom and refuse to join them—another fight over Okima. I suspect the truth, but all I hear are more lies. I can't take it. I call Maria and ask her to find me a shrink.

For the past few nights, Richard's been coming home at dawn, and I am getting used to it. He tells me he's been at the Hyatt with Robin, getting high and fucking girls. Then says he has a surprise, asks me to close my eyes, and wraps a full-length lynx around my shoulders. I wish it had been love instead. It's beautiful, but it's not enough. I need more than a fur coat to stay warm.

This evening, I come home and Richard's got two strange men with him in the living room. He introduces me but I've no idea who these "suits" really are.

I have begun seeing a shrink, Michelle. She is loving and very supportive. The first thing she says is, "I hope your marriage works out but if you have to leave it, you will not be devastated."

"That's good to hear, because I *feel* pretty devastated all the time."

October 13

I work today on one of those "what to do in case of a wreck"-films for Golden West Airlines. Richard has kept me up all night. I *am* a wreck. I have to deliver my reams of dialogue and am embarrassed by having to ask for cue cards.

Come home and Sugar Ray Leonard is here for dinner. He is absolutely adorable and looks up to Richard as though he's his big brother. He asks for Richard's advice; it seems that Sugar Ray's such a star now, he's afraid of getting swallowed up. Sugar belts down a few Jack Daniels in a row and Richard warns him about drinking too much. They both go off to the Store, leaving me quite alone.

I decide to go visit Paul and come home around dawn, after Richard. He goes nuts. "What's that white spot on the comforter?"

"Richard, I don't know what the hell you're talking about!"

"It looks like cum. Who did you fuck in the bed?"

"This is insane, Richard."

"Where were you?"

"With Paul and Sam at Paul's."

"Is that a girl or a guy?"

"Sam is a girl and Paul's my good friend!"

"Mama, you're lying and the truth ain't in ya!"

"Richard, please, we've both been up all night. Don't start. You leave me alone days at a time. How dare you ask me anything?"

"I'll slap the taste right out of your mouth," he says, locking the bedroom door. He rifles through my bag, taking my credit cards and money. Then he throws me on the floor and orders me to take off all my jewelry. "Go fuck yourself, Richard." The next thing I know I'm staring at the heel of a boot, an inch away from my face.

"Bitch, take all that fucking jewelry off or I'm going to kick your face in. You got it?" Got it. Big time. I got it. I hand over the new gold Rolex monogrammed "To My Wife," my ruby ring, and my earrings. Mission completed, he walks out of the bedroom. When I get free, I call Skip, who rushes over to mediate.

David Banks also shows up. Richard tells Skip he wants a divorce. David looks shocked. "But Richard, Jenny's got heart."

Then good old Skip tells Richard. "Fine, okay. Look Jennifer, it didn't work out so it's over," Skip says. "Let's get on with it. I can have the two of you divorced in no time."

I just bet you can, Skip. Dump the deal, go on to a new one. Jesus! We settle on a brief separation.

Richard leaves for Hana today and I begin going to daily therapy sessions. I'm happy that he's away. I focus on myself; sign new commercial contracts, work out, go to museums and art galleries, see my friends, go on interviews, go out to dinner, shop—good thing I asked Richard to put me on a clothes budget—and *listen* to Michelle when she tells me, "Think only of yourself."

She also has me writing letters to Richard that I sometimes read to him over the phone. These letters aren't angry or accusatory; in fact, *I* even apologize for my quick temper and for the times *I* behaved badly. But mostly, they're about my goals for us—to love each other, to have a home together, to build a good life together.

Michelle tells me I must learn to feel my pain instead of going straight to anger; anger necessary to my survival as a child, but now as an adult it's a crippling obsolesence. This is a terrifying concept, but I try. After one bad phone conversation with Richard, I send him pictures of me dressed up as a weeping angel, complete with a white jogging suit and white and silver wings that I found in a children's store.

October 31

Richard comes home and tells me he's taken an apartment in Century City for an "escape hatch," whatever *that* means. He also tells me that those two "suits" were detectives who've bugged the house and the phones.

"What did you find out, Richard?"

"That you love me."

Life with Richard begins again. I've gotten a commercial for Harlequin Books to be shot on the Queen Mary. Richard says he's happy about it, but again, keeps me up all night before the shoot. Big budget, big cast, and big crew. I play the part of a woman who's dreaming of being chased by a mystery man who's in love with her. No stretch for me! I have to run and run—all over the decks, up and down stairs. My fatigue and general emotional state make this secretly treacherous.

This coming and going of Richard's is beyond unpredictable. I wake to the stiletto click of his Maud Frizon boots on the hardwood floors and the sound of his hand jingling coins in his pocket at any and all hours of the night. I hold my breath as he comes in to check, to see if I'm here. Some nights he climbs into bed with me and watches TV. Sometimes he holds me and I pretend that *this* is the way it always is, thinking that if I believe hard enough this might become reality. Sometimes he'll make love to me, roughly and passionately. Life in constant crisis, feelings of danger. Do I like this? No. I know it well—I grew up this way. I can hear my Pat and Harry—the screams, glass breaking, the sound of midnight flesh. And I can feel the little girl shaking inside me. Fear of infanticide. Constant crisis. Dreams of Richard Speck. I think of Pat, staring into the bathroom mirror, inspecting her bruises. I see her raging and hitting, provoking my father. She was so many different women. I remember the promise I'd made to myself, "I would never be like them." I know I have forgotten it. I put on a pair of Richard's silk pajamas and try to sleep, wondering if I can really let go of the past.

November 14

We actually manage to string a few days of sanity together. Then this morning, while making breakfast, I say something to Richard about his cocaine habit. Suddenly the eggs in the carton on the kitchen counter become little white missiles hurling through the air. Egg in my face, in my hair. He pulls me down on the floor, punches and chokes me. I manage to scramble up, run into the guest room and lock the door. He's outside yelling, "I want to slit your fucking throat, bitch!"

I call my shrink, who calmly tells me, "Put the phone down and walk out the front door."

"But I'm not dressed."

"Jennifer, get out of there. NOW!"

Thank God I keep some clothes in here. I grab a T-shirt, some jeans, and the phone rings. "Daaarlinng, it's me. Come meet me at Janet Sartin."

"Barbara, I'm in danger. I'm leaving the house now. Come pick me up." I quietly slip out the front door, walk down the front steps, and begin sauntering down the road. No Barbara. By that time I reach the intersection at the bottom of the hill, she is still nowhere in sight. Finally the black BMW passes me like a shot. As I yell to her she slams on the brakes. In her best horror-movie syntax she says, "Ohhh, my God, Jennifer, I must have missed you. I knocked on the door and Richard opened it, glaaaaring at me. He said, 'Leave us aloooone, Barbara. We want to be happy.' I thought you were in there lyyyying in a pool of blood." Darth Vader meets the Black Knight!

"How did he look?"

"That's the strange thing."

"What?"

"He had on a gray cashmere robe, his haaaaands behind his back, almost noooo expression on his face. There was a sexuuuual tension between us." I decide that Barbara is really Sid Vicious's mother. I spend the night at her apartment. Back at the house in the morning, Richard doesn't even wait till I get through the door. He is still in a foaming-at-the-mouth kind of rage. "I'll kill you, bitch!"

My car is locked in the garage and I can't get it. I check into L'Ermitage. Ray Stark calls to tell me I'm being cruel to Richard.

"He's a sensitive artist, Jennifer. you must not expect too much from him. You should treat him gently."

"Ray, I just expect him to behave like a human being. Is that asking too much? You just care about your movie, anyway."

"Listen, Jennifer, yes, I care about the movie but I want to see the two of you happy."

"Well, at this point Ray, I'd be satisfied with survival."

"And remember, Jen, if you can get Richard to do *The Toy*, hell, I'll make you producer!" Good old Ray.

Another voice of non-reason is Mitzi Shore, who gives me a lecture on the delicate psychic makeup of comedians in her whining, nasal voice, "It's such a fragile psyche, Jennifer. They're so complicated and intense."

My lawyer's heard through the grapevine that Richard is furious that I've left the house and is having papers prepared. "Papers?"

"Divorce papers."

November 19

I move back into the house and into a new level of mind games. "Richard, do you have papers?"

"Yes. No. Maybe I do, maybe I don't."

November 22

Today Richard chases me out of the house threatening to kill me. After he slams the Rolls door on me, I go over to Paul's.

Thanksgiving

Amidst all the mayhem, I still cook a damn good turkey.

November 29

Natalie Wood has drowned. God, what a tragedy. I was on that boat once, in the very place where she died—Catalina Bay. This makes me feel closer to her death and vow never again to go on a boat with Richard. I met her once and she was very warm, very genuine. Her death has affected Richard as well. I tell him we must find the lesson in this, we must appreciate each other and our love as it could all end in seconds. In response he writes me a letter in which he admits his fears of love and tenderness. He also confesses his many indiscretions. Tell me something I don't know. I've kept all the notes and phone numbers he's left on the bedside table as souvenirs of my pain. But I don't say anything. He is trying.

December 1

Richard's 41st birthday, and he's leaving for San Carlos with his entourage to try out his new act at Circle in the Square. I give him a beautiful gold cross to protect him—mostly from himself.

I get reports from Lauren and Daniel, a friend of mine whom I've hired as his valet, that Richard is already fucking up. He's seriously out of control, drinking and drugging more than ever. Richard's begun the late night paranoid calls again, desperate to keep tabs on me.

December 7

Last night was the worst. The screaming and ranting calls and accusations. I begged him to stop, pleaded with him but he wouldn't hear me. Finally, I put all the buttons on hold so he couldn't get through. I fall asleep with my own repertoire of paranoia dancing in my mind, and remembering how close he came to murdering me once. It's early evening, the manicurist is here, my feet are soaking in a tub of warm water, my fingernails are being filed and buffed, when the doorbell rings. I hear Gladys call out, "It's a messenger for you, Mrs. Pryor."

I know in my heart it's a gift from Richard. He's sorry and wants to make amends. I leap up and run to the door, leaving wet footprints. "Mrs. Pryor?" Awfully well-dressed for a messenger. Very obviously not a box from Tiffany's.

"Yes?"

"I don't think you'll be too happy to receive this." The messenger hands me an envelope and a pen.

I sign and ask, "What is it?"

He stuffs the pen back in his pocket. As he turns away he says, "You've just been served with divorce papers."

Son of a fucking bitch! I want to kick his insensitive, arrogant ass down the steps. Stunned, I put my feet back in the water and pull the thick wad of papers out of the manilla envelope. I pick up the phone. "Richard, what the hell is this?"

"Well, I finally get a call."

Is it all and only about power, this love that I think is so important? Perhaps, like his marriage to Deboragh, it's an ending. This is the last thing I ever wanted to admit to myself, but it's looking as if he's married me to end our relationship.

December 9

The first night of shooting at the Palladium. Everything is a disaster. When Richard begins to perform, Paul Mooney, his friend and human cue card, is seated in the wrong spot, the sound system is off for the first several minutes, and the lights are way too bright. The too-red tuxedo that Daniel designed for Richard makes him look like a monkey on acid. And the entire atmosphere is like a circus tent, without the warmth and intimacy required for Richard to really cook on steam. He cannot get it together. The audience is filled with adoring fans who know him well enough to know when he's not being honest. The man who "tells it like it is," isn't. Richard can feel the disappointment and I can feel his. He stops in his tracks, in mid-sentence, and confesses, "I don't know what I'm doing here. I'm not funny anymore. It's better if I leave."

He places the mike on the stool and walks off to his trailer. A horrible silence comes over the audience. I run after him. He's locked himself in the trailer and already there's a crowd of very concerned looking people standing outside. I see Berry and Tony Perkins. Berry is crying. "Jen, that was awful. Is he all right?"

The trailer is slowly filling up with friends, all of whom I am convinced, simply want to witness his latest nervous breakdown—Quincy Jones, Altovise Davis, Reverend Jesse Jackson, Guy, Skip, Paul, and Daniel. Then the Reverend Jackson decides to lead an impromptu group prayer. Ol' Jesse's always has had an instinct for timing! We all hold hands and Jesse prays, "Dear Lord, please help Richard in his hour of need . . . " and everyone obediently recites, "Dear Lord, please help Richard in his hour of need . . . " and "give him the strength, dear Lord, to continue his work free of pain. . . . " We recite "give him the strength, dear Lord, to continue his work free of pain . . . "

This is insanely melodramatic and will only make Richard feel worse. I sneak a peak at him—he looks like a deer caught in the headlights of an oncoming car—trapped, frightened, and sad. Prayer completed. The trailer has the air of a subdued funeral party. Richard's present, but no one acts as if he's really there. Guy and Skip are discussing tomorrow night's performance and what needs to be remedied and I take the opportunity to tell them what I think of their organizational skills. Jesse pulls me aside and says, "I'd like you to come over to my hotel tomorrow to discuss Richard."

I look at him blankly. He continues, "What you can do for your husband, how to help him. You see it's been my experience. . . "

My blood turns hot and I stop him cold. "I think you should discuss Richard's problems with Richard. Stop flirting with me or coming on to me or whatever the hell it is you're trying to do. I've got nothing to discuss with you in your hotel room."

Teetering on the edge, I pop half a Quaalude. Richard's sanity is crumbling. Everyone here is a voyeur to the disaster. Richard tells Rashon to find the car and get me out of there. I ask Rashon, "But what about Richard?" I know that tonight he's is completely capable of killing himself.

Back at the house, I call Le Dome and speak to Robin. "Please go be with Richard. He's in trouble tonight. I'm very worried."

The fear I saw in Richard tonight was different. I know realize that he is not going to be able to "get it up" on stage anymore. I also realize that this means the end of our marriage. He has refused to face the truths about our relationship, and if he cannot find the truth, then he will no longer be able to find it anywhere. Richard's ability to find and to tell the truth has always been the essence of his work; the linchpin, the heartbeat.

December 10

Richard comes home around noon, frail and fractured, coked-out from his night of self-pity. I know that stiff, self-conscious walk, shoulders up to his ears, terror masked by phony bravado. I want to hold him, love his pain away, but I don't dare touch his brittle body. I can barely look into his eyes. I put him to bed. He's got another evening of shooting ahead.

A miserable, hot little rumor is snaking it's way through town. In order for Richard to get it up for this evening's concert, he'll have to beat me up. God, I have to face two facts—that it's common knowledge that I'm battered, and that *I am* battered! I do not go with him this evening. He's better? Afterward we go to Sammy and Altovise's where Robin, Candy Clark, and a few nameless others are hanging out. I don't like Candy; more to the point I don't like the fact that Robin cheats on Valerie so openly. Somehow I feel that this undermines my status as a "wife." When we leave, Richard says that he's going to follow some "dude" who's in the van in front of us and who's got a "great cocaine connection." I don't want to go but am told, "Bitch, you're coming with me."

"That's what you think." I hop out of the yellow Rolls, which is travelling around a mean, little curve in the road at a fairly good clip. Richard doesn't even slow down, but I manage to perform this dangerous maneuver, sort of skipping and running and I don't even fall. The next thing I know, Robin's beside me. "Get in the car, Jennifer. I'll take you home."

Then sweet Robin tells me, "I'm beginning to think my job is to pick you up when you escape from fights and fast-moving vehicles."

Ray Stark calls and tells me they definitely have to reshoot. "God, Jen, I wish I'd had the '79 concert with this crew." But even this far superior crew, which incudes Haskell Wexler as cameraman, cannot give this film the quality or the help it needs. So much of Richard's really good material has been lost to drugs and fear; either he doesn't remember a routine that worked in woodshedding or he's simply been too lazy to work on the more challenging ones. The care and discipline that had gone into the '79 concert are not in this one. It's rushed. One night at the Store, I heard a chillingly brilliant bit he was trying out about Jesus. Now, listening to the Palladium tapes, I'm sad remembering how close to the bone he was with the '79 material. Worst of all, Richard's told me that he "*bought*" that stupid milk-and-cookies joke about how he burned up. Jesus! He's really off his "truth" center. Richard's always written his own material, that's what he's always been about!

The most honest routine of the bunch is "Being Married." In it he discusses our relationship in a way that is both truthful and revelatory.

"My wife is white and the first two years we went together, she thought her name was 'white honkey bitch.' "

I'm wiped out; I've been taking tranquilizers and 'ludes for the past two days. Richard finally comes home. He's in his usual belligerent mood and makes a remark to Rashon about my "pussy." I lose it. I scream at him and start throwing things. Then, I develop a plan. I pull out my entire collection of his women's phone numbers and, pretending I'm Richard's secretary, call them all. "Richard wants you to meet him in the lobby of the Hyatt House tonight." Only one girl questions this.

"Are you sure this isn't Jennifer?"

"I'm sure, why?"

"Well, 'cause we all hear she's one crazy bitch."

I tell Richard what I've done. Furious, he chokes me, then decides to call my bluff. He goes to the Hyatt. A Pyrrhic victory. I call the doctor for a sleep cure. He injects me with a heavy dose of some mysterious liquid. Before going unconscious, I beg him to lay it on heavy with Richard. "Tell him I can't be fucked with anymore, I'm at the end of my rope." He lays it on a bit *too* heavily. "The doctor says you're really not well, Jennifer. I think maybe it's best if we put you in a hospital." Slick. Richard knows I set him up and he's paying me back. "No, no Richard, I'm fine. Just a little tired." I know he can legally commit me and that is the very last thing I need. I sleep for two days.

December 16

Go to Century City and buy the most beautiful ornaments—miniature antique reproductions of children's toys. The shops are filled with people and the air is filled with holiday spirit, but Richard is filled with nastiness.

December 17

On my way to a looping session for the Harlequin commercial, I pass Richard and Rashon at the dining room table. They're doing the last of an all-night batch of coke, crazier than two hoot owls. After looping, I meet Evelyn Dana at the Bistro for lunch. She's with Don Adams soon-to-be ex-wife and everyone commiserates about "life with a comic." I am getting sick of this particular bit of psychobabble. Afterward I do a little shopping at one of my favorite Rodeo Drive stores—Theodore's. Driving home, I've got the sun roof open in my black Mercedes sedan. Packages fill the back seat, I've got coke in one pocket and a wad of cash in the other. I am heading home to meet a real-estate agent to look at houses to buy. My famous husband awaits, as well as the maids and the manicurists and the masseuses. Isn't this is supposed to make me happy? Why do I want to head straight to the top of Mulholland and drive off a cliff? Instead, I steer the car onto Sunset and drive in slow motion back to my misery, praying that Richard is asleep, or nice, or something other than mean and crazy.

I walk back in on trouble; Richard and Rashon have scored more coke and are snorting up a brand new storm.

"These are not the same clothes you had on when you left his morning. When did you change? What's in the bag?"

"I went shopping. Leave me alone, Richard, you're ripped!" I am brave from the Chardonnay at lunch. "I'll see you later."

"And where do you think you're going?"

"The real-estate agent is in the driveway, waiting for me. We're looking at houses."

"Oh, no you're not."

"Excuse me?"

"You're not going anywhere, Mama." He opens his palm. "Give me those keys."

I stand my fool's ground. "No, Richard. you're not taking anything away from me.

"Give them to me, *now.*"

I clutch them tightly in my hand.

"Fuck you!"

He lunges towards me, trying to pry them loose. Unable to open my hand, he backs up, takes a swing with his right fist—straight to the jaw. The next thing, and the last thing, I remember is bouncing up off the couch, my fists closed and swinging.

I come to, seated on the couch, my head on Gladys's shoulder. I'd been knocked cold by Richard's right. I never even landed a punch. Rashon is smiling and talking jive. "Born fighter, Jen. You came up swinging those fists. Instant reflex. But you buckled and passed out. No matter what though, Jen, you got a great spirit, a real great spirit."

Somehow, this makes me feel better. Then I touch my jaw, which already feels like an overripe pineapple. Rashon and Gladys take me to Cedars Sinai for x-rays. This time, I tell the truth. "Mrs. Richard Pryor. My husband slugged me."

My face enters the house before I do. Maxine and the kids are here to decorate the tree and have eggnog. Shit, I forgot. I make a valiant stab at tradition, offering cookies and my stoic m.o. All I want to do is jump on Richard and leave marks. He's hiding out in the bedroom, wallowing in his guilt. That's his apology, his only one. I put on more Christmas music and pretend everything is just fine.

I turn down Christmas invitations and hide out in the guest room with my face and shame to keep me company. The bruise turns its different shades of blue and green. I keep the door bolted.

December 20

Prophett comes over to hang out with Richard and listen to his self-pity. They are snorting dope and playing dominoes and I over-hear Richard crying. "My career is over!"

I venture out of my cage to interject some truth: "You can't stop destroying it."

This exacerbates his mounting histrionics. He angrily announces that he's leaving with Prophett and I shouldn't expect him to come back.

Fine.

He walks out, slamming the door. I retreat to my chamber and bolt the door. A few minutes later, I hear him re-enter. Silence. What's he up to? An eery silence. Then I hear the mean, click-click of his boots on the hardwood floors as he leaves the house. Only he doesn't close the door this time. I wait till I hear him drive away. Why is the door open? I unbolt the door and brave the jungle of my home. I cross the living room. My heart is already in my mouth as I near the bedroom; I see that the terrace doors are wide open, and I see clothes, my clothes, in a path coming out of our bedroom heading straight into the pool. Clothes are floating, like dozens of dead bodies. Pantyhose drifts by, leather pants head for the bottom. I feel sick. Basile, Complice, Armani, Yamamoto, Miyake, Charles Jourdan shoes, Maud Frizon boots—the best-dressed pool in town. And not just my clothes, but horribly, some of my journals, my books of songs and poems, my testimonies to survival. All sinking. There's even a photograph of Richard in a silver frame with a poem I'd written to him for his birthday. As I pull it from the water I see that the words, "I love you" are running together. A blue and lavender nightgown is caught in a tree, a Chinese robe dangles from a nearby branch. I follow the path to its source—my closets in the dressing room. Sweaters, dresses, pants, shoes, pocketbooks, and belts, all over the sisal. An open dresser drawer spills bras and underpants and like a tributary they join the clothes river.

Jasmine, the night maid, and Raul suddenly appear. Without saying a word, they begin to retrieve the drowning clothes. It's a strange silent performance combing the water with the pool net, fishing to the bottom with the long steel handle. So sweet. So useless. So sad. Jasmine speaks. "Mrs. Pryor, we can save some of this."

I step on some soaked maroon leather boots. They drip "bloody" water. I go to the guest room, lock the door, and cry myself to sleep.

December 21

I begin shopping, literally lifting whole racks of clothes onto the check-out counters. My taste is not discerning. He'll "pay the cost to be the boss" all right.

With Liz and Rain we go to Hana for Christmas. He has apologized again and again. I tell him, words, words, words. But I do love hearing him say, "You mean everything to me, please, please, forgive me." We need some major healing over this holiday.

Christmas Day

A long string of pearls and then things slide downhill. Rain is her usual, miserable self, and in the middle of an argument, I call her a brat. Richard, without even asking what's happening, takes her side, which sends me into a frenzy. I yell at him and he slaps me as hard as he can in front of her, while she yells, "Shut up!" I am humiliated and enraged; Rain gloats. In a flood of tears I leave the house in the middle of a storm and speed recklessly down the slippery bumpy road, sloshing and splashing, until one monster puddle almost sends me spinning off the earth. The engine dies and I walk back home in the torrential rain. Merry fucking Christmas.

December 29

This morning Richard drags me out to the spot where we were married and tells God and me that he's sorry and that he loves me.

Another battle with Rain and again Richard defers to her. I throw a big china bowl and he comes after me, smashing my head against the wall, spitting in my face, threatening to break my jaw. I manage to break free, run into the kitchen, and pick up the blue-handled pair of scissors. I spin around, clutching them tightly in my hand. He's coming towards me. I raise them over my head and in a voice so calm it surprises me, tell him, "Don't come near me again Richard or I'll stab you."

He freezes, so do I. He walks away and I sleep in the den, gripping the scissors all night.

December 30

This morning I tell Richard a story. Years ago, my father represented a woman who'd killed her husband after years of abuse. The bastard came home one evening, threw the food she was cooking on the floor, tossed a steak at her, and said, "Cook this, squaw." When she refused, he knocked her down, put his foot against her shoulder and pulled her arm out of its socket. She got up, went into the bedroom, got his sawed-off shotgun, and shot the bastard through the heart. My father says that he told her, "Congratulations—you got a bull's-eye." Harry used the media to influence public opinion and the battered woman was never indicted.

As I tell this story, I become aware that I'm delivering a message to Richard and to myself: "Call the plane to take me back. I've got to leave. I'm afraid I'm going to kill you."

The pilot sighs as he closes the door to the plane. I watch Richard drive away and remember him waiting there the first time I came to Hana. It seems like a million years ago.

January 4

Back in L.A., I get myself a lawyer, just in case this is really *it*. I don't know what's going on with the famous "On-again, off-again" papers, so I also look at houses to rent, just in case. I see a really charming, fairy-tale house on North Beverly Drive.

Richard returns, stays in his apartment, and does a day of re-shoots on the concert film. Ray calls to tell me that they'll "work," but he doesn't sound happy.

Of course everything is on hold about our belated honeymoon cruise. We've chartered *The Silver Trident*, a fully staffed, hundred-foot yacht, which we're supposed to board in Barbados and then cruise through the Caribbean. So I visit a voodoo woman in West Hollywood to work a little of her magic. With incantations, kri-kri, and oil, she prepares candles for me. Each one is to heal some specific rupture in our relationship—there are a lot of candles! I put what must be two dozen in the shower in the guest bathroom and light them. They're safe in there, safe from fire and from Richard, should he show up.

He shows up. I'm on the phone in the bedroom and suddenly I hear this blood-curdling scream. "What the fuck is going on? What are you doing to me?"

I cannot convince him that the candles are for our own good.

January 6

Richard goes on our honeymoon without me, taking James as his companion. There is something tragically funny about this. I sign the lease for the house on North Beverly Drive, and prepare for life without Richard.

January 10

As usual, Richard displays uncanny instincts. Whenever I am prepared to let go and carry on without him, he throws me a disori-enting curve. Today, he calls from *The Silver Trident* on ship-to-shore radio. He wins me over—what else is new?

"Come down and meet me, I'm miserable without you."

"But Richard, we're miserable together."

"Only when I'm a mean, horrible, son-of-a-bitch."

"True."

"We'll fix it, Jen. I promise you. I mean it this time. I'm passing Teardrop Island. Please, Jen." I am laughing and crying.

"Jenny, there's Heartbreak Cove."

"Richard . . ."

"Sorrow Reef is coming up. Please come to me." I am drowning in a sea of tears, happy and sad. Lost in hope once again. This *could* be our last chance.

"What about those fucking papers, Richard?"

"I'll take care of them, get rid of them. Please, Jenny I love you."

January 11

I shop for cruise wear and call my lawyer.

"Yes, they're being rescinded. Don't worry, go away and have a wonderful time."

"Yeah, but I've heard this before."

"This time it's true. There's a lawyer flying down to Maui, going to the courthouse where they were filed, as we speak."

January 12

I fly all night to meet my husband. I am full of faith.

January 13

I fly into Kennedy and pick up a connecting flight to Barbados. There, a small private plane greets me and delivers me to tiny Union Island. I am quivering with excitement at being reunited with my man. As we land on the miniature runway, I see him waiting, nervous, and kicking the dirt, and it reminds me again of that first trip to Hana. I've never met a man who needed love so badly and resisted it so much.

I run into his open arms. He holds me. I look at his shy face and know I'm in the right place. Captain Raggs is with Richard and he looks like his name. He's a short, salty Aussie with a long moustache. He's missing two front teeth, has a tremendous beer gut, a hearty laugh, and a wicked gleam in his eye. His sturdy legs and wobbly knees are fully exposed beneath his uniform of tight, white Bermudas. Old Raggs looks as if he's spent a little *too* much time on the islands. I like him immediately.

In a small skiff, we motor out to *The Silver Trident*, which is moored far out in the bay. She's beautiful, and looks like a giant wedding cake: white, three-tiered, trimmed in blue and gold.

I walk into the large, luxurious living room as our female stew shows up. I can't believe my eyes. Betsy* is a drop-dead knockout, a true-blue WASP with bright eyes, dishwater-blond hair, good manners, and great legs. She waits on us in a short, navy skirt, and sexy, tanned, bare feet. Lord, Richard'll be after her in a New York minute. She makes me nervous but she's really great. She shoots me a knowing look that says, "You've got your hands full." Then I meet Kate* a high strung, English, anorexic, and a gourmet cook. The rest of the crew consists of Tony, the first mate from Malta, and three young Filipino men. I hope these nice people don't have to witness some of our up close and personal psychoses! James "In the Way" Anderson, who's still along on our honeymoon, is subtly hostile, acting as if I am the interloper. I am civil, but just that!

We motor over to the tiny privately owned island of Petit St. Vincent to dock for the night. We have rum punches and a delicious meal; Kate can definitely cook. Richard and I are still awkward with each other, which I believe to be a good sign. After dinner, the crew invites us to join them at the hotel for a "jump up." I go and have a fantastic time, while Richard chooses to stay behind with "In the Way."

January 14

Amazing hangover! I kneel on the white beach, vomiting pink goo and praying. Richard's adorable, holding my rum head and making jokes about pink goo and green water.

Captain Raggs takes us to the other side of the island and drops us off with a picnic basket full of Kate's treats. What an afternoon! No James. Just us chickens, a sweet yellow lab who decides to adopt us, and endless beach, warm aqua water, and true-blue sky. We play at the edge of the sea, take pictures of each other and hang out in the hammock under the trees after lunch. We hold each other as though for the first time. This is paradise; this is a fairy tale; please God, let us have a happy ending.

At twilight, we head for the island of Bequia. A romantic journey—full moon, stars, and stars. As we approach we see a beautiful array of sailboats—one belonging to Bob Dylan. After another delicious dinner, the lusty reggae music pulls me to shore and Captain Raggs escorts me to the local hotspot for another night of dancing. Again, Richard stays on board. When I get back, I know something's happened. Betsy and Richard are both sulking and no one's speaking. I can only guess.

January 15

Richard is the Incredible Sulk and the weird thing is that "In the Way" is mirroring his moods. Fuck it! I go ashore alone to shop and tour Bequia. They make sailboats here, including miniature ones, and I order one of these—a schooner with red sails—for my father. Back on board, Richard is drunk and surly. We fight about the boat I'd ordered. It seems that Richard's now jealous of my father. It turns out that "In the Way" is my bodyguard, too, as he restrains Richard.

We've become an attraction for the tourists and the locals. Homeboys arrive in battered, colorful rowboats and serenade us accompanied by their primitive, homemade guitars. We're a show for the crew, too, as they watch and wait for the next fight. And now there are many, over nothing. Now Richard's threatening to leave when we get to Mustique. He's even hired a plane to meet him there.

January 17

A choppy voyage to Mustique. Richard tells Raggs to cancel the plane. Bravo! We have lunch on the terrace of the Cotton House during the most beautiful part of a late West Indian afternoon, when the air is heavy and sensual. Richard and I are neither together nor completely isolated from one another. We eat chicken salad, drink white wine, and watch as the birds wait in line for their share of bread crumbs. I explain, "This is what a pecking order is."

We all laugh, enjoying the relief from our tension and the self-conscious atmosphere of this hotel. The help moves about in grand lethargy. Most of the guests are European, and they glide about on expensively oiled legs that seem too tired and too bored to walk. The men show off their miniature baskets while the women, all of whom are topless, wear strings of leopard skin or shiny fabrics, showing off their perfectly waxed thighs and hungry loins. There is no sensuality here. The mood is pretentious, rich, trendy and mean.

"In the Way" asks what E.C.—East Caribbean currency—stands for and I tell him, "Eece come, eece go."

Again we all laugh, Richard the loudest. I love making him laugh. I know how to do it, I do it well, and I do it a lot. Sometimes I get fucking sick and tired of doing it. Why is he always in such a bad mood? I feel myself get madder and madder, about everything.

We stand on the bow, watching the anchor being raised, happy to be leaving the sterility of Mustique. We slice our way back to Bequia in another star-filled, full-moon night. The sensual sounds of reggae music fill the bay. It feels like a homecoming. And I am filled with a sexy hope for a night of great love-making. It's been a while. Mostly we've just been fucking, our bodies slamming up against each other, all the passion now just a sloppy, nasty lust. He's cancelled that plane so I know he wants to make a go of it. I get dressed to kill in a black linen short skirt slit up the back, a white halter top, and white sandals. Richard dresses as well—white linen slacks, a black T-shirt, and those elegant black bare feet. We're in synch. Arms around each other, we are in love.

Betsy and Kate have caught on putting on fresh uniforms for us. Kate's prepared grilled flying fish and serves it with Château Margau, brie, and fruit. Small votive candles burn inside pale-blue frosted cups.

"How do you feel, Richard?"

"Married. Nervous."

"Richard, all I want to do is love you."

"That's what I'm afraid of."

After dinner, we take pictures and hang out, but we are still self-conscious when we go below to our cabin. I put on a black nightgown: Richard is waiting for me. I slip into bed beside him, trying to conceal my desire just a little. I feel so raw. I crave his tenderness, but getting it is never easy. We've perfected a technique, one that I've grown tired of. I submissively fawn over him and he pushes me away. I act appropriately wounded and he rewards me with the love he can't give freely. Let's not play tonight! I pick up a book. Richard makes a remark about reading and I deliver one of my own, "It's good for the soul, you should try it sometime."

In a flash he slams my head against the headboard, then he has both hands around my throat. As I struggle to get free, I fall off the bed, landing on the floor with an unattractive thud, tangling in the top sheet as I go. I feel all the familiar aches in my heart, in my throat, and in my eyes. I get up and sit on the side of the bed. We're both breathing hard. And all I wish is that he would take me in his arms. We could make passionate, crazy love, cry in each other's arms, and be sorry for all the hurt. But he's too angry and too scared of love. My ears are ringing, my face is stinging. I can taste blood. I turn and look at him. "This is the last time, Richard."

He pivots his head around, shooting me with one of his killer looks. He hates me. And now I too, hate. "You'll be sorry for that."

He's trying to catch his breath, get his shit together, but I know he's confused. This is a new reaction. I want to ask him, "'Bout fucking time, huh, Richard?" Instead, I go to the head and look in the small ship's mirror. My mouth is cut and bleeding. I see Pat.

We go to separate cabins. I don't sleep at all.

January 18

We leave Bequia this morning and go on to St. Thomas for fuel and water. Richard is ominously silent. I know he's got a plan. We head for Marigot Bay, St. Lucia without speaking. My head is aching. As we pass by the mountains of St. Lucia, I think why does my pain always seem to occur with beautiful backgrounds? Some weird trade-off? Why can't *I* match where I am? Richard fishes and fishes. And still I hope. Too late.

Marigot Bay is green and still, and wrapped in a mist that feels like a whisper. It is one of the most beautiful bays in all the Caribbean. Captain Raggs tell us this cove has a serious past; it was once a pirate hideout. Now it holds our future.

Our boat docks in front of the Hurricane Hotel—how appropriate. We find that we've arrived in the midst of an attempted Third World coup. Richard runs into the hotel. I follow him and watch him talking on the old black phone. A fan spins overhead as he leans against the straw walls. I am a sad, desperate woman in some old forties movie. I hear him say "Skip," and know the plan. When he finishes I feel like Ida Lupino and slide around the edge of the straw wall to the same phone. After several tries I finally get through to my lawyer. Yes, he just got a phone call. Divorce proceedings back on. Fuck. Those papers had never been rescinded. I'm furious and feel betrayed. There is only one phone and soon the two of us are amusing the hotel guets and the help, as we come and go from the boat passing each other on the gangplank, hysterically calling our lawyers. We eat dinner separately.

Then Captain Raggs informs us we're heading up to Rodney Bay in the morning. Great, another beautiful setting. Richard drinks martinis and I cry myself to sleep. The entire crew is depressed.

Janaury 19

As I'm eating breakfast on the terrace of Hurricane Hotel, Richard joins me. The sun is shining and a fine mist is falling. I know it's probably our last meal together. We exchange a few words but it's our pain that connects us now. We've begun too bloody a battle to retreat. And Richard does have a point about one thing—if we stay together he might end up disfiguring or killing me. We pick at our food and cling to our pride. And we can't swallow either. We even laugh at ourselves.

Rodney Bay cannot compare with Marigot's magic. It has a sour, stagnating quality, which I like better than all that fucking beauty. Gros Islet, a small fishing village on a nearby shore, looks sad and poor. Black teenagers mill about on the muddy bank and stare at our monster boat, probably thinking we have it all.

Richard's been on shore making phone calls and reservations. He's all greased up on martinis. Uncle Dicky is sick, and Richard has to go see him. I can't help asking, "Isn't Uncle Dicky always sick? I mean the poor bastard weighs three-hundred pounds."

We've begun fighting again—snotty, "off-side" remarks that sound staged. "In the Way" is just that—smack dab in the middle. Richard keeps knocking back martinis. It is time to call Maria and tell her to go to the house and get some of my things—especially my car. When I go to use the ship's phone Captain Raggs tells me that I'm not allowed to.

"What do you fucking mean, I'm not allowed to?"

"Mr. Pryor's orders. You're not allowed to use the phone until Mr. Pryor is off the boat."

"Captain Raggs, I have a right to use that damn phone."

"Well, Mr. Pryor is paying for the boat." Fucking pig.

"That, Captain Raggs is none of your goddam business. Then take me ashore so I can use the phone."

"Can't do that either. Mr. Pryor's orders."

That's it! I run from the kitchen to the deck yelling at the top of my lungs, "I want everyone to listen! You are all going to get into a hell of a lot of trouble here. We're in international waters and you motherfuckers are in over your heads. I will fucking swim to shore and have you all arrested for kidnapping."

The burned-out Aussie runs to Richard to talk this over. "I'll take you ashore, Mrs. Pryor."

Now that I've won my point, I don't need to go. Instead I've got a few more things to say. "You have no fucking friends, Richard."

"Look, you made James cry." I can't believe it. Alligator tears are streaming down "In the Way's" face.

"I'm crying because Richard might lose his uncle, the last connection with the past and he might lose you. Please stay on the boat when we leave." I can't believe this bullshit. "In the Way's" on a roll.

"And Richard does have friends, Jennifer. I am his friend. Richard is loved."

"You're on his fucking payroll, asshole." I rip back into Richard.

"One of the most disillusioning things about this relationship is finding out that you are not a decent human being. You are a man who manipulates people, connives, and uses others for your own end. You value no one, no human relationship, and most of all, you don't value yourself." He looks wounded and pathetic and it's breaking my heart, but I can't stop myself. It makes me even angrier that I care. I hate him for destroying us. My fury has taken on a life of its own. Rage is spurting out of me, a waterhose of venom, I am a poisonous snake.

"I know you feel like failure. I know you feel awful about your concert movie and you should, you compromised piece of shit. The sad truth is, Richard, you're not even a good artist anymore. How does it feel to be mediocre, Richard? Mediocrity is the torment of genius! Well, at least you don't have to worry about that anymore! You know how good it could have been? But you don't tell the fucking truth anymore. Even Ray Stark wishes he had the '79 material with the Palladium crew."

Richard is slumped over his martini, shrinking and sinking into his chair, too drunk even to respond. All he can muster is, "This boat costs $100,000 a month."

"That's right, Richard. It's all about money." Mean adrenalin courses through me. I want to bomb the fucking boat and all of us in it. I go collect my passport, airline ticket, and money, sensing that it's all destined for the deep blue sea, just like me.

Richard's bad mood and alcoholic stupor worsen. Now James is drinking martinis, too. I eat dinner outside on deck as Richard and "In the Way" dine inside. I listen to the belligerent, black, macho, dialogue. I refuse to react. Richard gets angrier and louder. Rage and misogyny are wrapped in bitter blackisms.

"I told that lily-white motherfucker to kiss my black ass." I put on some classical music.

"Can't live with the bitches, can't live without them." I am beginning to feel afraid; that's what he wants. I know this will escalate into some violent circus and I have no protection.

"The bitch deserved it." Always head for the safety of racism and machismo. I don't need a tree to fall on me. Tonight could easily be murder on the high seas. I go see Captain Raggs.

"I'm concerned for my safety. May I sleep in your office?"

"It's the observation deck."

"Whatever. Can I lock myself in?"

"All but one door. I'll have Tony stand guard." I give my passport, money, and tickets to Betsy to hold. Kate tells me that Besty's been fired because she refused to sleep with Richard that night in Bequia. I apologize to Betsy, even though it's not my fault. A few minutes later, Captain Raggs reappears with my things in his hands.

"You've got to take care of this stuff yourself. I can't have any of my crew involved."

"I understand but you'll be involved if I wind up in a pool of fucking blood." He gets it. He doesn't want a murder on his boat.

I make up the leather couch for a bed, although I know I won't sleep. The doors are locked, I've got a book, and I pray that Richard will leave me alone. I have stuffed some other valuables under the mattress in our cabin and I hope he doesn't find them. I've been dozing, so I don't know how much time has passed when I hear the sound of the silver handle on the mahogany door. The handle jiggles as I watch Richard's silhouette through the small round window at the top of the door. He leaves. A few seconds later, he's at the other door, rattling the handle. "I want to talk to you."

I don't move. I am terrified. Please God, let him leave me alone. All through the night he appears and reappears at the two locked doors and rattles the handles again and again. At one point, he comes with a key that he tries to fit into the locks. He presses his face against the small round window and in a low, creepy voice he says, "I need to talk with you."

There's no telling what he'll do if he gets in. In my heart, I believe my life will end. Richard has told me on this trip about his fantasies of killing me and throwing me off the boat and he's also told me that he's asked to have me killed. I knew that, just like I know that he's downstairs now, looking through my things. Thank God, I've got my stuff so I can leave. I doze, shake, and pray. I have a serious talk with God: If I make it through this night, I promise I will change.

I must give up my addiction to this misery, I must let go and find the courage to leave. I don't *need* to live like this—and I *won't* any longer. I am a miserable creature. And the worst thing is that the thought of change is almost as terrifying as the thought of what Richard might do if he gets in here.

Around dawn the silver handles stop moving. I have hit bottom. I *will* get out.

January 20

It's eight A.M., the sun is hot and the sea is rough. Rodney Bay is uglier than ever; it's a good setting. Captain Raggs tells me that Tony slept outside the unlocked door all night and I cry at the thought of someone caring. Breakfast is on the table and Richard is nowhere in sight. I hear the nerve-jarring sound of silverware.

Then Richard and James are in front of me. "I'll never hit you again, Jennifer."

He is dressed in loose white travelling clothes and carries a small suitcase. He turns to go and I feel as if I'm about to throw up. He stops and looks over his shoulder at me. "Will you be here when I get back?"

Bullfighters call this "The Moment of Truth." I don't answer. I just give him a quick glance and notice that he can't hide his shame. He and James are going down the stairs and I decide to watch him leave. I walk slowly to the other side of the boat to watch Richard as he gets into the silver Zodiac. Captain Raggs already has the outboard running—a quick getaway. This is the saddest day of my life; I am crying and he never even told me he was sorry. I sit down to eat breakfast and the crew seems more depressed than I am.

I am lonesome, my marriage has failed, but I'll be okay. I think I'll carry on to Martinique and fly home from there.

Richard calls and tells Old Raggs to wait for him and not to move the boat one inch. So much for Martinique. I'll leave tomorrow.

My last meal on the boat, a sad one, and I think: The Last Supper. Kate's outdone herself, the meal is just beautiful. I photograph it.

It's a long, bumpy ride to the airport. Looking tough and feeling shattered, I am an oxymoron. I am in another world in my third-world cab. I keep telling myself, *Remember why you're leaving.* There are strange moments when I've no idea where or even who I am. The terrain is more African than Caribbean. The St. Lucians along the road look more like shadows than people. The houses and the other cars are all bright blurs. I try to remember my prayers for courage. How can I do this? How can I change? Is there any simple way? God, I love him. But I cannot be hit or degraded anymore. I am not my mother. I remember the words: "Never compare yourself to others, only to the person you know you can be." I am crying now and the cab driver keeps nervously looking at me in his rearview mirror. I'll pull myself together as we heave over steep hills and dark, curves. I might find out who or what I am, or can be. I just have to get through the next five minutes. That's it, five minutes at a time.

I apply this technique the entire flight to Miami. Sobbing all the way. To make matters worse, some asshole sits next to me sporting a cap on his Cro-Magnon head that says, "Loose Women Tightened Here."

ME

You can gaze out the window
Get mad and get madder
Throw your hands in the air
Say "What does it matter?"
But it don't do no good
To get angry
So help me, I know.
For a heart strained in anger
Grows weak and grows bitter
You become your own
   prisoner
As you watch yourself sit
   there
Wrapped up in a trap
Of your very own chain of
   sorrow.

"Chain of Sorrow"
John Prine

1982

January

I am in the Ionosphere Club at Miami International Airport. There is a row of phones with different colored doctor's office-type chairs in front of them. While waiting for a flight, one can make business calls. I've got some business. First my lawyer, then Maria.

I order a beer from a surly waitress as I'm telling Maria to get my jewelry, my lynx, my car and anything else she can, out of the house. I call Gladys, who tells me that Richard's been in L.A. He left when he heard that I'm on my way back.

Amidst my hysterical phone calls, I hear, "You tell him it's Marvin Mitchelson. He'll take my goddamn phone call."

I approach him. "Excuse me Mr. Mitchelson, but I couldn't help overhearing . . . my name is Jennifer Lee . . . Pryor, and I am getting a divorce from my husband, Richard. Can we talk?"

He asks what flight I'm on and tells me to find him on the plane. "We'll talk there."

I find him slumped over his briefcase with a gin and tonic and I sit down beside him. As I begin divulging my tale of woe, he begins pulling press clippings out of the briefcase. Not a good sign. He commiserates "I will see to it that you don't get screwed . . ." and I make an appointment for the following afternoon.

January 22

Century City—a tall complex of sinister buildings-of-the-future —power central! Marvin Mitchelson's office is high up in one of these structures. I am sitting on one of the deep maroon couches in the waiting room. I think, here is where they all sat: Britt, Bianca, Michelle, Soraya—an endless stream of blond tits and Hollywood hustlers. I feel as if I'm in a bordello. After fifteen minutes, I am ushered into the inner sanctum.

Mr. Mitchelson himself appears, dressed in bellbottom jeans and a maroon-velvet, double-breasted blazer. I feel as if I'm now in the hands of an oversized velvet divorce machine. I compliment him, a required social amenity. "Really great looking office."

"There's a Jacuzzi just in the other room. I can put my robe on after work, fix myself a drink and relax." I bet!

I give him a five-thousand dollar retainer and tell him, "above all, no publicity; please keep this quiet." Roxanne Pulitzer's been all over the front pages and I have no desire to emulate her or her media coverage. "Don't worry about a thing, we'll take good care of you."

This afternoon, when I call Marvin about my missing car he's busy being interviewed by *People* magazine and a gigantic red flag goes up. This guy is a publicity seeker. This is how he does it!

Liz Smith calls to ask about my divorce. I say, "It's not true. Who gave you this information?"

"Someone in Marvin Mitchelson's office."

I tell Liz I met him on a flight from Miami and *that* was all. I send her a huge basketful of orchids. When I call Marvin's office to yell at him, they tell me he's away. "Tell him to call me. *Immediately!*"

Mitchelson calls from Vienna and I rip into him. "How dare your office let out that information to the press, you unethical mother-fucker. Priests, doctors, and lawyers are legally bound to keep their mouths shut! Give me back my retainer or I'll take you up before the California Bar."

(Liz tells me that her people and all the other columnists call certain lawyers like Marvin regularly to ask if there's anybody they should know about. I don't like it.)

I meet with two young Beverly Hills lawyers, which makes my *third* law firm, and I stress the importance of discretion.

"First we must tell you that nobody has ever done what you did with Mitchelson and gotten any part of their retainer back. Congratulations. And yes, of course we're very discreet. Did you hear about Kate Jackson's divorce?"

"Not until now."

"Exactly. We handled it. Not a word in the press, ever."

February

I'm now living in that sweet little house on North Beverly Drive. The cute blond hostess from "The Love Boat" lives next door. She's very wacked out on coke, twitches all over the place. God, I hope I don't look that way when I'm high. I sit on the brick terrace under the lemon trees, listening to Julio Iglesias and wonder how long it will take for my heart to heal. I go on interviews, meet with the lawyers, see my shrink Michelle, go to the gym a lot and see lots of movies. Time to take a lover!

Walked around Alvaro Street looking for crosses and serapes; found a wounded dove in a cage, bleeding from his neck.

March

I can't fucking believe it! Richard discusses our divorce on the Johnny Carson Show! Go to the Stanhope in New York with Barbara Steele and Teo Davis. It's freezing here, but it feels incredibly grounding. Maybe I should move back here.

April

My father's furious that I fired Mitchelson and says, "If you don't take my advice, I will have no further discussion with you about your divorce." Thanks Harry, but he does have one great idea, which is that I should sue for assault and battery as well as divorce. But no can do because I'm afraid of what Richard and all his big guns might do. Lawyers, money, and the power of stardom are lethal weapons. Visit Georgia in Bennington. Her child is fast becoming her clone—sad but true. Spend a day with Cindy and her kids in Stockbridge. She's become "The best mom in the world." Buy a car—a red, convertible VW Rabbit. Teo Davis helps me out with the purchase and says, "You're so nurturing. What Jennifer Lee needs is a Jennifer Lee." Amen.

May

Party at Barbara Steele's and meet a really adorable guy—Bruce Robinson. He's got that great, French existential look—actually he's English—with a cigarette hanging out of his mouth, and the burned-out demeanor of the suffering poet. Bruce is no slouch either. He's an actor and a writer. He wrote the screenplay for *The Killing Fields* and performed in *Romeo and Juliet* and *Adelle H.* I hear that he lived with Zeffirelli and that he still has a broken heart over Leslie-Anne Down, with whom he lived for years. He can use me as a milagro.

I am sitting, fantasizing about Bruce when Barbara calls with the news: Richard (who's been shooting *The Toy*) is in a hospital in New Orleans with a "heart attack" or "pneumonia" or something. More likely, it's an OD. I fight with myself not to rush to the airport and get on the first plane. Instead, I call Bruce. "Hi, remember me? Why don't you come up and take a Jacuzzi with me?"

We drink Bloody Marys, I have a couple of lines, and we boil together in my outside Jacuzzi. We make great love and I escape the temptation to fly to New Orleans. A few hours later, Bruce rides off into the sunset to do research in Los Alamos.

Beverly drops by tonight with a set of very good looking Italian twins who are high on heroin. Meet with Howard Rosenman at Paramount about an idea I have for a play called *Basé.*

Bruce is back. This afternoon, he has me dress all in white and sit in a huge Mexican leather chair, gets the fireplace roaring, puts Julio Iglesias on the stereo background, and asks me to tell him about the first time I ever "did it." The whole story really excites him and we end up making passionate love. We drive to Westwood, browse through bookstores, eat ice cream cones, and hold hands. Naive and wonderful. I've forgotten that people do this.

June

Lunch today with my new "best friend" Nancy Dowd, a screenwriter who won an Oscar for *Coming Home.* We talk about books and I think I am beginning to find my mind again, perhaps for the first time.

Producer Jack Towne* calls, saying he desperately needs to speak to me. I've never met him. So, I ask for a hint. He says, "A project Richard wants to do."

"What do I have to do with this?"

"Talk to me and you'll see."

Although Jack lives around the corner, he sends a car to pick me up. A maid greets me and walks me through the living room and through the open glass doors to the terrace. Jack introduces himself, approaching me as if I'm a long-lost friend. He's a legend in this town and certainly one in his own mind. I've heard gossip about this man for years. And Jack is true Hollywood, the "Perfect Man," with that seamless, strangely hued tan that must come out of a very expensive bottle. I stare at his sharp nose and remember the story of how it had almost dissolved from coke and had to be rebuilt with Teflon. I think of frying pans. Jack wears flawless white slacks and a cream-colored silk shirt; his jet-black hair is slicked back. He makes me nervous. I'm happy to see the chilled bottle of good white wine.

He begins. "There's a project I'm producing about the New York jazz scene. You've heard of it?"

"Hasn't everybody?" The gossip is that this film is already in trouble.

"Great story. Hang on." He runs into the house and returns with a big fat book and an advertising mock-up featuring a very prominent Richard.

"I want Richard to do it."

"Yes?"

"I need your help." I am definitely confused.

"My help?"

"I want to get you and Richard back together. I hear he is really miserable over you and I know you love him, right? You love him?"

"Yeah, I love him."

"So I thought, I have you two meet here and I'll get *E.T.* for you to watch together. I spoke with him and he said he'd love to see that with you."

"You spoke to him about me?"

"Yeah. I told him how much I loved my ex-wife. He told me how much he loves you."

"I don't think I can see Richard." "Perfect Man" looks worried.

"All right, I know it's emotional stuff. But think about it. Promise me you'll think about it. Read the book and think about it."

297

I leave with all this homework but I don't need to think about it. His intentions are clear—use me to get to Richard for the deal. Fuck Jack Towne and the horse he rode in on! I can just imagine what he's telling Richard.

It's a few days after this meeting and I know I can't see Richard. I am too vulnerable. I call "Perfect Man" who tells me he's spoken to Skip who says Richard definitely wants to do the project.

"Good. Then you won't need me." This upsets him.

"Please, trust me. I told him you're reading the book."

"It has nothing to do with anything except how I feel. I can't see him. I'm frightened, do you understand?"

"Completely. I'm just asking you to take a chance."

"I've done that! Anyway, I don't get anything out of this. It'd just be a favor for you." Now it gets good. Jack is hurt.

"A favor for me! I resent that! I get nothing out of this, in fact, I'd probably be putting myself in jeopardy. Check me out all over town, I've nothing to do with getting involved on a personal level. Richard's difficult—"

"Jack, I'm scared!"

"Well, I'll give you protection. You need it more than Richard." Oh, this is getting rich.

"May I call you my Godfather?" Now, he's not only defensive, but he's begun sneezing. I wonder why?

"Are you having fun, Jack?"

"I've been sneezing all day . . . you know I can get Harold Robbins to do this!" This motherfucker will not listen to me!

"This is my decision!"

"Listen, go away this week. Where do you want to go? I'll send you to Palm Springs. You like the Springs? I'll make reservations." There's no way I'd take a toothpick from this man, let alone a trip! "Listen, Jen, look upon it as an adventure. You can walk away after an hour."

"You deliver me and you get a deal, is that it? Jack, I'm sending your things back."

That's it! I'm outta here! New York, here I come!

A couple of days later, I see *E.T.* and cry.

July

Go to Richard Gere's party at the home of Nando Scarfi-otti—Bertolucci's set designer. God, I'm glad to be leaving this desperate town.

July 13

The money thing is all settled. I get into the elevator with one of my lawyers and he's so happy. "We got you that money. Now I can buy that little Mercedes I want." Then he kisses me on the cheek! What an insensitive son of a bitch. This is *not* a happy time for me. My prenuptial determined how much I would get. It didn't take a genius to extract what I was due. The lawyers took my case on contingency, so they get a third. What a dummy. (For the record, I didn't get $750,000 as has been reported; I got $250,000, before fees.) Go to court and got on the stand. "Do you swear in your petition of divorce . . ." It was over in moments. I will be officially divorced in six months. I was officially married for six months before we separated. Richard has been my life for four years. Is *this it?*

July 14

I've been unable to pack so I've hired Services Unlimited. The crew arrives and begins moving furniture and stuffing things into boxes. Still in bed, I listen to them, unable to face the fact that I am really leaving L.A., this house, and the man I love. They pack around me. Finally Jasmine shakes me. "Mrs. Pryor, it's time. They need your bed." I get out and hit the floor, curling up on the carpet until the last possible moment . . . Jasmine's crying. Then the limo door shuts with a thud and I'm suffocating behind a smoky glass partition.

I sit in first class, order champagne and start to cry. As the 747 taxis down the runway, I look out at the L.A. smog and think about what I'm leaving behind: Rodeo Drive, maids, cocaine dealers, haircuts with José, lunch at the bistro, hand-delivered manicures and leg waxes, my famous last name. I could turn into an avo-cado—one more coke-snorting ex-wife who becomes an interior decorator, a photographer, or a real estate agent. L.A. is insidious. The ennui is pervasive. It's too easy to get lost here. Unless you're a star you have nothing, are nothing. So you go to lunch and then ten years later you wake up and say "Where's my life? What happened to it?" No thank you to this bullshit. No fucking thank you! Ciao L.A.

Wainscott, Long Island

Rent a house by the beach, start writing, trying to do something with this pain. I love being here, getting up early, biking to the beach, swimming, reading, jogging. No cocaine and no famous last name. I will not turn into an avocado after all! I met a man on the beach several weeks ago and we jog together but he won't sleep with me. So one night, I put on a short, pink and green Chinese kimono and decide to pay him a little visit. Julio's wailing on the tape deck and by the time I spot his driveway, my heart's racing. I've only seen his house in daylight. I pull into the dark driveway and whoops! Wrong one! I slam the gear shift into reverse and feel a mighty thud. A ditch? At this hour? All I can hear is the sound of my wheels spinning. I stumble into the pitch-black house calling his name. A light goes on and finally, he's at the top of the stairs telling me to shut up. "What are you doing here?"

"I decided it's time we make love."

I'm so glad I've taken the bull by the horns, so to speak. It's ended my crush of lust. My car is impaled on a large wooden pot of impatiens.

September: Cap Estates, St. Lucia

I'm visiting Nancy Dowd, who's taken a house here for a month. Really fucking amazing—the very island my marriage ended on. Yikes! Corny, a friend of Nancy's who lives here, remembers the Silver Trident being docked at Marigot Bay. He saw two black men on the deck, waved and shouted, "Nice boat!" Being with Nancy is big fun, she drags us everywhere—old plantations in the south, or huge swims and snorkeling in Soufrière. Barbara Warner Howard is also visiting and we all sail to Marigot Bay where I have the opportunity to see the beauty without all the pain.

It's beyond beautiful—rainbow-colored boats, gorgeous coconuts, fish, and ganga-smoking fishermen. Nancy and I need some distance from one another—Jah knows!—so I've split with Corny to his house in Gros Islet. Now I am sitting in this magical little fishing village, which is on the shore of Rodney Bay—another hot memory spot. This trip, it keeps getting weirder—a good weird. It's as if I'm being called upon to re-experience this place with my present head and heart and perspective.

I love it here. The village wakes up around six A.M. to the multiple sounds of reggae, laughter, children, and the sea. The women shout orders while the men go fishing or head up the hill to work at the Hotel Cariblue. Breakfast is coconut juice, coffee, bananas, and fresh bread. Within an hour, I'm walking down the road, munching on a stalk of sugar cane, picking up fragments of patois, and taking lots of pictures. I'm glad to see the real side of St. Lucia.

October: NYC

Get a great apartment in a pre-war walk-up and a magnificent German Shepherd puppy whom I've named Tiberius. I get my boxes out of storage and when I unpack, all my clothes look like "cocaine clothes"—too colorful, too tight, too many zippers and studs. Living in New York requires more strength and more attention to reality. My fourth-floor walk-up reminds me that my life now lacks all that Hollywood glitter—I am confronted by the homeless in their refrigerator boxes and I see how insulated I have been. I go to the A & P, walk my dog, carry my laundry to the "fluff and fold." No illusions here, only real life. There is also *weather* here; there is none in L.A. And the light here is different—it's harsher; even the dirt here is different—it's grayer. The sunny, spandex-ed, blond-titted, whispery syntax of L.A. is a far away memory. Sometimes I miss some things about it, though. When I get my final divorce papers, reality hits me like a ton of bricks.

Christmas

Byron looks awful—pale, fragile, sad. He's living all alone in Cropseyville with all those childhood ghosts and current demons. Whoa! Harry and Yvonne are living elsewhere and I tell Byron that I think he's been a conduit for their problems.

New Year's Eve

Anthony Herrera and I throw a party. I don't know many of the guests.

1983

January

Lunch at the Russian Tea room with Howard Rosenman and some "brilliant" editor from Random House, Gary Fisketjon. He's definitely smart and definitely cute. Begin seeing Gary, who's very encouraging and gives me books, books, books. I love Harry Crews's *Childhood: A Biography of Place,* and *Stop Time* by Frank Conroy. Tiberius has a seizure and the grim diagnosis is epilepsy. Medication for the rest of his life.

Spring

Gary and I bring Tiberius to the obedience school run by the Monks of Newskeet in the Berkshires. The gold-domed monastery sits on a mountaintop in a beautiful setting. Each Greek Orthodox monk, in long brown robes, lives, eats, sleeps, and prays with the dog he's training. Wonderful concept!

Pick up the very well trained Tiberius. Gary and I visit Cropsey-ville and go on to see Harry and Yvonne. Byron is there, looking worse than ever.

I see a crowd on Park Avenue and then I see feet sticking above the hood of a car. White shoes protrude from the windshield; a maid has jumped fifteen stories to her death. Like crocuses, jumpers come out in the spring. It's as if they can't bring their dark wintery moods into the gorgeous light of a spring day.

Go to a reception for Bernard Malamud at Roger Strauss's house. He is quite frail and Ann is as strong and bubbly as ever. Happy to see them after all these years. Go to Studio 54 with Paul Jabara and see Sugar Ray, who's cuter than ever. And guess who was with him? James "In the Way" Anderson, all fat and friendly.

Summer: Paris

Going to meet Barbara Steele. We check into a Left Bank hotel and spend a day roaming around the Ile St. Louis. I buy antique postcards and a wonderful navy silk men's robe from a thrift shop around the corner. Cafés, Sacre Coeur, and back to the Ile— Barbara wants an apartment here. German shepherds all over Paris. I miss Tiberius.

Today after a wonderful lunch we take a long walk in the French rain along the Seine. Cobblestones glisten as I listen to the ghosts of Paris past. Lighting strikes and Barbara throws herself up against a white building with a red awning. I take a picture. There are red geraniums in a green windowbox and a small cruel smile on Barbara's lips. Her hair is tied back into a pony tail; her cheekbones seem higher than ever; she looks like an executioner. We end up in a beautiful crowded church in the Marais and listen to Mozart. Music washes over us and the flickering light from the small white votive candles fill the church. My soul lifts and I think, "A good friend, God, and Mozart, what more could I ask for?" So, I confess. "Barbara, I have something to tell you." She leans sideways to listen.

"You know that money that you think you screwed me out of?"

"What money?"

"That five hundred dollars, for the house. Well, you didn't. You had a credit at the Stanhope Hotel that I took the liberty of transferring to my name. It was exactly the amount you owed me." Barbara sits like Lady Dracula for several moments.

"I'm going baaaack to the hotel." I don't watch her walk away. It's still a great summer night in Paris even if I did fuck it up. I walk back to the hotel and wonder what payback awaits me.

Barbara's in a frenzy, packing her suitcases; she's leaving for Rome tomorrow morning. I'm about to panic, but won't show it. She tells me, "I thought thaat matter was all settled." . . . "Barbara, how could it be settled if we never talked about it?" She ends the argument by saying, "You are a much more confrontaaative personality than I am." This is not a compliment.

A gloomy morning. She's speaking to the maid in French in a cold officious manner, and then the door slams. It's raining and I am alone in the gray hot Parisian summer.

I move to a cheaper, more charming hotel on the Left Bank.

Alone, I wander the French streets, sit for hours drinking espressos in Place des Vosges. I shop, browse, look at art, eat dinner alone, and light candles in the church on the corner of Rue Jacob and St. Germain. I take pictures of every German Shepherd I see. I am thoughtfully melancholy. Time to get out of here. I decide to look up my pal Ann, in Greece. It's my last night here and after dinner, as I walk along crowded St. Germain, I hear someone call my name. It's Micky Knox, an old friend who lives in Rome. He takes me to a club for some smokin' "le jazz hot."

When my seven A.M. wakeup call comes, I am in no condition to get to the airport. Book a later flight; I hide behind my mylar Raybans and drink Bloody Marys all the way to Athens. I feel like a terrorist. I don't even know if Ann is in Mykonos.

I arrive in Athens with two hangovers instead of one. I am a dishevelled wreck. All I want is to sit on a beach somewhere, but I run into chaos in the domestic flight terminal. I kick and scream but still miss the last flight to Mykonos. I *can't* spend the night in Athens—maybe I can get a boat!

I ask the lady at the information booth. "Excuse me, can you please tell me about boats to Mykonos?"

She ignores me. I try again and finally she yells at me: "I don't know any boat. I can't help you."

I walk away. Then my hangovers, exhaustion, and loneliness collide and slowly I turn. I yell, "I've never been to this damn country before, I missed my flight to Mykonos because I don't know guerilla warfare. I asked for your help, but not only have you refused to answer my questions, you've been excessively rude to me."

In broken English, she screams at me, "You rude and stupid. I can't help you for to find a boat in airport."

We're both shouting when a good looking, dark-haired man in his early thirties addresses me in an English accent. "Excuse me, you seem to be having some difficulty. May I help you?"

"I'm trying to get a boat to Mykonos."

He speaks to my enemy in flawless Greek; she answers. He turns toward me, looking perplexed. "Why *are* you trying to find a boat in an airport?"

We laugh, and I join him for a drink. Hercules*—Herky for short—is Greek. He was educated in Paris and now lives and works in New York. He's separated from his wife and is now on his way home to the Island of Patmos. Sounds good to me. He makes hotel arrangements for me at the Grande Bretagne and asks if I'll join him in Patmos after my visit to Mykonos. After a long bath I go for a walk and find a café with a red, green, and white tiled floor and leather booths. I sit outside in one of the old red leather Rattan chairs. The waiters are all laughing old men with a few teeth who've been drinking too much all their lives. The pale, blue-gray twilight lingers till 10:30 or eleven. It's the Fourth of July and I'm in Athens—wish I had a sparkler. I have a great sense of well-being as I watch the world as well as the old men and their cigars. Barbara is far away, so is Richard and so is Cropseyville.

Mykonos, Greece

Ann's in Rhodes for a brief holiday, she won't be back till the end of the week. I've been staying in a lovely pension. One of the guests is Stefano*, an Italian who I think is a gangster (strange scar from his ear to his shoulder). He's been after me, but I haven't been interested. This morning, when I ask for his help in attaching a tiny turquoise cross to my bracelet, he gives me an angry sexual look and roughly grabs my wrist. Then, using a piece of wire, he ties the cross to the chain. The kind of intricate knot he makes sends chills down my spine. He gives me another slightly mean, challenging stare and splits. Now I want him, but he's got a girlfriend. I leave a note on his door for him to come say good-bye to me. At three in the morning there's a knock. "Where are you going?"

"Patmos. I'll be back."

"I really cared about you, Jennifer." Yeah, right! He kisses me. I pull him to me, inside my room, inside of me. We go to Panaramos beach and play *Swept Away*—swim naked in the sea, and make love on the sand. I feel safe since I'm leaving. And, thank God—Stefano's saying things like "You'll pay me to make love to you." Yeah—in your dreams!

Ann's back and now I'm on my way to see Hercules. All tanned and smiling, Hercules meets me at the boat. Then he tells me he's not legally separated. "Excuse me? Are you or aren't you separated?"

"Yes, but not legally." We have a great afternoon. I meet some of his family and tonight we make love. I really like him. Then he tells me that he's lied to me again. He *plans* on leaving his wife, he just hasn't told her yet. And to top it off there's a child. I hit the fucking ceiling. I give him my father's phone number and tell him to give me a call when he's separated. He's shocked I'm hurt, and I tell him that I'm out of here on the next boat—the day after tomorrow. "Now get out and leave me alone!"

A nice case of cystitis. I go to the front desk to find a doctor and suddenly Herky appears in the lobby. He's pale and shaking. "I'm not good at Trevor Howard roles." Whatever that means! I'm happy to see him. The next few days are bliss. He says he's leaving his marriage. Hope so, 'cause I'm in love.

July 26: NYC

The minute I get back Herky comes over. He is so sweet—says we musn't sleep together until he is separated—otherwise I won't believe that our relationship is important.

September

I'm visiting Cindy and her family and feeling blue. Something's in the air, I don't know what. Just autumnal melancholy?

Sunday, September 11

I am lying awake in my room above the kitchen. It's six A.M. and the phone is ringing. I hear Cindy's steps and her cautious hello. After several minutes of silence, I hear a blood-curdling "Nooooo . . ." and the phone hitting the floor. I rush to the kitchen. Cindy is clutching her mouth with both hands, shaking her head from side to side, sobbing, a wild look in her eyes. I pick up the phone. I hear my father crying. "Dad, it's Jenny—"

"Jenny . . . Byron . . . it's Byron." Harry's gasping. I can barely understand him.

"Dad . . ." I know, but I need to hear it. "He's dead, Jenny."

Everything's a blur. When we arrive in Troy, Dad is not in good shape. Yvonne gives us her analysis and tells us how Harry had passed out when he identified Byron. I want to kill her, but instead I ask for details. It happened in a sad little white house on Route 2 that Byron was sharing with a couple of other boys. There, Byron hanged himself from the stairwell with his belt. A friend was with him, but he was passed out on the couch. He came to, perhaps in time, and cut Byron down. But he couldn't administer CPR or get it together to call an ambulance because he was so out of it himself. I get crazy over all this and want the sheriff involved; I want answers. Dad just looks broken. Cindy says we have to get his things. Byron was the star in his group and these people will want his belongings. I go out there with Cindy's husband, John. Yellow tape and state trooper cars surround the house. There are people milling about. A boy who sits on the hood of a car looks over his shoulder at me with a cruel smirk on his face. I want to slap that expression off his white-trash face; it's the kid who cut him down. Inside, we go straight to Byron's room, passing the spot on the stairwell. We gather everything in minutes—pictures, clothes, papers and notebooks. I find a postcard I'd sent him from Maui. When I turn it over I see the words "fuck you" in green ink written over my message. I understand. Words, words, words.

September 12

The wake. I have tried to call Richard, but he's in Bermuda with Deboragh. He sends flowers with a note that simply says I'm sorry. Byron's dressed in his Jim Morrison leather pants. His hands look exceptionally large and Jesus, the expression on his face! It's that familiar knowing smile, as if he's gotten one over on everybody. A mischievous grin that contains his bright irony. I ask the caretaker if the expression was there when he was brought in. "No, as a matter of fact, it happened recently."

My mother is here. Pat stands in front of the open coffin looking bewildered. One hand props up her chin, the other supports her elbow. She tilts her head from side to side. She seems absolutely perplexed as she says, "He looks good, doesn't he?" She asks everybody this question.

I haven't seen Pat in a long time—not since Cindy's wedding. I sit next to her and Ace, her faithful Cro-Magnon, sits on her other side. I doubt if he even knows where he is. Pat looks me over. "You must be tired, Jenny." I say, "Yeah, haven't slept. Had to go to NYC and then fly back." She shakes her head and smiles. "You always were strong, Jenny. You always were strong." At this moment I love her, but it's almost too much to feel.

September 13

The memorial service. The church is packed, SRO. Cindy, Georgia, and I are each reading a tribute. Cindy can't make it through her reading, Georgia reads a passage from a book and I shake and rattle through something I have written especially for my brother:

> *Dear Byron . . . .I have lost you to that sorrow that blew like a cold wind through your heart—a wind I could hear and a chill I could feel. I knew you in many ways and yet not at all. But little Brother, I now know you forever as a part of me . . . I love you, dear brother, now as I have always loved you, and your spirit shall keep me company as I continue this journey. Your battles are over, the war is at an end and nobody won. Please still your eyes for you saw too much. Blow out the candlelight but remember dear one, this is not the end.*

As I stand by his coffin, I can feel his presence—there is life after death. I know, deeply, that he is not dead. The coffin moves away from us and enters the fire. The fire will not burn his soul.

I last saw Byron at the house in Cropseyville, in March. He wasn't home when I arrived so I went in to wait. I found his works. When I confronted him, he panicked. I begged him and threatened him and he promised to stop shooting up. How worthless my pleas and threats were! Why didn't I try to *really* help? Why didn't anyone? Byron was full of coke when he died. Everybody in the family is culpable.

It's a couple of weeks since his death. Herky has left his wife and wants me to join him in England but I don't want to. He's furious. "But I left her to be with you and now you won't come here!" I think he's hopelessly selfish.

"Sorry, there's been a minor change in my plans. My brother has died—remember?" He doesn't want to hear it; his loneliness is more important. But I know if I go to him, I will block my pain with externals—food, fucking, Veuve Cliquot. Instead I will go back to St. Lucia to face my pain and try to do something with it.

On my way to St. Lucia, I call my father from Barbados and I am in a rage. My anger at Yvonne and Harry has suddenly exploded and I scream and yell into the phone causing a minor scene in the airport.

October: Castries, St. Lucia

Nancy Dowd's bought a huge, old house on top of a hill above Castries. It's got a magnificent view of the harbor, a wrap-around porch, and it's filled with wonderful old Caribbean furniture. One minor catch, though; I *know* it's haunted, but that doesn't bother Nancy. She just laughs at me.

I am working, writing everyday. I'm at my desk on the veranda every morning by seven A.M. And I will be forever proud and pleased that I have come here instead of losing myself in hedonism.

My dreams are bad and there are many sleepless nights, but I can live with them. All through the night I hear footsteps in the attic above me and my huge four-poster sometimes rocks as though someone has grabbed onto the posts and is madly shaking away. A St. Lucian woman tells me "they" can come through a keyhole and make love to you while you're sleeping. I see UFOs in the night skies. I ask Gertrude, the housekeeper to smoke the house—burn incense throughout it—to exorcise any evil.

October 25

Grenada invaded. We listen to shortwave radio on the veranda late into the night looking out past the dark into the moonlit Caribbean.

Whitman Harper*, the Rastafarian refrigerator repairman, comes by for dinner. He's a little genius, whose talents with appliances have made him the most popular man on the island. As I look at Whitman and see his baggy pants held together by a safety pin—that safety pin does it—I decide to take him to bed. It's great until the religious icons hanging in my room begin falling off the walls. He leaps up and in fast forward—is out of there like a bat out of hell.

November: NYC

Herky is here and asks me to please join him in a little cottage by the sea in England where we can both recuperate. I take the Concorde to London with Clive Davis and Bob Feiden. When I arrive, drive down in Herky's yellow Morgan to Bawdsey, a small village on the sea outside of Woodbridge, in the county of Suffolk. The cottage is darling but the friend of Herky's who's joined us is not. And Herky starts acting weird and megamaniacal. "I visited the Christ in Rio and dark clouds covered his head. The guide said to me, 'You are not fit to gaze upon Christ's eyes.' " He gives me biographies of Winston Churchill and Alexander the Great. "Read these two books and you will understand me." Jesus! But he *is* a great lover, which has been a serious awakening.

Byron's birthday. I take a long walk down the foggy, rainy beach, and walk smack into the Ministry of Defense. Sirens go off, the guards come out and I am escorted back home. I call Cindy who tells me she had a dream about Byron's rebirth.

Back in London—Harry's Bar, Annabel's, San Lorenzo, Marks, race-car driver friends and endless sex. Herky says, "Yes, I care about the best table at the finest restaurant. So what if I'm superficial?"

December: NYC

It's the night of the ex-wife. She wears a full-length leopard skin coat looks sad, pinched, and tucked. I am feeling terrible. Her first words are "Is my husband here?" I offer her a drink and ask if she's all right. "Yes, I'm younger than you. You look one hundred and fifty years old." I tell her, "I feel it." Herky comes downstairs and asks why she's here. "I want to see the girl you left me for. I can't believe she lives in a building like this!" Herky remains passive.

She goes on and on along these lines until I finally tell her, "I'm not responsible for your failed marriage. Herky's just trying to get his dignity back."

"Dignity! How would you know? You were married to that nigger husband of yours."

That's it. "Herky, you can throw your wife out now. And why don't you go with her?"

1984

January: St. Lucia

It's been four months since Byron died. I have a dream about him singing "What's the matter? Where did it all go wrong?" He's wearing a blue mohair sweater and has tears in his eyes. I call Cindy and she tells me that yesterday morning she was paying a clerk in a store when she heard Byron call out, "Cin—the kids!" When she turned around, a huge oil barrel had just fallen off a truck and was rolling down the hill straight for Cindy's children. She ran and grabbed them in the nick of time.

April: Durango, Mexico

Here to do a small part in my friend Alan Sharpe's movie, *Little Treasure*, which stars Ted Danson and Margot Kidder! Alan gets me at the airport and we go straight to Ted's house. On the way, I tell Alan I don't want to be paid, just fly Cindy down. Margot's seen Richard, "Gee, Jennifer, he was in bad shape. Holed up in a hotel room in London with pipes and bottles all over the place. Missing you and very miserable." We shoot a scene where Margot, who's playing a stripper, strips down from a wedding gown. She's so high she almost falls down. What's really ironic about this is that Alan's got me pulling the key ribbons on the dress.

Cindy arrives! There are lots of parties in the villa where Alan, his kids, his editor, the editor's wife, and Cindy and I are all staying. Ted gives a party one night—what a hopeless flirt! When we dance, he holds me like some long-lost love. Then I watch him hold *everybody* like a long-lost love. Cindy and I get to spend lots of time together and I feel so close to her. I see her pain is still fresh, too. I love Alan and decide—*no*, truly platonic relationships between hetero men and women are *not* possible.

August: London

Herky's rented a millhouse in the country for the summer and I go see him but I know that this affair is sputtering to an end. I was so disgusted by the loud pastel bathing suit that he wore when we were in Montauk, somehow that said it all. I'm not at all comfortable here either; I feel like a Bosch character trapped inside a Turner painting.

Paris

On my way to see Richard in L.A., I stop off in Paris, where I head straight for the church on the corner of Rue Jacob and St. Germain and light a zillion candles to help ward off any and all psychic attacks. Barbara's here with Dan scouting locations for a mini-series on another one of those Herman Wouk books. Very cozy.

Los Angeles

Richard says he wants to work things out, but gee whiz, there's a girl "with child" in the picture. Hey, call me when you figure it out!

Hawaii

Fly to Honolulu to meet Richard for my birthday. Champagne and roses on the plane and a sweet dinner when I arrive. We go on to Hana, but our wheels are spinning. Okima's back and she's *not* washing the floor with vodka anymore. Wonder why? I tell Richard we have to see a shrink together if we're really going to put this back together. "Think about it."

November

I go to L.A.—Richard's thought about it. We start seeing a therapist, but after a week of sessions it's clear to me that this thing isn't any nearer to being resolved and I'm wasting my time. Rode hard and hung up wet!

Christmas: Tobago, West Indies

Here with Dad, Georgia, Cindy, and John, and their kids—Jane, Kate, and Johnnie. It's the first time since Byron's death that we've all been together and the purpose of this trip is to try and heal. Yvonne's not invited—in fact, Dad's been having an affair with

Lynn, an English doctor from Albany. Apparently, since Byron's death Yvonne's gotten really crazed. She's been drinking and taking lots of pills and hearing the Doors' music. And Dad's affair has really driven her around the bend. I hear that she showed up at Lynn's house with a fucking ax! I find something satisfying about controlling Yvonne coming unglued.

We have a grueling flight down—it takes two days on BWIA, and they manage to lose our luggage. We spend another two days straightening this out and then we try to have some fun. Dad and I get drunk together and do a little lightweight arguing. The place where we're staying reminds me of a setting in a Tennessee Williams play. The airport is too close and planes screech overhead all day and all night. I begin writing a play, *Christmas in a Third World*; the main character is the ghost of Byron.

The beaches are beautiful, the weather is good, but I am in so much pain that the only way to deal with it is to be the ultimate bitch and try to make everyone as miserable as I am. I'm still recruiting passengers for the "blame train." I write an endless letter of apology to Dad as he leaves to meet Lynn for a week of sailing. I also apologize to everyone else for my bitchiness. It's just that I'm so damn sad.

1985

January

My friend Peter Lester died of AIDS in London. He was just thirty-two years old. Go with John Schlesinger and Michael Childers to a screening of *The Falcon and the Snowman* at the Museum of Modern Art. Afterwards, there's a party at the Limelight, then we have dinner at Odeon with Whoopi Goldberg, Sting, Timothy Hutton, and David Suchet. Blah, blah, blah.

April

I go with Gwen Welles to a dinner party at Il Cantinori that's being given by Glenda Jackson for the cast of *Strange Interlude*. Glenda sits at the head of the long pine table. She's very much in control and having lots of fun, drinking and eating with complete abandon. At the party, I meet Brian Cox, an English actor who's in the play.

May

I saved a dog's life today—he'd been hit by a car on FDR Drive. I took him to the hospital. I'd have kept him, but the owner showed up.

I go see Brian in *Rat and the Skull*, a play about the IRA and a British soldier. Afterward, we have dinner at Elaine's with Albert Finney, who's a good friend of Brian's, and some English girl. Albert is so handsome, even though he's so bloated and wears his napkin tucked under his chin. He relentlessly attacks his soft shell crabs and orders bottle after bottle of great white wine. While we're eating, I take this opportunity to tell a really ridiculous story: "My ex-husband says he met you and your ex-girlfriend in London. He really liked her. He said she was wearing this seriously awful necklace that he felt you had given to her, and that it didn't suit her at all. He said she was really uncomfortable in it. Anyway, he really did like her."

Albert looks blankly at me, chews his crabs and orders another bottle of wine. I don't know why in God's name I've told this story. I'm turning into a social pariah.

My instincts have told me that it's time for some time out, and I've entered a quiet period in my life. I've been going to lots of Alanon meetings, sometimes two a day, trying to get a grasp on this "co-dependency" issue. It's a hard one to understand. I'm an "enabler." I can take care of someone else so well—fixing, picking up the mess, and filling in the blank spaces—it "enables" them to continue the behavior. They don't have to take responsibility or deal with the reality of their actions—I do it for them. Not only do *they* not have to change or grow, I don't have to deal with my *own* problems either. All my time and energy is focussed on them. Denying all the facts of my life and its pain, filling in all *my* blank spaces with the other person's life—they get worse so I take care of them better—what a vicious cycle! *Now* it's easy to see the source of this.

And, God, I'm getting so much from these meetings. They have some great maxims, like "once a victim, twice a volunteer" and "if

you meet three assholes in one day, check your spiritual condition."
I'd thought I could control the madness with Richard. But the truth
is that I was addicted to the madness and drama as well as to him,
so wrapped up in my rescue m.o. that I forgot about me. I even
lost touch with my own body—the drugs, the anorexia, I didn't even
know when I was preggers! That's out of touch! I almost died! I
denied all my instincts, believing that with will and determination I
could control and manage everything. I didn't understand that there
would be a high price to pay for my so-called "tolerance and love."
I used to think that being brave meant hanging in no matter what,
which included getting beaten. It's true that when a woman gets
hit, deep inside—deep in the marrow—she thinks that somehow
she deserved it, that she's bad. In her book, *When Battered Women
Kill*, Angela Brown cites studies which suggest that a woman who's
seen her mother being beaten is less skilled in self-protection and
is "more willing to believe that victimization is part of what is means
to be a woman." But even among these women there are those
who fight back, and those who do are considered to be only mildly
battered because they manage to hold onto a part of themselves
that refuses to be victimized. I've survived.

And I'm learning. I'm grabbing hold of my life in increments—one
day at a time, five minutes at a time—like last week, when the
vacuum cleaner broke down. Because of Tiberius, I need to vacuum everyday and strangely, that gives me an incredible sense of
accomplishment. I like to see the clean green paths of carpet
emerge from a field of dog hair, Milkbone crumbs, and down pillow
feathers. So I almost flipped out when my Celebrity Hoover Quiet
Series Canister stopped working. I decided to take care of it myself.
And I figured it out! I got out my Philips head screwdriver and took
it apart. I saw that the fan belt was broken, got a new one at the
hardware store, and fixed the machine. Voila! I'm making clean
green paths again! This was such a major event that when I was
asked to speak to an Alanon meeting about change and growth, I
talked about repairing my Celebrity Hoover. And the most amazing
thing is that they all got it!

1986

May

Saw *Jo-Jo Dancer, Your Life Is Calling* and it's made me nuts. It's so full of shit. When I got home, I immediately started writing an article, which I've sold to *People* magazine. I guess you can call it a "review" of Richard's film.

June

People article is causing a minor stir. I'm booked on "Good Morning America," "Regis and Kathy Lee," "Oprah," and "Live at Five."

July

On FDR Drive, I find a dog that's been badly battered and bruised. I bring her home thinking that she'll help Tiberius get through his seizures. It's worth a try. I name her Livia after Tiberius's mother—she's the one who poisoned everybody. Fitting because this dog is beautiful but very aggressive toward anyone she doesn't know, very obviously an abused animal.

August

Staying in East Hampton with Marysa Maslansky and her kids. My poor Tiberius has fallen into the pool, wacked out on phenobarbital, which hasn't helped his seizures anyway. They just seem to be getting worse. The vet suggests putting him to sleep. I can't decide. His seizures continue through the night.

"The Death of Tiberius." I feel like a murderess watching the vet overdose my darling under the big elm tree. I cry my eyes out and drink white wine to dull the pain. I feel that everybody and everything is going away.

September

Do the "Oprah Winfrey Show" with other "celebrity wives"—wives of Jerry Lewis, Michael Landon, and Wayne Newton. Really embarrassing experience. By the end of the show, my chair is miles away from theirs.

Toronto

I'm here to do a part in *The Believers*, which stars Martin Sheen and Helen Shaver. John Schlesinger is directing and Michael Childers is producing. It's a dark story about Santeria, a religion that originated in Africa as a combination of tribal religions and Catholicism brought by the missionaries. It gathered more rituals when it passed through the islands on its way to America, although when it is practiced here, Santeria is usually hidden behind the saints and icons of Catholicism. In the movie, I play "Jennifer," a rather sinister character who works for Harris Yulin's even more sinister character.

Mary Ellen Mark asks me to pose for some stills with two huge Dobermans. I'm a real sport and say yes. As I'm trying to get the Dobies to sit where I want them one just says, "Whoa, bitch, stop bossing me around," and places his gigundo jaws around my wrist. He doesn't bite me, just wants to make a point. Point well taken.

Back to Toronto to finish my part. We're in Wesleyville, a one-horse town a few hours out of the city, staying in a facsimile of the Bates Motel, appropriate because we're shooting at an abandoned power plant that looks like an enormous crypt. It's dark, damp, and really eerie. The gloomy space echoes with the sounds of film equipment being moved and the loud voices of the crew. The set is several hundred feet up in the pitch-black air and we have to wear construction helmets as we ride the elevator up and up and up. Already I'm nervous; I am terrified of heights. The scene we're doing is the killing of a child. I'm standing in the front of a small group of people, and we are chanting this African chant that is the prelude to the killing of the little boy. It's a real Nigerian chant that Malik Bowen, who plays one of the villains, has transliterated for us. A huge amount of incense is burning on the platforms above and below us; they're also using smoke machines to make the atmosphere even smokier. This incense thing worries me; although it's used to dispel bad spirits it can also summon them. This scene is taking forever, lots of complicated camera angles. And my vertigo has kicked in, so I have to be escorted on and off the set. The platform we are standing on is a metal grid—I think of barbecue grills—and when I look down I lose myself in terror. On our second day of shooting, an extra's necklace comes apart and I watch as it falls through the barbecue grill and the smoke—down, down, down.

By the third day, I'm feeling especially fragile; a hangover and PMS exacerbate my fear. It also doesn't help when one of the security people tells me that the power plant is haunted by someone who died here in a fall from the scaffolding. I think of this as I look at Martin Sheen, who's leaning over on the railing peering down and out into the abyss. The smoke and the lights hit his eyes and at that moment he looks seriously troubled, as if *he* is haunted. I am suddenly aware that the entire set may be possessed. There is an palpable and frightening negativity in the air and I think that many of us are unaware that we are being affected by it and its power. I'm also sure that the Santeria priestess who is a consultant on the film must be aware too. I suddenly feel the compulsion to jump. I try to shove away this dreadful thought but it's strong. I wonder if a *real* human sacrifice isn't being demanded by the dark side. The urge is too powerful, I cannot control my thoughts, I *must* jump. My palms are sweating as I start looking over the edges of the railings, searching for the longest drop. One side ends in a metal floor, but it goes down only thirty feet; another side has a net for the stunts; a third drops way the hell to Hell. Then I am stopped by the strangest thought. *If I do this, production will stop and John and Michael will be so mad at me.* It's not my death, but the thought of their anger that slows me down. In this instant of sanity, I grab the little cross around my neck and begin to pray, begging God for help. But the force reasserts its power and my mind has a mind of its own. My body is covered in sweat and my ears are ringing. I *know* I am going to die. I see myself running to the railing and leaping over it and then my body sailing slowly down through the dark space. Then out of nowhere, Martin Sheen is next to me; he's talking about Catholicism and the Ecstasy of St. Theresa. I can't believe it. Martin has made contact and broken the hold of the dark forces within me with talk of the divine—with God and angels. Somehow he *knows*. He has saved my life, and stays by my side all day.

During a break, he writes down part of a seventeenth century Benedictine monk's poem and gives it to me: "Uphold me, Lord, as you have promised and I shall live and do not disappoint me in my hope." When we go back to the set, he waits for me, walks with me, and takes my hand in a wonderfully reassuring way. He too has felt the dark presence here. He is my hero and I love him. But his absolute kindness and gentleness have inspired in me something purer and higher than any other desire. I want his friendship. I have lunch with Martin, his wife, and their daughter in his trailer. At the end of the day, he walks me off the set, makes sure that I'm all right and bids me safe journey back to Toronto.

The second I'm back in civilization, I call a masseuse. He works with a giant crystal, unblocking and removing what he says are the results of a psychic attack. Then I look for and find a beautiful Catholic church a few blocks from the hotel. The priest is in the rectory office and as I begin my tale, I know right away he is kind. I tell him about the movie, my fears, and Martin. He tells me that he is Martin's confessor and adds that they are also troubled by the film and its darkness. Now I know that I am safe. I tell him I need some protection and some direction, that I am a "former" Catholic, that I'm afraid to go back to complete the rest of the picture, and that I believe in God, Jesus, and myself. This last point helps! The priest gives me a book on Catholic theology and advises me to think about coming back to the Church. He also suggests prayer, and comforts me by saying that since I've found my way here, I am already receiving some guidance. Yeah!

Back to fucking Wesleyville. Well, at least I'll see Martin again. I go up on the barbecue grill again today—we're shooting my death scene. Whoa! They pad me all over the place and then I have to summon all of my courage to run around all over the metal grid with my high heels and my terror. I get shot in the back and crash on a huge table, biting the blood capsules in my mouth. I make it through my death and my wretched vertigo. Of course, Martin is there, lending a loving and supportive hand. Before I leave he gives me some books—*Catholic Theology and St. Theresa*. Martin also tells me that he came back to the Church, and his faith, after the heart attack he'd had while filming *Apocalypse Now*.

October

I'm back in New York. Warren Beatty calls and I stop by the Ritz Carlton to see him. I decide that I don't want to sleep with him, so I don't.

At the Columbus with Malik Bowen and Beverly Camhe, one of the producers of *The Believers*. Warren's there, and Mike Tyson.

Mike's heard how I shouted "go fuck yourself" at the would-be mugger who'd pointed a gun at me. He tells me I was lucky I wasn't shot.

November

L.A., and I go to visit Martin in Malibu. From the outside, it's a rather simple ranch-style house, and the inside is pretty basic and comfortable. But the landscaping behind the house is spectacular, with man-made rock formations, and waterfalls with footbridges, and beautiful foliage.

At first it's a bit bizarre. Martin and I are alone in the house. We just sit in the living room watching some football game on TV. I'm uncomfortable; I think he is, too. Then his daughter Renée shows up, as well as the "tap-dancing" son with a couple of friends, and Martin decides to organize a basketball game. It's rather fierce and I give it my all. As the juices start to flow, I begin feeling enormously competitive and am afraid that I look just as enormously unfeminine. I wonder, what's really going on here? (We're probably working out some sort of sexual attraction!) After the game, his son Charlie shows up. *The* Charlie Sheen, the newest little matinee idol who's got the teenage girls all crazy. He seems nice enough, but a typical Hollywood caricature—right down to his Porsche and his colorful Hawaiian shirt. Charlie's glued to the phone from the minute he arrives.

A bit later, Martin has a private talk with me about Richard, asking me if Richard has AIDS. I tell him no, but Martin insists on giving me the name of some psychic healer, anyway. The large coffee pot is brewing and other guests begin to arrive. Tomorrow, Martin's getting arrested with the Berrigan brothers again—protesting something. He is the consummate activist.

December: NYC

Party at John's and Michael's. Warren's there, and he takes the opportunity to tell me that he hated the *People* article. Who is he to judge me? Maybe it's because I don't want to sleep with him anymore. Fuck him and his Greta Garbo act!

1987

January

A nice letter from Martin telling me he's going to the January 27th demonstration in Yucca Flats on the thirty-sixth anniversary of the first atomic test at the Nevada Test Site, and plans on being arrested there. He adds that he and Mitch Snyder are organizing the March 3rd "Grate American Celebrity Sleepout" in Washington D.C. This is to lend support to the urgent "Relief for the Homeless" bill that is currently before Congress.

February

I get to see Anthony Herrera throw his soon-to-be-ex-wife's piano down the stairs. What a racket! She'd left him, and two weeks later, she calls for her piano. He tells her, "Come and get it. It'll be on the street in twenty minutes." It sure is, all right—in a million pieces, with piano larvae dripping all the way down the stairs. When the police show up, I tell them I've got a terrific broom and Anthony isn't arrested. I call Anthony "the piano tuner."

I got another really nice letter from Martin describing progress on the "Sleepout." He also says, "As I watched *The Believers* the other night, I fondly recalled our time working together and how inspiring and nourishing it was. You have a powerful energy and clear spirit working deep within. As St. John of the Cross reminds us, 'At the final twilight, we will be judged by love and by love alone. That love must start with love for ourselves.' " I've been feeling guilty, because I cannot bring myself to join the "Sleepout," and Martin's last words are a great comfort.

March

L.A., I see Richard, who's deeply depressed about the end of his marriage to Flynn. We watch *Manhunter* (Brian Cox plays Dr. Hannibal Lechter)—Richard's seen it now sixteen times. He says he's been fantasizing about killing Flynn, chopping her up into a million pieces, putting the pieces in a suitcase and leaving it on the freeway somewhere. But then he couldn't face having to tell his son someday what had happened. So, divorce was better. I guess so! I spend the night. In the morning, I discover a gun under my pillow.

April

Through a girlfriend, I meet Arno*, a darling little man-child. She didn't sleep with him, even though she wanted to. Some women are just plain uptight about sex. No matter, *I'll* sleep with him! He's fourteen years younger and a lyrical old soul. He's also savvy, smart, and sober—an ex-junkie—and sensual, too. Good combination.

May

Take a trip to Water Island with an old friend and find myself missing Arno. Write him a soul-poem:

> *cartwheels across a green lawn*
> *black garter belts*
> *dinosaur mornings*
> *Gibson guitars*
> *seriously worn-out cowboy*
>   *boots*
> *Shiner beer*
> *drive-in movies*
> *you.*

Arno pushed me down. I've threatened to throw his red 1969 Stratocaster out the window. I think the man-child will have to go.

October

Arno leaves this message on my machine, "I'm listening to Tchaikovsky, sitting on James Joyce's chaise lounge, and thinking of you." Well, he *is* cute.

1988

March

Doing some work in video production. This week I've been working on Tracy Chapman's "Fast Car" video—she's great! I'm also working part-time for Dr. Kathy Cox.

April

I work on a video for a Lisa-somebody—obviously forgettable. Get three days work on *Slaves of New York*, a small part in a party scene with Betty Comden. Jim Ivory wants to give me a few more lines but Betty wouldn't give up any of her interminable dialogue. Jim looks quite exasperated, but can do nothing! The production itself is very weird and I end up locking horns with some hostile p.a. who must think she's finding the cure for AIDS, her attitude is so self-important.

More video work—one with Jerry Harrison of the Talking Heads. It's a couple of days worth of true shit-work: long hours, low budgets. Go out to L.A. and see Richard. He looks pretty bad, but we hit the racetrack and manage to have a little fun together.

July

Richard's in New York. I don't know what's going on with him. Drinking and pilling up a storm, frighteningly thin, getting migraine headaches. He tells me he wants to die. He also tells me he's been to the Mayo Clinic for tests. Before he leaves, he promises me he'll see a shrink.

August: NYC

Richard's here to film *See No Evil, Hear No Evil*. He wants me to work with him—he'll put me on salary. I read lines with him and act as go-between to director, sweet old friend Arthur Hiller, and Marvin Worth, producer. It's the usual—do everything! The first thing I do is move him into the Plaza Athenée where I organize a little kitchen so I can cook and maybe get him to gain some weight. He's even more depressed about Flynn; she's had *another* child.

Flynn managed to get herself pregnant while she was walking out the door to get divorced. "Jen, she was naked under a fur coat. What could I do?" In addition to this new baby there's also another child—by an extra he met on the set of *Jo-Jo*. They travelled cross-country together and for the whole trip she was using birth control. When she saw the East Coast looming and the end in sight, some-where around Ohio, she threw her pills away. (She eventually won a generous monthly child support settlement. So somewhere in the Valley there's yet another child.) I suggest condoms might be a cheaper alternative. Despite his denials, I think he's getting high. He sits for hours staring at his video golf game, absolutely mute. He can't stand my energy, and keeps asking me to calm down and be quiet. What the hell is *he* on?

September

Oh, God, I feel as if I'm in love all over again. I've tried to stay detached but in my classic two-step fashion, I respond to all of Richard's loving gestures. He's asked me to open my heart to him, to "explore my leftover feelings," and says things like "We've wasted so much time. I'm so glad it's not too late and you're still in love with me." And like a fool, like a woman, I take the bait. Part of me hates that I still love him, that I should still feel any hope. I should *know* better. But I can't resist him. My heart has a mind of its own.

October

Richard lacks self-confidence and energy and walks like an old man. He says he's only taking the anti-depressants, Tofranil, but he vomits up his food the minute he swallows it. I am not surprised when I walk into the bedroom and see him coming out of the bathroom pushing his shirtsleeve over the blood running down his arm.
"Why, Richard?"
"I can't stand the pain. Don't worry. My doctor knows."
"Your shrink knows you do this? What does he say?"
"He doesn't like it, but he thinks I'll give it up when I'm ready."
"What is it?"
"Bunk."

I found his works hidden in a cigarette carton in a drawer. Then Richard tells me when he was at the Mayo Clinic in June, they diagnosed him as having multiple sclerosis and that's why he walks like an old man.

I get him to eat, he's gaining a little weight, and actually seems to be improving. For a while things seem pretty good. Lots of meetings with his agents and with writers and I'm reading some of these scripts. Eddie Murphy shows up, with his two giant body-guards, to discuss a film project he wants Richard for—but hasn't written yet. Bill Murray calls, wants to speak to Richard about something he won't discuss over the phone. We go to Snedens Landing and sit at the huge table in his living room. He tells Richard there's a joke in his new movie, *Scrooged*, that they want to keep but it depends on how Richard feels about it. It's a restaurant scene, where there's a small fire and Bill says, "Who do you think you are, Richard Pryor?"

Richard doesn't give a hoot. Business over, we have a couple of beers, sit outside for a while, ride out to see his wife's shop, promise to get together soon, and leave. I know we'll never see them again.

Everything with Richard is still a battle. He's as difficult as ever, but it's no longer captivating; in fact, it's boring. Thank God I'm still seeing Arno. On location in Connecticut with him one night, I was trying to watch the news and he was talking at the same time. When I asked him to be quiet, he told me, "I know someone who will listen to me."

Back in New York and he's acting distant and hostile. I suspect another woman. He is unable to sustain any level of intimacy for too long. Why am I surprised? I'm left with a million clues—notes on hotel notepads, room service bills, even her dog's food!

Today, I find out for sure that he's been entertaining some girl he met on Madison Avenue. This is such a sucker punch! I try to detach. Richard tells me he'll stop seeing her. Then she calls the hotel and when I repeat the name the operator has given me, at first Richard just looks blank. Then he says, "Oh, that's her. Tell her you know about her and it's over."

"That's your job. I don't want to talk to her, Richard."

"It's okay. It's better if you tell her. She knows I don't want to lose you. Tell her to stop calling. I told her never to call here anyway." I am a fool.

"Operator, put the call through." I hear the voice of the girl. She's named after a liquor I never drink.

"Richard?"

"No, it's Jennifer."

"Oh, hello. Jennifer. Richard has told me all about you." I can't believe this ballsy little bitch.

"Listen, Richard's asked me to tell you he doesn't want to see you anymore. It's over, so please stop calling."

"I want to hear it from Richard himself." I put her on hold.

"Richard, she wants you to tell her." I can't believe I have allowed myself to be sucked into this all-too-familiar game.

"No, I don't want to talk with her." Now I'm shaking.

"Richard doesn't want to talk to you!" I slam down the phone. He just sits there, sulking.

"Well, I guess I should have talked to her myself." I want to kill him.

"No shit, Sherlock. Richard, who the fuck is this little cocktail? She knows all about me!"

"Well, she cares a lot about me, no matter who I am. She says she'll never hurt me the way you have." I am numb. I am *dumb.*

"I better call her and tell her myself. I owe her that." I start to leave.

"I promise to stop seeing her. I don't want to lose you. When I think of it, I start walking like an old man." *Poor* Richard.

November

I was doing fine, ragged around the edges but okay, when Richard comes to town and we resurrect some old love, some new love, and a lot of fucking pain. I keep coming across this sorrow, as if I've been hiding, saving it, the way Livia hides a bone behind a pillow on the couch. I'm learning to dislike Richard all over again. His cock even gets harder when he knows he's hurting me.

I'm leaving town for the weekend to go see Cindy and her new farm. Before I go, I pay a visit to a shop on Lexington Avenue, where "the cocktail" works as a salesgirl. I go in and pretend to look at the clothes, which is hard since this place is an upscale version of J.C. Penney. I wait around till her name is called and check out this little hustler. I can't believe it! Short and dumpy, and plain enough to be called unattractive. She's the kind of girl who was never youthful. She's ten years younger than I am but her clothes and jewelry are matronly. This child is no threat.

Cindy's life is a good one—cows, kids, dogs and a happy marriage. All that love. I've brought Livia, who's in heat, to get knocked up by Cindy's big brown labrador, Moose. I want to put something in my life besides all of this Richard-misery—something life-affirming. We put Livia and Moose in the summer kitchen and I feel almost guilty that I've left my girl to be raped by this Lab that resembles a Kodiak bear! There's a lot of yelping. Richard calls during the big event and says to throw some cold water on Moose to make him stop. I tell him that would be a good idea for *him* since, most of the time, he has no idea where he puts his thing! Moose mounts Livia about five times during the weekend and the deed is done.

Back with Richard and this girl is in and out of the hotel and in and out of our lives. She calls from the lobby and I see her low self-esteem, her obsession, and I can see my old self in her. She wants to win and thinks she can and she might win, temporarily. It's as if she really wants to beat *me* more than she wants Richard.

November 16

I have managed to stay away a few days, but I'm here again and while I'm cooking dinner, "the cocktail" calls. I hear Richard tell her, "Well, I really can't talk because Jennifer's standing here, listening to everything."

Destructive visualization! I see myself taking the roast chicken out of the DeLonghi oven and throwing it at him, then taking the pan and pouring the grease all over his Comme des Garcons and Armani. Instead, I turn the oven off, pack my things, get Livia, and leave. Must let go!

November 17

Richard calls, begging to see me. I refuse, but he tells me there's something important he needs to discuss with me. We go off to Elaine's to meet his new agent and Skip, his lawyer. Nothing resolved. Things just sputter along.

327

November 28

Richard says he wants to go to the wrap party alone. No big deal, see you later. But it's later and later and I'm here at the hotel waiting, and then I know he'll be out all night, his last night.

November 29

I show up around noon and he's just gotten in. The air is thick with anger and resentment and my sadness.

"You spent the night with her?"

"Yeah."

I pack up some things. Lorne Michaels has sent me a tape from the "Saturday Night Live" show with Tracy Chapman as the musical guest. I put it on. "I love you/ Is all that you can't say," she sings, as I sit on the edge of the bed. My back is to Richard, and I am beginning to cry. I sit for a few moments with a rock in my throat, unable to move for fear of a flood. Then I hear Richard move. I look over my shoulder. His arms are reaching out to me and in sotto voce, "Come here, baby."

"Words don't come easily/ Like I love you I love you." My tears are stuck in my limbs. I could disintegrate. I smile vaguely, shake my head. I turn back to Tracy and again, I hear his voice. "Come here baby."

I look at him and my fucking heart is breaking. I want to fall into those arms more than anything I've ever wanted. I want to feel his flesh, let my tears spill out over his shoulder.

Instead, I say, "No, thank you." I have to leave. I know I'm going to break. "Richard, I've got some things to do."

The door slams behind me. I won't be back. I am crying now.

1989

January 5

In the middle of a snowstorm, Livia gives birth to nine spectacular puppies on my bed. I'd thought that the gestation period was three months, but when Livia began digging a hole in my comforter, I figured I'd better check. Out popped a little head. I call Cindy, screaming. Seven black pups, two blond. I make a bed for these sweet creatures out of a refrigerator box but it falls apart quickly. Nothing to do but build a bed! Get a hammer, nails, and some wood and *voilà!* I line it with serapes and a pillow. Mama Livia loves it and nurses her babes.

I feel as if I'm wrapped up inside a giant healing metaphor. I've spent the entire month in bed watching the little creatures and recuperating from Richard. I have broken the cycle of abuse. Life is renewed.

February

A little blond puppy totters over to my bed like a drunk—he wants *on*. I put him back into his own bed but a few minutes later, the little drunk is back at my bedside. He's chosen me. I name him Emmet Fox Kelly Lee.

Dad's joined a theater group for charity and I go see him in *You Can't Take it With You*. He's very good and full of his usual energy.

March

I'd done an interview with Richard for *Spin* magazine and they liked it. When I suggest one, with Miles Davis, they go for it. The only other time I've ever met Miles was with Richard, when we went to see him at New York Hospital.

The first night I go see him at the Essex House, the place is a real mess, the classic bachelor pad. The walls are covered with art—his own paintings, works by up-and-coming artists—sort of ethnic folk art. And the place is furnished in an early-sixties style—very low tables and couches, lots of bright colors, lots of mirrors. Musical instruments, electronic equipment, and dusty exercise apparatus create sculptural arrangements. There's a TV in each room, and the one in the sleeping area is on. Somehow I know that it's *always* on. I get a sense of isolation from Miles that's all too familiar. We start talking, and seem to get along pretty well. At one point I ask about the scar on his lip, if it's from playing the horn. "It's from making love for so many years," he says. What? "I'm kidding, it's from the horn. Come here, let me show you." And Miles puts his lips to mine and, using his tongue very lightly, acts as if he were blowing his horn.

The next night, I go back to finish the "interview." I've brought

Italian food for dinner. He answers the door and seems happy to see me. He's wearing a paint-spattered blue workshirt and baggy silk trousers. The place has obviously been cleaned, and I think that's sweet. I feel a bit as if I'm on a date. As I unpack the food, the doorbell rings. Miles opens it and it's his road manager dropping off some videotapes. No one has introduced me, so I say hello. When Miles goes to introduce me, he pretends he can't remember my name. Snapping his fingers, he says, "Uh, let me see. Uh, Renee, right?" I say, "I'm Jennifer Lee." They go off into the other room and I finish unpacking the food. They return a few minutes later and the road manager turns to leave. At the door he pauses and says, "Nice meeting you, Renée." Under my breath, I mutter, "Good-bye, asshole." Miles says, "He's really a nice guy, Jennifer." "I think he's a little rude, Miles."

This tension passes and we sit down to eat. My eye is caught by a large framed painting. I tell him that it looks like his music. Miles says, "Yeah, I've just figured that out." He points to a striking looking face on the canvas and adds, "That's my girlfriend Bridget. She taught me how to draw a nude." Then he takes out a pen and draws an abstract female figure on a napkin and gives it to me.

We're sitting in the sleeping area and during the entire interview, the TV is on. Miles pops videos in and out and flips channels as we talk. He tells me how he got his famous rasping voice: "I talked too soon after an operation on my vocal cords. I yelled at some motherfucker." And he tells me about his ex-wife Cicely Tyson: "She'd call all my girlfriends to see if I'd been with any of them. Then she'd sit on my dick. Just sit there and look at me. She turned me into an occupation." Everything seems to be going well until Liza Minnelli comes on the "Arsenio Hall Show." She's wearing some dated distressed-ripped sweatshirt and singing songs from her new album, produced by the Pet Shop Boys. I groan. Miles seems agitated and says, "I like her." I say, "Well, I don't." There's a palpable hostility in the air. Miles does not like to be disagreed with. I figure it's time to make tracks; it's started snowing, anyway. He asks if I'd like to spend the night. "No thanks, I want to walk my dogs in the snow."

As I'm putting on my coat, I ask, "Miles, why did you get hostile a few moments ago?"

"Bitch, don't pull that white shit on me!"

"Excuse me?"

"You heard me."

"Yeah, I did Miles." I just want to get the hell out of there.

"Do you need cab fare?"

Now this strikes me as strange, as I'd brought dinner and he hadn't offered to pay for that. Just another mean control freak!

"Will you call me when you get home?"

"Probably not." Again I ask, "Miles, your remark—"

"What remark?"

"About me being white . . . that was out of line, don't you think?"

He's yelling now. "Bitch, *you are acting white!*"

I walk out, slamming the door behind. All the way to the elevator, I can hear him fumbling with the locks. The napkin with his drawing is crumpled up in my fist. What a sad, bitter man. Fuck the interview!

NOW

"God made time to keep it all from happening at once."
—*Mickey Newbury*

1989

August 31

My birthday. Alone and happy! Invited to Bridgehampton "without the dogs—not even Emmet." Thanks but no thanks! Rather spend my birthday in the hot city with my sweet animals. Controlling friendships are over, too! I light the candles on my birthday cake and sing "Happy Birthday," to me! For the rest of my life, I will be the best party I'll ever have.

I have lived with a deep sadness, but I have learned that it's not what you live through that makes the difference, it's what you do about it. I was motivated by anger when I began to write, but now I'm motivated by what I have learned through writing. Although it can't provide answers for me, it has helped me to piece together what I *do* know, to make sense of it all and in this way I am coming closer to the truth.

I have been looking for the truth about Byron's death, and have found out that there were other people present at the house that night, as well as copious amounts of drugs. No one seems to know exactly what happened or why, but apparently, the kids panicked and ran, leaving my brother alone with the kid who was passed out on the couch. And Byron put his head in the noose. Whether or not he could have been saved, we will never know. Sober, Byron didn't really want to die, although he talked about it. Drunk or stoned, he almost always wanted to die and fucked around at the edges of death. If you fuck around long enough, one day you "win." We lost Byron. I have tried talking to some of his friends about that night, but I've only encountered fear; I've gotten no answers. *The River's Edge* has come to Cropseyville. The bottom line is Byron's gone.

His friends have told me that they were worried about him. As one of them said, "Byron always had these shitty jobs. He didn't have to work, but it was never good enough for your father." He and Harry ended up in a vicious cycle of Byron being unable to accept responsibility and Dad refusing to give him any. I also believe that Yvonne had a role in the breakdown that led to Byron's end. Shortly before he died, Byron confided in Cindy his passionate hatred of Yvonne—he'd even begun fantasizing about killing her. I recall the way Yvonne reacted when Pat told Cindy she was not Harry's daughter. Rather than comforting the poor kid, Yvonne exploited and exacerbated Cindy's pain, telling her that it "made sense," and then detailing the genetic similarities between Cindy and the man Pat claimed was the "real" father. We have also heard Yvonne tell Byron that his troubles stemmed from his "inherited" insanity. Byron was deaf in one ear and had significant learning disabilities and this talk must have underscored his stoned belief in his inevitable doom. After Byron's memorial, I overheard Yvonne repeat her theory to some friends.

And where was Harry in all this? I believe that his need to have someone fill the gap caused by Pat's departure was so strong that he couldn't or wouldn't risk losing Yvonne. (He eventually married her.) So he closed his eyes and withdrew. Over the past twenty years, he has donated much of his time and money to aiding mentally ill people and battered women. In appreciation for his efforts one group has named a building in his honor. I know now that Harry deeply regrets ever having hit my mother, and I feel his pain for not being able to save his son.

I have a dream. I'm in the country, sitting at a picnic table under the trees and Byron comes and joins me. He's barechested, wearing only his leather pants. He says, "Jenny, I didn't mean to do it. But it's done and I'm okay."

Georgia called one day and told me a friend of Byron's was

living in New York and wanted to see me. He came into my life looking like the answer to some loneliness. He called himself the "last decent man" and I believed him. I felt comfortable with him, he knew my family intimately, I didn't have to give any exposition, or short cut to love. He was sexy and he liked my dogs. I also liked the fact that this guy was a home-boy—down to earth, with little sophistication—I've had plenty of that. I also believed Byron had sent him to me to help shed some light on the mystery of his death. Instead, he turned out to be another test. After the smoke of infatuation cleared, he was revealed as a major grifter. He was involved in various nefarious activities, as well as seeing another woman. And he had no answers about Byron; every lead led me in circles. The *pièce de résistance* was when he took an ugly little oil painting out of my stairwell that a neighbor had jokingly signed "Monet," and announced he'd had it appraised. "It's authentic Jen, and it's worth eleven million." Check!

There comes a point where you either grow and clean up your act or you stay stuck in the mire. I'm no longer willing to do this. This grifter-thing proves that I must be vigilant. I am, after all, a veteran of co-dependent love, the dance of death, the two-step, the seeker and the sought, push-pull, come here go away, the escape from true intimacy. At first glance, a hundred miles of rough road can look like an exciting dusty highway. But there comes a point where you just want to park your car by a pond. I've also said good-bye to Arno.

There were times I have raged against my family because I was so wrapped up in a hurt I didn't really understand, and I couldn't understand theirs. I know now that Pat was never fully there, that part of her was always lost in her own painful childhood and the terrors: the breakdown and the electroshock treatments she'd had as a young woman. She still isn't well, but I see that in the context of her current life, her mental illness is not the problem it was for her in our family. Maybe trying to take care of four kids and a demanding husband while making Beef Bourguignon for a dinner party, all in the middle of the woods, would have driven me around the bend, too! She's still living with Ace, who's still talking to the sink and making spider webs out of string. And she seems to have found some sort of peace. I can appreciate her now, although then, I needed a mother. And I have come to appreciate everyone in my family for their love and for what they have given me—and it has been plenty! Despite the sadness and craziness of my upbringing, it was a privileged existence, filled with opportunities and experiences that few have. There were lots of good times, and Harry's generosity and Pat's artistic nature made a difference. Three of us children have survived, and Cindy is my best friend. I no longer think in terms of evening up a score. As they say: If you seek revenge, you'd better dig two graves. Of course, there are certain things that I find myself still unable to forgive or forget. As I once heard a salesgirl in Fred Segal's say, "I'll figure it out in recarn."

1991

April

I hadn't spoken to Richard since he was making *See No Evil* in New York in 1988. I vowed that I'd never to talk to him again; I even changed my telephone number to seal the deal. But after I heard that he was extremely ill I sent him a card. What we went through was too much, too good, and too bad to ever forget completely. In fact, I was looking at some old photos from that time when I received a telegram pleading with me to get in touch.

I call the number; it's the office. A secretary takes my number; Richard will call me back. Aah, some things never change. Five minutes later, he calls. After a few awkward moments of pleasantries, we seem to pick up where we'd left off. "I saw *Always* last night and it reminded me of us, of our relationship," says the spider to the fly. I tell him I haven't seen it, though I know it's about "eternal love." I don't feel myself go all gooey inside. My trust and gullibility are finally gone. I am thrilled, sad, and a little embarrassed by this non-reaction.

I change the subject and mention that I'd been looking at a photograph of Okima a few minutes earlier, wondering why he had never leveled. He gives me that all-knowing secretive laugh that drives me crazy. "Richard, after all this time, tell me the truth. Why was sweet dear little Okima mopping the floor with vodka and crying all the time?" More laughter, but a little more nervous. I'm waiting.

"What?"

"Did you, Richard? Sleep with Okima?"

"Yes . . ."

"So I wasn't crazy. I hate you for making me think I was." We both start laughing, and our laughter is followed by a companionable silence.

After this conversation, I see *The Grifters,* a movie about hustlers, cons, and gangsters. I think of Richard several times during the film. The next day he calls and says, "I'm sorry I hurt you, Jennifer."

"For what?" Silence. I'm supposed to know. "Oh, Okima. I'm not hurt. I *was* hurt. Don't worry about it. Frankly, I'm surprised you've admitted it."

"So am I."

I am surprised, but I'm also slightly upset. Then I realize that it's the deceit that still lingers, not the fact that they exchanged bodily fluids. After all, I did marry Richard knowing that he wasn't monogamous—but wishing that he could/might be. It was the deception that hurt; that's painful. Then there's the fact that he can still push all the right buttons. "Youse is nothing but a grifter, Richard."

I did go out for a visit. Richard greeted me at the door of his bedroom. He was holding onto the wall, looking as if he were going to tip over any minute. I walked him back to the bed and he moved as if he were on stilts. His arm felt painfully thin under my tight grip. Richard is seriously ill.

Since that visit, Richard and Flynn have begun divorce proceedings—Flynn's wife number six and seven. Ostensibly, it's because of me, but all the principal players know better. Flynn wants out, and I'm as good an excuse as any.

Now I'm on my way back to L.A. to see Richard a second time. After the first trip, I swore I wouldn't go back. It's too painful. But clearly, there is some unfinished business and it has to do with the difference between knowing something in your mind and experiencing its reality.

I've brought my dogs, Emmet and Livia, this time. It's easy to do on these MGM first-class flights. Mike Nichols and his film cans are today's featured dignitaries. Neil Sedaka, who looked like a white version of "Baby Doc" Duvalier, and his wife were the stars on the last trip. At first Richard agreed to my bringing "the children." But then he started waffling. I finally told him, "I come with baggage now. It's no longer just me and my toothbrush. 'Love me, love my dogs!' " Anyway, I'm going out there for a substantial length of time and I won't leave the canines for more than a few days.

Majella, the sweetest housekeeper in the world, greets me and takes my bag to the guest room. Now Richard's in worse shape than ever and it's too much for him to get up and meet me at the bedroom door. He's even thinner, all skin and bones. I spot the same wooden-handled .357 Magnum on the bed. He sees me see it and begins to put it in the nightstand drawer. But he's slow, it takes more of an effort than it should; the gun is now too heavy for his hands.

"I know you don't like guns, Jenny."

"Yeah, especially that one!"

Livia still remembers Richard from his last visit in 1988. She loves Richard; Emmet does not. When Richard gets up and tries to get to the bathroom, a big event with his MS, Emmet backs away and starts barking at him. Richard tries to hit Emmet with his cane, like some grouchy old man. Of course, this sends me into a mild rage and I try to explain that to Emmet, he is like some strange apparition with his rickety walk. Richard explains that he doesn't like being barked at in his own house.

Majella loves the dogs but Virginia, the other housekeeper, is terrified, especially since Livia's bitten the gardener. This has made Richard nuts because he's sure he's going to get sued. He starts calling her "Livia Lechter" as in Hannibal's wife (with her muzzle on, she looks the part). I try to explain to Richard that people without green cards aren't likely to sue, and anyway, it's not a bad bite. We give the gardener a few hundred dollars and tell him to take the week off. He leaves for good. So now I have to have the security people at the Bel Air west gate call us whenever anyone's coming, so I can pen the dogs up in the tennis court. Richard acts extremely inconvenienced by this. I think it's just too much real life for him. Children and dogs: he can't control them, they're not on staff. However, I think that any little bit of hard-core life is good for Richard's sadly isolated one. Basically, he's jealous about all of the attention I pay to my canine kids; he admits it. The dogs make me feel safe when Richard launches into one of his tirades—he simply can't fuck with me too much. Also, they give me something of my own in the midst of all this private splendor—the Richard-ness, the his-ness of it all.

We watch *The Grifters* on his big screen and reminisce about things that remind us of people we've known. Short con, long con. Uncle Dicky's name comes up, some appreciative giggles, but this is also a painful subject—Uncle Dicky has recently died. I miss him, and I can imagine how Richard feels. Good old Uncle Dicky had kept hitting on Richard for serious cash, right up to the end. Suddenly I *feel* the past. Drug-dealer Joe's name comes up, and I ask, or tell, Richard, "I take responsibility for the black out. But why the hell did you let him FUCK ME and then stand there and not only watch but photograph it?"

He shakes his head. "I'm sorry."

I'm sorry too. But sometimes that's all there is.

We're watching a rap show and somebody says something that bothers him. "Some white folks imitating black folk—'youse and dem dose,' you know how they do, baby."

I want to kill him. "Not nice, Richard."

"I always blamed it on my baby, didn't I?"

"Yeah, but I let you. I'm not a racist. I know that, even if you don't."

"That's right. You're not. But I've been listening to it for years—as a child, you know."

"Yeah, but you didn't let it stop you. You did something with your life Richard, regardless of all those words."

This makes me think about all our fights about racism and guilt—*my* racism and *my* guilt. Richard looks for the weak spots in his friends, family, and lovers in order to control them, and for years he's bullied me about this issue. His attitude has always been that it's impossible for a white person *not* to be a bigot. Therefore, there was nothing I could do to defend myself, to make him realize that I was not a bigot, that I loved him past his color, that I fell in love with him despite his color. My guilt was as plain as the white skin on my face—end of discussion. And, as the victim of my supposed racism, Richard was absolved from having to look at or deal with his own. This was enormously frustrating for me. I understood his rage, but not the fact that he made me its object. The world is not a fair place, but I did not cause that. I know this now, and, in fact, I'd begun to understand it when I'd read *The Autobiography of Malcolm X*. It's a relief to hear that he's finally gotten it, too.

Then I decide to ask Richard a question that's been bugging me for ages. Richard has a "street" phrase that I've never heard clearly and he's refused to translate. It's one particular blackism he's withheld from me for years, probably because he knew how much I wanted to know it. When I ask him this time he says, "Okay, Jenny, here it is: *Must be is 'cause must ain't don't sound right.*" I finally know the words. Now I have to figure out what it means. But now I'm frightened. I wonder, why is he finally telling me? Does he think he's dying?

Richard's troubled about the divorce from Flynn, whom he calls Idi Amin. He'd married her this last time with no prenuptial, because, he claims, she caught him when he was weak and vulnerable after his last heart attack. She called up the preacher mighty quickly. She's managed to get him to finance a movie project to the tune of approximately three-quarters of a million dollars. And in the past year he'd also bought her beaucoup jewelry—the serious kind. Richard tells me this adding that he wishes that he'd bought more tasteful jewels for all his women. I tell him, "I would've been happy just to have kept mine." He does the old Dangling Carrot Routine, "So when I get Flynn's jewelry back, I'll give you some."

The housekeeper leaves, and the house has a hollow, eerie feeling to it. The alarms don't work; Richard has a mirror rigged up in front of his bed, so he can see who's coming in his door. I ask him *how* he sleeps and he says, "With the door locked and the gun by my side." I think of all the money and jewelry he's got stashed here and it makes me envision a Charlie Manson reunion tour. I'm still afraid of Richard, that he might kill me in my sleep, or even worse, that I might kill him. I am intensely uncomfortable here. I fight these thoughts, put my arms around him, and hold him the way I used to—tight and close. This will dispel these dark thoughts. Does. I'm jumpy and can't really sleep, dozing off only for a few minutes at a time.

Around three A.M. I hear a low siren go off somewhere. "Richard, I thought the alarm was broken. What the hell is that?"

"I don't know. I've heard it before, though."

This makes me feel worse. "Richard, don't you think you should do something?"

"Here's what I do." He presses the conference button on the phone. "I listen to hear if someone's in the house."

Yeah, very comforting.

"Richard, this is insane. You don't have to live this way."

But Richard, and everyone around him, is in intense denial about his condition. This is all too familiar and all too dangerous.

Majella has taken the weekend off and Virginia is sick. There's no one to take their places, so we're alone in the house. I play cook, microwaving the food Majella's left for us, and home health aide, cleaning up after Richard and changing his sheets, which he soils regularly.

He's in the shower leaning on a walker that had been hidden in a hall closet until I found it and put it in the bathroom to help him. Suddenly, I hear a scream. Richard has fallen on the slippery marble floor and is caught in the metal walker itself. The shower is pummeling him; he looks wounded, in pain. I disentangle him and struggle to get him out of the wet, marble room. He clings to me. He is shaking, cold and terribly frightened. All the intimacy this moment holds, all the love, and the end of it all fills me with such a horrifying sadness. I give up feeling, otherwise I won't be able to complete this task. I keep saying, "You're okay, Richard. Nothing's broken. Everything's all right." I know I have to get him up and out of there, quickly. I shift into nurse mode; I pretend I am strong. I lift the love of my life and am amazed at how light he is. He feels like a young child and looks like the world's oldest man. I get him over to his big leather barber's chair, sit him down and towel him off. He is terrified. "Jenny, I'm scared."

I'm silent. I'm scared, too.

"What am I going to do?"

"Richard, it'll be all right."

"No one else could have picked me up like that. You're the only one who could have done that."

I don't know what to tell him, but I know it's time he faces his illness. "Richard, if I weren't here what would you have done?"

"I would've been there all night with the water pouring on me."

"Richard, this has got to be dealt with."

I look at his frail body. The excruciating pain that has occupied his heart and soul for years now occupies his body.

I sit down on the edge of the bathtub, trying to catch my breath. "Jenny, you're bleeding."

I look down. There is blood on the marble floor, coming from my ankle. "Oh, I must have caught it on the shower door. I didn't even feel it."

It reminds me of all the things I didn't feel when they happened. "Remember that time on my birthday when I drove myself bleeding to the hospital to get stitches?"

"Jenny, I have flashbacks of punching you in the eye that time that I can't bear. I wake up screaming from it."

We're both sad; we're both silent.

He calls me "mommie" and I don't know why. I don't know how to respond.

He's all cleaned up and we watch movies. Richard is his old petulant, moody self. He tells me, "You know, I wonder if anybody ever loved me?"

"How dare you, Richard. I loved you for years, you motherfucker. You just threw it away."

He looks ashamed.

I think of all the abuse, all the hurt and humiliation. It took me so long to get over it. Yeah, denial. Blinded by love. He took advantage of these feelings, I let him, and we eventually destroyed them. I can't help it. I tell him, "You blew it with me, do you know that?"

He sighs, whimpers and looks away. "Jen, I couldn't believe anyone could love me."

"You also couldn't believe you could love somebody. It used to make you angry how you felt about me."

"I don't know . . ."

The conversation sputters to an end because it's now focused on a theme, not just on him.

We go to the dentist. Richard has gum disease and has had a number of teeth removed. He refuses to wear the temporary replacements, saying that they bother him. But today's visit is to have other work done. Little by little, he's having all the amalgam replaced in the teeth that remain. There's a theory that he saw on a "60 Minutes" segment, that the old amalgam can cause a form of blood poisoning, which in turn can cause multiple sclerosis. He hopes to be able to walk when all the old fillings are out. Richard gets dizzy in the car on the way there, and shouts because we didn't take a different road with fewer curves. It occurs to me at the dentist's office that he needs to have a "wife" with him and it's very sad that he is alone. He is dependent on his staff for every move. And what a staff! These new secretaries genuflect more than any of the others I've ever seen, which, of course makes them of no real help. They *do* have titles though. There's Sheila, who's the "executive assistant" and Jennifer, the "executive assistant's assistant" (only in L.A.).

During the course of my visit, I manage to get some things in order for him. The burglar alarm is repaired, a mobie arrives—for the long trips to the bathroom, Virginia starts spending the night, and another housekeeper is hired. Some light is shed into the dark denial.

Richard hasn't been able to perform sexually for some time. He asks me to wear a short black skirt and to try to resurrect this failure—the great white hope. But I fly out of the room when he even broaches this subject. I suggest that he invite a "friend" over.

I'm downstairs, in the kitchen when he rings the intercom. "Jenny, pick up the phone. My friend Gina won't come here while you're here."

"Gina? Hi. Listen, I'm an ex-wife and a friend. Please feel free to visit. Richard and I are only friends."

"Which one?"

"Number five."

"No, I mean which wife?"

"Oh! Jennifer Lee."

"Yeah! You're the one who called all the girls and had them go to the Hyatt."

Computer search. "Oh. Were you the one who said 'Are you sure this is the secretary and not Jennifer? She's crazy!' "

"Yeah, I'm Gina!"

She says it as though I'd remember and as though I'd feel bad about it.

"Oh, Gina, well, gee, sorry about that. Anyway do come visit Richard."

An hour later I open the front door and Gina rushes in, past me, runs halfway up the stairs, pauses and says, "You cut your hair."

Well, two things are clear. Gina needs to show me how familiar she is with Richard and wants me to know that she's seen me when I hadn't seen her. I guess she's been around more than I'd thought. I don't give a fuck about either.

I bring them each something to drink and sort of get a weird kick out of playing "hostess-with-the-mostess"—a surreal revenge—because I know it's me he wants. Then Richard asks me to join them. A threesome? I do an imitation of Richard sulking and Gina gets a real kick out of this. "Rich, honey, that's just how you are."

We have a brief discussion about the power plays of the new executive assistant and her assistant. Gina starts showing off. "Well, you know what I do, Jenny, when they get grand with me? I just ask 'em, how long you know Rich? I've known him twelve years. That shuts 'em right up."

They are listening to "their" song, a song that, earlier in the day, Richard had been obsessing about finding. I am a bit non-plussed by this blatant "their" song business, and unfortunately, I inquire. "So what's the origin of this?" . . . "Well, it was on the boat . . ." Gina begins. Red flags.

"Boat? What boat?"

"*The Silver Trident.*" She begins to sing, "*Silver Trident . . . Silver Trident . . .*" I can't believe what I'm hearing. Then Richard pipes in, imitating ship-to-shore radio talk, a duet of sing-songy sadists. "*Silver Trident . . . Silver Trident . . .*" The arrow has hit its mark. Are they oblivious to my feelings? I search for hidden meanings, intentions. Now I feel embarrassed, for them and for me. "What's this about . . . ?"

"Oh, Jenny, it was after you left. I joined Richard on the boat. And then we had this song."

This story is getting richer. Blood running hot and cold. "Excuse me, but this is making me feel a tad uncomfortable," I say.

"Oh, Jen! I was cleaning up the mess you made . . . the heart-break. Not easy to do."

I want to say, "Sort of like following dogs or children?" but don't.

I wander over to the pile of CDs.

"Hey, Jen, how long have you known Rich?"

I hate when she calls him "Rich." People who don't know him well, but want to look as if they do, call him that. "I've known Richard, fourteen years."

After Miss Gina leaves, Richard asks me *many times*, to listen to the song with him. I hit the roof. "You destroy a relationship, have this low-rent routine stand in for me on my fucking honeymoon—on my honeymoon boat—where the two of you find a little music to accompany this insensitive, maudlin act, and now you have the nerve to ask me to wallow in your self-pity alongside you, for something you are responsible for destroying? . . . Go fuck yourself!"

He laughs, appreciatively. I don't.

Suddenly I realize that while Richard causes pain, he's also been collecting women and the wounds they inflict, real or imagined. And basically all of us women have been interchangeable. Sad but true. Now he has physical pain to go along with the rest.

"I knew I was bad but, Jenny, was I *this* bad?"

"Richard, do you think this is some sort of retribution?"

"Of course it is."

I know he has never been the same since the fire.

The chaos that exists between the secretaries—excuse me—the "executive assistant" and the "executive assistant's assistant," further clarifies this whole pathetic scene. Richard keeps everybody hopping, jumping, off center, trying to please. I've been a puppet in this sad game, and this game is now killing him. He may feel brief remorse for an old cut above my eye but it doesn't stop him from lashing out in brand-new, venomous rages. All those years of serious drugs, of visiting the dark side over and over till the angels get so worn out they won't travel with you the way they used to. Eventually you come back with the demons, carrying them to the bright side. And the demons have extracted their price. When I look at Richard, with his missing teeth, skeletal body, and painful, rickety movements, it is difficult to see traces of the man I first met. I realize that if Richard were taken out of context—removed from his surroundings, the trappings of his wealth—and placed on any street corner in L.A. no passerby would suspect that this was a successful man. They would see a homeless man. They would not think he was a sick man; they would think he was a junkie. I, too, see this and it's a painful sight; it hurts me. Richard is all alone. Did he bring it on himself? Only God knows. I do know that his illness has not changed him, rather, it's made him worse. His selfishness and self-deceit, are no longer discernible as separate parts of his character, even to him. It's all merged. There are no boundaries, it's all just one big mass of confusion and manipulation. But now he is the victim. I tell him I took his abuse when I didn't know any better, didn't want to know any better, but that's gone. I tell him I cannot accept abuse because he's sick. I can't stay.

Sheila delivers a ring. The stone is a large and very serious diamond that has been at the jeweler's being reset. Richard's been asking about it for days. When it arrives he expresses no emotion, puts it on, and lights a cigarette, obviously aware of how the ring looks, almost showing off. As he leans back against his pillows, the sun bouncing off the huge diamond sliding around on his bony finger, it occurs to me that somehow he is comforted by it.

The executive assistant enters the bedroom again, bringing in a piece of legal-sized paper. "Here's what you asked for." I ask him what it is.

"What times the trailers for the film are on TV."

I assume he means *Another You*. When I wander in the bedroom that afternoon, he tells me, almost yelling, "Here it is, Jenny! Watch this!"

Suddenly on his giant television screen is a blazing inferno. "What is this, Richard?"

"This is that movie—about fire." *Backdraft*.

I stay for the screening of his new movie *Another You* much to the assistants' dismay; the business of seeing Richard's movies is clearly their territory. And the attitude that the producers of this epic cookie-cutter have reminds me of why I no longer live in L.A. One of them refuses to acknowledge me, the other kisses my ass. I'm very uncomfortable and the movie is mediocre but hey, I'm outta here tomorrow. Richard is shaky and very obviously sick in every frame of the film. The director had lied when he told Richard that he'd "fixed it" so that no one would be able to tell how ill he really is. The movie ends with a freeze frame shot of Gene Wilder and Richard. They have their arms around each other and they are smiling. Suddenly I am crying. It feels as if this is Richard's last movie. He asks me about his performance and refers to himself in the third person. "Could you tell if Richard was sick?"

I lie. "No, Richard. You were only really visibly shaky in one early scene, when you're driving away from the mental hospital with Gene, but it matches the broken-down, grifter character you play."

"So Richard was good, Mommie?"

This "mommie" shit is jarring. I hate it.

I say good-bye to the land of "executive assistants" and fuchsia jogging suits and I'm back on the MGM plane with my "kids," who are safely drugged in their pet-porters. I think about it all. I had spent so many years in love with this man, unable to let go, hoping we would walk off into the sunset. (I think Harry still loves Pat.) Richard is so sad now, confined to his bed. He did have the world in his hands but his genius is also comprised of his flaws. He can't admit it but I can feel his regret like a steel rod through me. He believes it's retribution, a concept that keeps him the victim. And he cannot discuss the physical and emotional havoc he's brought on himself. All the bad choices, the non-choices. Hitting just because he had the impulse. All the unplanned children. Getting high because he wanted to. Working for the man just for the money. The deal became God, eclipsing his talent. What happened to all that magical painful truth? Richard had wanted so badly to get good parts. And the deal-makers gave him a company, money to develop projects, but he couldn't, wouldn't, didn't want the responsibility. Richard was someone who helped me tell the truth, gave me more courage to do so. When I think of Richard I try to remember him strong and full of dreams, the Richard of his first concert movie, before he started making major bucks.

I remember a phone conversation I had with him not long before this visit. I asked him, "You busy, Richard?"

"I'm lonely."

"So, you're a very busy man being lonely."

"Jennifer, that's a song . . ."

I didn't write the song, but I did try a verse:

> He's a very busy man being lonely
> Running from everyone who ever cared
> He's a very busy man being lonely
> Climbing the ladder to nowhere.

I can see clearly now, without the obstruction of the obsession. I loved Richard deeply and I know that I will never love like that again—but who would want to? I want to love with a clear head and a strong heart. I want to nurture and be nurtured. I feel ready, I feel whole.

May

I've sent Pat a card and roses for Mother's Day and she's sent me back a note: "The color of the roses is not available to my mind. However, I would describe the shade as a light orange with some shading of various tones." She sends her love to my dogs. I've given her pictures of them that she has hanging on her wall. Pat calls Livia her granddaughter and Emmet her great grandson. I remember her gardens . . . the love there. I mourn for my mother and for myself—for any woman who is abused.

I see my life as a gift—the good, the bad, the ugly, have all been part of the process. I thank God that I've had the strength and the faith to live it fully. I feel privileged to have known the people I have known, and to have done the things I've done. For all the wild times, particularly the early ones, people were generous with me and protective of me, for the most part. And as angry as I have been at Richard, I am grateful for all I have learned and for having shared my heart and part of my life with him.

I have found a spiritual path, and reclaimed my faith in something higher (what does dog spell backward?). Though not a card-carrying Catholic, I am grateful I was raised one. It imbued me with a faith in something higher—in a neverending hope and a sense of right and wrong, mystery and wonder—a foundation for the existence of the spiritual realm. As a child, this led to my constant search for talismans, magic places, magic fawns, and guardian angels. This has carried me through the rough and the rocky and allowed me to see my life as a series of lessons. I'm beginning to trust myself again.

INDEX

350

Warfield, Marsha, 157
Warhol, Andy, 27-28, 33, 235
Washington, Buck, 9
Weinstein, Hannah, 218, 227
Weintraub, Bruce, 73, 75, 76, 135
Welch, Frankie, 28
Welch, Raquel, 71, 73
Weld, Tuesday, 51
Welles, Gwen, 80-81, 313
Wells, Kitty, 55
Wenta, Stefan, 76, 82
Westbrook, Jim, 8
Westbrook, Liz, 8
West, Mae, 262
Wexler, Haskell, 273
Whips, Andrea, 28, 29
Whitelaw, Sandy, 34, 37
White, Mrs., 23, 24
White Whore and the Bit Players, The, 17
Wholly Moses, 210, 212
Why Shoot the Teacher, 87
Wilder, Gene, 71, 217, 221, 345
Wilding, Chris, 248
Wild in the Streets, 47
Wild Party, The, 73
Wiley, Andrew, 64
Williams, Hank, 60, 62, 77, 88
Williams, Jack, 57, 58
Williams, Jackie, 38, 44
Williams, Mrs., 75
Williams, Robin, 262-263, 272
Williams, Treat, 239
Willow, 65
Wilson, Connie, 59-60
Wilson, Eddie, 59
Wilson, Flip, 124
Wilson, Mitchell, 56
Wilson, Stella, 56
Winfrey, Oprah, 316
Winkler, Henry, 259
Wizard of Oz, The, 174
Wood, Natalie, 78, 85, 269
Woods, Jimmy, 64
Worth, Marvin, 323
Wouk, Herman, 312
Wynkin, 34

Y

Yankee Doodle Dandy, 83
Yasmin, 23

You Can't Take it With You, 329
Young, Andrew, 107
Young Frankenstein, 72
Yvonne, 26, 34, 57, 66-67, 74, 84, 120, 193-194, 238, 301, 302, 306, 308, 312-313, 333

Z

Zarem, Bobby, 18
Zeida, 131
Zevon, Warren, 89